THE CULTURES OF
COLLECTING

THE CULTURES OF COLLECTING

Edited by John Elsner *and*
Roger Cardinal

HARVARD UNIVERSITY PRESS

CAMBRIDGE, MASSACHUSETTS

1994

First published in the United States of America
in 1994 by Harvard University Press,
Cambridge, Massachusetts

Published in Great Britain in 1994
by Reaktion Books, London

Designed by Humphrey Stone
Jacket designed by Ron Costley
Photoset by Wilmaset Ltd, Birkenhead, Wirral
Printed and bound in Great Britain
by The Alden Press, Oxford

Library of Congress Catalog Card Number 93-81-271

ISBN 0–674–17992–7
ISBN 0–674–17993–5 (pbk.)

The editors and publishers would like to thank
Editions Gallimard for permission to publish a translation
of Jean Baudrillard's 'Le système marginal', a chapter of
Le Système des objets (Paris: © Editions Gallimard, 1968);
and the University of Chicago Press for permission
to publish a revised version of Naomi Schor's
'*Cartes Postales*: Representing Paris 1900', which appeared
in *Critical Inquiry*, XVIII (Winter 1992), a journal
published by the University of Chicago Press.

Contents

Photographic Acknowledgements

The editors and publishers wish to express their thanks to the following for supplying photographic material and/or permission to reproduce it: The Alte Pinakothek, Munich: p. 189 (photograph, Bayerische Staatsgemäldesammlungen, Munich); The Library of the Australian National University, Canberra: p. 132 [lower]; The British Library, London: pp. 183, 187, 196, 202; Detroit Institute of Art Founders Society (a Founders Society Purchase, Director's Discretionary Fund): p. 206; The Freud Museum, London: pp. 225, 228, 231, 232, 233, 242, 251; *The Independent*: pp. 53, 65 (65 [upper]: photographer Marc Hill; 65 [lower]: Edward Sykes); The Kunsthistorisches Museum, Vienna: pp. 149, 153; Lay & Partners, London: pp. 60 (60 [upper]: photographer QFT Photography Ltd, 60 [lower]: Pio Photos); Marlborough Fine Art, London (photographs Prudence Cuming Associates): pp. 79, 81, 85, 91, 94; Robert Opie: pp. 37, 41, 44; Guy Peellaert: p. 57; Peale Museum, Baltimore (photograph, Baltimore City Life Museums): p. 220 [upper]; Pennsylvania Academy of the Fine Arts, Philadelphia: pp. 220 [lower], 22 (the former from the Collections Fund, the latter from the Joseph Harrison Jr Collection, a Gift of Mrs Sarah Harrison); Philadelphia Museum of Art, George W. Elkins Collection: pp. 210, 215 (the former a Gift of the Barra Foundation); Naomi Schor: pp. 267, 270, 271, 272, 274; The Trustees of Sir John Soane's Museum: pp. 163, 174 [upper]; The Dixson Library, State Library of New South Wales, Sydney: p. 131; The Trustees of The Tate Gallery, London: pp. 77, 89; Nicholas Thomas: pp. 117, 119, 132 [upper].

Notes on the Editors and Contributors

JOHN ELSNER is Lecturer in Classical Art at the Courtauld Institute in London. His book-length study, *Art and the Roman Viewer: The Transformation of Art from the Pagan World to Christianity*, is due to be published in 1994.

ROGER CARDINAL is Professor of Literary and Visual Studies at the University of Kent at Canterbury. He is the author of *Figures of Reality* (1981) and *The Landscape Vision of Paul Nash* (Reaktion Books, 1989); he has also written on German Romanticism, Expressionism, Surrealism and Outsider Art.

JEAN BAUDRILLARD, who lives in Paris, taught sociology at Nanterre University from 1966 to 1987. The author of *Le Système des objets* (1968), an analysis of consumerism, he is best known in Britain for his dazzling diagnosis of the postmodern condition, *Simulations* (1983), and for the melancholy reflections of *Cool Memories* (1990).

ROBERT OPIE collects packaging and commercial artefacts, and curated the exhibition 'The Pack Age – A Century of Wrapping It Up' at the Victoria & Albert Museum, London, in 1975. In 1982 he gave up his job as a market researcher to set up the Museum of Packaging and Advertising in Gloucester, which opened to the public in 1984 as a national centre for the preservation and study of consumer products. He is the author of *Rule Britannia: Trading on the British Image* (1985), *The Art of the Label* (1987), *Sweet Memories* (1988) and *The Packaging Source Book* (1989); both *A History of Advertising* and *A History of Packaging* are due to appear in 1994.

JOHN WINDSOR regularly contributes articles on collecting and the art market to *The Independent* newspaper. Having spent two years (1973–4) with the Maharishi Mahesh Yogi, who introduced the Transcendental Meditation technique to the West, he taught the TM technique full-time for ten years; he now both teaches and writes.

MIEKE BAL is Professor of the Theory of Literature at the University of Amsterdam, and Adjunct Visiting Professor of Visual and Cultural Studies at the University of Rochester, New York. Her books include *On Story-telling: Essays in Narratology* (1991), *Reading 'Rembrandt': Beyond the Word-Image Opposition* (1991), and *On Meaning-Making: Essays in Semiotics* (1993).

NICHOLAS THOMAS is a Senior Research Fellow at the Australian National University, Canberra; his books include *Out of Time: History and Evolution in Anthropological Discourse* (1989), *Entangled Objects: Exchange, Material Culture and Colonialism in the Pacific* (1991) and *Colonialism's Culture* (1993). His research interests range from contemporary Pacific Islanders' art to eighteenth-century British travel writing and anthropological thought.

THOMAS DACOSTA KAUFMANN is Professor in the Department of Art and Archaeology at Princeton University. His books include *Drawings from the Holy Roman Empire, 1540–1680* (1982), *The School of Prague: Painting at the Court of Rudolf II* (1988), which won the Mitchell Prize for the History of Art, *Art and Architecture in Central Europe, 1520–1620: An Annotated Bibliography* (1988), *Central European Drawings, 1680–1800* (1989) and *The Mastery of Nature: Aspects of Art, Science and Humanism in the Renaissance* (1993). His broad interpretative survey of art, culture and society in Central Europe from the Renaissance to the end of the *ancien régime* is forthcoming.

ANTHONY ALAN SHELTON is Keeper of Non-Western Art and Anthropology at the Royal Pavilion, Art Gallery & Museums, Brighton, and Research Fellow in Museum Ethnography at the University of Sussex. He has published widely on aspects of Mexican ethnography, Pre-Columbian art and critical museology; his most recent publication, edited by J. Coote, is in *Anthropology, Art and Aesthetics* (1992).

SUSAN STEWART is Professor of English at Temple University, Philadelphia, and the author of several books on literary and aesthetic theory: *Nonsense: Aspects of Intertextuality in Folklore and Literature* (1979), *On Longing: Narratives of the Miniature, the Gigantic, the Souvenir, the Collection* (1984) and *Crimes of Writing: Problems in the Containment of Representation* (1991), as well as two books of poetry, *Yellow Stars and Ice* (1981) and *The Hive* (1987).

JOHN FORRESTER is Lecturer in the History and Philosophy of Science at the University of Cambridge. He is the author of *Language and the Origins of Psychoanalysis* (1980), *The Seductions of Psychoanalysis: Freud, Lacan and Derrida* (1990), and, with Lisa Appignanesi, *Freud's Women* (1992). He co-translated into English Jacques Lacan's *The Seminar: Books I & II* (1988), and is co-founder of the Psychoanalytic Forum; the Cambridge Group for the History of Psychiatry, Psychoanalysis and Allied Sciences; and the group Unofficial Knowledge, also based in Cambridge.

NAOMI SCHOR is the William Hanes Wannamaker Professor of Romance Studies and Literature at Duke University, North Carolina, and co-editor of *Differences: A Journal of Feminist Cultural Studies*. Her books include *Breaking the Chain: Women, Theory and French Realism* (1985), *Reading in Detail: Aesthetics and the Feminine* (1987) and the recently published *George Sand and Idealism* (1993).

Introduction

JOHN ELSNER AND ROGER CARDINAL

Noah was the first collector. Adam had given names to the animals, but it fell to Noah to collect them: 'And of every living thing of all flesh, two of every sort shalt thou bring into the ark, to keep them alive with thee; they shall be male and female. Of fowls after their kind, and of cattle after their kind, of every creeping thing of the earth after his kind, two of every sort shall come unto thee, to keep them alive' (*Genesis* 6.19–20). Menaced by a Flood, one has to act swiftly. Anything overlooked will be lost forever: between including and excluding there can be no half-measures. The collection is the unique bastion against the deluge of time. And Noah, perhaps alone of all collectors, achieved the complete set, or so at least the Bible would have us believe.

Noah represents the extreme case of the collector: he is one who places his vocation in the service of a higher cause, and who suffers the pathology of completeness at all costs. Noah's passion lay in the urge to save the world – to save not just single items as they chanced to occur but the model pairs from which all life forms could be reconstructed. Here is saving in its strongest sense, not just casual keeping but conscious rescuing from extinction – collection as salvation. Noah was no scholar, yet the contents of the Ark, like some definitive *catalogue raisonné*, inventorize and then re-found all the categories of living things. In Noah, the act of collecting up that which had been created and was doomed became inseparable from the creation of a new and better world. In the myth of Noah as ur-collector resonate all the themes of collecting itself: desire and nostalgia, saving and loss, the urge to erect a permanent and complete system against the destructiveness of time.

Classification precedes collection. Adam classified the creatures that God had made; on the basis of his nomenclature, Noah could recollect those creatures in order to preserve them. Of course without the prior *existence* of the animals, they could not have been named; equally, without their endowment with names they could not have been collected. In effect, the plenitude of taxonomy opens up the space for collectables to be identified, but at the same time the plenitude of that which is to be collected hastens the need to classify . . .

The science of classification is, in Stephen Jay Gould's words, 'truly the mirror of our thoughts, its changes through time [are] the best guide to the history of human perceptions'.[1] And if classification is the mirror of collective humanity's thoughts and perceptions, then collecting is its material embodiment. Collecting is classification lived, experienced in three dimensions. The history of collecting is thus the narrative of how human beings have striven to accommodate, to appropriate and to extend the taxonomies and systems of knowledge they have inherited.

And the world itself, certainly the social world, has always relied on its appointed collectors. Civilization could not exist without tax collectors and gatherers of information, harvesters and hoarders, census takers and recruiting officers, rent collectors, ticket collectors, refuse collectors, undertakers. . . . Jesus enjoined his followers to give unto Caesar, and Matthew gathered in Caesar's pence. 'To every thing there is a season. . . . A time to plant, and a time to pluck up that which is planted. . . . A time to cast away stones, and a time to gather stones together. . . . A time to get, and a time to lose; a time to keep, and a time to cast away.' (*Ecclesiastes* 3.1–6). The rhythms of collation and dispersal, of accessioning and de-accessioning, replicate the natural cycles of seasonal growth and decay, of dynamism and entropy. The collapse of the Roman Empire coincided with the failure of its bureaucracy to collect taxes and therefore to sustain an economy and a structured state. The social order is itself inherently *collective*: it thrives on classification, on rule, on labels, sets and systems. Notions such as caste and class, tribe and family, priesthood and laity, privileged and poor, prescribe a grid into which actual people and objects get allocated. That which is plucked up has at one time been set out in furrows.

If the peoples and the things of the world are the collected, and if the social categories into which they are assigned confirm the precious knowledge of culture handed down through generations, then our rulers sit atop a hierarchy of collectors. Empire is a collection of countries and of populations; a country is a collection of regions and peoples; each given people is a collection of individuals, divided into governed and governors – that is, collectables and collectors. In early modern Europe, secular authority collected slaves, while the Churches collected souls. This kind of public collecting was a mission expressing concerns both earthly and spiritual: capitalism and Christianity exhibit reciprocal extremes of collecting in their orientation towards the material and a dimension beyond the material. Of this, Gogol's *Dead Souls* offers a droll yet chilling parable in its portrayal of the landowner Chichikov, who scours the countryside collecting the souls of deceased serfs.

In the light of the social perspectives of containment and regulation, one's identity as an individual may depend on the difference between one's personal collection and that of one's parents, or of anyone else. As one becomes conscious of one's self, one becomes a conscious collector of identity, projecting one's being onto the objects one chooses to live with. Taste, the collector's taste, is a mirror of self. Yet taste – all too often inherited taste – may constitute little more than an inherited reflex: the preciously defined self discovers that it is merely another item in the cabinet of social display. The more interesting dream is to resist the criteria inculcated by one's generation and class, and to collect against the grain – to wriggle out of belonging to an established set. Sometimes one collects so as *not* to submit to social expectation, or to 'belong'. The myth of the truly tasteful collector, the one who creates taste instead of merely promulgating it, is that one is collecting rather *recherché* things or that one has a different approach from everyone else – that, somehow, one's own collecting is 'best': for taste, that process of distinguishing between things, itself aspires to be seen as distinctive and distinguished.

Such socially admissible collecting – whether a manifestation of bureaucratic dictates or of tolerated foibles – enables the rhythms of communal life to play according to their accustomed beat. But collecting can also attempt to challenge the norm, and cock a snook at the accepted patterns of knowledge into whose regulative frame the interests and energies of the world have been corralled. Outside the boundaries of social recognition arises the myth of the pioneering, the experimental collector whose vocation may be to parody orthodox connoisseurship, to challenge the expectations of social behaviour, even to construct a maverick anti-system. The supreme pioneer is the totalizing collector, the 'completist', like Noah. Such a collector can brook no constraint, can show no hesitation, in the compulsion to possess a complete category in each and every of its variations. To collect up to a final limit is not simply to own or to control the items one finds; it is to exercise control over existence itself through possessing every sample, every specimen, every instance of an unrepeatable and nowhere duplicated series. It is to be unique. For the collector is then like God – not the God who created the world, but the God who chose to obliterate his own creation. Absolute control is only realized at the pitch where it can actually extinguish that which is controlled.

When bureaucracy underwrites the totalizing impulse, collecting is at its most dangerous. The Holocaust can be seen as a collection of Jews, gypsies, homosexuals, the insane and other 'vermin', differentiated by a specious scientific classification that was then corroborated by a zealous bureaucracy. In its ambition to achieve its own perfect 'set', to install the absolute of the master race, the Third Reich, in a monstrous parody of connoisseurship, exerted godlike mastery over the vermin that didn't fit, and through parallel processes of labelling and denigration made a negative definition synonymous with a decree of extinction. The Holocaust is collecting's limit case; for it combines the pathology of the compulsive individual, who will not compromise to attain his end and who innovates by finding a perversely new series to be collected, with all the norms and powers of totalitarianism. Yet one wonders whether the latterday Nazi hunters, fifty years on, are not possessed of the same collector's zeal.

In the West, the *history* of collecting objects of cultural and aesthetic virtue has tended to be presented as a sub-set of the sociology and the history of taste. The great canonical collections, with their temple-like architecture, their monumental catalogues and their donors' names chiselled in stone, testify to the paradigm of Beauty as the exclusion of all ugliness, to the triumph of remembrance over oblivion, to the permanence of Being over Nothingness. Absurdly and dementedly eternalist as they are, they carry such weight as to seem incontrovertible, while the histories to which they give rise appear equally impervious to query. One of our ambitions in this book is to challenge such self-assurance, and to ask whether collecting, as a cultural and behavioural phenomenon, can be adequately *understood* if one looks only at the official norms – the public art collections, the museums, the sacred stations of the Grand Tour.

No history of collecting has addressed the Holocaust, nor has the positive appreciation of taste been adequately explained in its dependency on the negative perception of waste. It is true that we have not attempted here to tackle intertexts of such wide-ranging moral and aesthetic resonance. Nevertheless, our aim in gathering this magpie's nest of disparate essays has been to follow a strategy of alternating foci that seeks, at least, to probe more deeply into the nature of collecting by honouring the extremist as much as the conformist, by assessing the eccentric alongside the typical, and by juxtaposing the pathological with the normative. Sceptical of the glowing mirage of uniformity and orderliness that the standard histories of collecting have tended to conjure up, we wish to be reminded that collectors' thoughts stray as much to dying as to eternity; and we seek to contemplate some of the less cosy aspects of collecting, where envy, frustration, depression and despair are the obverse of success and triumphalism.

Anthropology suggests that the clean presupposes – indeed necessitates – the filthy: that our identity thrives only because we posit an 'Other' that will never be taken for ourselves. But if the cultural criterion of the desirable excludes anything tainted by shit, if the definition of a collectable rests on an implied ritual of cleansing (whether literal or figurative), and if we never touch anything that is not already in a sense 'our own', then all conventional collecting can really offer is kitsch – that aesthetic ideal which, as Milan Kundera has suggested, 'excludes everything from its purview which is essentially unacceptable in human existence'.[2] Against the sleek amplifications engineered by scholarship and curatorial publicity that direct our admiration towards the treasure-houses and the masterpieces, we feel there is much to be learned by listening in to the quieter, subversive voices rising out of that 'unacceptable' residue lying in culture's shadow.

At the margins of social convention lie the urges sublimated in careful arrangements and informative labels: desires for suppression and ownership, fears of death and oblivion, hopes of commemoration and eternity. Collections gesture to nostalgia for previous worlds (worlds whose imagined existence took place prior to their contents being collected) and also to amusement. Across history there have been innumerable 'trivial' collections (few of which have survived, for obvious reasons), based on ironic whim, on personal reverie, on casual caprice. Yet even amusement (which hints at the muses and at museums) is in some sense an aesthetic category, so that casual pleasure – no less than social climbing – bears testimony to the standards and rules of the mighty cultural system of which collecting is part.

The Cultures of Collecting offers a *bricolage* of theoretical, descriptive and historical papers whose collective ambition is not to invoke canons and confirm taste, but to lay bare a phenomenon at once psychological and social, one that not only has its less than obvious material history, but is also a continuing contemporary presence. There is, so to speak, a past that is another country, but there is also a past that lies right here. If collecting is meaningful, it is because it shuns closure and the security of received evaluations and instead opens its eyes to existence – the world around us, both cultural and natural, in all its unpredictability and contingent complexity. The narratives we have found to be most enlightening have not been those of the careers of collectors like Henry Clay Frick, J. Paul Getty or Charles Saatchi, for whom building a collection of things is inseparable from building up wealth and prestige. Instead we have been drawn to the less publicized stories of those less perfect collectors whose vocation sends them across the confines of the reasonable and the acceptable. These last – people like John Soane, Charles Willson Peale, Kurt Schwitters, Sigmund Freud and Robert Opie – exemplify a genuine exposure to existence: indeed their project, at times melancholy, even morbid, and perhaps ultimately tragic, often carries with it an intimation of the failure that is always on the cards once mortal desire reaches the limits of what can and cannot be done. Suddenly such collectors emerge alongside Noah, at the margin of the human adventure, that pivotal point where man finds himself rivalling God and teeters between mastery and madness.

I

The System of Collecting

JEAN BAUDRILLARD

Among the various meanings of the French word *objet*, the Littré dictionary gives this: 'Anything which is the cause or subject of a passion. Figuratively and most typically: the loved object'.

It ought to be obvious that the objects that occupy our daily lives are in fact the objects of a passion, that of personal possession, whose quotient of invested affect is in no way inferior to that of any other variety of human passion. Indeed, this everyday passion often outstrips all the others, and sometimes reigns supreme in the absence of any rival. What is characteristic of this passion is that it is tempered, diffuse, and regulative: we can only guess at its fundamental role in keeping the lives of the individual subject or of the collectivity on an even footing, and in supporting our very project of survival. In this respect, the objects in our lives, as distinct from the way we make use of them at a given moment, represent something much more, something profoundly related to subjectivity: for while the object is a resistant material body, it is also, simultaneously, a mental realm over which I hold sway, a thing whose meaning is governed by myself alone. It is all my own, the object of my passion.

THE OBJECT DIVESTED OF ITS FUNCTION

The fact that I make use of a refrigerator in order to freeze things, means that the refrigerator is defined in terms of a practical transaction: it is not an object so much as a freezing mechanism. In this sense, I cannot be said to possess it. Possession cannot apply to an implement, since the object I utilize always directs me back to the world. Rather it applies to that object once it is *divested of its function and made relative to a subject*. In this sense, all objects that are possessed submit to the same *abstractive operation* and participate in a mutual relationship in so far as they each refer back to the subject. They thereby constitute themselves as a *system*, on the basis of which the subject seeks to piece together his world, his personal microcosm.

Thus any given object can have two functions: it can be utilized, or it can be possessed. The first function has to do with the subject's project of asserting practical control within the real world, the second with an enterprise of abstract mastery whereby the subject seeks to assert himself as an autonomous totality outside the world. The two functions are mutually exclusive. Ultimately, the strictly utilitarian object has a social status: think of a machine, for example. Conversely, the object pure and simple, divested of its function, abstracted from any practical context, takes on a strictly subjective status. Now its destiny is to be collected. Whereupon it ceases to be a carpet, a table, a compass, or a knick-knack, and instead turns into an 'object' or a 'piece'. Typically, a collector will refer to 'a lovely piece', rather than a lovely carving. Once the object stops being defined by its function, its meaning is entirely up to the subject. The result is that all objects in a collection become equivalent, thanks to that process of passionate abstraction we call possession. Further, a single object can never be enough: invariably there will be a whole succession of objects, and, at the extreme, a total set marking the accomplishment of a mission. This is why the possession of an object of whatever kind is always both satisfying and frustrating: the notion of there being a set of objects to which it belongs lends the object an extension beyond itself and upsets its solitary status. Something similar can be said to operate in the sexual sphere: for if it is true that the amorous impulse is directed at the singularity of a given being, the impulse of physical possession, as such, can only be satisfied by a string of objects, or by the repetition of the same object, or by the superimposition of all objects of desire. A more or less complex pattern of connections and correlations is vital if the individual object is to achieve a degree of abstraction sufficient for it to be recuperated by the subject within that experience of embodied abstraction known as the sense of possession.

The product of this way of dealing with objects is, of course, the collection. Our everyday environment itself remains an ambiguous territory, for, in ordinary life, function is constantly superseded by the subjective factor, as acts of possession mingle with acts of usage, in a process that always falls short of total integration. On the other hand, the collection offers us a paradigm of perfection, for this is where the passionate enterprise of possession can achieve its ambitions, within a space where the everyday prose of the object-world modulates into poetry, to institute an unconscious and triumphant discourse.

THE LOVED OBJECT

'The taste for collecting', suggests Maurice Rheims, 'is like a game played with utter passion'.[1] For the child, collecting represents the most rudimentary way to exercise control over the outer world: by laying things out, grouping them, handling them. The active phase of collecting seems to occur between the ages of seven and twelve, during the period of latency prior to puberty. With the onset of puberty, the collecting impulse tends to disappear, though occasionally it resurfaces after a very short interval. Later on, it is men in their forties who seem most prone to the passion. In short, a correlation with sexuality can generally be demonstrated, so that the activity of collecting may be seen as a powerful mechanism of compensation during critical phases in a person's sexual development. Invariably it runs counter to active genital sexuality, though it should not be seen as a pure and simple substitute thereof, but rather a regression to the anal stage, manifested in such behaviour patterns as accumulation, ordering, aggressive retention and so forth. The practice of collecting is not equivalent to a sexual practice, in so far as it does not seek to still a desire (as does fetishism). None the less, it can bring about a reactive satisfaction that is every bit as intense. In which case, the object in question should undoubtedly be seen as a 'loved object'. As Rheims observes, 'The passion for an object leads to its being construed as God's special handiwork: the collector of porcelain eggs will imagine that God never made a more beautiful nor rarer form, and that He created it purely for the delight of porcelain egg collectors . . .'.[2] Such enthusiasts will insist that they are 'crazy about this object', and without exception, even in circumstances where no fetishistic perversion is involved, they will maintain about their collection an aura of the clandestine, of confinement, secrecy and dissimulation, all of which give rise to the unmistakable impression of a guilty relationship. The boundless passion invested in the game is what lends this regressive behaviour its sublimity, and reinforces the opinion that an individual who is not some sort of collector can only be a cretin or hopelessly sub-human.[3]

Hence the collector partakes of the sublime not by virtue of the types of things he collects (for these will vary, according to his age, his profession, his social milieu), but by virtue of his fanaticism. This fanaticism is always identical, whether in the case of the rich man specializing in Persian miniatures, or of the pauper who hoards matchboxes. This being so, the distinction one might be tempted to make between the collector as connoisseur – one who adores objects because of their beguiling singularity and differentness – and the straightforward collector, whose passion is to fit his acquisitions into a set or series, breaks down. In either case, pleasure springs from the fact that possession relies, on the one hand, upon the absolute singularity of each item – which means that it is equivalent to a human being, and eventually the subject himself – and, on the other, upon the possibility of envisaging a set or series of like items, in which is implied a prospect of limitless substitution and play. The quintessence of the collection is qualitative, while its material organization is quantitative. For if possession entails a certain intimate delirium as one fondles and scrutinizes the privileged piece, it equally involves activities of seeking out, categorizing, gathering and disposing. Actually, there is a strong whiff of the harem about all this, in the sense that the whole charm of the harem lies in its being at once a series bounded by intimacy (with always a privileged final term) and an intimacy bounded by seriality.

Surrounded by the objects he possesses, the collector is pre-eminently the sultan of a secret seraglio. Ordinary human relationships, which are the site of the unique and the conflictual, never permit such a fusion of absolute singularity and indefinite seriality. This explains why ordinary relationships are such a continual source of anxiety: while the realm of objects, on the other hand, being the realm of successive and homologous terms, offers security. Of course it achieves this at the price of a piece of sleight-of-hand involving abstraction and regression, but who cares? As Rheims puts it, 'for the collector, the object is a sort of docile dog which receives caresses and returns them in its own way; or rather, reflects them like a mirror constructed in such a way as to throw back images not of the real but of the desirable'.[4]

THE PERFECT PET

The image of the pet dog is exactly right, for pets are a category midway between persons and objects. Dogs, cats, birds, the tortoise or the canary . . . , the poignant devotion to such creatures points to a failure to establish normal human relationships and to the installation of a narcissistic territory – the home – wherein the subjectivity can fulfil itself without let or hindrance. Let us observe in passing that pets are never sexually distinct (indeed they are occasionally castrated for domestic purposes): although alive, they are as sexually neutral as any inert object. Indeed this is the price one has to pay if they are to be emotionally comforting, given that castration, real or symbolic, is what allows them to play, on their owner's behalf, the role of regulating castration anxiety, a role that is also pre-eminently that of the objects which surround us. It can be said that the object is itself the perfect pet. It represents the one 'being' whose qualities extend my person rather than confine it. In their plurality, objects are the sole things in existence with which it is truly possible to co-exist, in so far as their differences do not set them at odds with one another, as is the case with living beings. Instead they incline obediently towards myself, to be smoothly inventorized within my consciousness. The object is that which allows itself to be simultaneously 'personalized' and catalogued. And there is never a hint of exclusivity about such subjective inventorizing: any thing can be possessed, invested in, or, in terms of collecting, arranged, sorted and classified. The object thus emerges as the ideal mirror: for the images it reflects succeed one another while never contradicting one another. Moreover, it is ideal in that it reflects images not of what is real, but only of what is desirable. In short, it is like a dog reduced to the single aspect of fidelity. I am able to gaze on it without its gazing back at me. *This is why one invests in objects all that one finds impossible to invest in human relationships.* This is why man so quickly seeks out the company of objects when he needs to recuperate. But we should not be fooled by such talk of recuperation, nor by all that sentimental literature that celebrates inanimate objects. We cannot but see this reflex of retreat as a regression; this sort of passion is an escapist one. No doubt objects do play a regulative role in everyday life, in so far as within them all kinds of neuroses are neutralized, all kinds of tensions and frustrated energies grounded and calmed. Indeed, this is what lends them their 'spiritual' quality; this is what entitles us to speak of them as 'our very own'. Yet this is equally what turns them into the site of a tenacious myth, the ideal site of a neurotic equilibrium.

A SERIAL GAME

Of course, this recourse to objects looks superficial: how could consciousness be so easily fooled? But here is where subjectivity demonstrates its cleverness. The recourse to the possessed object is never superficial: it is always premissed on the object's absolute singularity. Not in real terms: for while the appropriation of a 'rare' or 'unique' object is obviously the perfect culmination of the impulse to possess, it has to be recognized that one can never find absolute proof in the real world that a given object is indeed unique. On the other hand, subjectivity is entirely capable of working things to its advantage without such proof. It is true that one peculiarity of the object, its exchange value, is governed by cultural and social criteria. And yet its absolute singularity as an object depends entirely upon the fact that it is *I* who possess it – which, in turn, allows me to recognize myself in it as an absolutely singular being. This is of course a colossal tautology, yet it never fails to hasten the intensity with which we turn to objects, and the ridiculous facility with which they afford us a glorious, if illusory, gratification. (True, there will always be disappointment in store, given the tautological nature of the system.) But there is more: while the same sort of closed circuit can also be said to regulate human relationships (albeit with less facility), there are things inconceivable in the intersubjective encounter that become quite feasible here. The singular object never impedes the process of narcissistic projection, which ranges over an indefinite number of objects: on the contrary, it encourages such multiplication, thus associating itself with a mechanism whereby the image of the self is extended to the very limits of the collection. Here, indeed, lies the whole miracle of collecting. For it is invariably *oneself* that one collects.

We are now in a better position to appreciate the structure of the system of possession: a given collection is made up of a succession of terms, but the final term must always be the person of the collector. In reciprocal fashion, the person of the collector is only constituted as such by dint of substituting itself for every successive term in the collecting process. We shall see that there is, at the sociological level, an exact congruity of structure with the system of the series or the paradigmatic chain. For we shall find that the collection or the series is what underpins the possession of the object, which is to say, the reciprocal integration of object with person.[5]

FROM QUANTITY TO QUALITY: THE UNIQUE OBJECT

The weakness of this hypothesis might seem to be the decisiveness with which the passionate collector reaches out for a given piece. But it should be clear that the apparently unique object is, precisely, no more than the final term embodying all previous terms of a like kind, the paramount term of an entire set (whether virtual, invisible or implicit, is of no consequence). In short, the unique object epitomizes the set to which it belongs.

In one of those literary portraits in which La Bruyère demonstrates how curiosity can be the most extravagant of passions, we meet a collector of engravings who voices the complaint: 'I suffer from an affliction I cannot ignore, and it will oblige me to give up collecting engravings for the rest of my days. I now possess the whole of Jacques

Callot, apart from just one piece, which is, in truth, not even one of his better productions. On the contrary, it is one of his weakest, and yet it is the one I must have to round off Callot. For twenty years I have striven to lay my hands on that engraving, and now I've got to the point where I've given up all hope. It's so cruel!' Here we may discern, in strictly arithmetical terms, an equation between the entire set minus one item, and the single item missing from that set.[6] This last, for lack of which the set at large remains meaningless, is a symbolic summation thereof: it is thereby imbued with a strange quality, the very quintessence, so to speak, of the entire preceding cavalcade of quantities. Certainly, as an object, it is perceived as unique, given its absolute position at the end of the series, which ensures its illusory air of embodying a special finality. This is not so remarkable, we might think; yet it is worth noting how quality is in fact activated by quantity, given that the value concentrated within this single signifier is one which spreads along the entire run of intermediary signifieds making up the paradigmatic chain. Here we find what might be called the symbolism of the object, in the etymological sense (*symbolein*) whereby a chain of significations is subsumed in a single one of its terms. The unique object is indeed a symbol, not of some external factor or quality, but essentially of the entire series of objects of which it constitutes the final term (while simultaneously being a symbol of the person who owns it).

La Bruyère's example allows us to draw out another law, which is that an object only acquires its exceptional value *by dint of being absent*. It is not just a matter of the glamour of a mirage. What we have begun to suspect is that *the collection is never really initiated in order to be completed*. Might it not be that the missing item in the collection is in fact an indispensable and positive part of the whole, in so far as this lack is the basis of the subject's ability to grasp himself in objective terms? Whereas the acquisition of the final item would in effect denote the death of the subject, the absence of this item still allows him the possibility of simulating his death by envisaging it in an object, thereby warding off its menace. This gap in the collection may be experienced as painful, but it is equally that rupture through which is signified a definitive elision of the real. We should therefore congratulate La Bruyère's collector for not having tracked down his last Callot, since he would otherwise have ceased to be the living and passionate individual he still was! It could indeed be added that the point where a collection closes in on itself and ceases to be oriented towards an unfilled gap is the point where madness begins.

Another anecdote, relayed by Rheims, confirms this way of seeing things. A bibliophile with a magnificent collection of unique books learns one day that a bookseller in New York has placed on sale an item identical to one of the volumes he owns. He takes the plane, purchases the book, and then arranges to have a notary public present when he sets fire to the second copy, in order to ensure a formal attestation as to its destruction. Whereupon he slips the attestation inside the first volume and retires happily to bed. Does this act represent the annulment of a series? Only apparently: in fact, the unique volume owes its value to all virtual volumes, and the bibliophile, in destroying the second copy, merely re-establishes the perfection of a symbol that had been compromised. Whether denied, forgotten, destroyed or virtual, the *series* always remains operative. As much in the humblest of everyday objects as in the loftiest of rarities, it is the indispensable nourishment of ownership and the passionate game of possession. Without the series, there would be no possibility of playing the game, hence no possibility of ownership, and, strictly speaking, no more object either. Indeed the truly unique object – absolute, entirely without antecedent, incapable of being integrated into any sort of set – is unthinkable. It exists no more than does a pure sound. And just as in music the harmonic series exists to help identify the particularity of the note we hear, so do the paradigmatic series or sets implicit in collecting, in their greater or lesser complexity, promote the symbolic propensity of objects, at the same time as they prepare them for the human processes of possession and play.

OBJECTS AND HABITS: THE WRIST-WATCH

Any object may be said to float midway between a practical specification or function, which can be likened to its manifest discourse, and its absorption within a collection or set, where it enters a latent and repetitive discourse, the most elementary and tenacious of discourses. This discursive object-system is homologous to the one which informs our everyday habits.[7]

Now, habit has to do with repetition, and also with discontinuity (rather than continuity, as common usage might suggest). It is through our cutting up of time into those patterns we call 'habits' that we resolve the potential threat of time's inexorable continuity, and evade the implacable singularity of events. Likewise, it is through their discontinuous integration within sets and series that we truly dispose of our objects, and thus truly come to possess them. Here we confront the very discourse of subjectivity, of which objects represent one of the most privileged registers – interposing, in that space between the irreversible flux of existence and our own selves, a screen that is discontinuous, classifiable, reversible, as repetitive as one could wish, a fringe of the world that remains docile in our physical or mental grip, and thus wards off all anxiety. Not only do objects help us master the world, by virtue of their being inserted into practical sets, they also help us, *by virtue of their being inserted into mental sets*, to establish dominion over time, interrupting its continuous flow and classifying its parts in the same way that we classify habits, and insisting that it submit to the same constraints of association that inform the way we set things out in space.

The wrist-watch is an excellent example of this sort of discontinuous and 'habit-like' functioning.[8] It epitomizes the dualism inherent in the way we deal with objects. On one level, the wrist-watch keeps us informed about objective time: chronometric exactitude being, of course, a factor indissociable from material constraints, social intercourse, and death. Yet, all the while it makes us submit to this temporal tyranny, the wrist-watch, as an object, also helps us to make time our own. Just as the car 'eats up' miles, so the wrist-watch-as-object eats up time.[9] By treating time as a substance that can be cut up, it turns it into an object of consumption. Time ceases to be the perilous dimension of praxis and becomes a domesticated quantity. Not only does civilized man know what o'clock it is, but also, thanks to an object which is his and his alone, he can now 'possess' time, enforcing its ceaseless registration within his presence. This fact has become part and parcel of the experience of modern man, his very security. Time is no longer situated back at home, within the beating heart of the grandfather clock, but is now, through the wrist-watch, registered throughout the day, with the same organic satisfaction as the throb of an artery. Thanks to the wrist-watch, time allows me full latitude to objectify myself, on the same footing as a domestic possession. In truth, any kind of object might support this analysis of the recuperation of the dimension of objective constraint: because of its direct bearing upon time, the wrist-watch is simply the most clear-cut example.

OBJECTS AND TEMPORALITY: THE CONTROLLED CYCLE

The problematic of temporality is fundamental to the collecting process. As Rheims observes, 'a phenomenon often associated with the passion of collecting is the loss of all sense of the present'.[10] Yet are we speaking merely of nostalgic escapism? A collector who elects to identify with Louis XVI, down to the very legs of his armchair, or who is infatuated with sixteenth-century snuffboxes, is naturally at odds with the present day by virtue of this historical alignment. However, in this context, such an alignment is a secondary issue, for what really matters is the systematic of the collection as it is experienced. In fact the profound power exerted by collected objects derives not from their singularity nor their distinct historicity. It is not because of these that we see the time of the collection as diverging from real time, but rather because *the setting-up of a collection itself displaces real time*. Doubtless this is the fundamental project of all collecting – to translate real time into the dimensions of a system. Taste, curiosity, prestige, social intercourse, all of these may draw the collector into a wider sphere of relationships (though never going beyond a circle of initiates): yet collecting remains first and foremost, and in the true sense, a *pastime*. For collecting simply abolishes time. Or rather: by establishing a fixed repertory of temporal references that can be replayed at will, in reverse order if need be, collecting represents the perpetual fresh beginning of a controlled cycle, thanks to which, starting out from any term he chooses and confident of returning to it, man can indulge in the great game of birth and death.

This explains why it is that to be surrounded by our personal possessions – the collector amid his private collection being the extreme example – is a dimension of existence as essential to us as it is imaginary. It means every bit as much as our dreams. It has been said that if, in an experiment, one were to prevent a person from dreaming, severe psychological disturbances would rapidly ensue. It is equally certain that if a person were deprived of the possibility of escaping-and-regressing within the game of possession, if that person were prevented from marshalling his own discourse and running through a repertory of objects imbued with self and removed from time, mental disarray would follow every bit as promptly. We are incapable of living in the dimension of absolute singularity, in uninterrupted consciousness of that irreversibility of time signalled in the moment of our birth. It is this irreversibility, this relentless passage from birth to death, that objects help us to resolve.

Naturally enough, such equilibrium can only be neurotic, just as the panic reaction is regressive: for we have to concede that time is indeed objectively irreversible, and that even those objects whose function is to shield us from this fact must in due course be snatched away by time. And naturally enough, the strategy of discontinuous defence at the level of objects cannot be anything less than a constant paradox, given that the world and mankind form a continuum. All the same, can one really speak of normality or anomaly here? To seek refuge within a synchronic haven might be seen as a denial of reality and a form of escapism, if it is indeed thought that objects are being invested with what 'ought' instead to be invested in human relationships. And yet the immense power of objects to regulate our lives depends on just this option. In our era of faltering religious and ideological authorities, they are by way of becoming the consolation of consolations, an everyday myth capable of absorbing all our anxieties about time and death.

We should dismiss the cliché that man survives through his possessions. Creating a safe haven has really nothing to do with securing immortality, perpetuity or some sort of afterlife by way of a *mirror-object* (man has never really maintained any serious belief in this), but is a far more complex game which involves the 'recycling' of birth and death within *an object-system*. What man wants from objects is not the assurance that he can somehow outlive himself, but *the sense that from now on he can live out his life uninterruptedly and in a cyclical mode, and thereby symbolically transcend the realities of an existence before whose irreversibility and contingency he remains powerless.*

Here we find ourselves not so far away from that ball which, in Freud's analysis, the child makes vanish and re-appear in order to experience the alternating absence and presence of its mother – *fort / da / fort / da* – the anguish of lack being dispelled by the sustained cycle of re-appearances of the ball. Here we can appreciate the symbolic resonances of serial play. Indeed we might be prompted to say that *the object is that through which we mourn for ourselves*, in the sense that, in so far as we truly possess it, the object stands for our own death, symbolically transcended. That is to say, by dint of introjecting the object within an enactment of mourning – in other words, by integrating it within a series based on the repeated cyclical game of making it absent and then recalling it from out of that absence – we reach an accommodation with the anguish-laden fact of lack, of literal death. Henceforth, in our daily lives, we will continue to enact this mourning for our own person through the intercession of objects, and this allows us, albeit regressively, to live out our lives. The man who collects things may already be dead, yet he manages literally to outlive himself through his collection, which, originating within this life, recapitulates him indefinitely beyond the point of death *by absorbing death itself into the series and the cycle*. In this respect, it would make sense once more to invoke the analogy with dreams: to the extent that each object is, in terms of its function (be it practical, cultural or social), the mediation of a *wish*, it constitutes equally, as one term among others within that systematic game we have just described, the articulation of a *desire.* And this last is that which, on the indefinite chain of signifiers, brings about the recapitulation or indefinite substitution of oneself across the moment of death and beyond. It is by a not dissimilar compromise that, just as the function of dreams is to ensure the continuity of sleep, objects ensure the continuity of life.[11]

THE OBJECT CONFINED: THE JEALOUSY SYSTEM

Pursuing regression to its final stage, the passion for objects climaxes in pure jealousy. Here possession derives its fullest satisfaction from the prestige the object enjoys in the eyes of other people, and the fact that they cannot have it. The jealousy complex, symptomatic of the passion of collecting at its most fanatical, can exert a proportionate influence over the reflex of ownership, even at the most innocent level. What now comes into play is a powerful anal-sadistic impulse that tends to confine beauty in order to savour it in isolation: this sexually perverse pattern of behaviour is a widespread feature of object relations.

What does the object come to represent when thus isolated? (Its objective value is secondary, for it is the fact of its confinement that constitutes its charm.) If it is true that one is hardly inclined to lend another person one's car, one's pen, one's wife, this is because these objects are, within the jealousy system, the narcissistic equivalents of oneself: and were such an object to be lost or damaged, this would mean symbolic castration. When all is said and done, one never lends out one's phallus. That which the jealous person commandeers and guards in close proximity is, beneath the disguise of an object, nothing less than his own libido, which he endeavours to neutralize within the system of confinement — the selfsame system thanks to which the collection deflects the menace of death. The jealous owner castrates himself through fear of his own sexuality; or rather he enacts a symbolic castration — the confinement of the object — in order to dispel the fear of literal castration.[12] It is this desperate endeavour that gives rise to the awful pleasures of jealousy. One is always jealous of oneself. It is always oneself that one watches over like a hawk. And it is always in oneself that one takes pleasure.

Clearly this pleasure steeped in jealousy stands in stark contrast to the background of utter disappointment that accompanies it, since regressive behaviour, however concerted, can never completely cancel out one's awareness of its inadequacy in the face of the real world. And so it is with the collection: its sovereignty is a fragile one, and the superior authority of the real world lurks behind it as a constant menace. Even so, this very sense of disappointment can be seen to be part and parcel of the system.

For it is the fact of being disappointed, quite as much as being satisfied, that activates the system: this is because disappointment is never focused on the world, but always on the next term in the series, so that disappointment and satisfaction emerge as the stages of a cyclical process. It is this built-in disappointment that often makes the system seem so frenzied and neurotic. The series tends to rotate ever faster upon itself, with the result that differences get worn away with the acceleration of the mechanism of substitution. Then it is that the system may rush headlong towards its own collapse, equivalent to the self-destruction of the subject. Rheims cites examples of collections that are violently 'done to death' in this way, in a kind of suicide reflecting the impossibility of ever circumventing death itself. Within the jealousy system, it is not at all uncommon for the subject to end up destroying the very object or being he has confined, driven by his sense of powerlessness at ever being able to withstand the encroachments of the world and of his own sexuality. This is the logical and highly irrational outcome of the jealousy system.[13]

THE OBJECT DESTRUCTURED: THE SYSTEM OF PERVERSION

The efficacy of this mechanism of possession is in direct ratio to its regressiveness. And this regressiveness echoes the modalities of perversion itself. If it is true that, in terms of object choices, perversion manifests itself most classically in the form of fetishism, we can hardly overlook the fact that, throughout the system, the passion for, and possession of, an object are conditioned by comparable purposes and modalities, and can indeed be seen as what I would call a *discreet variety of sexual perversion*. Indeed, just as possession is coloured by the discontinuity of the series (be it real or virtual) and by the targeting of just one privileged term, so sexual perversion consists in the inability to grasp the partner, the supposed object of desire, as that singular totality we call a person. Instead, it is only able to operate discontinuously, reducing the partner to an abstract set made up of the various erotic parts of its anatomy, and then exercising a projective fixation on a single item. Whereupon a given woman stops being a woman and becomes no more than a vagina, a couple of breasts, a belly, a pair of thighs, a voice, a face – according to preference.[14] Henceforth she is reduced to a set whose separate signifying elements are one by one ticked off by desire, and whose true signified is no longer the beloved, but the subject himself. For it is the subject, the epitome of narcissistic self-engrossment, who collects and eroticizes his own being, evading the amorous embrace to create a closed dialogue with himself.

This mechanism is neatly illustrated in the opening shots of Jean-Luc Godard's film *Le Mépris*, where a sequence of 'naked' images is accompanied by the following dialogue:

> 'How do you like my feet?' the woman asks. [Be it noted that, throughout the whole scene, she inspects herself, detail by detail, in a mirror. This is hardly innocent, for what she is doing is to valorize herself as a set of separate, ready-framed images.]
> 'I love your feet.'
> 'How do you like my legs?'
> 'I love your legs.'
> 'And my thighs?'
> 'Oh yes,' he repeats, 'I love them.'
> [And so on, from bottom to top, until they have reached her hair.]
> 'So, you must love me all over?'
> 'Oh yes, all over.'
> 'Me too, Paul', she says [as if to sum up the situation].

Conceivably the film-makers meant to convey the algebraic brilliance of a passion entirely undisguised. It remains the case, nevertheless, that this absurd ticking-off of the desirable is fundamentally inhuman. Reduced to a set of anatomical parts, the woman becomes a pure object, and is subsumed within the series of all object-women, of which she is but a single term among hundreds. Within the logic of such a system, the only conceivable room for manoeuvre is the game of substitution. And this we have seen to be crucial to the fulfilment of the passion of collecting.

This kind of step-by-step destructuring of the object within a perverse, auto-erotic system is less likely to occur within a true amorous relationship because of the partner's integrity as a living being.[15] On the other hand, it is typical of all cases where there is an orientation toward non-human objects, and especially fabricated objects of sufficient complexity to lend themselves to mental fragmentation. I might, for instance, refer to the car I drive in terms of '*my* brakes', '*my* steering-wheel', '*my* bonnet'. And no-one thinks twice about saying '*I* braked', '*I* changed gear', '*I* drove off'. Each component, each mechanical function can be referred back to the subject in the modality of possession. This is not to be seen as an activity consolidating the social persona, but as an activity of self-projection. It is located not within the order of having, but within the order of being. If we turn to the example of the horse, historically one of man's most astonishing instruments of power and transcendence, we find that this kind of assimilation fails to work. This is because the horse is simply not made out of component parts, and above all because it has a sex. I might refer to 'my horse' or 'my lover', but that is as far as the possessive denomination can go. That which has a sex is resistant to fragmented projection, and thus to that mode of passionate appropriation that we have seen to be a species of auto-eroticism and, at the extreme, a perversion.[16] Faced by a living creature, I might say *my*, but I can never say *I* in the way I do when symbolically appropriating the functions and components of the car. It is impossible to regress any further. One could list a whole clutch of symbolic meanings that have been invested in the horse (it represents headlong sexual lust, it embodies the wisdom of the centaur; its head is a terrifying phantasm linked to the image of the Father, while its composure reflects the strength of Chiron seen as protector and teacher). Yet the horse can never yield to such simplified, narcissistic, primitive and infantile forms of self-projection as can the component parts of the car (reflecting an almost delirious analogy with the dissociated components and functions of the human body). If there is a symbolic dynamic to the horse, it operates precisely because it is impossible to enumerate each of the horse's parts and functions; hence it is equally impossible to exhaust the relationship by way of an auto-erotic 'discourse' focused on isolated elements.

This regressive reduction to component parts implies a particular *modus operandi* or method on the part of the subject, concentrated within the sphere of the part-object. Thus the woman translated into a syntagm of separate erogenous zones is assigned the single function of giving pleasure, to which corresponds the erotic method. This is of course a method that seeks to objectify and to ritualize, so as to camouflage the anxieties of the personal relationship and at the same time establish a valid alibi (gestural and plausible) while the system of perversion runs its phantasmatic course. It can be argued that every mental system is 'indebted' to reality in that it requires some concession, some technical 'ratification' or pretext. Thus the accelerator in the phrase 'I accelerated', the headlamp in the phrase 'my headlamp', or the entire car in the phrase 'my car', represent the material technical underpinning of that whole enterprise of narcissistic recuperation that seeks to ignore materiality. The same holds for the erotic method, deliberately pursued: be it noted that, at this level, we are no longer dealing with the genital order that abuts upon reality and pleasure, but with the anal-regressive order of the serial system, for which erotic activity serves only as a cover.

It is obvious that such a method is far from being consistently 'objective'. It can be objective if it is socialized, or absorbed within a technology, or when it informs new structures. But when it operates within the realm of the everyday, it offers a space ever more conducive to regressive fantasy, given that the potential for destructuring is always so close at hand. When assembled and fitted together, the components of a technical object embody a coherence. Yet the structure betrays its fragility once confronted by the mind: from the outside it may cohere by virtue of its function, but for the *psyche* it is a form open to manipulation. Although the components of a structure may have been organized as a hierarchy, at any moment they can fall apart and lapse indiscriminately into a paradigmatic system within which the subject can rehearse a private repertory of meanings. The object is *a priori* lacking in cohesion; it is easily destructured by thought. All the more so where the object (and especially the technological object) is no longer associated, as in the past, with a human gesture, a human dynamic. If it is true that the car is superior to the horse as an object of narcissistic manipulation, it is largely because the control one exercises over a horse is muscular and rhythmical, and involves physically balancing oneself, whereas one's control of a car is simplified, functional and abstract.

REAL MOTIVATION AND SERIAL MOTIVATION

Throughout this analysis, we have worked on the assumption that it is not important what sorts of objects are being collected: we have concentrated on the systematic and ignored the thematic aspect. Even so, it is clear that one does not collect paintings by Old Masters in the same spirit that one collects cigar-bands. It should be stressed that the concept of collecting (from the Latin *colligere*, to select and assemble) is distinct from that of accumulating. The latter – the piling up of old papers, the stockpiling of items of food – is an inferior stage of collecting, and lies midway between oral introjection and anal retention. The next stage is that of the serial accumulation of identical objects. Collecting proper emerges at first with an orientation to the cultural: it aspires to discriminate *between* objects, privileging those which have some exchange value or which are also 'objects' of conservation, of commerce, of social ritual, of display – possibly which are even a source of profit. Such objects are always associated with human projects. While ceaselessly referring to one another, they admit within their orbit the external dimension of social and human intercourse.

On the other hand, even in cases where external motivation remains strong, the collection can never exist without an internal systematic (at the very least it will create a compromise between the two). For although the collection may speak to other people, it is always first and foremost a discourse directed toward oneself. The serial aspect of its motivation is evident in all cases. Research has shown that customers who invest in publishers' 'collections' (such as the paperback series *10/18* or *Que sais-je?*) get so carried away that they continue to acquire titles which hold no interest for them. A book's distinctive position within the series is sufficient to create a formal interest where no intrinsic interest exists. What motivates the purchase is the pure imperative of association. A similar behaviour pattern would be that of the reader who cannot settle down to read unless he is surrounded by his entire library of books: at which point the specificity of a given text tends to evaporate. There is yet another stage when it becomes clear that it is not the book that matters so much as the moment when it is safely returned to its proper place on the library shelf. Conversely, the customer devoted to a series will find it hard to 'pick up the thread' if he once drops it: he will not even bother to buy titles in which he has a genuine interest. These observations are enough to enable us to distinguish quite categorically between the two types of motivation: each is perfectly distinct, and they coexist only by virtue of a compromise, and with a pronounced tendency, created by inertia, for serial motivation to take precedence over 'real' or dialectical motivation in the identification of preferences.[17]

Notwithstanding, it can happen that pure collecting intersects with genuine interest. Someone who starts out systematically tracking down all the titles on the *Que sais-je?* list will frequently end up orienting his book collection towards a theme: music, say, or sociology. A certain quantitative threshold in one's accumulation allows one to envisage the possibility of selectivity. But there is no absolute rule. It *is* possible to collect Old Master paintings or cheese labels with the same regressive fanaticism; on the other hand, stamp collecting among children is invariably associated with swapping and therefore social contact. So that one can never declare absolutely that because a given collection happens to have a marked thematic complexity, then this is proof that it affords authentic access to the real world. At most, such complexity can offer a clue or a presumption.

What makes a collection transcend mere accumulation is not only the fact of its being culturally complex, but the fact of its incompleteness, the fact that it *lacks* something. Lack always means lack of something unequivocally defined: one needs such and such an absent object. And this exigency, modulating into the quest and the impassioned appeal to other people,[18] is enough to interrupt that deadly hypnotic allure of the collection to which the subject otherwise falls prey. A television programme on the topic of collecting illustrated this point rather well: as each collector presented his collection to the public, he never failed to mention the very specific 'item' he didn't have, as if soliciting his audience to procure it for him. Hence the object is capable of shifting over into a social discourse. Yet at the same time one has to recognize that *this shift is typically engineered through the absence of the object rather than its presence.*

A DISCOURSE ORIENTED TOWARD ONESELF

It remains characteristic of the collection that there comes a point when the self-absorption of the system is interrupted and the collection is enrolled within some external project or exigency (whether associated with prestige, culture or commerce makes no odds, only assuming that the object ends up confronting one man with another, thereby constituting itself as message). On the other hand, whatever the orientation of a collection, it will always embody an irreducible element of independence from the world. It is because he feels himself alienated or lost within a social discourse whose rules he cannot fathom that the collector is driven to construct an alternative discourse that is for him entirely amenable, in so far as he is the one who dictates its signifiers – the ultimate signified being, in the final analysis, none other than himself. Yet in this endeavour he is condemned to failure: in imagining he can do without the social discourse, he fails to appreciate the simple fact that he is transposing its open, objective discontinuity into a closed, subjective discontinuity, such that the idiom he invents forfeits all value for others. This is why withdrawal into an all-encompassing object system is synonymous with loneliness: it is impervious to communication from others, and it lacks communicability. Indeed we are bound to ask: can objects ever institute themselves as a viable language? Can they ever be fashioned into a discourse oriented otherwise than toward oneself?

In practice, the collector is unlikely to turn into an irremediable maniac, precisely because he collects objects that, one way or another, prevent him regressing toward total abstraction or psychological delirium. By the same token, the discourse voiced through his collection can never rise above a certain level of indigence and infantilism. The process of collecting is necessarily recurrent and finite; its very constituents – being objects – are too concrete, too discontinuous for it to be capable of articulating itself as a real dialectical structure.[19] If it is true that 'he who collects nothing must be a cretin', he who does collect can never entirely shake off an air of impoverishment and depleted humanity.

Translated by Roger Cardinal

2

'Unless you do these crazy things . . .'

AN INTERVIEW WITH ROBERT OPIE

John Elsner and Roger Cardinal visited the collector Robert Opie at his home in Ealing, west London, on 3 August 1993. Opie lives in a terraced house surrounded by the fruits of a lifetime's dedication to collecting. Despite the removal of a large proportion of its contents to Gloucester in 1984, where Opie founded the Museum of Advertising and Packaging, the house remains the true locus of his collection, with boxes, tins, bottles, trade signs, books and other objects occupying almost every available inch of living space.

Q. We know that your parents, Peter and Iona Opie, studied the lore of schoolchildren. Were they not also collectors?

Opie: Yes, my father built up an outstanding private collection of children's books, and after his death it went to the Bodleian Library, along with his private papers. My father was also interested in the artefacts we live amongst, particularly relating to children . . .

Toys and games . . . ?

Toys and games and general ephemera. He did actually save very small amounts of packaging – microscopic amounts compared to what I have now. Literally a couple of boxes of oddments, amongst them an early frozen food-packet.

With the food inside?

Without the food inside, thankfully; that's the reason it survived! It was a Findus packet showing the change from their being called fish-sticks to fishfingers. He was aware that these things were transient, so part of that was instilled in my upbringing.

Your parents were largely interested in oral culture, weren't they?

Yes, very much so, and this is not something that people generally realize, that you can also collect things that don't necessarily have a physical being. But the two things go hand in hand – you need the actual object but also the oral back-up, to know what people thought about it. Thus, if you have a packet of cornflakes, is it something nice to eat? You don't know, unless you ask people. 'Well, look, there's a packet of cornflakes, and 'it's the best thing since sliced bread'. You don't know whether that's true or not. All that is the manufacturer's own opinion.

We often have foreign guests who like the look of Marmite *and then spread it on too thick . . .*

Yes, that's because they haven't been shown how to spread *Marmite*, and they don't have that childhood link. Often things we have grown up with, we tend to like more.

But is it true you started collecting because your parents were collecting?

Who knows? Most children collect things, don't they? I think it's instinctive to collect things, or maybe just gather things. There are many different levels of collecting, and the first one is to just gather things together; and indeed the first thing I ever collected was a round stone which I pulled out of the garden path when I was two or three. I ran to show my mother and it was a fossilized sea-urchin. It became the basis of a collection of stones and things like that. Then I went on to collect stamps and coins, and the Lesney *Matchbox* series. I suppose my first comprehensive collection was when I did a scrapbook for the Coronation at the age of six, for which I won first prize at school: there were many older children and there I was, winning first prize. Nevertheless, as all parents do, they gave me guidance, but they weren't allowed to touch. There were all these swimming pools of glue, and I was told how to position the pictures.

Do you think scrapbooks are a good way to preserve things?

Scrapbooks have been very useful – a lot of things have survived. There was this great craze of putting scraps into scrapbooks, and later on people would say 'Oh God, they've the cut the corners off', or 'They've trimmed it, what a shame', but if it hadn't been for that, they wouldn't have been saved in the first place.

How did your collecting develop?

With hindsight, I was doing my apprenticeship in collecting throughout childhood. So when, for instance, I decided to start on the Lesney *Matchbox* series, my father would say: 'Well look, you save the box, you write the price it cost you and the date you got it', and this would have been in the late 1950s. I can't remember when I did start. That was obviously useful, because here were pieces of packaging, and one got used to not just buying the item but also gathering information about the company, the advertising material and so on, and making sure you got everything as it came out. So this was collecting contemporary items in the same way that I was collecting the new Post Offfice issues as well as looking back at the earlier stamps.

What age were you at this point? Being so systematic, one wonders . . .

I guess eleven or twelve, that kind of age.

You keep the Matchbox *toy, but you've also got a record of it, the price and the provenance.*

On the box itself. That's the best way of doing it.

You don't have a separate catalogue?

I do not have a separate catalogue. My whole basis is that everything is filed in such a way that it *is* the catalogue. So there may be a bank of a thousand boxes, each with a label on it which says what the contents are and inside there is the story of that company or that brand, and in a sense that is the catalogue. So long as you know where that box is you don't need a catalogue.

Is it alphabetical or associative?

It depends what you mean. Cataloguing is very difficult in this context because if I were to catalogue everything of Cadbury's, I would have to put an enamel sign in with a fragile piece of paper, in with a three-dimensional box which would then get crushed. So, generally speaking, it has to be split into six or seven different sections. One category would be enamel signs, but you would have all those together, and you would remember there was a Cadbury's enamel sign in there. Because I have that kind of mind, I can remember that type of thing. Then the chocolate boxes will be boxed as Cadbury's chocolate boxes, all the small paper Cadbury items would be filed under Cadbury's, all the chocolate bars would be filed under chocolate bars, all the small tins would be filed under the small tins. . . . It's easy for me to say this, but it probably doesn't happen strictly like that – there'll be all kinds of different rules. You can't be very strict about this, because you would go crazy.

So it's the nature of the object that governs the way it's kept?

You tend to put tin with tin and paper with paper. If a tin goes rusty it'll affect the paper, so you have to file it in a way that is easily retrievable, and to ensure from a conservation point of view that you're not going to damage them by putting the two together.

I'm intrigued that you move between the materials and the size of the objects. These things are made up as you go along.

You have to make things up for two reasons. The first is because you don't know how much there is. If I'd known how much stuff I'd be able to save I wouldn't have started this system. You begin thinking 'Well here are a thousand objects and here is a system to cope with a thousand objects'. You don't think 'How is that system going to react when I put in a hundred thousand objects?' With my collection of *Oxo* items, I will have one box for *Oxo* tins, one for paper *Oxo* containers and one for playing-cards and ancillary items. I can go upstairs and show you. I have about six or eight boxes, I forget how many; I would have started off with perhaps one box, and every time it filled up, you would split it, like an amoeba – it has to divide down.

In a way, you would have to keep re-cataloguing it?

That's right, the system has to be ever-expanding.

You don't have space that can be extended indefinitely, though.

I remember showing my father the things I could find. I remember doing a small exhibition in this very room and he was astonished that I had been able to find what I had found. I started collecting packaging, at the age of sixteen, that was just contemporary packaging and advertising. It wasn't until the end of 1969 that I realized that one should be saving the earlier material, in fact that one could still find the earlier material.

The first response was just not to throw things away?

When I was down at Portsmouth, doing a business studies course, I had a circuit of maybe twenty or so CTNs (confectioners, tobacconists, newsagents) in Southsea and Portsmouth and so on, on a regular once a week or twice a week basis, and gathered any display material they had, any advertisements they were throwing out and things like that. Then I would come back and re-display them myself and look at these wonderful boxes of dummy chocolates. In those days you could still get a box of *Black Magic* chocolates with individual plaster moulds for each chocolate, each in its individual doily, and they would make a dummy display up for the shop window – it was a work of art in its own right. In exactly the same way, I would go and spend my one-and-sixpence buying the latest in the *Matchbox* series of miniature toys, and think, 'Gosh, what a marvellous piece of engineering. How clever for all that detail to be put into one tiny little box.' Likewise one would go into the post office, buy the latest stamp, and think, 'Gosh, what lovely colours and look at all that intricate detail and design work. Isn't that amazing.' I think that as a child one does study down to that detail. A lot of what I'm trying to do is to put that excitement of childhood back into our everyday life and show how exciting it actually is. A trip round the supermarket is as exciting as when we were children.

That's an interesting axis, because one might have thought there was nostalgia for the past, an irretrievable past as it were. Do you feel a special affinity with the objects of the 1950s?

Absolutely, but only partly because it's nostalgic. If I haven't seen something for thirty or forty years it will give me that intense 'punch' of nostalgia, which happens to everybody. The last time it happened was with an advertisement for a cereal packet which showed the things that you could cut out. I suddenly 're-sensationed' that particular moment: I can remember cutting out from the *Weetabix* packet all those little cars that you mould up, the feeling of the colour and the cardboard, and the way the cardboard cuts. . . . All that sensation comes back to you in an instant and can have an enormous personal effect. People in the museum in Gloucester can get that sensation, and you can hear their cries when they see things. That can be really extraordinary.

As a child did you perceive yourself as different?

No, I certainly didn't. I always assumed that every home should have its own little museum in it, like my home had, and why didn't other houses I went to visit have the same thing? You grow up in an environment and to you as a child, that is the accepted norm and everybody else is different. I grew up in this house where there were books everywhere, every corridor was lined with books, one's father was working at home and that was the acceptable thing.

Why did you choose at age sixteen to focus on packaging?

After the Lesney *Matchbox* series (which was very much a regulated collection because you could only collect as much as was being pro-duced), I started collecting other things, especially stamps in 1954. That was parental influence. On each page were the six best examples of the stamp I could find, so there were six ha'pennies with the least postmark on them. Me and my brother both used to collect stamps (my brother not as hard), and we had alternate days to collect the post when it arrived. If it was your post day, you were able to take off the stamps you wanted. My father used to get quite a lot of correspondence. Elevenpenny stamps were hard to find as they were hardly ever used; we only had two or three of those.

It's quite aesthetic in a sense, because these were clean stamps?

Yes, but nicely postmarked.

Did you count the postmark as part of what you were collecting?

Oh yes. Otherwise you would just go out and get a mint one, which one couldn't afford anyway, but that was like cheating. This was to get the most perfect example; you didn't want one with a great big postmark that would destroy the stamp but a nice circled one, not taking up too much of the stamp.

How did you conserve the stamps?

I think it was Christmas 1957 when I got my first proper stamp album with all the countries in it. The floodgates were open and everything took off from there. I think my parents would have said this was the first thing I really got interested in. You start collecting every stamp, but as every stamp collector knows, it's too much, and you have to start narrowing down the field. So eventually I narrowed down my collection to anything that wasn't an adhesive stamp, then I was collecting anything that was issued over the counter in the post office. Postal stationery, greetings cards, telegrams, things that my friends did not collect. This brings out the explorer in one, like in the 1920s and 1930s you would go out and traipse into Africa, where no white man had gone before. Both my grandparents were very much of that ilk, both in far-flung corners of the Empire. One was a surgeon in India, the other a pathologist in the Sudan and Egypt.

Did they collect?

No, I don't think so.

So, in effect, you found your exotica at the post office rather than in stamps from all over the world?

Indeed yes, I shifted my ground to that because I felt it was something that other people had not done before. Slowly I found other people were studying it. It was useful in a way because it gave you somebody to talk to.

In your packaging collection, would you say you were pioneering within this country, or in the world? Do you have any idea of the overall picture?

Well, a pioneer only in a sense. It's rather like climbing Everest: since time immemorial someone's been trying to get to the top, but who is the pioneer? Is it the man who actually got to the summit first, or is it the man who first made it to Base One? It's the same with packaging. I've known collectors from the 1930s who've saved packaging, and of course people save things for different reasons. They may not think of themselves as collectors of packaging, they may just see themselves as collectors of matchbox labels . . .

All these different things – is there any limit to what you are prepared to collect?

No. My whole philosophy is that there should be no limit, because otherwise one is limiting the collection. There are some collectors of postcards who will only collect ones that fit into their album. If they get a postcard that won't, because it's a fraction of an inch too big – dammit! You know, they virtually chuck it away because it doesn't conform. I know collectors who collect tins of a certain size because that's all they want to do. They're not really collectors, to my mind, they are just gatherers, people who want to put things up on a mantelpiece to look interesting. I could take you through an analysis which will say 'There's nothing which I cannot find a reason for saving'.

How did you first realize you were committing yourself to this sort of universal preservation?

Have you read that account of the blinding flash of light and all that?

The Munchies?

The *Munchies*, yes. The trouble again is with hindsight, how much one knows is reality and how much is made up when you're asked by a journalist years later.

That's interesting too, because in a way your moment has been recollected and reconsumed too.

The factual side of it I know is true. In September 1963 I had been with my father and mother at the British Association for the Advancement of Science in Aberdeen. My father had been President of the Anthropological Section. I had been subjected to a week of high-powered talks and meetings, dinners with all these highbrow intellectuals. So my mind was in overdrive. We had then gone down to Edinburgh, I remember, to the Museum of Childhood, and I was the person who had claimed to set the world record at cup and ball. You know the cup and ball? Unless you know how to do it, it's impossible, but I think I managed to do about fourteen or fifteen in succession, which amazed the curator there, he'd never seen anything like it in his life. Then my parents returned home and I had an invitation to go to the very top of Scotland to stay with some friends. I stayed overnight at Inverness, on a Sunday.

It was impossible to get anything to eat on a Sunday, at least in those days in Scotland. I found a vending machine and purchased a packet of Mackintosh's *Munchies* and a packet of McVitie & Price's *Ginger Nuts*. Those machines made a good sound in those days – a real 'crunch' when they came down. I got back to my room at the hotel and as I was consuming the *Munchies*, I suddenly looked at the pack and thought, 'If I throw this away I will never, ever, see it again, and yet here is a whole wealth of history.' It was something along those lines. But you see, I was looking at this packet as if it were a stamp, something that I had been saving for thirteen or fourteen years up to this point. So I had had my 'apprenticeship' and it had come to this pivotal moment. I can virtually remember the room I was in. The sudden realization came to me that this was something I should be saving, and I thought what an enormous part of social history I was about to throw away. That packet was going to change and develop into other things. It was no longer going to be priced at seven pence, it would soon be priced at eight pence, or whatever it was. Yet I was about to throw it away, damage it. I knew I should be saving these things. The next packet was the McVitie's one. I still have these things, and they have a date on them. It still says 'wrapped in Sellophane' on them. Spelt with an 'S'! I had my training – as with the *Matchboxes*, I would write the prices on and the date and everything else. When I went up to see my friends in Scotland, I was already saying, 'Can I have those packets?' When I got home, my mother was told about this momentous event and from that time on, I have saved every packet that I've consumed the contents of.

And you can say that categorically?

Well, I can't be totally categorical about this – had I saved every milk carton, I would now have a collection of 100,000, all exactly the same; so there are some things I buy of which I know I will throw the container away. But by and large, when I go around the supermarket I am looking primarily for the ones I'm going to need, to update the collection.

So in the end the contents aren't as important to you?

Only in that I might go around the supermarket a second time and think, 'Have I actually got anything for dinner?' I might have only bought things that I didn't want. Then I'll think 'Can I find something I want to eat that is also useful for the collection?'

When you buy something you don't actually eat, do you keep the whole thing?

Well it depends, you have to empty some things out! If there's a yoghurt which I really don't like – I will eat yoghurts . . . I now have 10,000 different yoghurt cartons because I was in at the beginning of the yoghurt boom. I will buy four yoghurts and maybe only consume three of them because there's only a certain amount you can eat and some of them are pretty ghastly anyway. Sometimes I will buy things knowing I won't eat the contents, but by and large I try and find things whose contents I'll eat.

What else do you eat that one might not think of? Do you eat meat, and would you save wrappers from it?

Well there aren't many meat wrappers. My whole collection is rather biased towards packaged products.

Factory produced?

Factory produced. Well not when it comes down to that detail. For example, take this sugar wrapper – once you have ten, how many more do you want?

Well, that's an interesting question. I thought they could all go in?

Well, they could all go in. People bring vast collections of things to me at the museum, and say 'here you are, here's a thousand of – whatever – and I think 'so what?' At the end of the day, if I did a display of a thousand sugar wrappers, how many people are going to stop and look at them, except to think 'God, how stupid!' I'd much rather have a hundred *Bovril* jars! Variety is what the human mind actually likes, and variety is what one wants to show them. How interesting is something going to be in ten years' time, in fifty years' time, or now? But having said that, you almost have to save everything, because you don't actually know what is going to be interesting in ten years' time, or fifty years' time. Things that I was saving in the 1960s. . .there was a whole new craze for slimming products, *Limitts* and things like that. All those *Limitts* packets turn out to be quite interesting – we went through that phase in the history of the nation. Whereas to show a sugar-packet which hasn't actually altered . . . Well, so what? It's that play between what's useful to save and what's boring to save. Also there's the price of things. One doesn't have limitless resources, and if I did, I wouldn't be buying packaging, I would be buying collectors' art. I'd buy a Gainsborough or something.

Was it a matter of conditions being absolutely right for you to become a packaging collector?

I was blessed, in a sense, with the right combination of ingredients. I was born into the right family background, I had the upbringing which meant I could perceive the right way of looking at things, I had a family that was tolerant of collecting because they were collectors themselves – I didn't have a mother who tidied the room and chucked everything away. I also needed to have a certain kind of mentality, to put up with the chaos, to see light at the end of the tunnel, to be made in a specific mould. I do have moments when I think I am going crazy, or maybe I shouldn't be doing this – but something makes me keep on going. I see people going through all the initial phases and they give up, because of all kinds of reasons. Space, time, money, maybe they get married, the wife doesn't like it, all kinds of reasons. Children come along, you've got to have more space, work pressures – there are a thousand and one reasons.

On the whole you've not hesitated in thirty years to keep everything? Have you never had periods when you've stopped?

I can look back at collections I've done: my collection of stones petered out, my Lesney *Matchbox* series petered out because they started to become expensive and other people were collecting them as well. If other people are collecting them, then let *them* get on with it! My stamp collection has stopped – I don't go out and get the latest stamps because everyone else is doing it. Also I've tended to give up the postal stationery. It's not as exciting as it used to be and other people are doing it, so what is the point?

None of those other collections have the Munchie *moment?*

They don't, no. I suppose it's much better to discover something than to to be told what to discover.

Would you say this was religious?

Not really, but it depends what you mean by religious. . . . To give you an example, I remember going into shops and looking at the wonderful packets of sweet cigarettes and thinking 'I must collect those'. But knowing that I hadn't started collecting them two or three years earlier and missed a lot, how could I start collecting them now? Then forcing myself to buy them, and now I have a nice collection of sweet-cigarette packets which are wonderful. Because they show you all the early television characters.

They don't sell them anymore?

Oh no, they still sell them. I've got the Jurassic Park one that's just come out. They call them sweet-sticks or something now – candy-sticks. But you see, there they all are, from Lenny the Lion to Batman. The older ones are a microcosm of what was going on in children's television. That is the era in which they made their presence felt. That kind of thing goes back much further – now, chocolate cigarettes, that's probably 1900-ish. All these things go back much further than one thinks. Of course if one doesn't buy them anymore, one thinks they've died out. It's like parents thinking their children no longer play in the playground, with all their naughty ditties and so on, but of course children don't talk to their parents in that kind of language. Parents tend to think it's all disappeared, when it hasn't. People go round an antiques fair looking for one thing and you're looking for another. I will see my things and they will see their things. They'll come to me and say, 'Oh did you see any teapots?', and I'll say, 'No, I didn't see any teapots'; but there were probably teapots everywhere. One's eyes are focused onto a particular subject which one sees because that is what one is actually looking for, and that is why people say, 'How do you find these things?' But they are everywhere, and you just need to understand where and how to look for them.

You remember we asked you before and you said there weren't any strict limits, but you've given ground slightly by saying there are one or two things that you don't now collect, like stamps. Are there objects of which you would say 'I wouldn't have one of those in the house'?

'Trying to trace the history of the major brands . . .':
Ty-Phoo tea-packets over the years.

There are all sorts of limits. I am interested in furniture, but I can't collect it because it costs a fortune and it takes up a lot of space – but I do have lots and lots of furniture catalogues! I can produce all the images but without necessarily having all the objects.

If there is a remit, how would you define it? Packaging? Boxes and ephemera? We could go on. Printed, fabricated . . .?

Yes, the way I treat it now is different from how I started off. The initial thing was to save the packaging and advertising that was around, the most common examples, until I realized I could find the earlier examples and then it was trying to trace the history of the major brands. At first I didn't know what I was doing because I didn't know what one could find. I remember getting terribly excited the first time I went down Portobello Road with the new concept. I'd been down Portobello Road many times before looking at things in general, but here I was trying to find early examples of containers like we have in the present day. I can remember finding Sainsbury's potted meat jars from Edwardian times, ceramic pots and things like that. Of course that intensity, that adrenalin that you get. . . . I can remember the physical joy . . . I can't really find a word for it, it's almost like the nostalgic buzz like when you see something you haven't seen for years. Often you see something that you don't know existed, but you know it's essential when you see it. I always have this mythical list of a thousand items that I'm looking for, some of that list I will know, and some of that list I won't know, because I don't know some things exist until I actually find them.

When I first started I found a chemist's in the Bull Ring in Kidderminster which originally had fourteen storerooms full of stuff. There was this man, Mr Trevithick, who couldn't resist a bargain, so when a travelling salesman came in and said, 'I'll give you five of these for the price of four', he would say yes. During the War this was a bonanza because he had stuff that no-one else had. By the time I found him, he only had two storerooms left, but still there was a lot there. I wasn't at that time saving all this material, I wasn't looking for old packaging. Why it didn't occur to me then to start saving earlier material, I just don't know. I gathered some of it together, and got my brother, who had a car, to come up and take it away. Eventually it got back to London.

Were you ever choosing things for aesthetic reasons?

Yes, but I can't say it was totally aesthetic. Undoubtedly part of the collecting instinct – and I think that instinct has to be strong in anyone who's a collector – is that you are prepared to tolerate the physical space these things take up. You have to have that collecting instinct to be able to keep going at it. I think for a lot of people, as they mature, that dissipates and one gets interested in other things. For some people it remains as strong, with others perhaps not as strong, depending on the individual.

Your archaeology is the everyday life around you?

This is it. I've not been out today to look at the headlines on today's papers, which I should have done because I saw there were a couple of interesting ones which I should buy, and if I don't do it now it's going to be even more difficult to do tomorrow, because I know they won't save them if I don't get there before 8 o'clock in the morning.

I didn't know newspapers were part of all this.

Well they are now, I'm afraid, and this has only been going on for the last few years. It's quite a recent branch. They're daily papers like the *Sun* and the *Mirror* and so on, because they have the best headlines. One of each unless there's reason to buy more. Two or three examples out of the spread.

So you might be able to do comparisons with the coverage of a particular story.

Yes, that's right. I did buy five, for instance, when each tabloid carried the same picture.

That's interesting. I mean historically.

Yes. If you look at packaging in its widest sense, the newspaper headline is trying to grab your attention in exactly the same way as a piece of packaging.

All this suggests a fascination with history. And eventually you did become not just a collector but also the curator of a museum, didn't you?

Yes, but I don't see that as pivotal – not like some other things. You have the collecting instinct, but then you have to *look* at what you've got. Those are two very independent processes. There are some people who collect things and stick them into their album until they have the complete set, and then go on to the next set. They're not really interested in why stamps started, or why they are stuck onto envelopes, because they're simply collecting little pieces of paper. The second stage is understanding that the little pieces of paper represent the history of the postal service. So there are two steps. The first is to get one item and then to get another hundred; the other is to work out what these things actually mean. How were they used, when did they first start producing them. For example, when did the first sugar-lump happen? I don't know, although I could give a guess. I saw one of the earliest sugar-lump adverts the other day – one of those mythical things I never knew existed, but there it was.

A brilliant insight, making them cubed rather than round!

Absolutely, a round one might be better but you wouldn't get as many in a box. I think there are two very distinct types of people. There are those who just want to collect, and there are those who want to think about it all. One of my great philosophies is to think about a subject, putting it into an environment, a context, rather than as a defined subject, and that's leading back to your earlier question about limits. My answer is, there are no limits, but that doesn't mean I want to save everything – that is the difference between being sane and being mad. If one is sane, one doesn't need to *collect* everything, but one does need to *understand* how everything relates to each other. The trouble is, as soon as I start talking about packaging, I'm talking about brands and products. Packaging is just the evidence that a given product existed, because by and large mine don't have their contents in them. But I'm not just interested in the packaging, I'm interested in the brand, the product, also the manufacturer, the way it's distributed, the way it's promoted, the way it's advertised, what people think about it, how it's marketed, how it's retailed and how it relates to all the competition around it, and then the worldwide scenario. What I'm saying is that one has to understand the whole concept.

Take the *Oxo* cube. How extraordinary that they got all that flavour into a little cube in the first place, then they've got to fit six *Oxo* cubes into a tin, then that tin is put into a larger box which is sold out of a display carton on the shelf in the shop, which it's got to get to; then they've got to sell it, they have to put up great hoardings everywhere, point-of-sale material, eventually publicize it on television to get you into a shop to actually buy it; then you've got the competition, the twenty other brands that were competing with it, twenty imitators – you need to have representations of all those, and you need to understand how the *Oxo* cube came out in 1910. In fact, there were *Liebig* cubes before *Oxo* cubes. One needs to understand all that history and then how it all fits into the shopping list. It's not just *Oxo* that someone goes out to buy, but there's everything else. So there's the shopping basket; and then some people would telephone their orders through or they would send their servants down to pick it up, and how does that all work, and when did the motor car come in, and all these other differences in the social framework. But you also want to see what the kitchen looked like and so on, you want to understand the whole circle of life. My whole framework is this: instead of narrowing my subject from collecting worldwide stamps down to one reign, then to one set of stamps and then the perforations, I do literally the opposite. What I want is to understand how this whole consumer revolution has affected us over the past 150 years; in which case, I have to understand everything that is affecting people on an everyday level, and that goes into every blessed thing that we have around us in our homes, in the street and in the shops.

So your Oxo *cube is really the universe. Do you think this was implicit in the* Munchies *moment? Or was it a development?*

'It's not just *Oxo* that someone goes out to buy . . . there's everything else':
part of the collection of *Oxo* items.

'Every blessed thing that we have around us . . .':
some types of packaging.

It was a development. I couldn't in my wildest dreams have thought the
Munchies moment would have ended up like this!

*I imagine the exhibitions you've done are a way to get other people
interested, so they will go out and collect.*

Yes, the Victoria & Albert Museum exhibition I did in 1975 was slightly
difficult from that point of view – it started other people collecting, and
now I find I'm competing. But one of the important things was to prevent
people throwing things away. I know big, big brands and companies who
say, 'We don't need that archive', and chuck it away, and within five
years they'll be saying 'Christ, we'd better start gathering it all together
again'. It's mindless. It always comes down to individuals in charge – they
can clear out things in a day or two, saying, 'We don't need this, we need
the space.' You get one person who doesn't understand, and he can wipe
out history. In exactly the same way, in a different context, someone
somewhere is throwing away something right now from my top one
thousand list. Part of what I do is to broadcast the fact. The thing that I'm
looking for at the moment is the first *Sqezy* washing-up liquid bottle. The
last six or seven interviews I thought might produce this thing – all I've
had is two people 'phoning up, one from Lever brothers and saying
'we've got one here', and one from the company that produced it, BXL,
who said, 'We gave ours to the Science Museum.'

Why the Sqezy *bottle?*

It's a pivotal brand from my point of view because it's the most important
of the products that took on the new flexible plastic. It had a metal top
and a metal base, which means it doesn't survive because it goes rusty and
disintegrates. There's probably a crate in someone's shop or back larder
somewhere, and then comes what I term the '30-second gap' between
'out it goes' and 'I wonder if anyone might be interested in that?'

Do you not sometimes feel you're fighting a losing battle?

Of course, everything that I'm doing is a losing battle, but unless
somebody does it . . .

*Could I ask you indiscreetly, do you ever sell anything from the
collection?*

I don't. I can't think of the last time I actually sold something. I may occasionally swap things – if I've got duplicates, but, generally speaking, swapping and selling things takes time. I have many reasons for having duplicates, because if I'm asked to recreate a shop for a museum or a television serial I need them. Indeed, I have exhibitions in other places, so I send duplicates and so do not deprive the museum.

I want to find out how passionate you are about inventorizing and making sure everything comes back.

I'm not as good as I should be, frankly, because it takes a lot of time. I can be working under such pressure that I tend to do what people are asking for rather than what could be done tomorrow. It's very difficult to tell you exactly how it works.

Your life and your collection are not really separate are they?

Well, they can't be. I live in it.

It runs your life?

It does, pretty well. I try and run it occasionally, but generally speaking it does run my life. The best thing to have happened would be to find someone else doing it sufficiently seriously, then I wouldn't have had to worry about it! Perhaps I would have found something else.

You seem to hint at the sometimes oppressive nature of collecting. Do you feel you ever need a holiday from this?

Well, I do take holidays. I've been to China, Japan and Hong Kong this year. That was partly work. I was doing an exhibition out there. I had to open the exhibition and that was about it. I love the packaging in Japan. They're still using the Codd bottle out there, the one with the marble inside the top. It took me about half an hour to persuade someone to give me one, because you normally drink it on the spot and return the bottle. Fortunately, while I was trying to get this bottle, the American wife of a Japanese man came up and helped me, doing lots of interpreting and persuading, and trying to work out why he needed this bottle back. It turned out that if he didn't return his full quota of bottles he would be

'I live in it': Robert Opie with some of his collection.

chopped off the distribution list! Eventually I started recording it with a camera and then he gave up and handed it over.

You haven't moved onto other memorabilia, like photographs, have you?

No, because photographs are generally covered extremely well. I do occasionally take photographs, like one of a telephone kiosk with all the call-girl cards in there, or photographs of shops. I do have quite a number of those from the first years of this century. If a photograph comes along that has some use to it, then yes, I will go after it. Only I don't go round collecting photographs as such.

I was noticing these albums here, children's annuals, how do they fit in?

They fit into the wider scheme of things. I've always tried to think – should I really save this, or should I be saving something else? I do try to think about what I'm trying to achieve. I don't necessarily agree with the opinion that I reach. There are reasons I cannot get over psychologically. I say to myself 'I shouldn't be collecting that', but I can't stop collecting it. I can see a reason why I should stop but I can't physically do it. To give you an example, to get the Museum properly established, I ought to give up collecting, but I still can't give it up. It probably means that I can't get the Museum established in the way that it should be.

How do you see people who don't collect?

Saner than I am, probably!

How do you think they see you?

I don't know, it depends who they are, it depends on what level they're looking, and how much they see of what I'm doing. For example, I had an Australian film crew here going round saying 'Oh my God, this is ridiculous.' I didn't really care because I knew we wouldn't see their programme over here. They got to the stage of saying, 'Well I think this house is going to collapse', or they would focus on a pile of yoghurt cartons and say 'Well isn't this ridiculous!' They only saw the snapshot, they didn't get the total picture. Everything has to be put into the social context for us to understand what is actually going on. This is really what

I'm trying to do. To put everything, no matter what it is – us as people, living in this curious world – into its environment, its context.

Can the world be understood, do you think?

Well, I think we should jolly well try. I don't think one should start out by saying 'It all sounds a bit complicated, no I don't think we should'. It's rather like saying, 'Collecting packaging – why, we'll need a million packs every year! We'll give up before we start.' But let's try and isolate the key brands in our society, let's try and follow them through, let's try and understand that, and let's see how many other things we can do. Unless you start you will never achieve anything, and this is the whole thing about exploring Africa – 'tsetse flies, crocodiles, let's stay at home this year!' Unless cranky, quirky people do go out there and explore Africa. . . . I see myself almost in relation to all those other people who have done these crazy sorts of things. Unless you do these crazy things, you don't start to understand. Sending a man to the moon may have been perceived as the most stupid thing imaginable but think of all the benefits of that technological leap.

In a way, you have to be crazy to take that first step. But you obviously don't perceive yourself as crazy.

I try not to, but I might tell you a story which would make me seem crazy. If a television presenter did an interview and wanted to make me look crazy, it would be very, very easy. They could just isolate those things which made me sound crazy, photograph those things which make me look crazy. I have to tread a fine line between getting publicity, which usually has to relate to something which sounds rather extraordinary, and getting it to sound sufficiently sane to make most people think that I am doing something worthwhile.

It is extremely difficult. I suppose I think, now I've got to this stage in my life, do I really want to spend the rest of my life doing the same thing and then at the end of my life find myself saying, 'I haven't really lived my life.' There's no doubt, I'm not really doing some of the things I would really like to do. I'm not travelling as much as I would like, because I don't have the time. I was at one stage going to the States quite a lot and going to France, but mainly on packaging trips, mainly with a reason for going. Now it has become increasingly difficult over the last few years to do that. I should be saying, and I do say, am I actually doing what I want to do? Could I be achieving other things? But if I didn't do the things I am doing, there would be this gap, this void, because there's nobody else doing it.

Success in a curious way would defeat you, because if everybody did collect this stuff and brought it to you, you wouldn't be able to cope. You're getting close to it. Have you filled up the whole house?

This house? Oh yes, many times over, that's part of the reason why we have the Museum, to help divest myself of as much material as possible.

Are there any other storage places around?

It's all down in Gloucester. There are 7000 square feet of space down there, and do you realize how much space that is?

When will it be full?

Well it's pretty full now.

How many objects are there in the collection?

Well I don't know. The figure I quote in the Museum leaflet is 300,000 items. It doesn't really matter, it just gives people a figure that says there are a huge number of items. It could be twice as many, it may not even be that many. Is a pack of playing-cards 52 items or one? Are a thousand duplicates a thousand items or one?

This bottle, for instance. Does it ever occur to you to just go for the label on the bottle?

No. My whole philosophy is completeness. If you can give me a crate of lime-juice bottles, I'd be only too delighted to have the whole crate as it was delivered to the shop. Because inside the crate there probably would have been an advertisement as well. The next best thing is a full bottle with its label, its foil cap, everything.

I was thinking, when you are eighty the world will have gone on and more and more packaging will have been produced.

I know. It's going to be frantic isn't it? I'm looking forward to the day when there isn't such a thing as packaging any more!

But you'll still be looking to fill in the holes?

Oh absolutely, yes. I've been looking to fill in the holes since the year I started. After all, there's still that *Sqezy* bottle that I'm trying to find. It's there, if only someone knows that I want it. Even if it's rusty, don't throw it out!

3

Identity Parades

JOHN WINDSOR

The texts of the Veda of India – reputedly the oldest record of human experience – contain a word or two of interest to today's collectors. In a certain state of consciousness, they say, the fulfilment of the individual becomes pitifully dependent on the objects and circumstances of the outside world. In such a state, one's perception of the world is fragmented and changeable. Fragmented, because diversity rather than unity appears to dominate. Changeable, because the loss or gain of an object makes all the difference between unhappiness and happiness. In this state the attention is drawn hither and thither between different objects of desire without being nourished by the underlying unity experienceable from within. Object-referral instead of self-referral. Its symptoms are tiredness and frustration.

The most comforting thing that can be said of this state is that it is an illusion or *pragya paradh* – 'mistake of the intellect'. Whether or not our feeble minds are gripped by the diversity of collectable objects paraded before us, the elusive truth is that the uni-verse is both unified and diverse. Those who have tried to own the whole of it, object by object, have always come unstuck. The name of this state of consciousness is *ignorance*. In the Veda this is not an insult but a technical term – *agyan*, literally lack of *gyan*, or knowledge. What is more, we are (apart from a handful of suspects I could name) all in it. It is by no means a totally unpleasant state to be in. Although its incumbents make constant complaints about objects and circumstances, most of us, like fish in water, seem to have got used to living in it. Its peak experiences, even the enlightened might admit, are spectacular. Sotheby's New York, until recently an art-of-the-state purveyor of top-grade illusion, used to lend money to a select few, enabling them to experience the ecstasy of purchase at auction of paintings of aquatic plants or medical practitioners for tens of millions of pounds. Some who had acquired objects in this way went on to explore the experiences of bank forclosure or bankruptcy, just for the contrast.

Although the Veda offers the original and most complete critique of pure ignorance, machine-age scholars and commentators in the West, typified by R. H. Tawney and his *The Acquisitive Society* (1921), have independently formed the opinion that man's fatal attraction to 'the object' (Vedic shorthand for the outside world) is the primary determinant of the human condition. Seek not whether a man is a Catholic or a Protestant, a Darwinist or a Fundamentalist, a Liberal or a Conservative. Ask him what objects he collects.

Sarat Maharaj, lecturer in the Department of Historical and Cultural Studies at Goldsmiths College, London, lectures on 'The Ambivalence of Objects in Differing Contexts', which is in part a neat line in the excremental in art, spanning the outpourings of Joyce and the canned excrement of Manzoni. He describes collecting as 'the chief mode of our culture'. Not politics, not religion, but collecting. I think he is right. In more vernacular vein, a recent light essay in *The Independent* newspaper (15 May 1993) by the broadcaster Martin Kelner under the heading 'Martin Kelner's Theory of the Meaning of Life' was entitled 'The Importance of STUFF'. According to Kelner, 'this theory states that life is all about acquiring STUFF, then acquiring more STUFF, maybe changing your STUFF round a little, then acquiring even more STUFF, then getting a bigger place because there's no room for all your STUFF, getting rid of some STUFF, then getting a smaller place because you haven't got as much STUFF. Then you die'. I think he is right, too. Vedic seers, I am sure, would have nodded agreement, although the state Kelner describes is not exactly what they were used to.

The most succinct psychological analysis of collecting STUFF that I have come across is that of Susan Pearce, director of Leicester University's Department of Museum Studies. Lecturing on 'Collections, the Self and the World', she divides collecting into just three categories: systematics, fetishism and souvenir collecting. Systematics is the construction of a collection of objects in order to represent an ideology, such as the Pitt-Rivers Museum's portrayal in Oxford of the natural history of evolution, intended in its day to combat the ideology of revolution. Fetishism is the removal of the object from its historical and cultural context and its re-definition in terms of the collector. In souvenir collecting, the object is prized for its power to carry the past into the future. The collector does not attempt to usurp its cultural and historical identity. Where would Pearce place the fine-art collectors lit up in the glitter of Sotheby's, New York? 'Fetishists', she said, and would not budge when I suggested that her classification might offend Mr Getty. Be it a pair of knickers or a Van

Gogh painting, the owner or observer becomes a fetishist by identifying with it – the same mistake of the intellect that used to cause the seers of old so much amusement. It is hardly surprising that she regards souvenir hunting as the healthiest of the three.

These days, the way They expect Us to relate to objects in museums has become an issue. Both Pearce and Maharaj were speakers at a conference on the 'Politics of Collecting' organized in June 1992 by Walsall Museum and Art Gallery, at which the 'constructive representations' of reality offered by museums to the public came under fire.[1] The star turn was Steven Newsome, director of the federally-funded Anacostia neighbourhood museum in Washington D.C., who has relegated George Washington's false teeth to a store-room in favour of displays portraying 'the Afro-American experience in Washington'. He told the audience, consisting mainly of museum middle-management: 'Cultural identity is the last big war. Museums have been perpetrating a myth of white culture as the best and only definition of culture. I hate to tell you guys, but it's not you who are the arbiters of culture, it's the people.' At the conference was Walsall Museum's 'The People's Show', an exhibition of popular collecting including collections of plastic frogs, egg-cups and carrier bags, one of fourteen concurrent exhibitions by Midlands museums stung by jibes of elitism. It was an attempt to 'empower' the people by inviting them to usurp the museum curator's role and 'valorize' their own cultural identity. As another speaker put it: 'Collecting has to do with our need to make visible our own reality.' Indeed, the constructive representations of frogs, pigs, 'all things purple' and keepsakes had placards bearing self-justifying quotations from the collectors, who were invited to blend with their exhibits as if 'in their natural habitat', as the *Museums Journal* put it. Mrs Edna Bailey, frog collector, dyed her hair green for the occasion. This makes one wonder whether she was being encouraged by Them to become anything less of a fetishist than bidders for Sotheby's fine art. STUFF the politics of liberation, you might say: if all it offers is deeper and deeper bondage to 'the object' of our choice, it's time we all got a smaller place, got rid of our STUFF, and died. The seers, ever sympathetic, had a less drastic solution for those malingering on the path to enlightenment. 'The best way of getting rid of a desire', they advised, 'is to satisfy it'.

Thank goodness for that. I therefore propose that, while apprehensively awaiting the onset of liberation, we should participate fully in all three of Pearce's modes of relating to the objects of our desire, selecting different ones as the occasion demands, perhaps combining one with another, but always sufficiently clued-up to explain to passing academics why we have dyed our hair green.

Let us start with something middle-of-the-road and traditional, something for forty-somethings who cannot afford a Van Gogh but are capable of crushing a plastic frog underfoot. In a softly-lit Georgian antiques shop on the narrow corner of Vigo Street, Mayfair, opposite the house in which Dr Livingstone's body once lay in state, presides Christopher Gibbs, antique dealer.[2] He is an arbiter of good taste, the originator of the 'battered country house' look. For 30 years he has been indulging his fastidious taste at auction on behalf of his customers, heritage-conscious style followers who, having slaved over a hot computer screen in the City or a hot guitar in a recording studio, have at last been able to afford an oak-beamed country house. Such people are willing aspirants on the path of ignorance (technically speaking of course). They unashamedly want to identify, and have decided what they want to identify with. They cannot wait to slough off the identity which childhoods surrounded by shell pictures and Taiwanese pottery have imposed upon them. They want to be one with the gentry – if only they knew what objects to buy. Without Gibbs's help they could end up buying mean, dim Georgian furniture, tight uncomfortable little chairs, tables with drawers which are too small, or over-ornate Victorian chairs with a Louis XVI knee, a Louis XV toe and a Louis XIV back. The most at-risk among them might decorate their walls with framed original illustrations from children's books. If Gibbs catches sight of such horrors in his clients' homes, especially awful furniture, he says 'Chuck it out, chuck it out!' It is no good protesting; his response will be 'Sit on the floor, then, until you get the right thing.' The right things are Adam, Chippendale, architect-inspired Victorian furniture; Chinese blue-and-white ceramics or refreshing Meissen sculpture, which brings dark-panelled rooms leaping into life. Objects never seen before and unlikely to be seen again, things with a strong personal flavour of someone gone by – like the old walking-sticks he picks up at country house sales. Old ethnographic objects fashioned from wood and stone by primitive peoples in the far corners of the world before the vulgarizing influence of the machine age. Antique flints, fragments of sculpture. Thrilling materials: basalt, porphyry. Amphora, krater, kantharos. Anything Cycladic. Fetishism for his dimmest clients, certainly. But the Gibbs formula for the succour of would-be gentry is more subtle than it might seem, whether or not his clients are aware of it. For him it is not simply a matter of cramming a country house with good things into which the fetishistic

John Windsor's collection of 'tat'.

owner imperceptibly blends. No doubt some clients want him to help them do just that. But for him – 'I'm not interested in creating a dazzling impression of richness.' Instead, he favours the spare look, where every little bit is telling. No cluttered museum-style interiors to give guests a Pitt-Rivers-style history lecture, but with Lord Rosebery's horse-whip leaning idly in a corner, a hint of the souvenir hunt.

Towards the nadir of the wonderful world of objects are some things that those of moderate good taste would never be seen dead with, let alone identify with. They may yet be collectable – indeed I have collected them myself. I refer to *tat*.[3] Tat is a certain kind of junk. Its residue, in fact. When you have extracted from junk the sort of rubbish that dustmen collect and the sort of kitsch Jeff Koons leaps on, you will be left with tat – second-hand fancy goods. At first glance, tat might seem to be the quarry of souvenir-hunters. After all, much of it is marked 'Margate' or 'Costa del Sol'. But think again. How do you relate to it? The hapless exhibitors at the Walsall People's Show were encouraged to parade their attachment to such things. One placard read: 'I bet there's not a week goes by when I don't buy a frog.' Fetishism, pure and simple. Forget for a moment your political correctness, your deference of the people's right to collect what

it likes. When you see a plastic frog or a plaster elephant or a wall
decoration of praying children or a plastic tankard marked 'Went to P,
leave this drink alone', do you not suppress a curl of the lip? If you do not
keep your lip under control, what was tat will magically transmogrify into
kitsch. Kitsch is self-conscious – self-consciously awful. Tat is simple-
minded. To bring about the change, all you need do is to withhold your
attachment to the object, refuse to identify with it. Then, if it can speak for
itself, it will. Most tat does. Like many kinds of souvenir, it was made in a
spirit of nostalgia for the Good Old Days. Put together a pile of it and you
will find a miniature world of things past which you can revisit in the palm
of your hand. Shire horses toss their heads, jingling polished brasses on
genuine leather straps, while inside tiny rose-entwined cottages (in plastic
frames) there are tiny warming pans and tiny gongs to bang for tiny teas.
There are tiny sword-and-shield wall decorations that squeak of the
gallantry of old, tiny ornamental ladies in crinolines made from shells,
coloured prints in ramin-wood frames of good old things like steam
engines, and vintage automobiles in which the squire cradles his trusty
old-fashioned firearms on his way to a shoot.

It is not until you assemble a collection of tat that you realize that its
picture of the past is a coherent, though not necessarily accurate, one.
Individual bits of tat are fetishism for some, souvenirs for others, but *en
masse* tat is capable of constructively representing that amalgam of
sentimental interpretations of history that constitutes modern British
nostalgia. You can judge by the picture of my own collection of tat shown
here. Is not the impression of the whole greater than the sum of the parts?
Is not the construction of such wholes the very essence of collecting? As
self-appointed curator I have, of course, had the opportunity of making a
selection that could be hopelessly biased and unrepresentative.

Would-be tat hunters should be warned that market traders are forever
trying to turn cheap tat into pricey kitsch, especially Deco pieces. In Brick
Lane street market I was asked £20 for a tat pink plastic table lamp in the
form of a Deco-style lady that should have been priced at 50 pence. I know
of only two places where tat is preserved in its simple-minded purity: one is
in Walsall, the other is 'Wally's North London No. 1 Antiquated Shop' at
217 Stoke Newington High Street, London N16. Whisper who dares.

Modern tat is today's picture of yesterday, but every age has produced
ephemera that innocently mirrors the reality of its own time. Collected
with an eye to historical context, printed ephemera can provide a vision
of past times undistorted by today's nostalgia. Robert Opie, founder of
the Museum of Packaging and Advertising in Gloucester, where some

300,000 of his million cartons, paper packages and shop-counter displays are housed, thinks of himself more as a curator than a collector.[4] He says: 'The point of collecting things is not just to concentrate on objects but to understand how things have evolved in the historical context in which you are collecting. The way I see it, collecting is like putting together a gigantic jigsaw puzzle with millions of pieces. Sometimes you see a picture forming. Sometimes you get the pieces the wrong way round. The philosophy is: everything is connected with everything else.' The seers would approve of that.

If you were to walk out of Opie's museum and into a 'T.G.I. Friday',[5] one of the American franchised 'bistros' with a nostalgic 'urban America' theme, at first glance you might think that the same mind had been at work. The walls of every Friday's are cluttered with nostalgic junk, including advertising signs, with plenty of big and expensive pieces like rowing-sculls and American petrol-pumps with transparent gas cylinders. But this is not a meticulous museum-style reconstruction of past reality. Genuine period stuff it may be, but as a collection it is more akin to modern tat than Opie's attempt at authentic reconstruction. What is stimulated in Friday's is not what the past was really like, but what its customers like to *think* it was like. Friday's designers expect their customers, aged 25 plus, to identify strongly with it. The original Friday's designer, Rush Bowman, told me: 'I like to show them something they would have seen in their early lives – something not quite remembered but capable of jogging their unconscious.' He chooses gear that, instead of forming a coherent historical picture, tugs at the customers' heart-strings, begging them to form an attachment. Friday's souvenirs invite fetishism, while Opie's souvenirs rank as systematics.

The price of junk in the United States has risen tenfold since Bowman started buying in the Sixties (he accepts some of the blame). Having assessed the different pulling power of different items of junk, he now specifies the same favourite pieces for every new bistro. As if to validate the sureness of his eye, the Friday's in Bedford Street, Covent Garden, is reputedly the busiest restaurant in Europe, its 260 seats having yielded a turnover of £180,000 in a single week. His standard 'wants list' of nostalgic junk could therefore be regarded as a guide to the world's most fetishistic collectables. Here it is:

2 sleds, 1 buggy, 2 trikes, 2 pedal cars, 1 hobby-horse, 2 scooters, 2 sets of skis, 2 sets of snowshoes, 1 manikin, 1 dress form, 1 fire extinguisher, 2 carpet-sweepers, 1 bird-cage, 2 suitcases, 1 washboard, 2–3 wheels of

different kinds, 1 organ pipe, 1 pattern mould, 1 large ship's propeller, 4–6 containers (boxes, trunks), 50–60 assorted metal signs, 1 telephone sign, 8–10 lettered glass, double-sided light-signs, 8 wooden signs, 10–15 brass signs, 10 US vehicle licence plates, 2 large thermometers, 1 Nipper (HMV's dog), 2 large sign letters, 6 ditto small, about 100 pictures, 1 giant pointing hand, 4–6 brass items, 1 small bathtub, 1 ironing-board, 1 wall-clock, 1 wall-telephone, 1 lavatory seat, 1 large fish, 1 small fish, 1 gaming-wheel, 7–8 hats (period), 1 old radio, 1 pair ice-tongs, 4–5 different pairs of shoes (skating etc.), 3–5 trophy cups, 1 copper urn, 1 copper heater, 4 spittoons, 2 sets US traffic lights, 6 light-up advertise-ments, 1–2 tubas, 2 big drums, 1 cello, 1 double-bass, 15–18 small musical instruments, and so on, until the walls enclosing an average 8,500 square feet of restaurant space are filled.

The fostering of fetishism is, of course, an occupation that dare not speak its name. The burly Bowman, from Arlington, Texas, would never consider himself to be in the bondage business. In Walsall it is a seditious, undercover political activity inspired by strange beliefs about turning plastic frogs into empowered princes. But in the United States the Elvis Presley collecting cult openly wallows in its fetishism, much to the dismay of Graceland Enterprises Inc., official purveyor of Elvis memorabilia of the least tasteless sort.[6] While Graceland's turnover in naff but respectable Elvis tee-shirts and badges is approaching £9 million a year, there is a flourishing and fetishistic undercover trade in Elvis relics: toe-nail clippings, warts, even Elvis sweat preserved in glass phials. This is fetishism as you and I knew it, before academics started inventing new definitions. When I telephoned Graceland Enterprises in an attempt to buy some Elvis sweat I was told 'We don't sell such things. It's not good to sell tacky souvenirs.' Litres of 'Elvis sweat' are still in circulation among collectors. Some of the genuine examples – if genuine they be – are supposed to have been distilled from a stage-floor covering of wood-shavings on which Elvis perspired copiously. But any genuine examples are now vastly outnum-bered by spoof products such as the plastic phial of liquid offered with a greetings card published by Maiden Jest (sic) in 1985. It says it 'ABSOLUTELY contains a few *precious* drops of Elvis's perspiration' and is headed: 'Prayers answered. The King Lives. Elvis Sweat! LIMITED OFFER ONLY for the most *devoted* fan'. And, ecstatically: 'The IMPOSSIBLE has happened! Elvis poured out his soul for you, and NOW you can let his PERSPIRATION be your INSPIRATION. Yes, dreams *do* come true. In loving memory, send his greeting and show the world you *really* care!'

Guy Peellaert, *Elvis's Last Supper*. 'Elvis Presley is the King. We were at his crowning . . .'.
Clockwise: Tommy Steele, Vince Taylor, P. J. Proby, Billy Fury, Tommy Sands,
Rick Nelson, Elvis Presley, Tom Jones, Eddie Cochran, Terry Dene, Ritchie Valens,
Cliff Richard, Fabian.

Both official and unofficial Elvis markets describe their wares as
souvenirs. But, with the benefit of the Pearce classification we know
better. It is hard to decide which is more fetishistic, Graceland's
ownership in perpetuity of the Elvis 'image', sometimes described as a
legalized form of immortality, or the market in Elvis necrophilia. It is the
quality of devotion that turns an Elvis souvenir into an Elvis fetish.
Professor Christine King of Staffordshire University, a specialist in the
history of religion and the Third Reich, lectures on 'Elvis as Religious
Icon'. She points out that he lived a life of permanent adolescence and
immortality, surrounded by his twelve 'disciples', otherwise known as
the 'Memphis Mafia'. He flirted with the idea of becoming a pastor, held
Bible classes at Graceland, studied fringe religions and expressed a crude
form of Christianity in his gospel records and films – which occasionally
identify him with Christ. His legend, like that of gods, saints and heroes,
has grown since his death seventeen years ago. His fan-clubs pride
themselves on their charitable work, and the annual pilgrimage of
15,000–20,000 devotees to his tomb at Graceland is quiet and reveren-
tial. *Cognoscenti* argue among themselves whether, when he died on the
lavatory, he was reading about the Turin shroud in *The Face of Jesus*, or
Sex and Psychic Energy.

Some fans believe Elvis had mystical powers, and there have been reports of his re-appearance after his death. His stepbrother and bodyguard, David Stanley, wrote a chapter 'My Brother the Mystic' in his book *Life with Elvis*, in which he alleges that Elvis could heal by touch and move clouds in the sky.[7] When threatened with a violent thunderstorm during a car journey 'Elvis stuck his right hand out of the sunroof and started talking to the clouds. "I order you to let us pass through" . . . and the amazing thing was that the clouds did exactly as he asked them to. They split right down the middle.' There is a straight-faced, but rib-tickling, description of a risen-again Elvis delivering a gift of his sweat in Greil Marcus's *Dead Elvis*. The recipient is a cartoon-book author who decided not to publish a satire on Elvis: 'A phosphorescent shape appeared before me. It was vague and wavering . . . but there was no mistaking the cocky stance, the white jumpsuit or the slow, resonant voice that spoke my name. I forced my unwilling lips to speak, and I promised Elvis that I would cancel the book. . . . He stretched out a shimmering hand. "Thanks", he said. "Here, this is for you." I reached out and Elvis placed a small object in my palm, closing my fingers over it lightly. "Don't look until I'm gone", he said, and then he faded from sight. . . . Slowly I opened my hand. There in my palm was the gift Elvis had given me – a tiny droplet of sweat, sealed in a genuine plastic vial.'[8]

Graceland Enterprises takes such devotional claptrap in its stride, but the pseudo-fetishistic following that really flies in the face of its attempts to sanitize Elvis's image is that of Joni Mabe, the Elvis exhibitionist. Her touring show of Elvis memorabilia – wart and all – includes artworks of her own that are twisted fantasies of sex with Elvis. Her pop-art collage commemorating the first anniversary of Elvis's death is a make-believe fan letter surrounded by photographs of herself, bare-breasted and in intimate contact with an effigy of Elvis. The letter says in part: 'I could have saved you, Elvis. We could have found happiness together at Graceland. I know that I could have put your broken self back together. It's as if you could have discovered that sex and religion could be brought together in your feelings for me. I worship you. . . . I no longer know the difference between fact and fantasy. Elvis, I have a confession to make. I'm carrying your child. The last Elvis imitator I fucked was carrying your sacred seed. Please send money. Enclosed are the photographs of myself and the earthly messenger you sent. Love sick for you baby . . . Joni Mabe.'

Penetration might be the sincerest form of identification. But the art of Joni Mabe is not intended as simple-minded fetishism.[9] For the *cognos-*

centi it is a selfconscious and – for Graceland, at least – an embarrassingly well-observed parody of the varieties of ecstatic experience available to Elvis fans. The 'I could have saved you' fantasy is a familiar one among female fans, and Mabe's concoction of sex, religion and extra terrestriality is authentic Elvis cult stuff. However distant from Pitt-Rivers the art of Joni Mabe might be, you have to give it its due for attempting an accurate 'constructive representation' of the reality inhabited by Elvis fans. It may still be a fetish for devotees or a souvenir for the collector of pop memorabilia, but for the connoisseur of cultural and historical statements it is a 'systematic'.

The cure for embroilment in fetishism, boredom with souvenirs or intellectual nausea engendered by systematics is to choose a collectable that you loathe and then manufacture it. John Hine's company, near Aldershot, Hampshire, has a £20 million turnover in those miniature, painted pottery cottages designed by David Winter.[10] Hine did not plan it. Buyers from American gift shops came knocking at the door of his tiny workshop after collectors developed a fetish for his innocent limited edition souvenirs of Olde England. They have since sent prices soaring to over $40,000 for rarities. Hine indulged in a peak experience that would have been the envy of many a collecting addict seeking to kick the habit when he personally smashed up 4000 of his little houses. The edition was called The Grange, a Tudor half-timbered house. It had metal balconies that kept falling off, and Hine announced in a fit of pique that it would be discontinued, forgetting that 4000 were still in production. In order to guarantee the value to collectors of the 1500 or so already sold he bought a club hammer and goggles, hired a skip – and smashed the 4000 to smithereens. It sounds like the ultimate liberation from object-referral. You will be lucky to spot a David Winter cottage in Hine's home. He has never formed a collection of his own. But American fanatics have now pushed up the price of The Grange from £60 retail to over £1000.

Careful analysis of what makes a collectable tick has produced the first synthetic collectable – Swatch, the cheaply-made, fantastically-designed plastic wrist-watches that has saved the Swiss watch industry from oblivion.[11] As new edition follows new edition the Swatch collectors' market has become a cross between philately and high fashion, a wildly speculative circus that has already swept Europe, the Far East, Japan and America. Swatch is the first 'instant collectable'. You do not have to wait for limited editions to circulate in the 'secondary' (second-hand) market before they acquire a collectors' price tag. Limited edition 'specials' or 'variants' of standard designs command an above-retail premium even

Swatch: Chandelier's Christmas special, 1992.

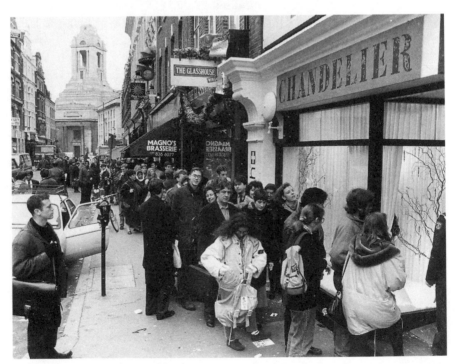

Queuing outside a Chandelier shop in London for the Swatch Christmas special.

before they hit the official Swatch shops. The unofficial futures market in new issues will pledge £250 or so for guaranteed delivery of a 'variant' about to retail at only £50.

In Paris, Leo Scheer, an advertising agent, television producer, sociology graduate – and Swatch collector – explained to me: 'Swatch is the first post-crisis product. Manufacturing industry has been experiencing a crisis in demand. People were becoming unsure of their needs. Swatch has shown that demand can be created for a product with neither a need nor a use. You do not even have to use your Swatch – it stays in its packaging – nor even have a need for it. This is an important phenomenon.' A collectable that transcends the established boundaries of collecting? The first collectable of the Age of Enlightenment? Hardly. Swatches are even more fetishistic than Joni Mabe's sexy sagas. Lust for these squidgy, spiky, furry timepieces has hooked 100,000 people worldwide. Over £40,000 has been paid for a rarity.

The Swatch collectors' market is manipulated in a deliberately capricious way by Swatch's creator, the 67-year-old Nicolas Hayek, chairman and chief shareholder of the Swatch company SMH. Collectors never know which countries he is going to starve of a certain model or which will be the unexpected sole recipients of a highly limited – and valuable – edition of a variant. He kick-started the sluggish American collectors' market of Swatches by supplying only America with a yellow version of the 1990 Bora-Bora. Their retail value, about £30, doubled on resale. Although they were not numbered editions (which would have made them even more valuable), they are now worth about £400 at auction. Special editions presented to celebrities are worth thousands. Nigel Mansell sold his presentation Swatch designed by Mimmo Paladino in 1989, one of only 120, for £13,200 at Christie's, and gave the money to charity. Press reporters attending the launches of specials like those designed by Vivienne Westwood (20 models so far) can be sure of receiving potentially valuable press-only variants. Hayek tends to get a good press. Swatch speculator/collectors are not so adulatory. They are obliged to second-guess how Hayek intends to outwit them. They do not always win. As fax and telephone lines buzz with news of the discovery of yet another unannounced variant a continent away, they mutter 'Love the product, hate the company'. Scheer explained: 'Collectors play against the company and the company plays against them. It is an information game.'

The insanities of the Swatch market or the miniature-house market or the Elvis market make the traditional accumulation of artworks by the wealthy seem comparatively simple-minded. Did we really think that Mr Getty's devotion to the treasures of antiquity was an indication of a complex personality? Does this collection contain any of the unique three Popswatches – shaped like a cucumber, a red pepper and eggs-and-bacon – which Hayek ordered to be wrapped in paper and sold from a New York grocery stall for around £50 each following his adept publicity to lure collectors? (They fetched about £2000 at auction in Zurich the same year, 1991.) The accumulation of riches, whether or not in the form of artworks, is, after all, the simplest and commonest form of fetishism as defined by Pearce. 'I am what I own', whether cattle or coin, concubines or Canalettos, has been the guiding principle of the technically ignorant throughout the ages. If that sounds unfair, think how few owners of big art collections have fitted the mould of the self-effacing curator, detached from the objects of his perception. There is generally some attempt to parade ownership in a fetishistic way. Prince Johannes of the German family of Thurn und Taxis, for example, now left with only seven of his family's 32 art-crammed castles, still insists that his footmen wear powdered wigs. His young wife ordered a cake with 60 candles shaped as penises for her husband's 60th birthday party.

In this generation, fetishistic collecting has overtaken souvenir collecting. The reason has been the increase in home ownership. More people are buying collectables as interior decoration, to identify with in the 'I am what I own' mode, than to hide away in albums or specimen cabinets. Significantly, the BBC's recently launched collecting magazine, the product of market research, is titled *Home and Antiques*. The battered country house look, as popularized by Christopher Gibbs, is but one manifestation of the trend towards home-making as the creation of identity-cocoons. A plunge into even deeper ignorance? But did not the seers say that satisfying desires was legit? Just so. Perhaps you did not hear them giggle when they said it. They never recommended the satisfaction of desires as anything more than a practical, pre-enlightenment *faute de mieux*. Remember that they also had up their sleeves spiritual techniques of transcendence capable of allowing the attention of the practitioner to escape the pull of the objects of the outside world and spontaneously turn within, experiencing boundlessness instead of boundaries.

Correctly applied, such techniques gave freedom from bondage. But they were not, as the West tends to assume, intended to induce the population at large to throw away their artworks and become recluses. According to the Vedic teaching the material and spiritual are not different worlds, but different aspects of the same world. There is no either/or choice. It is possible to live 100 per cent of both. By alternating experience of the boundaries of the material outside world with the inner experience of boundlessness – the basic, spiritual constituent of creation – a balanced perception of reality is attained. In practical terms this means that, established in boundlessness, the perceiver is able to experience the objects and circumstances of the outside world without risk of being bound by them. Unity, rather than diversity, dominates perception. Nothing has changed – except the consciousness of the perceiver. It is the spiritual equivalent of having one's cake and eating it.

The sole surviving example of a collecting tradition that fosters such principles of enlightenment is the Japanese tea ceremony, still taught today, even in England. The prized utensils – bowls, lacquer tea-caddies, dishes, serving trays – are handed down from generation to generation. Whole collections rarely come to auction, but when they do they fetch fantastic prices. Christie's raised £550,000 in London in 1989 for the Peony Pavilion collection, 400 lots of ceramics made in China for Japan around 1580–1650. The purpose of the tea ceremony is pure enjoyment, but there are near-inscrutable undercurrents. In presiding over the ceremony the host displays his high level of enlightenment and probes the level of enlightenment of his guests. *Chado*, the way of tea, has long been a route towards social and spiritual acceptance. Those who would rise in Japanese society must first display at a tea ceremony *wa* (harmony), *kei* (respect), *sei* (purity) and *jaku* (tranquility) – or, as the Japanese saying goes, 'that there is tea in them'. At a *chanoyu*, or tea ceremony, instead of being presented with fetishistic Sunday-best china, you are likely to be served tea in a bowl that is out of shape or has bald patches in its glaze. The host will offer it to you with its best side towards you before bowing to the floor. Support the bowl in your left hand and turn it twice clockwise 90 degrees so that the best side faces the host. Then drink the green tea.

This is not, as might appear, an arid ritual. Enjoy the light-hearted harmony of the occasion. If laughter comes, laugh. If tea is accidentally spilled, laughter will come soon enough. If you choose to make conversation, remark upon the bowl's bald patch. Praise its rustic simplicity, the carefree flourish of the potter's glaze. Clues to the behaviour expected of you will be found in the pictures on the tea ceramics themselves. In glazes splashed on in effortless abandon you will see rustic scholars in contemplation besides rushing streams, emblematic of the simple, enlightened lifestyle to which all *chajin*, tea ceremony

devotees, are expected to aspire. The four centuries old *chado* aesthetic –
known as *wabi* – nourished all that is pure but unpretentious, scruffy but
enlightened. *Chado* was the ideal device for exposing bores and impos-
ters. Japanese city merchants whose consciousness had not progressed
beyond fetishistic greed were soon found to have 'no tea in them'.

Britain's only tea-master, Michael Birch of the Japanese Urasenke
Foundation, who teaches from his home in Blackheath, London, tells his
pupils: 'Starting with the awareness of a single bowl or tray, we
floodlight the whole, while spotlighting a part'. It is the familiar unity-in-
diversity characteristic of the Vedic description of the state of enlightenment. Today, we see traces of the *wabi* aesthetic in the carefree scruffiness
of the British gentry – tweed suits with frayed trouser turn-ups, well-
worn Fair Isle sweaters. Most youngsters like to put on a bit of *wabi* –
such as jeans with holed knees. Both conceits feign virtuous non-
attachment. Modern *wabi* that is *par excellence* is, of course, the battered
country house look – if only the incumbents could comprehend the virtue
of not pretending that they are what they own.

This, of course, is the point: whether collecting is becoming more or
less of an 'identity parade'. It does seem to me that, although more and
more home-makers are collecting for display, and the Christopher Gibbs-
designed country house interiors give endless scope to the poseur, such
designer-collecting is a playful phenomenon; the horrors of full-blown
acquisition-fetishism are in retreat. Identity-creating through collecting
has become a selfconscious game, with objects being collected partly as a
joke, partly as a demonstration of the collector's wry view of social
history. The collecting of printed ephemera – unconsidered scraps of
everyday life such as playbills or tradesmen's cards – has become
particularly popular. Even Queen Victoria's knickers, lavatory paper and
airline sick-bags claim devotees willing to explain to open-mouthed
dinner guests the place of such things in their socio-historical context,
while at the same time assuring them that they are not to be taken
seriously. The catch is that such collectors are likely to be as attached to
their own cleverness as their own collectables. Their choice of art is a
conscious attempt to design their own smart identity. Collections of high
art, especially in battered country houses, declare: 'I am rich and have a
well-developed taste.' Quirky collections of kitsch and emphemera say
'Look how quirky but clever I am'. It is possible to come unstuck at this
game. For example, collectors of naff Thirties Deco ceramics like Shorter
ware should remember to curl their lip as soon as new guests enter their
homes, for fear of being misunderstood.

Ian Maxted, a collector of lavatory papers.

David Bowen, a collector of airline sickness bags.

One enlightened aspect of the designer-identity game is the trend towards selling one's collectables and buying afresh as taste and markets change, particularly home-interior goods such as pictures and period ceramics and furniture. Material things are increasingly looked upon as disposables rather than the bondage-gear of a lifetime. An entire collection of gas stoves was recently sent to auction by a single living owner, and we may yet see the sale of the first collection of vintage television sets by a canny dealer who spotted them as a collectable of the future and stockpiled them. Yesterday's obsession becomes today's liberation as the finds of a quest lasting several years are knocked out to new owners. It seems healthy enough to me.

There is also a growing weariness on the part of collectors and dealers alike with what might be described as the collecting equivalent of consciousness consumption. The main butt of this change in attitude is the Grosvenor House Antiques Fair, which still offers the world's richest and most dazzling annual array of top-priced art. Although its prestige remains unchallenged, in recent years its organizers have been puzzled by complaints by both press and exhibitors that the fair has become 'too glitzy'. What, one might ask, is wrong with glitz? Both the seers and Pearce's formula could have whispered an answer. It is that expensive artworks presented for sale without reference to their historical context are aimed at fetishistic identity-seekers rather than enlightened knowers of reality. The fair has become an affront to what might punningly be called collective consciousness.

Peter Watson, writing in *The Observer* newspaper (6 June 1993), contrasted the glitzy ambience of the 1993 Grosvenor House fair with the London gallery of Giuseppe Eskenazi, which has defied the recession by selling oriental artworks priced in millions. Eskenazi's secret is to thoroughly research the historical context of his objects at the earliest opportunity through the Chinese and Japanese archaeological journals his wife translates. His knowledge is five or six years ahead of rivals who wait for English translations, and this places him in a position to educate taste.

Is there any conclusion to be drawn from the West's bittersweet attachment to artworks and the commentaries on acquisitive behaviour offered by Vedic seers and their successors, such as Pearce? In the absence of enlightenment, the seers recommended satisfaction of desires through ownership, but in the West renunciation of ownership is written into both religion and politics. Both recommendations are pre-enlightenment stopgaps. After all, it is not ownership itself that results in bondage but the absence of enlightenment, the inability to perceive the boundlessness in all that one owns.

The only collectors who might produce proof of non-attachment to their collectables are Romanies.[12] Chris Hill, who refurbishes horse-drawn gypsy caravans in Suffolk and has come to know the Romanies well, tells me that they cherish Edwardian Aynsley china. It can fetch over £75 for a cup and saucer. He once saw a Romany in a caravan sit down on a built-in upholstered chest so crammed with Aynsley that the lid would not close. He accidentally crushed the lot. Everyone laughed. There's non-attachment for you. The Romanies, it is said, originated in India.

The means of attaining enlightenment? Certainly not by collecting – unless you collect like a Romany. As it happens, the ancient Vedic spiritual techniques have been restored. But that is another story.

4
Collecting and Collage-making: The Case of Kurt Schwitters

ROGER CARDINAL

To collect is to launch individual desire across the intertext of environment and history. Every acquisition, whether crucial or trivial, marks an unrepeatable conjuncture of subject, found object, place and moment. In its sequential evolution, the collection encodes an intimate narrative, tracing what Proust calls 'le fil des heures, l'ordre des années et des mondes'[1] – the continuous thread through which selfhood is sewn into the unfolding fabric of a lifetime's experience.

A friend of mine is a passionate (if erratic) collector of secondhand books. For years he has subjected each fresh find to a kind of *rite de passage*, taking formal possession by signing the flyleaf of the book and adding, beneath his name, the place and date of acquisition. He then copies the title and date into a notebook, which acts as a primitive inventory. He may leave the book out for a while until there is time to read or at least scan it; but at some point he will enjoy sliding it into a suitable place on his shelves.

Such routines articulate an awareness of categories and of transitions between categories. In a shop, a given book remains in a sense neutral so long as it is open to anyone to pick it out. That my friend notices and grabs it often means he is hastening to forestall any rival. If the book is both unusual and cheap, he may feel particular satisfaction in establishing private rights over it. In signing it, he ensures that his ownership will never be in dispute; at the same time, he may be drawing attention to his choice, narcissistically hoping that it will reflect his literary discrimination. His rituals of accession express an emotional investment, refined by the intellectual sense that the book fills a perceived gap, or extends a particular theme or set.

Though he does buy brand-new volumes, the bulk of my friend's collection is secondhand, which means his books often bear traces of previous ownership: indeed his rituals may be seen as an attempt to 'disinfect' the purchase, to sever it from its origins and draw it decisively into the orbit of present possession, thus designating the item as a signifier within the chain of signifieds that is his personal library (in turn a species of autobiography). Sometimes his signature will figure under that of a previous owner, which fact might prompt the thought that, although the book is retiring from circulation for the time being, there is a fair chance it will survive its new owner, and that the record of a desire fulfilled will in due course be read by some future bibliophile. In such moments one may dimly perceive how it is that meaning can 'thicken' within objects, functioning as they do as natural signs of the passage of history, of the serialization of moments of individual consciousness.

Jean Baudrillard observes that some collectors commit themselves to limited sets, of King Penguins, say, or first editions of Hemingway – finite series that are, in principle, possible to achieve. Such collectors, he suggests, hardly ever *use* their collectables, while Walter Benjamin even makes a case for defining the true bibliophile as one who never reads his books.[2] In this sense my friend must be an imperfect collector, in that though there are a few decorative rows he scarcely touches he generally tends to make good use of his library. (It is true that he is loath to lend anything!)

To open up a book and start reading is at once to travel beyond the single object of desire, in so far as every text opens onto the horizonless prospect of textuality at large. As an object, the book is so blatantly a *semiophore* – Krzysztof Pomian's term for an object in which meaning has been invested[3] – that it cannot conceal its participation in that universal discourse, that collection of collections, we call Literature. But books are not just intertextual signifiers; aside from those rare specimens that flaunt an aesthetic of self-sufficiency, like the ethereal sonnets of Mallarmé, texts tend to be referential, informing us of realms of material experience located outside the bookshop and the library. It is important to note that their phenomenal immediacy also intrudes decisively. It may be that the more fastidious type of collector – of gold coins, say, or of the rarest minerals – will suppress the circumstances of acquisition and, preserving each item in a velvet-lined drawer, cherish his possessions as immaculate, timeless things, abstracted from the Everyday. But the collector of secondhand books has only to glance at his shelves to be faced with the messier register of contingent existence. The torn and discoloured spines of my friend's collection are conclusive evidence that he belongs to that grubbier fellowship of bargain-hunters whose elective terrains are the market-stall and the basements of London's Charing Cross Road. Moreover, while some collectors fret over the integrity of their collection and negotiate bequests to spare it from decay and dispersal, my friend acknowledges that his sort of collection is doomed. Once he is gone, he knows that nobody else is likely to keep his shabby shelves intact. He and his collection are in a sense inseparable; without his presence, those uneven rows of paperbacks might not even be perceived *as* a collection.

Inexorably classified as we are under the category of mortals, we may envisage collecting as an existential project that seeks to lend shape to hapless circumstance. To collate and arrange any objects, culturally marked or otherwise, is to invent a space of privileged equilibrium offering at least some respite from the pressures of life. What is curious to behold is that, for many collectors, existential tensions tend to derive not just from the plain business of living, but also from the collecting activity itself, by means of which they had hoped not to repeat life but to transcend it. I see the collector as one caught in a constant vacillation, between the hankering for perfection and the need to tolerate imperfection, between an ideal of wholeness and the anxiety of incompleteness, between mature composure and the immature thrills of hunting and scrounging. Whatever the collection, its true history can never be an even one; its narrative is always informed by both design and accident, coverage and lack, permanence and impermanence, the unique and the redundant; and, within it, deeper meaning is often obliged to co-exist with the platitudinous.

THE CASE OF KURT SCHWITTERS

To draw these ideas into sharper focus, I shall devote this essay to a marginal, yet highly instructive, case of collecting. Many of the aspirations and preoccupations I have been evoking are exemplified in the activities of the German artist Kurt Schwitters (1887–1948), best known for the two thousand and more collages he produced throughout his career, from his days as a Dada experimentalist in Germany at the end of the First World War to his death in exile in England three decades later.[4] My contention is, first, that Schwitters's obdurate habit of collage-making itself represents a fascinating variant within the overall sphere of collecting; and, second, that his achievements, quite apart from their value as art, give rise to a problematic of reception and interpretation that has characteristically twentieth-century resonances, bearing as it does on the relations between the aesthetics of Modernism, the social history of modern Europe, and the ways in which private individuals image their participation in a specific cultural epoch.

COLLAGE-MAKING COMPARED WITH COLLECTING

There are certain perhaps surprising yet quite definite analogies between collecting in the broad sense and the modern artistic practice of collage-making.[5] Collages are pictorial compositions made by glueing separate scraps of paper onto a surface. So simple is this procedure that one can say that no training is required for a person of average nimbleness to produce one or two collages, just as it is true that that same person can start a casual collection. On the other hand, dedicated collage-making, like dedicated collecting, is of rather deeper resonance. To combine a few scraps may seem simple and innocent. Yet we must ask: what sort of combination, and exactly which scraps? Where did they come from, and what signifying purpose are they now being asked to serve? Whenever we sense that material bits and pieces have been amalgamated by human hand, we cannot but impute intentionality, and therefore expressivity, to their arrangement. To recognize that the components of a given collage have corporate impact is to acknowledge that they form a systematic ensemble. It follows that the collage is in fact a collection – by which I mean *a concerted gathering of selected items which manifest themselves as a pattern or set, thereby reconciling their divergent origins within a collective discourse.*[6] In many instances of collage, the criteria of selection and patterning are easy to account for: for instance, coloured bits of paper may be used to depict a recognizable figure. In other cases (as with abstract or decorative collages), the pieces simply 'fall into place' spontaneously, in accordance with what we may choose to call the maker's intuition, or instinct, or aesthetic sense. (But then, we remember that collectors are frequently unable to explain why some things 'belong' in their collection while others don't.) The final element that, I believe, clinches my comparison is that there is almost always an intention eventually to place the collage or the collection on display. Both ultimately exist to be *shown*, and implicitly to be shown to impress. We can say that both aspire to be noticed, inspected, admired, even envied.[7]

SCHWITTERS AND THE *MERZ* PROJECT

As a practising artist, Schwitters undoubtedly intended that people should see his collages. His artistic career began when, after military service in the First World War, he simultaneously committed himself to the Dada movement, with its anarchic challenge to establishment values, and to the task of establishing a network of communications across Europe. By the late 1920s his work was being widely shown in exhibitions across Germany and abroad. What is notable is that, despite the lure of Berlin as the artistic capital, Schwitters opted to remain based in Hanover, the city of his birth. Despite being accused by some Dadaists (notably Richard Huelsenbeck) of being bourgeois and provincial, he seems to have been content to follow his own path and to develop his own creative formats. While these in fact vary considerably (he was, for instance, also an accomplished typographer and experimental poet), it is in his approach to collage-making that he is at his most characteristic and inventive, and it is also here that he most obviously mimes the activities of the collector – or perhaps it would be more accurate to speak of the scavenger.

The beauty of my example lies in the fact that, unlike most of the collectors addressed in this book, Schwitters seems hardly a tasteful and nuanced discriminator. His maverick appetite opens onto the least seemly range of objects on offer in the world: dishevelled remnants, discarded scraps, things so decidedly secondhand and unserviceable that they are routinely subsumed under the generic label of 'rubbish' – defined, that is, in the unredeemably negative terms of utter worthlessness. But my point will be that, whereas Baudrillard sees fit to dismiss the collector as an impoverished creature (see page 24 above), Schwitters deserves consideration precisely because his chosen speciality is that of impoverished things: the paradox is that this man is a collector resourceful enough to have made something out of *what everyone else dismisses*.

Schwitters once spoke of his art as a campaign to combat chaos by salvaging the broken pieces left after the Great War.

Out of frugality, I drew on what came to hand, for we were a poverty-stricken country. One can still cry out by way of bits of rubbish, and that is what I did, by glueing or nailing them together. This I called *Merz*. . . . Nothing was left intact anyway, and the thing was to build something new out of the broken pieces.[8]

From an early stage Schwitters seems to have been disinclined to present his work under the collective banner of Dada, preferring to use the term *Merz* as an emblem of his singularity. No less nonsensical an expression than 'Dada', *Merz* derives from the accidental cropping of the letterhead for the *Kommerz- und Privatbank* in Hanover. Later, Schwitters pointed out a play on the verb *ausmerzen* (to eradicate), and we may also note an echo of the French *merde* (shit). But what I hope to show is that such connotations of meaninglessness, fragmentation, destruction and waste are in truth the negative obverse of what is better appreciated as a constructive, or rather re-constructive, project. What Schwitters seems to have done, in the aftermath of the German defeat, is to deliberately retreat to a zero position. Within the overall campaign which Dada wages against bankrupt tradition, Schwitters adopts a specific, ironic angle of attack. His response to the cultural order which had sanctioned the waste – the indefensible nonsense – of the Great War is to 'cry out by way of bits of rubbish', as it were adopting the dustbin-lid as his heraldic shield and fighting to redeem the smithereens of cultural meaning.

In practical terms Schwitters's project manifested itself in particular collecting procedures. Day by day he walked through Hanover in search of trash, scouring the pavement, the gutter and the dustbin, elective fields as fertile as they were disgusting. As if to caricature the posturings of the rich connoisseur, the virtue of whose cabinet of curiosities is that it comprises exquisite *artificialia* and *naturalia* transported with great difficulty across vast distances, the partisan of *Merz* limits himself to *artificialia* that anyone can pick up for nothing, located as they are in the most banal and close-by of sites, albeit sites that lie outside the periphery of normal attention, let alone of aesthetic concern.

An unrepentant scavenger, Schwitters would return from his excursions with pockets and bags crammed with paper litter and other varieties of refuse. Once in the studio, these lose their status as waste and become the raw material of art. Now it is that the typical collecting activities of searching, gathering and ordering give rise to *bricolages* or new artistic amalgamations. Schwitters saw these as falling into three broad types, the *Merzzeichnung*, the *Merzbild* and the *Merzbau*, terms of his own devising that parody the traditional academic divisions of drawing, painting and architecture.

The term *Merzzeichnung* (literally, '*Merz* drawing') in fact refers not to something made with pencil or pen, but to a pictorial work of modest dimensions (often as small as a postcard) made up of scraps pasted to a flat surface: in short, it is synonymous with 'collage'. The typical *Merz* collage comprises paper-based elements of variable size, shape, colour and consistency: tram-tickets, sweet-wrappers, shreds of newsprint, cigarette packets, serviettes, cloakroom tickets, playing-cards, envelopes, receipts, blotters, parcel paper, and so forth.

The term *Merzbild* ('*Merz* picture') refers to a relief picture on a larger scale, whereby three-dimensional components are fixed to a wooden surface: it corresponds to our more recent term 'assemblage'. The novelty of Schwitters's approach in 1918 is encapsulated in the story of his introducing himself to Raoul Hausmann in Berlin with the quip 'I am a

Kurt Schwitters, *zollamtlich geöffnet (Opened by Customs)*, 1937–8.
Tate Gallery, London. © DACS 1993

painter and I nail my pictures together'. Typical materials are timber offcuts, sections of plywood, wheels from children's toys, washers, cogwheels, chicken wire, umbrella spokes, coins, buttons, broken hinges, broken plates, shoe-leather, fragments of cloth, shards of metal. Schwitters liked to use frame-makers' tacks to fix the items discreetly in place (though he sometimes used cruder nails, which protrude more visibly).

The third format is the *Merzbau* ('*Merz* construction'), a sculptural assemblage whose scale borders on the architectural: we might nowadays speak of an 'environmental work'. It represents the most ambitious attempt to create a new whole out of disparate elements, and in this sense is a milestone in the history of the collage principle. I shall discuss it in some detail before returning to my main concern, the *Merz* collage proper.

Begun *c.* 1923 inside his Hanover home at 5 Waldhausenstrasse, Schwitters's first and greatest *Merzbau* grew from a single column into an immense structure of interlinked sculptural and architectonic forms, largely of wood and plaster. As if catering for some live organism, the artist cut holes in the floors of the house to allow the construction to extend up to the attic and down to the cellar. The *Merzbau* also proliferated in its detail, encompassing walls, arches, buttresses, ribs, spiky protrusions, painted panels, niches and hidey-holes. These last served as reliquaries, secreting all kinds of found objects and mementoes – a lock of hair, a half-smoked cigarette, a friend's shoe-lace or tie, personal letters, photographs, items of underwear, a sample of urine in a phial. The *Merzbau* was also a space for hanging framed collages and fetishistic assemblages, and even provided accommodation for pet guinea-pigs.

Eventually coinciding with the entire house, the *Merzbau* constituted a multi-functional environment, at once dwelling, studio, storehouse, exhibition space, walk-in artwork and totalizing collection. Schwitters devoted much thought to its elaboration as a kind of absurd museum with distinct galleries: 'The Cathedral of Erotic Misery', 'The Grotto of Love', 'The Cave of Deprecated Heroes'. In their eclecticism, the museum's holdings reflected the plurality of its maker's interests in culture both refined and popular, in events both public and private, in specimens both explicable and baffling. Schwitters's criteria were certainly idiosyncratic. While it superficially resembled those gatherings of matches, tools and bits of glass that are hoarded by such creatures as the wood-rat, of which William James reminds us that they are in fact accumulations rather than true sets,[9] the *Merzbau* none the less had the air of a coherent composition, its rationale being partly spatial and formal, partly chronological and associative.

Given its longevity – it was only in 1937 that its maker abandoned it when he was obliged to go into exile – the Hanover *Merzbau* parallels a whole epoch in Schwitters's existence, amounting to a compendium of his obsessions and caprices. The reverence with which things cropping up in his daily life were inserted into the multilayered design and even buried deep within it may suggest echoes of Egyptian mortuary ritual, as if the artist were cornering valued parts of his experience and embalming them in order to defy the ravages of time. As Brian O'Doherty observes, there are several kinds of dialectical interplay at work here – experience and structure, the organic and the archaeological, the city outside and the utopian space within: the *Merzbau* is 'a chamber of transformation',[10] whose sacred function is to transport its contents to a mythic dimension beyond contingency and dissolution. In this sense, the Hanover *Merzbau* was not only Schwitters's *Wunderkammer*, but also his mausoleum, a time-capsule, a refuge from history. In the event, the work was totally annihilated by Allied bombing in 1943, an intrusion of history that no artistic ritual could counter.[11]

THE STRATEGIES OF THE COLLAGE-MAKER

I propose to confine the rest of my remarks to the *Merz* collages alone, bearing in mind that, whether they eventuate as pocket-size collages, bulkier assemblages, or massive environmental structures, all Schwitters's creations are of a piece in their fundamentals. For every work he makes originates in acts of collecting and ordering; each can be construed as a display of select items supplied by his scavenging expeditions; each is analogous to a showcase or a cabinet of curiosities. Above all, I suggest, the stages of *Merz* creativity invariably follow the same sequence, mirroring aspects of collecting practice. An outline of the 'narrative functions' of collage-making should therefore illuminate the *Merz* project at large as a paradigm of collecting.

1. *The artist /collector goes prospecting in public spaces where he has no personal rights of ownership.*
In Hanover, Schwitters hunted in streets, squares, cafés, theatres, shops, railway stations and public vehicles. On journeys abroad he no doubt sought souvenirs in similar places. Sometimes he was allowed to dig around in the cellar of a Hanover printing-works, where waste paper was dumped. While the bulk of his material was undoubtedly 'scrounged'

from public sources, it should be noted that he occasionally recycled scraps from his own litter-bin, including printed copy from the graphic design agency he ran (entirely seriously, albeit under the name 'Merz-Werbezentrale'), as well as proofs from his literary publications.

2. The artist /collector gathers up his booty and thus removes it from public circulation.

3. Returning to his private space, he unpacks his acquisitions, of which he is now the undisputed owner.

4. He sifts the disparate items, appraising them and identifying those which qualify for accession into his collections.
Once filtered through an intelligence, amorphous litter takes on meaning: the scraps now mutate into semiophores worthy of being studied and preserved.

5. He rejects anything falling short of his criteria.
I surmize that for each finished collage, there must have been handfuls of unusable stuff that were consigned to the waste-bin for good, thus doubly rejected. Conceivably, some scraps smelled or looked too disgusting; others may, despite Schwitters's apparent evenhandedness, have offended him aesthetically. Metallic scraps too slippery to glue down may have been set aside for use in *Merzbilder*. Very probably, a stock of paper fragments was kept in indefinite limbo until a final decision was taken as to whether to elevate or to jettison them. Furthermore, many collages contain very thin parings and oddments that look suspiciously like trimmings swept back from the floor after a working session, in much the way that goldworkers will scrupulously recycle any spilt dust. In this regard, it can be said that Schwitters was constantly playing with the boundaries between waste and art.

6. He handles his chosen items and subjects them to special treatment.
Collectors are often said to fondle and polish their favourite pieces. I don't claim that Schwitters literally did so, but he is known to have washed dirty items before inserting them into a composition. I believe he sometimes used an eraser. It is certain that he regularly adjusted the shape of a piece before it entered the work, sometimes folding or crumpling it, most commonly snipping it with scissors or tearing it. All these attentions equate to little rituals of accession and possession.

7. He disposes the items in a pattern.
In fact, Schwitters's approach to collage lay-out seems to range between

studied design and a nonchalance more reminiscent of Hans Arp arranging collages 'according to the laws of Chance'. Hence an individual collage may either confirm the assumption that collecting thrives on systematic ordering, or draw attention to that assumption through ridicule.

8. *He imparts permanence to the pattern, thus establishing a set.*
The collage elements are fixed to a flat surface, usually thick paper or card, by means of home-made sizes of flour and water, boiled glues or tube adhesives. My guess is that the flimsier collages would have needed only a thin paste and an hour or two pressed under a heavy book to ensure they dried without buckling. The collage is now done, and can be deemed a completed set.

9. *He prepares the completed set for private display.*
Schwitters always trims the edges of a collage so as to construct a clearcut rectangle, which he mounts on a larger rectangle of stiff card. It is amusing to note that here the otherwise rebellious artist respects one of the conventions of Western visual culture, the rectangular shape of the image: I know of only one oval collage.

10. *He routinely labels the completed set with a number and a title.*
Thus, for instance: 'Mz [= *Merzzeichnung*] 26, 45. Sch.', a typical case of the artist titling the work by citing a typographical fragment from its surface, in this case one cropped to mimic part of his surname: '*Sch*'. Such annotations modulate into the catalogue entries which will be faithfully transcribed by dealers, curators and scholars like myself. Whether or not Schwitters himself logged his works in a master-list, the practice is symptomatic of a collector's scrupulous devotion to itemizing and listing. One imagines Schwitters getting vexed if two collages were ever tagged identically!

11. *He signs and dates the set by year.*
Such a practice might begin as a private act of possession, akin to signing a book just acquired. On the other hand, an artist's signature is also a gesture for public consumption, part of the agreed code of artistic behaviour. The artwork is now authenticated, so there will be no doubt as to its credentials when it later enters the circuits of the art market. Already the artist is rehearsing a leave-taking, a de-accessioning.

12. *He puts the completed set on private display, or stores it alongside other sets.*

Kurt Schwitters, *Mz 26, 45. Sch.*, 1926.
Marlborough Fine Art, London. © DACS 1993

Like most artists, Schwitters would hang finished works in his studio, or rather within the *Merzbau*, but his rate of production was such that he must have stored the bulk in cupboards or portfolios. Again the collage-maker behaves like the collector.

13. *The artist /collector later engages in more rigorous acts of selection, this time preparing certain sets for public display and sale.*
That is, he identifies the most 'suitable' works, frames them under glass, and arranges to exhibit them in commercial galleries. It could be argued that this pivotal function merges with that of the dealer, who likewise collaborates with any other sort of collector who has decided to de-accession certain pieces.

The last stage in this narrative announces a new cycle. Whereas certain favourites will remain in Schwitters's private hands, the typical collage is now poised to re-enter the public domain. A collection of recycled fragments, the individual piece will be evaluated as an element within the discourse of the artist's public *œuvre*, itself part of the discourse of art at large. As an autonomous and desirable collectable, its destiny is to circulate within the élite spheres of the art-market, and eventually to be lodged in someone else's art-collection.

APPROACHING THE COLLAGE AS AN AUTONOMOUS ARTWORK

If one is to assess a typical *Merz* collage, the first and obvious consideration must be its status as an artwork, given that Schwitters was undeniably a practising artist and that the critical consensus in our century has long since ascribed aesthetic virtue to the products I have described. And while it is true that Schwitters was enough of a Dadaist to want to resist being stereotyped, there are clear mannerisms of style and recurrent themes in his theoretical statements which facilitate an outline of his aesthetic position.

Many commentators still insist on seeing Dada in purely nihilistic terms, but my own sense of the broad character of the movement is that it cultivated negativism as a strategic disguise for a programme of positive restructuring. Individual Dadaists can be situated at varying points on the line that links the negative and positive extremes, while Schwitters may be said to have drifted ambivalently between the two. In this he was able to fulfil an ambition that at least one Dada practitioner and apologist, Hans Richter, saw as the essence: to generate anti-art impulses which would destroy and supplant existing art, thereby in effect creating art after all.[12]

Schwitters's perverse cultivation of materials resistant to aesthetic accreditation led to a dramatic revaluation of art in the modern period, and its reverberations are, I believe, still refreshing in so far as it reminds us that the aesthetic category must always be open to renegotiation. The *Merz* project enacts a symbolic conversion and subversion in that it redeems what society has belittled or repressed, conjuring up value by switching contexts, so that the negligible scrap from the dirty gutter turns into the admirable semiophore on the spotless wall of the gallery. I can't imagine Schwitters not revelling in this cheeky little revolution each time he saw one of his works on public display.

What needs to be recognized is that, whereas the basic temper of his collage materials hardly varies over three decades, his compositional strategies do. Some collages are awkward and scrappy; others are suave and entirely 'tasteful'. The fact is that, while Schwitters was essentially a Dadaist, he was also tempted by the polished, abstractive model of contemporary Constructivism.[13] As early as 1921, he began cultivating a relationship with Theo van Doesburg and the De Stijl circle in Holland. It seems clear that at least part of the *Merz* programme was aligned with

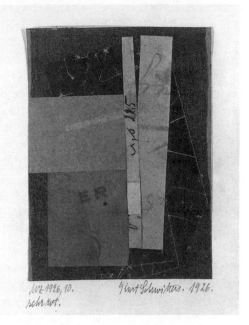

Kurt Schwitters, *Mz 1926, 10. sehr rot (Very Red)*, 1926.
Marlborough Fine Art, London. © DACS 1993

that trend within Modernism that seeks to legitimize a model of the artwork as something sealed off from ordinary circumstance. Schwitters himself enunciates an unequivocal doctrine of aesthetic autonomy when he writes in 1923, in the first issue of his *Merz* magazine: 'The picture is a self-contained work of art. It refers to nothing outside of itself.'[14] Several theoretical essays invite the viewer to respond to his compositions purely in terms of properties such as shape, colour and abstract rhythm.

To envisage Schwitters as an out-and-out formalist is to suppose that his intention was to dip into the trash-can much in the spirit that a van Doesburg or a Mondrian might dip into the paint-pot, addressing himself simply to colours and textures and distributing them across what is ultimately an abstract surface. Raoul Hausmann's yarn about Schwitters fishing out scissors and a tube of glue during a lull in their rail journey across Czechoslovakia, so as to touch up a collage which lacked 'a little piece of blue paper in the lower left-hand corner',[15] is redolent of a refined, almost effete aestheticism. But is this really how we should see *Merz*? Was Schwitters really making art for art's sake?

Of the inter-war collages, it is impossible to deny that a good many appear clean or aseptic, reflecting the meticulousness of a craftsman intent on precision and perfect finish. Schwitters indeed spoke of taking each element he used and drawing off its *Eigengift* – its individual 'poison', its characteristic tang – so that it would serve as a docile ingredient within the overall aesthetic concoction. In theory, this would imply that each element is dissociated from its past and stripped of any tell-tale trace of origin. Of course, Schwitters did sometimes use paper fragments in mint condition: but, as I have said, he also ritually cleansed some paper pieces. It is also clear that he took pains to glue down the scraps neatly and firmly. One report has him soaking the paper fragments thoroughly in paste and then skidding them about with his fingers across the slippery surface until their alignments were judged satisfactory.[16] This again looks to be a procedure governed by aesthetic principles. A final marker of aesthetic intention is the precise trim he gives to the work's boundaries.

Schwitters's practice elsewhere is certainly consistent with these suppositions. Even in the case of the more awkward *Merzbild*, where bits tend to poke out as if to snag at the viewer's coat, the artist would nail or glue his components with care, often adding a good lick of paint as a definitive confirmation of cohesion and 'belonging'. In much the same way, a furniture-maker will smooth down the rough joins of his construction before varnishing the whole. In either case, there is a concern to mask all trace of treatment and to define the piece as an autonomous work (and indeed to launch it on its career as a collectable).

THE GUTTER ORIGINS OF THE COLLAGE

On the other hand, if we were to assent without reservation to this model of the artist as unimpeachable Constructivist, I think it would be most embarrassing then to be asked to respond to a collage such as *Mz 172. Tasten zum Raum (Groping towards Space)*. The etiquette of Modernism might inhibit us from noticing, let alone interpreting, a blemish left on the surface of a canvas by someone like Mondrian. But can we bypass the lavish smears and scuffs on the surface of this *Merz* specimen? Can we sustain the myth of aesthetic autonomy when so many of Schwitters's collages blurt out tales of dirtiness and contamination?

In fact I must hasten to concede that a good many excellent collages are entirely worthy of the Constructivist ideal.[17] What I *am* arguing, though, is that the majority tend to fall short of what might be called the minimum standard of aesthetic hygiene, as if still registering too much *Eigengift* to pass the test of abstract purity. The notion of a thing newborn and indeed high-born cannot always be defended when the collage confesses its mongrel genealogy or lets slip its gutter origins.

Another reason why so many collages disqualify themselves from purely aesthetic appreciation is their composition. Schwitters has a knack of snipping his papers into abrupt slivers, of juxtaposing discordant textures, of letting uneven shapes collide and overlap incoherently, with apparent disregard for harmony. One may even feel that a collage has been interrupted before quite being finished, so that its arrangement, after all, seems only provisional. The impression of unregulated bursts of energy tempts me to take the title of a wonderfully restless collage of 1946 and apply it more widely: many of the collages are so *windswept*[18] in their appearance that, despite the glue, one can imagine their elements ready to fly away at any moment. In a work such as *Bild mit Raumgewächsen / Bild mit 2 kleinen Hunden (Picture with Spatial Growths / Picture with 2 Small Dogs)*, the visual rhythms are too turbulent for the eye to dwell evenly. Some collages evince such centrifugal energy that it is impossible to gaze at them without feeling vertigo. The viewer's characteristic reflex is to abandon the search for compositional regularity and to take refuge in close scrutiny, poring over the pictorial elements one by one, as if deciphering a text letter by letter.

The comparison of the collage to a *text* is not an idle one, for the unkempt look which hampers aesthetic appreciation is in large measure due to what I can only think is a deliberate, because so prolix, recourse to printed typography. Here is perhaps the key device in Schwitters's repertory. Whenever we peer at a collage, we seem to encounter enigmatic capital letters or staccato nonsense syllables; and when we do find sentences in a language we can follow, they are strewn higgledy-piggledy. Very often reading is frustrated because texts are obliterated by overlapping material (it is odd to see the laws of Chance apeing the styles of censorship!). Peremptorily, the collage throws us off balance, as we wonder whether to wrestle with its jerky script or to retreat and let our gaze hover unfocused across the picture plane. *Merz* is indeed a little uncanny in offering these alternatives. Ordinarily, to *read* and to *scan* are separate ways of seeking meaning, for when we read, our eyes follow letters and words in linear sequence, and when we scan they dart about freely in search of pattern or *Gestalt*. The fact that we want to do both at the same time, but cannot, may explain much of the singularity and mystery of the *Merz* style.

(Such a wavering between verbal and visual cues is, to be sure, a feature of Dada and Surrealism alike. It corresponds in my view to a fundamental intuition concerning the antagonism *and* reciprocity of the two modes within the semiotic habits of our culture. Our everyday urban environment is indeed so dense with similar ambiguities that it is possible that modern intelligence is fundamentally marked by the simultaneity of the challenge to elicit meaning from words and to construe visual configurations. I might add that, in either case, we are 'collectors' in so far as we gather in discrete particles of information and then try to set them out in consistent series, that is: messages, or integrated ensembles of meaning.)

APPROACHING THE COLLAGE AS A SOCIAL DOCUMENT

Let us return to the primary scraps and remnants that Schwitters processes, and question their import as semiophores *in their own right*, trying to imagine how they might first have struck the collector. I surmise that, when he emptied his pockets out onto his worktop, he was at a peak of pleasurable anticipation, and that, in handling those paper fragments, he experienced all the gloating pleasures of the collector, savouring their multiplicity, their variegated colours, their sharp or torn edges, their sheer *scrappiness*. Perhaps indeed those little bits and pieces were so intrinsically quirky and exciting that they invoked a complicity, seducing him into letting them pass through his hands without being neutralized. Maybe his patrolling of the aesthetic boundary was less rigid than he let on. Maybe he was, after all, less than meticulous in filtering off the *Eigengift*. Indeed, might not the washing of certain papers approximate more to a ritual of fertilization than one of sterilization? The formalist claims which Schwitters voices, and which many commentators emphasize, could have been partly an alibi, a way for the artist to cover up – even from himself – his tendency to fetishize, his neurotic impulse to hoard. I believe that to say these things is not to discredit the collage as a carrier of meaning, merely to re-orient our approach to such meaning. Our society teaches us not to rummage around in litter, but once we accept that the *Merz* invitation is to do just that, we may come across unexpected rewards.

What, indeed, is to be gained if today's viewer treats the collage as a literal slice of history, a dossier of circumstantial evidence compiled at such and such a time, and in such and such a place? We know that, broadly speaking, the constituents of Schwitters's early art originate in a narrowly defined environment and era. Because of the direct indexical link between each artwork and the streets of Hanover, the collages may be seen as unfalsifiable testimony, much like forensic evidence in a criminal trial. They have the character of miniaturized maps, or again

Kurt Schwitters, *Mz 172. Tasten zum Raum (Groping towards Space)*, 1921.
Marlborough Fine Art, London. © DACS 1993

(since we are looking specifically at remnants), they could be compared to those rubbish pits that transmit a narrative of daily life to archaeologists concerned with the material culture of a lost society. Viewed as a total corpus, Schwitters's *Merz* production constitutes a collection of artefacts dateable to a specific stratum of historical time. These fragments are part of a material discourse that is inseparable from the history of Hanover, and by extension of Germany, eventually of Europe. Today's political historian with no taste for art could undoubtedly draw on such evidence, given that Schwitters frequently preserves newspaper cuttings from the critical period of unrest and inflation that led to the Nazi seizure of power. A social historian might be struck by things like chocolate wrappers and theatre tickets, tokens of everyday social experience. The collage *Mz 172 Tasten zum Raum (Groping towards Space)* packs in quite a lot of information. We can, for instance, learn that in 1921 a tram journey in Hanover cost only 25 *pfennig*. The tickets had a standard format (comparable to tickets from Düsseldorf, samples also included here), with serial numbers and the name of the terminus of each line set in a box for the conductor to punch. The student of the history of lettering will note that the printed type on these tickets is already in plain roman, in contrast to the traditional *Fraktur* of the daily papers. The handwriting on the parcel dispatched by the Reinhardt publishing house in Munich, like the artist's annotations under the collage, are in the old-fashioned hand still current throughout this period. The student of urban history can deduce from the label 'Bezirk 138' that there were at least 138 districts in Hanover in 1921 (assuming that this otherwise unmarked label did figure on the original parcel sent to Waldhausenstrasse).

I submit that the most cursory inspection of Schwitters's Hanover collages cannot fail to pick up elements of 'local colour'. However worthless, human trash always secretes cultural meaning. And the predominance of print, however damaged, must enhance the probability of legible allusion. A theatre ticket can pinpoint a venue and a dated performance; there may be a price on a food-wrapper, a date on a newscutting. (Admittedly, my experience is that Schwitters tends to snip dates off news-cuttings in the collages, behaving with more archival scruple in the ones pasted intact into his scrapbooks.) However erratic and tenuous, all these samplings of an epoch and a locale help construct and memorialize social history, somewhat like the tins and wrappers of Robert Opie's packaging collection (see chapter 2).

An initial inference might be that the *Merz* images reflect a secure middle-class environment. Franked envelopes and parcel paper make plain that the mail still ran smoothly through those years; sheets from a wall calendar, cloakroom stubs, playbills, tradesmen's receipts, occasional snapshots – this is rubbish of a certain 'quality' or expressiveness that seems to speak of a world of economic and cultural harmony, of a rather comfortable state of affairs. Fragments from Schwitters's office, such as invoices and letterheads, testify to orderly economic process. The artist has a soft spot for the 'Directions for Use' labels on commercial goods, as if drawn to the idea that things in Germany are running smoothly. But, bearing in mind his dictum about crying out by way of bits of rubbish, might this not be a form of irony? Does the scavenger's eye-view in fact conduce to bourgeois cosiness? A secondary scanning of the Hanover material might suggest a more working-class bias. The discourse of the *Merz* assemblages in particular draws on a workaday vocabulary of nails and screws, worn tools, wheels, cogs and spokes. The collages likewise conjure up vignettes of everydayness: catching the tram for work, snatching time for a quick cigarette or a coffee, and so forth. As an orchestrator of predominantly human and urban signs, Schwitters privileges working-class culture through tokens of usage, of wear and weathering.[19]

If it is axiomatic that the common denominator of Schwitters's fragments is that they have been touched by human hands and then discarded, then the Hanover collages function as tiny showcases in a museum of inter-war history. Further, their serial discourse exudes a characteristic aroma of decay. Crumpled, torn, threadbare, tarnished, rusty, used up, obsolete, these could be dead letters spelling out entropy and collapse. Yet although one might expect the collages to be lifeless relics or 'embalmings', I think there is never quite a sense of inertia. It is as if those discarded tram-tickets and slips of muddied newsprint were still chattering cheerily, unashamed of their gutter origins, streetwise and defiant.

Solidarity with the downtrodden may indeed be an implication of the artist's choice of certain news headlines alluding to left-wing political protest. Since we must assume that Schwitters was perfectly capable of censoring such items, we must also assume he deemed them 'fitting' for his collection. Does this mean he was engaging in committed commentary, rather than neutral documentary? Here it is worth recalling Schwitters's reluctance to join in the overt politicking of the Berlin Dadaists. My sense of his political orientation is that he is best described as a pacifist, a man horrified by violence, authoritarian rhetoric and social hypocrisy. Certainly he is prepared to hint at economic deprivations in a way that clearly marks him out from the average bourgeois patriot. Left-wing sympathies can be inferred from cuttings like the one about the metalworkers' strike of 1919, found in the collage *Mai 191* of that year; although I believe there is no instance of Schwitters manipulating any Fascist propaganda material (presumably after 1933 Hanover litterbins also contained leaflets bearing swastikas), nor did he make anything resembling the satirical photomontages of John Heartfield. I do not mean to say that Schwitters was passive and compliant, but simply that the general tonality of the collages, their lack of stridency, conveys a quiet resoluteness, with the occasional flicker of irony or rage. If this is a committed art, its mode is that of surreptitious defiance: it is almost as if Schwitters were using code, broadcasting messages about the current situation that are acute and informative, yet would pass as harmless if intercepted.

Under Nazism, Schwitters suffered the effects of the Party's antagonism towards any sort of experimentation in the arts. The fact that four of his works were chosen for the *Entartete Kunst* exhibition that Joseph Goebbels masterminded in Munich in 1937, and that the list of 'degenerate' works confiscated by the Ministry of Propaganda from museums across Germany mentions thirteen of his pictures, are unequivocal signs that a passion for trash was incompatible with an ideology of purity and sublime aspiration. In the face of the Fascist menace, Schwitters activated long-prepared plans for escape, and left for Norway on the first day of 1937. While obliged to wrench himself away from the *Merzbau*, he did take with him a clutch of works, including the 1920 *Picture with Spatial Growths*, which measured almost two feet by three. (I take it to have been carried unrolled, given that it was half collage, half relief, and comprised stiff pieces of wood – hardly a typical refugee's indispensable hand-luggage!) A couple of years later, Schwitters revised the work, renaming it *Picture with 2 Small Dogs*. A rare handwritten label to this effect was stuck onto the collage; dated 24 November 1939, it situates completion to his spell at Lysaker outside Oslo.

In this work, it is noteworthy that practically all trace of lettered material in German has been obliterated by printed scraps in Norwegian, nearly all mentioning Oslo. The place-name appears at least a dozen times: on tickets for the National Theatre, a standing-room ticket for a choral performance at the University, sweet-wrappers from the Freia factory, pages from a local magazine, local train tickets, a postmarked envelope. A page from a tear-off calendar reads 'Onsdag 8 – 11 – 39'. I take it that this composition, with its ritual burial of material from over two decades earlier and its emphasis on present time and location, represents a symbolic farewell to a Hanover he would indeed never set foot in again, and an expression of radical dislocation. Delicately exerting an archaeologist's trowel, we may disinter other narratives from these fraught years. In the collage *Opened by Customs*, customs labels date-stamped 3 August 1937 tell a tale of the ignominy of the exile who, receiving a parcel from home, discovers that the officials in Hanover have already rummaged in it. (I surmise that the handwritten address 'Norwegen' is in the handwriting of his wife, Helma.)

When, some three years later, German forces invaded Norway, Schwitters was obliged to flee anew, this time to Britain, where he would spend the remaining seven and a half years of his life. Classified as an enemy alien, he had to spend the first seventeen months of this period in various internment camps. To the British viewer, the collages of the years 1941–7 leap into focus as legible evidence, for English litter now takes

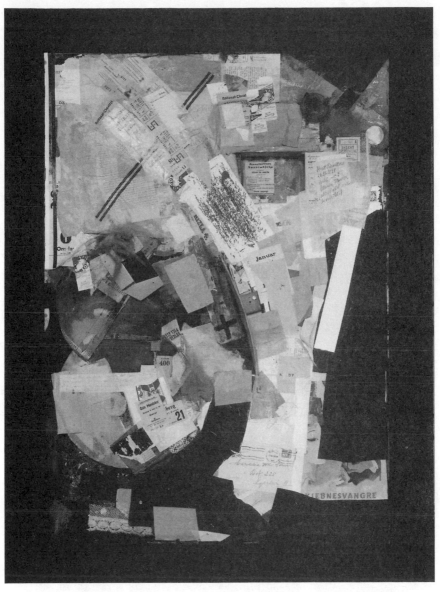

Kurt Schwitters, *Bild mit Raumgewächsen / Bild mit 2 kleinen Hunden
(Picture with Spatial Growths / Picture with 2 Small Dogs)*, 1920 and 1939.
Tate Gallery, London. © DACS 1993

over from Norwegian and German as Schwitters's natural medium. (It is reported that Schwitters refused henceforth to speak German, though his grasp of English was far from perfect.) One collage made in London in about 1944 includes a newspaper ad for a (satirical?) American film entitled *The Hitler Gang*, a clue to the artist's perception of events in his homeland. Allusions to penury and suffering, perhaps even martyrdom, are unmistakeable in the 1941 collage *Brown and Green*, where a pathetic strip from a shabby overcoat hangs next to the ripped-off sole of a shoe with several twisted nails still showing.[20]

This kind of reading-for-clues is reminiscent of detective-work, and some will say that a magnifying lens is not really the right equipment for the serious art historian. Nevertheless, I contend that such investigatory games are a legitimate extension of the momentum generated by the *Merz* project, which now emerges not as the pursuit of abstracted beauty but rather of human meaning. It is important to recognize the change in our habits of reception that this implies. The significance of the *Merz* collage is that it obliges the viewer to engage in different ways of looking at art, ways regulated less by aesthetic models and refined cultural connotation, than by the commonsensical, associative semiotics on which we rely in our everyday lives. When we notice the label from a jam pot, it may be expected that we should spontaneously (unconsciously) think about the jam inside the pot. If we see the name of a town on a train ticket, it is natural to think about travelling to that town. We may not be familiar with an outdated banknote, but we *do* recognize it as money, and wonder about its purchasing power. The notion that a collage like *Mz 30, 15. (ENIX)* incarnates an aesthetic epiphany exempt from all worldy reference seems by now ridiculous. I think it far more likely that the average viewer will look at it and think, 'Oh, here's a clutch of tram tickets Schwitters picked up in The Hague, I wonder how often he went there?', or 'So it was in Holland that he was able to get hold of American rolls of film in 1930'.

The simple fact of the matter is that *Merz* art persistently confesses its material origins within a volatile social context, and, by extension, invites us to speculate about its handling by the artist as scavenger-collector. This truancy from pure aesthetics may seem playful, but is of enormous import for the status of Schwitters's art. I would be surprised if speculation of this kind were prompted by many other early Modernists. It is true, we may chance upon a slice of common wallpaper in a Cubist composition by Braque, or be told that the bottle-rack exhibited by Marcel Duchamp was bought at the haberdasher's: but is our curiosity

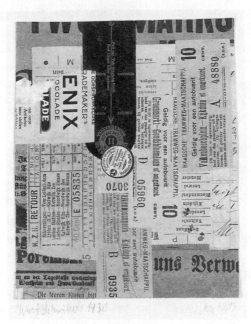

Kurt Schwitters, *Mz 30, 15. (ENIX)*, 1930. Marlborough Fine Art,
London. © DACS 1993

really whetted as to the mundane circumstances of their acquisition?[21]
For his part, Schwitters often thrusts a little trophy right under our nose,
as if to say, 'There! Guess where I got this?' Despite their superficial
neutrality and impersonality, the shreds of litter he collates are invariably
invested with glimmerings of aura and eloquence.

Robert Harbison offers a helpful analogy when he likens the scrapbook to the catalogue, defining both as 'collections of beginnings'.[22] We
can go further and bracket the collage with the same pair, since it too
encourages fragments to speak to us about the absent wholes whence
they originated. Just as mere titles or descriptions in a catalogue can
stimulate some collectors, so the fragment in a scrapbook or a collage can
activate an image of something fuller that happens not to lie within
immediate reach. This mode of representation is metonymic (the attribute signalling the thing itself), or synecdochic (the part in lieu of the
whole); and I would dare suggest that the whole virtue of the *Merz*
collage, as indeed of the *Merz* assemblage and the *Merzbau*, lies in its
capacity to constitute itself as a miniature of the real, as a microcosm
whose link to the macrocosm outside its frame – first to the local streets
of Schwitters's suburb, then more widely to Hanover, to Germany, to

Europe – is one of exemplary invocation. Indeed the fact that, before entering the *Merz* discourse, the chosen fragment is typically torn in two, or abruptly scissored, suggests to me a perverse trick to amplify its power of suggestion. The more maltreated or truncated the slip of paper, the more energy and meaning it seems to concentrate: its understated utterance has all the quality of a whisper made paradoxically more urgent the more it is muted.

APPROACHING THE COLLAGE AS A PERSONAL EXPRESSION

I have argued against treating Schwitters simply as a passionless aesthetic manipulator because I feel that the alternative view of him as a socially involved collector has the advantage of foregrounding the practicalities of *Merz* activity, which must surely have absorbed a lot of physical and emotional energy. I daresay this will be no surprise if we appreciate that Schwitters's art originated in the feverish days of early Expressionism. But I will go further, and, remembering just how self-engrossed and self-indulgent collectors can be, ask whether it might not make more sense now to approach the collages from yet another angle, not as a transcript of collective experience in certain places and times, but rather as the log-book of one man's personal impulses, a diary in which the individual subject records his struggle to hold together a few meagre certainties in a world that is being torn apart.

Envisaged as the phenomenological trace of a singular sensibility, the *Merz* cycle opens up yet further prospects of meaning. We are familiar with the idea that temperament is often obliquely registered in the range and disposition of a collector's curios. The little *Merz* exhibits of shards and splinters reflect that concern to 'make special',[23] which captivates us simply because we warm to the extravagant vision of the same one individual marshalling, fixing and signing each one so fervently, as an embodiment of expressive intent. What picture of Schwitters do these collages conjure up? It has been said that he passed for a respectable businessman, yet I cannot but think of the idiosyncrasies of a man who, after all, went to the considerable trouble of *scooping up* all that rubbish, wearing coats with capacious pockets, never tossing away a cancelled ticket, constantly bending down to pavement or gutter, even snooping in dustbins. Did he not risk disease? Did he blush if witnesses caught him pocketing an irresistible yet filthy scrap?[24] Was he obliged to go plundering under cover of darkness? I wonder what explanation Schwitters thought up if, passing through customs on one of his foreign trips, he was ever required to open up his portfolio of unfinished collages

or his case bulging with litter. What sort of psychological effects arise if
one sifts through detritus so intimately, year by year? In the bourgeois
mind, only children, mad dustmen or senile dropouts could possibly take
pleasure in handling rubbish. It is as though, spurning Baudelaire's model
of the gloved and scented *flâneur*, Schwitters made common cause with
those alternative figures whom Baudelaire was inclined to admire from a
safe distance – the ragpicker, the tramp, the down-and-out. Such figures
may be said literally to inhabit the experiential field of rubbish: but this
was precisely Schwitters's elective domain as an artist, his happy hunting-
ground as a collector.

It is amusing to observe that the urban scavenger does occasionally
stumble across an exceptional find amid the dross. Whenever 1920s
Hanover yielded a treasure, Schwitters would pounce. Another echo of
Baudelaire comes to mind: the propensity to isolate choice objects as foci
of exotic reverie. Like all ephemera collectors, like all curators of a
cabinet of curiosities (and perhaps like a good many tramps), Schwitters
knows how to treat a rarity. The disc given pride of place at the centre of
Mz 30, 15. (ENIX) testifies to his eye for a 'fine piece' (in this case, the
pristine label from a tube of cobalt-blue gouache, arguably a favourite
colour). Schwitters was partial to a good smoke, but his reverent
installation of an intact tobacco-label from North Carolina in *Duke's
Mixture* (1921) – how did he turn *that* up in Hanover? – and his graceful
interpolation of a packet of Egyptian cigarettes in *Miss Blanche* (1923)
are ritual acts that sacralize and sublimate, in a cult more of the
metaphysical than the material. Such exotica evoke the journeys
Schwitters could make in fantasy if not in fact (in reality, he crossed
neither the Mediterranean nor the Atlantic). They are emblems of that
bittersweet yearning directed across space and time that we call nostalgia.

Susan Stewart has said of the souvenir that 'the possession of the
metonymic object is a kind of dispossession in that the presence of the
object all the more radically speaks to its status as a mere substitution and
to its subsequent distance from the self'.[25] It may indeed be the case that a
sensation of hollow longing is the underlying keynote of the collages at
large. I suggested earlier that things like worn leather or parcel paper may
have impressed Schwitters as tokens of actual usage, as metonymies of
human desire intersecting with real time. But the fact is that, even as he
salvaged them, that usage had already been extinguished. It may be more
plausible to see them as alluring emblems of a situation and a circumstance which, even in the pivotal gesture of recovery (as the collector
bends down in the street), were themselves perceived as beyond

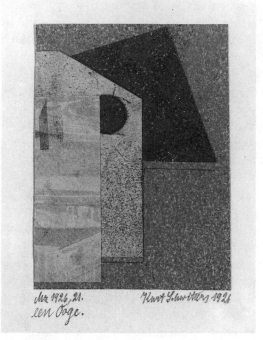

Kurt Schwitters, *Mz 1926, 21. een Ooge*, 1926.
Marlborough Fine Art, London. © DACS 1993

redemption. Emblems are substitutions, not actualities: the ticket collected is no longer the ticket that can be used on a real journey. So it is that
the notion of metonymic immediacy may, after all, be obliged to yield to
one of metaphoric suggestivity, the colour of distance. In this sense, when
we in our turn encounter the *Merz* memento, decades after its discovery,
we may not be picking up whiffs of actual desire, evinced at a certain time
and place, but more re-enacting the desperation of the fetishist who must
always stumble upon the scene after the fact. We might almost imagine
that the used-up tram-ticket from 1926 will shrink away if we stare too
hard, the shy-est piece of a world that will in any case always elude its
ravisher. Upon which, the fundamental emotion snared by *Merz* turns
out to be one of sweet frustration, the yearning for the out-of-reach, for
what fingertips can graze yet never grip – the touchable/unclutchable. In
this sense, Schwitters's non-fictive micro-narratives may in fact be
shrouded in the dust of a nostalgic illusionism, any pleasure they give us
being a function of poetic suggestion rather than historical authenticity.

This line of interpretation is no doubt exaggerated, yet I do sense that a high percentage of the collages have a tendency to dip away from sharp historical pertinence (the referent of literal hunger, as it were) and into the haze of figurative yearning (the order of the imaginary, the repleteness of reverie). At which point it is inevitable that, in seeking to pinpoint the presence and meaning of *Merz*, we should come up against the implied presence of its initiator. The poetic expressiveness of the collages is that of a creative subject whose imaginings blur chronology while purporting to invoke it. There is always a year mentioned *under* the collage, but rarely one *inside* it: the act of dreaming can be dated, but dream content is timeless. Typical of Schwitters's English series is *En Morn* (1947), which offers glimpses of lively desire in the form of a peppermint chocolate-wrapper and a label from a can of *Golden Morn* peaches, set beside the face of a pretty girl torn from a magazine and the legend 'These are the things we are fighting for'. The high quotient of sweet- and chocolate-wrappers in the works of this period is evidence not just of a childlike sweet tooth, but of a yearning for a paradise entirely beyond historical reach. And while it may be true that Schwitters was conscious of handling the myths and mirages that help soothe the collective libido, documenting the little gratifications of contemporary Londoners in an epoch of austerity, his compilations of cigarette wrappers, food ads and jam labels can equally be read as a sublimation of private longings and grievings.

It might, therefore, be axiomatic that, although *Merz* processing certainly does fix objective 'quotations' from social time, it cannot insulate the discourse of the collage from metaphoric or mythic contamination, nor quell the murmurings of dream and desire. Those little hints of fantasy and delectation are, so to speak, the unswept residue that lingers after the marks of pragmatic actuality have been audited. Moreover, the aroma of nostalgia the collages insinuate to us has to be measured against our own proclivity to romanticize the text of the past. We should not underestimate the fact that, for us, notions like 'Hanover in the 1920s' or 'wartime London' are themselves inseparable from the allure of the bygone – another sort of exoticism, sponsored by our own curiosity about origins. And where one can boast of authentic personal exposure to a given locale and epoch, auratic idealization is even more prevalent. Given that my London childhood overlaps with the period of Schwitters's British exile, I cannot look without a Proustian twinge on collages that allude to *Marmite* and *Ty-phoo Tea*, or which boast such enviable specimens of the selfsame London Transport bus tickets I began myself to collect in the year Schwitters died.

If there is any 'moral' to the narrative of collecting, it must be that the collector who allows his desires free sway risks becoming the lonely inhabitant of a narrow corridor along which his finds are arrayed like successive diary entries: and yet it may be said that to savour one's singularity (the collector's coincidence with his unique serial system) while acknowledging one's vulnerability (the mortal's inability to outlive his collection) is really the best prelude to understanding one's place within the 'collection' that is the human society of one's age.

Of course, I cannot claim that to recover an idea of my own past through Schwitters is the same as recovering Schwitters; yet I think I am now closer to appreciating (and perhaps to reviving) his project, that of a rather superior collector who is as much receptive to ideas as he is to things. Or perhaps it is simply that *Merz*, that doctrine of scattered aphorisms, really boils down to one elemental truth – namely that, like the complementary aspects of the Saussurean sign, semiophores can only have import because they are material things, while they can only become 'objects' (objects of consideration, objects of desire) because meaning is able to inhabit them. In *Merz*, the Unconscious of the twentieth century is imaged in the *artificialia* of the city; though there is still an echo here of the yearning that prompted Novalis, in a yet more distant epoch, to muse on the intricacies and textures that are the hieroglyphs of Nature, illegible for routine consciousness.[26]

Romantic idealism aside, it is the ragpicker's espousal of marginality that was the foundation of Schwitters's mordant anti-aestheticism, and it continues to sustain the Dadaist's challenge to our modern sensibility, still conditioned as we are by approved standards of purity relating not just to post-Romantic or Modernist aesthetics but to plain daily hygiene. Putting it bluntly, *Merz* means accepting that meaning lurks even in human waste, and that things which happen to be soiled, imperfect, broken or nondescript can still be treasured as vehicles of insight, reminding us of our lapsed affinity with matter. In this sense, Schwitters upsets the apple-cart of puristic collecting criteria by celebrating the phenomenal richness of what lies under our noses and our feet – that bitty world that is all the more desirable for being substantially still uncatalogued and uncollected.

5
Telling Objects:
A Narrative Perspective on Collecting

MIEKE BAL

It is a definite social relation between men, that assumes, in their eyes, the fantastic form of a relation between things.

KARL MARX[1]

In the same process that constructs the world as a view, man is constructed as subject.

MARTIN HEIDEGGER[2]

When you leave fiction you rediscover fictions.

JONATHAN CULLER[3]

NARRATIVE INTRODUCTION

This paper comes from two directions, reflecting two major interests I have been pursuing for some time. The one concerns narrative as a discursive mode; the other, collecting. It seems to me that an integration of these two interests is worth the attempt, and the subject of this collection of essays the best opportunity I can imagine.

To begin with a narrative of my own: I have been working on narrative through the eras of structuralism and poststructuralism. In the beginning, I was interested in analysing literary narratives, and when my search for reliable tools was frustrated, I stepped aside to fix a few, develop some others, and construct one or two more. But I became dissatisfied, for a while, with what I had, or perhaps I lost interest in simply 'applying' those tools. A sense of purpose was lacking. As soon as I understood how narrative was made, I wanted to know how it functioned. Thus I got caught in the question of how narrative functions socially, ideologically, historically; how it changes and what people do to make it change, and to what purpose. All along, the question of what kinds of texts can be called narrative, what makes a narrative special, was part of what I was trying to understand.

Although there are many aspects to narrative, the one I was most fascinated by is the interplay between subjectivity and the cultural basis of understanding, whether you call it objectivity or intersubjectivity. Not that these two concepts are identical, of course; but they both claim to cover the status of things *outside* the individual subject. This is, of course, the paradoxical status of all art and literature, of all cultural expressions. On the one hand, both in the production and in the reception, subjectivity is the bottom line. Yet, the object produced and interpreted must be accessible, materially (object-ively) and discursively (semiotically, *qua* meaning that is). Cultural objects must signify through common codes, conventions of meaning-making that both producer and reader understand. That is why they have to be inter-subjectively accessible. A culture consists of the people who share enough of these conventions to exchange their views (*inter*-subjectively), so that making cultural artefacts is worth some subject's while.

Here lies my particular fascination with narrative – and, as I will bring up later, with collecting. In narrative, I discovered, this paradoxical situation is doubled up. Objectively, narratives exist as texts, printed and made accessible; at the same time, they are subjectively produced by writer and reader. Analogously, the discursive mode of narrative feeds on this paradox. They are ostentatiously 'objective': in terms of speech-act theory,[4] narratives are *constative* texts: like affirmative sentences, they make a statement – describing situations and events, characters and objects, places and atmospheres. Like newspaper reports – a narrative genre – all narratives sustain the claim that 'facts' are being put on the table. Yet all narratives are not only told by a narrative agent, the narrator, who is the linguistic subject of utterance; the report given by that narrator is also, inevitably, focused by a subjective point of view, an agent of vision whose view of the events will influence our interpretation of them. In my previous works I have given this subjective presence in narratives the name of *focalisor*, and the activity in question, *focalisation*.[5] In many analyses of narratives I have since been engaged in, this concept turned out to be crucial for insight into the tension between socially accessible objecthood and the characteristic subjectivity of narratives. This makes all narratives by definition more or less fictional; or, conversely, it makes fictionality a matter of degree.[6]

Narratives fascinate me because of this dual ambiguity that makes them almost exasperatingly difficult to understand; a difficulty that is at odds with the widespread use of this mode. Not only are the large majority of verbal texts narrative, it is also obvious that verbal texts are not the only objects capable of conveying a narrative. Language is just one medium, perhaps the most conspicuous one, in which narratives can be constructed. Images, as the tradition of history painting demonstrates, can do so as well, not to speak of mixed media like film, opera and comic strips. I began to wonder if the exclusive focus on language in the study of narrative didn't limit the range of observations in a somewhat arbitrary way. But here as with the subjectivity question, one way of exploring the impact of such doubt is to take an apparently extreme counter-example, and see if that it is the exception that *breaks* the rule. While stretching the concept beyond its confining force, one must also ask the question: how far can you go? What if the medium consists of real, hard material objects? Things, called objects for a good reason, appear to be the most 'pure' form of objectivity. So examining the question of the inherent fictionality of all narratives can as well begin here. In other words, can things be, or tell, stories? Objects as subjectivized elements in a narrative: this possibility adds a third level to the duality of narrative's paradox.

From the other direction comes a totally private interest in collecting. Not necessarily in collections, but in what might be called the collector's mind-set, or the collecting attitude. Whereas it is virtually impossible to define collecting, and, narratively speaking, to mark where that activity begins, a collecting attitude is unmistakable and distinct. Yet, definitions of collecting tend to be irremediably fuzzy. Thus Susan M. Pearce's useful textbook for museum studies, *Museums, Objects and Collections* (1992), defines collecting through a definition of museum collections, which 'are made up of objects' that 'come to us from the past', and which have been assembled with intention by someone 'who believed that the whole was somehow more than the sum of its parts'.[7] If, we take the 'past' element loosely, as I think we must, as loosely as the existence of museums of contemporary art and of contemporary 'exotica' forces us to take it, this definition appears to hold equally for interior decorating, the composition of a wardrobe, and subscribing to a journal or book series, even for finishing reading a book. Starting an inquiry with a definition of its subject-matter inevitably leads to frustration: either the definition is too narrow and doesn't cover the whole range of its objects; or it is so broad that a lot of other things are covered by it too. But perhaps – and here my private interest joins the academic one – these attempts at a priori definition are themselves contingent on a view of knowledge that is ultimately at stake in the problem of collecting. As enigmatic as this may sound, knowledge that begins with definitions is very much like knowledge based on collections and classifications of objects.

If one begins reflecting on collecting in a narrative mode, it is equally hard to say when collecting begins to be collecting, as opposed to, say, buying a thing or two. If you buy a vase, and you then come upon a similar one, you can buy the second one because it matches the first one so nicely. That doesn't make you a collector, not yet. Even when you buy six vases, in different sizes but in matching colour and similar in material, style and historical provenance, you can still argue that you need six different sizes to accommodate the different lengths flowers come in, and you like the matching for the harmony it provides within the house. As someone who lacks the collecting spirit, that is how far I would go myself. But my friend who has the spirit in him pushed on after vase number six, and now he has 50, all beautiful, undamaged period pieces of roughly the same style, and the flower justification doesn't work any more. He doesn't need any justification, because one day he happily found himself a collector. Since then, I have kept an eye on his buying behaviour in general. I see it happening much earlier now, when he starts to collect some new 'series' of objects – a special kind of moulded plastic box, cheap little things; or baskets, or books in first impressions, or bits of stained-glass windows. Sometimes I can see the attraction, and shyly go for an item for a collector's reason myself, but so far it hasn't really happened to me in any serious way.

If I try to integrate my professional interest in narrative with that private one in collecting, I can imagine seeing collecting as a process consisting of the confrontation between objects and subjective agency informed by an attitude. Objects, subjective agency, confrontations as events: such a working definition makes for a narrative, and enables me to discuss and interpret the meaning of collecting in narrative terms. Perhaps it can bring to light aspects of the topic that tend to be overlooked. This, then, will be my particular focus on the subject in this essay. I will discuss collecting as a narrative; not as a process about which a narrative can be told, but as itself a narrative.

COLLECTING AS A NARRATIVE

Briefly put, I need the following concepts to discuss narrative, in the subject-oriented sense in which I choose to consider it. I understand narrative to be an account in any semiotic system in which a subjectively focalised sequence of events is presented and communicated. A few terms need clarification here. The sequence of events, brought about and undergone by agents, is the *fabula*, more commonly called plot; the agents – subjects of action – on this level are called *actors*. As I said earlier, the subjectivisation is called focalisation and its agents, focalisors.

The subjectivised plot is called *story*: it is what is being told in signs –
words, gestures, images or objects – that others can understand. The
semiotic subject producing or uttering that account is called the *narrator*.
The distinction between focalisor and narrator is necessary because a
narrator is able to subsume and present the subjective view of another, as
in 'I felt her quiver at the sight of her nerve-wrecking father', where the
first-person narrator renders in the compound *nerve-wrecking* the
subjectified vision of the other person. This split between narrator and
focalisor can even accumulate in several degrees, as in 'He saw that she
realized he had noticed that she was aware of the lipstick on his collar'.

   According to Aristotle, Western cultural history's first narratologist, a
fabula has a beginning, a middle and an end. The story, precisely,
manipulates that order, as when it reverses beginning and middle in the
structure called *in medias res*, and the possibility of such manipulations is
the very characteristic feature of narrative. More often than not,
chronology is mixed up in narrative. To consider collecting as a narrative
makes us focus, precisely, on the non-obviousness of chronology. So, our
first inquiry might be: where does it all begin?

BEGINNINGS: MANY

Looking back at the story of my friend's vase collection, it is noticeable
that the beginning is exactly what is lacking. One object must have been
the first to be acquired, but then, when it *was* first it was not being
collected – merely purchased, given or found, and kept because it was
especially gratifying. In relation to the plot of collecting, the initial event
is arbitrary, contingent, accidental. What makes this beginning a specifically narrative one is precisely that. Only retrospectively, through a
narrative manipulation of the sequence of events, can the accidental
acquisition of the first object *become* the beginning of a collection. In the
plot it is pre-historic, in the story it intervenes *in medias res*. The
beginning, instead, is a meaning, not an act. Collecting comes to mean
collecting precisely when a series of haphazard purchases or gifts
suddenly becomes a meaningful sequence. That is the moment when a
selfconscious narrator begins to 'tell' its story, bringing about a semiotics
for a narrative of identity, history, and situation. Hence, one can also
look at it from the perspective of the collector as agent in this narrative.
Would that make it easier to pinpoint the beginning? I think not. Even
when a person knows him- or herself to have the collector's mind-set, the
category of objects that will fall under the spell of that attitude cannot be
foreseen. The individual one day becomes aware of the presence of an

eagerness that can only be realized *after* it has developed far enough to become noticeable. Initial blindness is even a precondition for that eagerness to be developed, hidden from any internalized ethical, financial or political censorship. It is of the nature of eagerness to be accumulative, and again, only retrospectively can it be seen. Stories of collecting begin by initial blindness – by visual lack. So this beginning, too, is of a narrative nature.

Between the object and the collector stands the question of motivation, the 'motor' of the narrative. Just as Peter Brooks asked the pertinent question, 'What, in a narrative, makes us read on?'[8] – so we may ask what, in this virtual narrative, makes one pursue the potential collection? Motivation is what makes the collector 'collect on', hence, collect at all. Most museologists have that question at the forefront of their inquiry, and in a moment I will survey some of their answers. From the narratological perspective of this essay, the question of motivation underlies the unclear beginning, the false start. This question is called to replace, or repress, that other beginning, which is that of the object itself *before* it became an object of collecting. Motivation is, then, both another narrative aspect of collecting and its intrinsically ungraspable beginning.

When we look at explanations of motivation, however, articulation of understanding recedes and yields to another narrative. Pearce begins her discussion of motivation with yet another beginning:

The emotional relationship of projection and internalization which we have with objects seems to belong with our very earliest experience and (probably therefore) remains important to us all our lives. Equally, this line of thought brings us back to the intrinsic link between our understanding of our own bodies and the imaginative construction of the material world . . .[9]

This view is part and parcel of the story of origins of psychic life as constructed by psychoanalysis, in particular the British branch of object-relations theory.[10] Although I cannot go into this theory and its specifically narrative slant here,[11] the unspoken assumption of this quotation is directly indebted to that theory, and therefore deserves mentioning: the desire to collect is, if not innate, at least inherent in the human subject from childhood on. This type of explanation partakes of a narrative bias that, in its popular uses, both explains and excuses adult behaviour.

From motivation in childhood Pearce moves to phenomenologically defined essential humanness – and storytelling is again an indispensable ingredient:

The potential inwardness of objects is one of their most powerful characteristics, ambiguous and elusive though it may be. Objects hang before the eyes of the imagination, continuously re-presenting ourselves to ourselves, and telling the stories of our lives in ways which would be impossible otherwise.[12]

According to this statement, collecting is an essential human feature that originates in the need to tell stories, but for which there are neither words nor other conventional narrative modes. Hence, collecting is a story, and everyone needs to tell it. Yet, it is obvious that not every human being is, or can afford to be, a collector. The essentializing gesture obscures the class privilege that is thereby projected on the human species as a whole. From this doubly narrative perspective, Pearce goes on to discuss as many as sixteen possible motivations. It is worth listing these, for the list is significant in itself, and each motivation mentioned implies a story in which it unfolds: leisure, aesthetics, competition, risk, fantasy, a sense of community, prestige, domination, sensual gratification, sexual foreplay, desire to reframe objects, the pleasing rhythm of sameness and difference, ambition to achieve perfection, extending the self, reaffirming the body, producing gender-identity, achieving immortality. Most of these motivations have a sharply political edge to them, and the more difficult they are to define, the less innocent they appear when one tries. Thus the aesthetic impulse, probably the most commonly alleged motivation and the least obviously political one, is defined by the French sociologist Pierre Bourdieu in terms that are both tautological and political-utopian:

The aesthetic disposition, a generalized capacity to neutralize ordinary urgencies and to bracket off practical ends, a durable inclination and aptitude for practice without a practical function, can only be constituted within an experience of the world freed from urgency and through the practice of activities which are an end in themselves.[13]

In other words, you can only bracket off practical ends if you truly do so, and to have this disposition (or 'capacity'!) you need to be rich – so rich, that the rest of the world hardly matters. The means are projected first as disposition, then as capacity: I recognize again the essentializing move that defines humanness through an extension of a feature of one privileged group.

Pearce's list is both troubling and compelling. What makes the list so compelling is the sense of increasing urgency in the 'collecting drive', from relative luxuries like aesthetics to needs as 'deep' as extending body limits, constructing gender identity, and, climactically in the final position, achieving immortality. The trouble with the list, however, is its character *as* list, the enumeration of what thereby appear to be different motivations, none of them explicitly political. Discussed one by one, each motivation is neutralized by its insertion in this mixed list. But the paradigmatic character of this presentation conflicts with the implicit systematic, which appears when the items are ordered differently. The desire for domination, inconspicuously mentioned somewhere in the middle of the list, might receive more emphasis were the list to be turned into a coherent set of aspects of the same impulse, connected, that is, with the construction of gender identity, the achievement of sexual gratification, and the divine – or childish – desire for immortality, to mention only the most obvious ones. Underlying most of these motivations, I would suggest, is another kind of developmental narrative, that of the many strands, developments and framings of a concept capable of connecting them all: fetishism.

This missing term is the one that has a long tradition of connecting the psychoanalytic narrative explanation to the Marxist-political critique. Yet fetishism conflates and sums up the large majority of the motivations in Pearce's list. To help get this concept and its implications for the beginning of collecting as a narrative into focus, let us turn to James Clifford's seminal essay, 'On Collecting Art and Culture'.[14] In answer to the question 'Why do we collect?', the question that enmeshes explanation and origin, articulating the one through narration of the other, Clifford qualifies a certain form of collecting as typical of the Western world:

In the West, however, collecting has long been a strategy for the deployment of a possessive self, culture, and authenticity.[15]

And Clifford goes on to explore the relevant aspects of that particular collecting attitude. Such an attitude, then, is predicated on a particular view of subject-object relations as based on domination. The separation between subject and object this entails makes it impossible for a subject, caught in the individualism characteristic of that separation, to be part of, or even fully engage with, a group. To the extent that this is a cultural feature, one cannot simply escape it; the most one can do is 'make it strange', make it lose its self-evident universality.[16]

This merciless separation between subject and object makes for an incurable loneliness that, in turn, impels the subject to gather things, in order to surround him- or herself with a subject-domain that is not-other. Small children do this, collecting gravel, sticks, the odd pieces that grown-ups call junk but which, for the child, has no quality other than constituting an extension of the self, called for to remedy the sense of being cut-off. Adults are likely to disavow the similarity between their own forms of collecting and this childish gathering: they would rather claim that the collection makes their environment more 'interesting'; but 'interesting' is a catch-phrase destined to obscure more specific *interests* in the stronger sense of German critical philosophy.[17] This stronger sense of *interests* becomes painfully obvious when, as tends to be the case, the object of gathering is 'the other'. For then, objects of cultural alterity must be made 'not-other'. Clearly, the act of collecting then becomes a form of subordination, appropriation, de-personification.

This process of meaning-production is paradoxical. The 'not-other' objects-to-be must first be made to become 'absolute other' so as to be possessible to all.[18] This is done by cutting objects off from their context. It is relevant to notice that the desire to extend the limits of the self – to appropriate, through 'de-othering' – is already entwined with a need to dominate, which in turn depends on a further 'alterization' of alterity. This paradoxical move, I will argue, is precisely the defining feature of fetishism in all senses of the term.

In Clifford's analysis, collecting defines subjectivity in an institutional practice, a definition he qualifies, with Baudrillard, as both essential and imaginary: 'as essential as dreams'.[19] Essential, but not universal; rather, this particular need is for him an essential aspect of being a member of a culture that values possessions, a qualification that might need further qualification according to class and gender. And it is imaginary to the extent that it partakes of the formation of subjectivity in the unconscious, which is itself the product of the collision and the collusion of imaginary and symbolic orders. Deceptively, collections, especially when publicly accessible, appear to 'reach out', but through this complex and half-hidden aspect they in fact 'reach in', helping the collector – and, to a certain extent, the viewer – to develop their sense of self while providing them with an ethical or educational alibi.

BEGINNINGS: ONE

With this reflection as background it becomes easier to understand the narrative nature of fetishism as a crucial motivation for collecting. The literature on fetishism is immense; I will limit myself here to the common ground between the three most directly relevant domains: psychoanalysis, social theory – say, in the guise of Marxist analysis – and visuality. As for the anthropological concept of fetishism, it will be conceived here as largely a Western projection, and as such integrated in both Freudian and Marxist views. Psychoanalytically speaking, fetishism is a strong, mostly eroticised attachment to a single object or category. As is invariably the case in this discipline, that attachment is explained through a story of origin – the perception, crucially visual, of women's lack – and of semiotic behaviour.

It is a story that has been told and retold.[20] The child 'seeing in a flash' that the mother has no penis, identifies with this shocking sight in a first metaphorical transfer of 'absence of penis' to 'fundamental, existential lack', and acts on it. This negative 'presence' in the mother, because of its negativity, can only be the product of symbolization; visual as the experience is, there is nothing object-ive about vision. 'Lack' is not the object seen, but the supplement provided by the seeing subject. If this negative vision is as crucial in the formation of subjectivity as it appears to be in Freudian theory, I wish to emphasize the crucial negativity of vision it implies. Vision, then, is both bound up with gender formation and with semiotic behaviour; it is an act of interpretation, of construction out of nothingness. If the penis must have this founding status, so be it. But then, it is not the member that makes members of the ruling class, but its absence that is the foundation of vision as a basically negative, gendered, act of fictionalization.

The child denies the absence in a second act of symbolization. This time, he denies the negativity. Superposing fiction upon fiction, the absence becomes presence, and the child is back to square one in more than one sense. Later on, the fixation of this denial results in the displacement of the absent penis onto some other element of the body, which must then be eroticized for the grown-up child to become fetishistic. This constitutes the third act of symbolization. This other element of the body – this object that must become the paradigm of object-ivity: semiotically invested objecthood – is subjected to a complex rhetorical strategy. In this strategy three tropes contribute to the perversion of meaning: *synecdoche*, the figure where a part comes to stand for the whole from which it was taken; *metonymy*, where one things stands for another adjacent to it in place, time or logic; and *metaphor*, where one thing stands for another on the basis of similarity, that is, something both have in common.

Examples of these tropes in general use are well known. A sail stands for a sailboat as a synecdoche: it is part of what it signifies. Smoke stands for fire as a metonymy: it is contiguous to fire, both in space, since you see the smoke above the fire, and in time, since it develops out of the fire; and even in logic, as is suggested in the expression 'no smoke without fire'. A rose stands for love as a metaphor: both rose and love are transient, beautiful, and have the potential to hurt. These rhetorical strategies work as follows in the structure of fetishism. First, the substitute for the penis is synecdochically taken to stand for the whole body of which it is a part, through synecdoche: a foot can become eroticized in this way, for example, or 'a shine on the nose', as in Freud's case history of the English governess 'Miss Lucy R.' in *Studies in Hysteria* (1895). Or the substitute can be valued as contiguous to the body, through metonymy: for example, a fur coat, stockings, or a golden chain. But second, the whole is defined, in its wholeness, by the presence of a single part that is in turn a synecdoche for wholeness, the penis whose absence is denied. In another world this body-part might not have the meaning of wholeness, and therefore of the lack 'we' assign to it. But, if taken synecdochically, the penis can only represent masculinity, whereas the object of fetishism in this story is the woman's body, essentially the mother's. Hence, metaphor intervenes at this other end of the process, in other words, the representation of one thing through another with which it has something in common. The wholeness of the female body can only be synecdochically represented by the stand-in penis that is the fetish, if that body is simultaneously to be metaphorically represented by the male body.[21]

Note that this entire rhetorical machine, which puts the female subject safely at several removes, is set in motion by a *visual* experience.[22] This multiple removal allows us to get a first glimpse of the violence involved in this story, which might well become a classic horror story. I contend that it is this intrinsic violence that connects this Freudian concept of fetishism with the Marxian one, at least, as the latter has been analysed by W.J.T. Mitchell in his seminal study of discourses on word and image distinctions.[23]

Mitchell compares and confronts Marx's uses of the terms *ideology*, with its visual and semiotic roots, *commodity* and *fetish*, and brings to the fore a number of fascinating tensions in those uses. Fetish, Mitchell reminds us, is the specifically concrete term Marx used in order to refer to commodities, a strikingly forceful choice, especially when one considers it against the background of the developments in anthropology at the time. 'Part of this force is rhetorical', Mitchell states:

The figure of 'commodity fetishism' (*der Fetischcharacter der Ware*) is a kind of catachresis, a violent yoking of the most primitive, exotic, irrational, degraded objects of human value with the most modern, ordinary, rational, and civilized.[24]

The anthropological notion of the fetish is clearly needed for the rhetorical purpose of this contrast in the well-known process of radical 'othering' of other cultural practices – which is why it seems inappropriate even to bring it in as anything other than this Western projection. Mitchell pursues this rhetorical analysis of the concept in a footnote that is worth quoting in full:

The translation of *Ware* by the term 'commodities' loses some of the connotations of commonness and ordinariness one senses in the German. But the etymology of 'commodities,' with its associations of fitness, proportion, and rational convenience (cf. 'commodious') sustains the *violence* of Marx's figure, as does the obvious tension between the sacred and the secular. The origin of the word 'fetish,' on the other hand (literally, a 'made object') tends to sustain the propriety of the comparison, insofar as both commodities and fetishes are products of human labor.[25]

The violence, both in the Freudian and in the Marxian conception of fetishism, is brought to light through rhetorical analysis, and consists of multiple degrees of *detachment*.

In both cases, it is also through the *visual* nature of the event (Freud) or object (Marx) respectively that this violence is necessary. Mitchell's analysis of the way the visual metaphor functions in Marx's cluster of concepts – ideology, commodity, fetish – convincingly demonstrates how crucial this visuality is for Marx's rhetoric. For my purposes the insistence on vision of both Marx and Freud in their accounts of the (narrative) emergence of fetishism and of fetishism's essence, respectively, matters primarily because of the paradoxical subjectivation of objects that is the intrinsic other side of the objectification of subjectivity described in these theories. What gives visuality its central relevance is the deceptiveness of its object-ivity. Vision is by no means more reliable, or literal, than perception through the other senses; on the contrary, it is a semiotic activity of an inherently rhetorical kind. The violence Mitchell points out is not due to the rhetoric itself, but to the need to obscure it.

This paradox enables Slavoj Žižek to push this subject-constructing power of objects one step further, and to come up, not with a Marxian Freud, but with a Lacanian Marx. In his discussion of ideology he writes:

we have established a new way to read the Marxian formula 'they do not know it, but they are doing it': the illusion is not on the side of knowledge, it is already on the side of reality itself, of what the people are doing. What they do not know is that their social reality itself, their activity, is guided by an illusion, by a fetishistic inversion.[26]

And a little further on he 'translates' this relational social reality onto the objects that are positioned in it. Putting it as strongly as he can, Žižek writes:

The point of Marx's analysis, however, is that *the things (commodities) themselves believe in their place*, instead of the subjects; it is as if all their beliefs, superstitions and metaphysical mystifications, supposedly surmounted by the rational, utilitarian personality, are embodied in the 'social relations between things'. They no longer believe, *but the things themselves believe for them*.[27]

Žižek goes on to argue that this is a Lacanian view to the extent that it is a conception of belief as 'radically exterior, embodied in the practical, effective procedure of people'.[28] The function of ideology – Žižek's concern here – is, then, like the junk accumulated by the child, or the objects collected by our hero the collector: 'not to offer us a point of escape from our reality but to offer us the social reality itself as an escape from some traumatic, real kernel'.[29]

There is no point in pushing the similarity between Marx and Freud too far, however. On the contrary, the concept of fetishism needs to be rigorously reinstated in its full ambiguity as a *hybrid*. True, both appear to be not only fixating on the visual aspect of fetishism, but also in its wake on the twisted relation between subject and object to the extent that, for Lacan, they can change places. They both articulate these aspects in a narrative of origin where vision as both positive knowledge and perverting subjectivity constitutes the core event. Yet, it is in the plot of their respective narratives that their crucial difference lies. Freud's story is that of individual development, of the little boy growing up with the burden of his early negative mis-vision. Marx's story is the grand narrative of History. In both cases, there is a discrepancy between the narrator and the focalisor. The narrator 'tells' his story in a non-verbal way, the Freudian subject by acting out his erotic fetishism, the Marxian subject by living his historical role, including the acquisition of commodities, perhaps in the mode of collecting. For Freud, the narrator is an adult male agent, for Marx, the historical agent. This narrator is by necessity stuck with a double vision, embedding the focalisation of adult and child, of lucid agent and deceived idolator, indistinguishably. Freud's focalisor has fully endorsed the doubly negative vision of the child, including the remedial denial and the fetishistic displacement. Marx's focalisor is a selfconscious agent standing within the historical process and endorsing as well as denouncing false consciousness and the idols of the mind.[30] Far from demystifying commodity fetishism from a transcendental position outside history, Marx turns commodities themselves into figurative, allegorical entities, 'possessed of a mysterious life and aura'.[31] The self-evident acceptance of motivations listed by Pearce is an acknowledgement of the inevitability of this double focalisor.

If this double focalisor can be retained as the most central feature of fetishism in both Freud's and Marx's sense, and, in turn, this double-edged fetishism as a crucial element of motivation, then it becomes easier to see, not the self-evidence but the inevitability of the impulse to collect within a cultural situation that is itself hybridic: a mixture of capitalism and individualism enmeshed with alternative modes of historical and psychological existence. In other words, rather than presenting that impulse through a list of independently possible motivations that sound innocent, collecting must become, through an analysis of its complex of motivations, a true *problematic*. A problematic is a complex epistemological problem that is at the same time a political hybrid; it is neither dismissible as simply ethically objectionable, subject to the moralism that sustains liberalism, nor is it ethically indifferent and politically irrelevant. In contrast, the hybrid notion of fetishism, able to account for the entanglement of agency in a political *and* individual history, should be assigned its rightful – because productive – place as the *beginning* of the beginning of collecting seen as narrative. This is why there is no unambiguous beginning. For its very search is bound up with, as Naomi Schor put it in her interpretation of a broken gold chain in Flaubert's *Salammbô*: the 'original and intimate relationship that links the fetish and the shiny, the undecidable and the ornamental'.[32] Collecting fits this bill more than nicely.

MIDDLE

Aristotle wasn't stating the obvious when he insisted that narratives also have a middle. For whereas the beginning is by definition elusive, it is the development of the plot that is the most recognizable characteristic of a narrative. The retrospective fallacy that alone enabled the speculative beginning is itself the *res* in whose middle the structure of *in medias res* takes shape; the beginning *is* the middle, and it is constituted as beginning only to mark the boundaries of the narrative once the latter is called into being. Conversely, once a beginning is established, it becomes easier to perceive the development of the plot of collecting. Again, one can focus on either the objects or the collector as narrative agents, and again, their stories do not converge. The objects are radically deprived of any function they might possibly have outside of being collected items. According to an early theorist of collecting, this deprivation is so fundamental as to change the nature of the objects:

If the *predominant* value of an object or idea for the person possessing it is intrinsic, i.e., if it is valued primarily for use, or purpose, or aesthetically pleasing quality, or other value inherent in the object or accruing to it by whatever circumstances of custom, training, or habit, it is not a collection. If the predominant value is representative or representational, i.e., if said object or idea is valued chiefly for the relation it bears to some other object or idea, or objects, or ideas, such as being one of a series, part of a whole, a specimen of a class, then it is the subject of a collection.[33]

If this change in the nature of the object is not taken as an articulation of a definition but as an event, it might be illuminating to see this event of deprivation as the core of collecting as itself a narrative, particularly as such a change in nature is a *narrator's* decision. Note the strikingly modern semiotic vocabulary employed: objects are inserted into the narrative perspective when their status is turned from object-ive to semiotic, from thing to sign, from collapse to separation of thing and meaning, or from presence to absence. The object is turned away, abducted, from itself, its inherent value, and denuded of its defining function so as to be available for use as a sign. I use the words 'abducted' and 'denuded' purposefully; they suggest that the violence done to the objects might have a gendered quality. This will become more explicit below.

The new meaning assigned to the object, Durost suggests, is determined by the syntagmatic relations it enters into with other objects. These relations may be synecdochic ('part of a whole', 'one of a series') or metonymic ('valued chiefly for the relation it bears to some other object or idea'). But this relation is also always metaphoric ('a specimen of a class'): the object can only be *made* to be representative when it is made representational, standing for other objects with which it has this representational capacity in common. This insertion, by means of rhetoric, of objects defined by objecthood into a syntagm of signs is the body of the narrative that emerges when we choose to consider collecting so. Violence is done to the objects in each episode of collecting, each event of insertion that is also an act of deprivation. This is not a one-time act, for meaning changes as the collection as a whole changes. As the narrative develops, each object already inserted is modified anew.

This narrative development can perhaps be made clearer through apparent counter-examples. Aberrant plots like single-object collections, aborted collections, as well as anti-collecting – the accumulation of objects *not* related – demonstrate the plotted nature of collecting conceived through the objects. Another way to emphasize this aspect of collecting is the frequently occurring change in the ordering of an extant collection, or a number of different collections whose intersections are reorganized. A striking example of this re-plotting is provided by Debora J. Meijers's analysis of the new organization by Christian von Mechel around 1780 of the Habsburg painting collection.[34] Whereas the objects in the collection remained virtually the same, the collection itself was set up in such a different way, conveying, through this re-plotting, such a different conception – not only of this particular collection but of collecting itself as a mode of knowledge production – that Meijers is able to argue for an epistemic break as the meaning-producing agency. In terms of the present discussion, the objects as things remained the same, but the objects *as signs* became radically different, since they were inserted into a different syntagm. The act of insertion, accompanied by the act of deprivation of objecthood as well as of previous meanings, propels the plot forward as it constitutes the development of the narrative. In spite of the anti-narrative synchronicity of Meijers's Foucaultian perspective, in which the two epistemes, before and after the break, are compared in their static epistemological make-up, the dynamic 'life' of the objects during the process of their insertion into a collection clearly stands out in her analysis.

Considering the collector as a narrative agent, the motivation itself is subjected to the development of plot. Unlike the suggestion emanating from Pearce's listing of motivations, motivation changes according to its place in the narrative. The notion, developed above, that a complex and hybrid kind of fetishism – indebted to childhood gendering as well as to submission to political history, to memory as well as to lived experience in the present – underlies collecting in the Western world, implies a fundamental instability of meaning. If initially – always retrospectively understood – the predominant aspect of the fetishism that informs collecting is anchored in anxiety over gender, this emphasis is likely to shift on the way. It may shift, for example, from obsessive attachment to each one of the objects in itself to investment in collecting as an occupation; or from accumulating to ordering. But more significantly, the relation to the fragility of subjectivity itself may shift. In one episode of this narrative, the extension of subjectivity through investment in the series of objects fit to stand in for the absent attribute of the past may overrule other affects. In another episode, not gender but time – death – can get the upper hand. In accordance with Freud's concept of the death instinct, subjects constantly work their way through the difficulty of constituting themselves by re-enacting a primal scenario of separation, of loss and recovery, in order to defer death. Collecting can be attractive as a gesture of endless deferral of death in this way; this view provides

Pearce's 'achieving immortality' with a meaning more intimately related to narrative. As Peter Brooks has argued,[35] this need to repeat events in order to hold off death is the very motor of narrative.

But this elaboration of collecting as a narrative of death can also come to stand in tension with its other side: the desire to reach the ending. What if, to recall another of Pearce's categories, the perfection, or completion, strived for is actually reached? Of course, it is not a question of real, 'objective' perfection – although when the series is finite, completion is quite possible. Perfection, as a subjectively construed standard of idealization, may come so dangerously close that the collector cannot bear to pursue it. Unlike what one might tend to assume, this is not a happy, but an extremely unhappy, ending of our narrative.

ENDINGS

If completion is possible, perfection is dangerous. Completion may be a simple way of putting an end to a collecting narrative – defining it, so to speak, as a short story – in order to begin a new one. The collection that harbours all items of a given series will have no trouble extending itself laterally, and will start a new one. Perfection, the equivalent of death in the sense that it can only be closely approximated, not achieved 'during the life time' of the subject, is one of those typically elusive objects of desire like happiness, or the satisfaction of any other desire. Perfection can only be defined as the ending; as what brings collecting to a close by default. It is an imaginary ending that owes its meaning to the contrast between it and what can be called the contingent ending. The latter is the product of such contingent happenings as running out of space, disposing of collections, changes in desires, changes in forms of storage, sales, gifts or death – not death as constitutive force in subjectivity but as arbitrary event.

Again, in order to make sense of this random set of notions, a narrative perspective can be helpful. According to the logic of plot, or of theories of fabula, of structuralist genealogy, the particular combinations of beginnings, middles and endings that make up a story of collecting allow illuminating specifications of collectings. Reduced to its bare minimum, the structuralist model designed by Claude Bremond, for example, which is the simplest of its kind, presents 'narrative cycles' as processes of amelioration or deterioration of a situation, according to the wish or desire of a primary agent. The possibilities Claude Bremond lists in his model are not so much 'logical' in the general sense (as he claims), but rather, specifically, ideo-logical and psycho-logical.[36] Thus a fetishistic subject whose gender and historical identity heavily depend on the possession of certain objects supposedly undertakes to acquire these. The episode leading up to the acquisition of each object that so contributes to this subject's sense of self and fulfilment constitutes one step in the process of amelioration for this subject. The accomplishment of acquisition constitutes the closing of the cycle, which opens up the next one: either the renewed desire for a similar object that typically indicates the collector's mind-set, or the desire for a different kind of fulfilment that signals the premature ending of the story of collecting. Rendered in this way, the process of amelioration takes place at the intersection of private and public, psychic and historic existence, and the episode contributes to the shaping of this subject as much as the subject shapes the episode.

This structure can, and indeed must, be complicated in two ways. The position of the initiating subject can be filled in differently. A process that brings amelioration to the collector, for example, can bring deterioration to the object-being as it forfeits its function and, by extension, to the subject who held, used or owned it before. Thus, the same process needs to be assessed twice over, in order to expose the subjective nature of the meaning of the event. The second complication is constituted by a further specification of the amelioration itself – or the deterioration. Bremond distinguishes processes like accomplishment of a task, intervention of an ally, elimination of an opponent, negotiation, attack, retribution. These types are obviously derived from folk tales, and their relevance for collecting seems far-fetched. Yet, their allegiance to a specific type of plot – one in which hostility is a major factor – unexpectedly illuminates a side of collecting that was already present in Pearce's list: competition, domination. Each of these – and others are of course conceivable – turn the event into something other than what it seems in the cheerful light of most of the many isolated motivations.

For at the intersection of psychic and capitalist fetishism, the narratives such analyses entail turn collecting into something else again: a tale of social struggle. This struggle over 'ameliorations' by means of an attack on someone else's property with the help of money; negotiation over prices; elimination of a rival; accomplishment of the task of developing 'taste'; expertise competing with that of others – all these plots engage subjects on both sides of the 'logic of narrative possibilities', and on both sides of gender, colonialist and capitalist splits. If the plot evolves so easily around struggle, then the collector's opponents are bound to be the 'other': the one who loses the object, literally by having to sell or otherwise yield it, or, according to the visual rhetoric of Freud's little boy, by forfeiting that for which the collector's item is a stand-in. Paradoxically, the narratives of collecting enable a clearer vision of this social meaning.

6

Licensed Curiosity: Cook's Pacific Voyages

NICHOLAS THOMAS

While the museum is associated primarily with the public and the state, and with a condition of permanence, collecting – which provides its contents – is usually understood as a private and impassioned pursuit. The museum expresses a detached mastery over the objects and fields of knowledge that constitute its strengths; the collector, who may become the museum's donor, has a personal preoccupation, frequently of a surreptitious or illegitimate kind. The institutionalized collection stands as a detemporalized end-product, as an array of works abstracted from the circuits of exchange; the collector, on the other hand, is situated in the highly contingent time of market or non-market exchange, and often also in the culturally displaced and morally ambiguous position of the colonial traveller.

This juxtaposition might effectively capture the differences between major state museums and the desire of many individual enthusiasts, but of course cannot accommodate the peculiarity of many private, particularized museums, or institutional collecting of the kind engaged in by many nineteenth- and twentieth-century, museum-sponsored expeditions. I am concerned in this essay not to characterize collecting as a process actually pervaded by desire, but to explore its construction in such terms. Although the psychology of this particular form of acquisitiveness can no doubt be generalized about, passionate curiosity is particularly crucial for the vocabulary of collecting and, in an indirect way, for its attendant visual representations in Britain in the late eighteenth century. For this period, which I discuss with particular reference to the 'artificial curiosities' obtained on the voyages of Captain James Cook in the Pacific, it is sometimes argued that science justified imperial expansion, but it would seem closer to the mark to suggest that imperialism legitimized science. In the second half of the eighteenth century, the status of natural history was in no sense secure: collecting was not self-evidently scientific, and science was not self-evidently

A carved Maori chest, illustrated in John Hawkesworth, *An Account of the Voyages undertaken by the order of His Present Majesty for Making Discoveries in the Southern Hemisphere* (London, 1773).

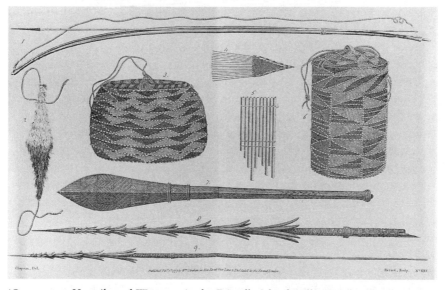

'Ornaments, Utensils and Weapons in the Friendly Islands', illustrated in James Cook, *A Voyage Toward the South Pole and Around the World*, 2nd edn (London, 1777).

deserving of public approbation. If not exactly antithetical, curiosity and virtue were far from readily reconciled; curiosity, collecting, curiosities, and licentiousness were uncomfortably connected, despite the best efforts of scientists to represent their interests in terms from which passion was evacuated.

The starting-point of this essay is a puzzle: why, in the official narratives of Cook's voyages, were ethnographic artefacts such as masks, clubs, spears, ornaments and head-dresses illustrated through engravings in which particular pieces were highly decontextualized? This would seem paradoxical, because the books, illustrations and public perform-ances that capitalized on the popularity of the voyages in Britain privileged the exotic appeal of the peoples encountered, and often idealized the Tahitians in Primitivist terms (or responded critically to that sort of idealization). Given the degree of manifest preoccupation with the newly-discovered peoples, why should ornaments and weapons be depicted in ways that distanced them from Polynesian life? Why was a public often appreciative of the noble savage presented with material in a fashion that was disconnected from activities that might valorize it aesthetically or morally, that placed it almost beyond the reach of reprobation or appreciation?

This question may seem to bestow undue significance on an esoteric and unimportant class of images. It should be noted, however, that voyage publications were extremely popular, that engravings were considered crucial to the success of such works, and that a significant minority of the illustrations were of this type, of utensils and weapons. The oddity of this sort of image may require emphasis, because a development of its eighteenth-century forms, usually depicting a larger symmetrical array, became increasingly common in nineteenth-century travel books, and persisted in photographic forms well into the twentieth century; even if late twentieth-century viewers have not encountered much of this material, photographs of tribal art in an analogously vacuous isolation are certainly familiar. The point, then, is that the subsequent tradition of decontextualized representation, and the fact that it is now self-evident that artefacts may in some sense be specimens, can leave us unprepared for what is problematic in these representations, which should, I suggest, be located in the peculiar space the objects are made to occupy. The images had parallels at the time, in the plates of the *Encyclopédie*, and earlier, in depictions of classical relics and specimens in herbal manuals;[1] the question that arises does not concern the origin of this mode of depiction, but its salience and appropriateness for these publications.

J. K. Sherwin after William Hodges, 'The Landing at Middlesburgh,
one of the Friendly Islands', from James Cook's *A Voyage Toward the South Pole
and Around the World*, 2nd edn (London, 1777).

The extent to which depiction in isolation carries with it a kind of
discursive deprivation can be signalled crudely by the contrast with
engravings of another kind in the same publication; these depicted
Cook's landings on various islands in the south Pacific, and were made
after paintings by William Hodges. Some of these showed peaceful
encounters; others violent ones; all embodied the sense of historical
significance that the voyage of exploration possessed, one that was
manifested not only in the expansion of strictly geographical knowledge,
but also in the commerce and intercourse that ensued between Europeans
and islanders, commerce that was considered fateful and morally
ambiguous, that would induce progress through trade and the introduction of manufactured articles, as it would also corrupt the characters and
bodies of natives, emblematically through the introduction of venereal
disease. The topographic sites of these encounters on the edges of land
and sea, civility and barbarity, the inclusion of the ship – expressive of the
voyage and British naval power – and the juxtaposition of the dignity of
the classicized islanders and the grandeur of Cook's arrival, are immediately reminiscent of established traditions of history painting – which, of
course, found more appropriate subject-matter in Cook's death in 1779
on a beach in Hawaii during the third voyage.[2] The 'landing' pictures are,
in other words, saturated with human purpose, with human difference,
with an encounter that was, and was at the time understood to be,
historically constitutive.

It is precisely this contextualization in human action – action that is accorded some moral or historical significance – that is at the greatest remove in the images of curiosities. Though the objects are of course the products of human work and craft, they are abstracted from human uses and purposes; the very possibility of displaying 'weapons and ornaments' in a single assemblage indicates the extent to which the things imaged are decontextualized, and their uses made irrelevant. While the meanings of objects normally subsist in their functions and in their perceived and encoded significance, and are hence clubs and head-dresses rather than merely pieces of wood or shell, such differentiations seem subordinated or forgotten here in the perception of forms; while it would no doubt be going too far to suggest that the associations with particular practices are entirely erased, we must be at a severe remove both from any sort of narrative and from the ordinary flow of experience, when fighting, fishing and self-decoration can be rendered equivalent in this fashion.

These images have immediate affiliations with natural history illustrations, but there is also a kind of painting they are reminiscent of. The genre of still-life, Norman Bryson suggests, offers several insults to the kind of 'human-centered dignity' we are used to in other genres of painting, and of course in narrative and representation more generally: 'In history painting we see the human form more or less idealized, and in portraiture we see the human form more or less as it is, but in still life we never see the human form at all'; the viewer is, moreover, 'made to feel no bond of continuous life with the objects which fill the scene'; the objects depicted 'lack syntax: no coherent purpose brings them together in the place where we find them'.[3] Bryson argues that some still-life, and particularly that of Chardin, humanizes and refamiliarizes its objects through a casualness of vision, implying households and domesticities rather than showcases, and hence there is scope for a counterbalancing contextualization that mutes the genre's objectifying fetishism. But it would seem that, in the images of the kind of artefacts mentioned above, there is no such amelioration of abstraction, and that Bryson's proposition that the genre displaces or excludes humanity is true in a more extreme way. The disconnection between human viewer and an array of things has particular determinations in these cases, which go beyond what characterizes Dutch still-life (a defamiliarizing treatment of otherwise familiar bread, fruit and vessels); dissociation is magnified not only by the peculiar conjuncture of objects belonging to quite different domestic and non-domestic domains of human activity – tattooing and warfare are two important examples – but also by a simple fact that can only be considerably less arresting for the museum-going, late twentieth-century viewer: namely, that in the 1770s Maori carving was indeed radically novel and strange, and, to a greater or lesser degree, so were many of the other artefacts and designs brought back from the Pacific in Cook's ships. Of course, some things were readily recognizable as spears, bows or bowls; but others, such as a Marquesan headdress of feathers, shells and tortoise-shell fretwork, and the garment of the chief mourner in Tahitian funeral processions, were considered extremely curious, perplexing and (in the words of Joseph Banks) 'most Fantastical tho not unbecoming'.[4]

A further, and more fundamental, sense in which these images radically exclude and alienate humanity arises from the space the objects occupy; while, in the second half of the nineteenth century, artefacts were sometimes arranged on walls in a fashion reminiscent of the printed images of that period, which gave much greater emphasis to symmetrical appropriations of form, there is no sense here that what we have is a representation of a wall or of any other natural space, upon which or within things are set out. Rather, the absence of shadow, the de-emphasis of tone associated with any particular light source, the frequent lack of any framing or border on the page, and the inclusion of a variety of implements of quite distinct sizes, presupposes an abstract, non-spatial field in which weightless things might equally be standing vertically or laid out on a surface. The strange counterpoint to the uninflected realism of the objects' treatment is the wholly imaginary field that they occupy, which could be seen as no less abstract and unnatural than the painted surfaces of Pollock or Rothko. If the latter immediately strike us as paintings rather than paintings *of* anything, the former is just an area of blank paper on which things have been printed, not an area that imitates a real space of any other kind. The suppression of scale, and the fact that one piece can appear twice within an image – from different angles, in its entirety and in a detail – not only suggests a comprehensive abstraction from any normal physical domain, but raises a question about the position and the character of the viewers: is there some correspondence between the unworldliness of the specimens' non-space, and their own vision and interest in the objects? That is, can that interest be positively constructed as an engagement that is correspondingly dehumanized and objective, free of inflected motivation, or is it intelligible only as a kind of alienation, a failure that is ensured by the severity of the images' decontextualization?

This is the point at which it becomes important to ask what is meant by calling artefacts 'curiosities'. Of course, this term had been employed earlier, as it was subsequently and is sometimes still, though after the mid-nineteenth century 'curio' was more widely used; given this diversity of context it cannot be suggested in some trans-historical way that this labelling is especially revealing.[5] In the eighteenth century, however, it is notable that travel writing (concerning Europe as well as more distant regions) is pervaded by the idea of curiosity, that the nature of curiosity is not fixed but morally slippery, that the legitimacy of curious inquiry is uncertain, and that this area of semantic conflict is directly associated with responses to ethnographic specimens, since 'curiosities' were frequently characterized as being 'curious' and as arousing the 'curiosity' of people for whom they were exotic. If the ambiguities of curiosity had sixteenth- and seventeenth-century histories, which Krzysztof Pomian has charted recently with great erudition, they acquired a distinct salience in the second half of the eighteenth century, in the shadow of debates about luxury, novelty and commercial society, that impinged on the perceptions and practices of collectors who, even in the south Pacific, could not escape the play of passion and power that European argument had invested in questions of acquisition, taste, property and corruption.[6]

The *Journals* of Cook himself, and those of the naturalists and officers on his voyages, are replete with references to artefacts – garments, adzes, head-dresses, ornaments, and so on – that are 'curious' or 'curiously carved'.[7] What is specific to this moment is a field of meaning within which naming (the thing is a curiosity), adjectival characterization (it is curious) and subjective response (one's interest is passionately curious) would seem intimately connected, though not necessarily in a harmonious way; in the late nineteenth century, in contrast, a 'curio' was more immediately legible as a sign of idolatry or cannibalism that would provoke quite specific moral responses, rather than the form of desire I will suggest was marked by its ambivalence and vacuity. To put this another way, and in quite anachronistic theoretical terms, the eighteenth-century associations implied a relationship between exotic object and knowing subject that was profoundly hermeneutic – a thing could not be considered a curiosity without reference to the knower's intellectual and experiential desire: discourses, inquiries and relations were curious, not just their objects – while subsequent attitudes tended to objectify the tribal specimens as expressions of a savage condition, a barbaric stage founded in the order of social development rather than in the responses and pleasure or displeasure of a particular civilized person.

There is an implication of risk, for the eighteenth-century engagement with a novel and exotic object, that appears not to arise in other contexts. Cook noted that the artefacts offered by islanders in barter 'generally found the best Market with us, such was the prevailing Passion for curiosities, or what appeared new'.[8] This enthusiasm was so extreme as to prompt indigenous parody in Tonga: 'It was astonishing to see with what eagerness everyone [the British] catched at every thing they saw, it even went so far as to become the ridicule of the Natives by offering pieces of sticks stones and what not to exchange, one waggish Boy took a piece of human excrement on a stick and hild it out to every one of our people he met with.'[9] This passion had a more general and apparently unproblematic form: in 1788 George Keate could assert that the general significance of Cook's voyages was 'the great spirit of enquiry' they excited – 'an eager curiosity to every thing that can elucidate the history of mankind'.[10]

If a spirit of enquiry might be thought to be irreproachable, the moral character of such scientific enthusiasm could only be imperilled by some wider, positively hazardous, associations of the notion of curiosity. Though the idea of legitimate inquisitiveness is often encountered, there are many forceful statements in a variety of genres to the effect that curiosity is feminine, unstable, somehow tarnished, and licensed in the sense of licentiousness rather than in that of authorization: a memorable passage in Burke's *Enquiry* (1757) infantilizes it radically, and finds the desire for novelties superficial and indiscriminate, possessing always an appearance of 'giddiness, restlessness and anxiety'.[11] Lord Kames noted that 'love of novelty . . . prevails in children, in idlers, and in men of shallow understanding'; while curiosity might legitimately be 'indulged in' – it evidently was still a matter of indulgence – in order to acquire knowledge, 'to prefer anything merely because it is new, shows a mean taste, which one ought to be ashamed of: vanity is commonly at the bottom, which leads those who are deficient in taste to prefer things odd, rare, or singular, in order to distinguish themselves from others'.[12] The echoes here of Smith's pessimistic account of the consumerist pursuit of trinkets and baubles as the means to 'vain and empty distinctions of greatness' mark the extent to which curiosity was deeply, almost causally, linked with commerce – the desire for novelties being postulated as the stimulus to trade – and with the moral ambiguities and latent corruption of commercial society.[13] If it was 'the first and simplest emotion', as Burke put it, curiosity, blended with vanity and opulence, could become an irrational passion that governed men, that narrowed and cheapened their sense of enterprise to the detriment of public virtue.

In the private spaces traversed by the novel, curiosity is often more explicitly promiscuous. It might be suggested that its dependence on external things, and its arousal and risk, in the context of a masquerade in Fanny Burney's *Cecilia* (1782), is paradigmatic: 'in her curiosity to watch others, she ceased to observe how much she was watched herself'.[14] A curiosity (an object), can also figure in this way, as in James Harlowe's contrivance in *Clarissa* (1747–8) to leave his sister alone with her unwanted suitor, a Mr Solmes: James Harlowe,

> arose from *his* seat – Sister, said he, I have a curiosity to shew you. I will fetch it. And away he went, shutting the door close after him. I saw what all this was for. I arose; the man [Solmes] hemming up for a speech, rising, and beginning to set his splay-feet (Indeed, my dear, the man in all his ways is hateful to me!) in an approaching posture. – I will save my Brother the trouble of bringing to me his curiosity, said I. I courtesied – Your servant, Sir – The man cried, Madam, Madam, twice, and looked like a fool. – But away I went – to find my Brother, to save my word. – But my Brother, indifferent as the weather was, was gone to walk in the garden with my Sister. A plain case, that he left his *curiosity* with me, and designed to shew me no other.[15]

Even in its more legitimate aspect, where it directly prompts the pursuit of knowledge, curiosity peculiarly blends laudable and negative attributes, as is apparent from Kames's reference to indulgence, and the paradoxical gloss in Samuel Johnson's *Dictionary* (1755): to be curious is to be 'addicted to enquiry'. Enquiry may be a proper and essentially masculine activity, but addiction, like the impassioned desire for a novel commodity, or an extreme instance of passionate attachment, entails a complete or partial surrender of self-government before an external object or agent; it is certainly an anxious, restless and giddy condition.

What is powerful, yet shallow, insecure and morally problematic at home, may nevertheless figure as an appropriate disposition abroad: Gibbon expressed the commonplace with respect to his own Grand Tour: 'in a foreign country, curiosity is our business and our pleasure';[16] and it seems entirely natural for Johnson to note censoriously that a writer who failed to ascertain the correct breadth of Loch Ness was 'very incurious'.[17] The apparently logical character of this shift, arising from the different status that a preoccupation with the novel has in familiar circumstances and in foreign parts, does not, however, render curiosity unproblematic in the context of travel; it is not as if the external situation of the objects of inquisitiveness insulates knowledge from the implication of impropriety. For John Barrow, in 1801, discursive authorization was evoked through curiosity's exclusion: 'To those whom mere curiosity, or the more laudable desire of acquiring information, may tempt to make a visit to Table Mountain [above Cape Town], the best and readiest access will be found directly up the face next to the town . . .'. But what was the difference between being curious and desiring information? He wrote that the mountain's summit was 'a dreary waste and an insipid tameness', which prompted the adventurer to ask 'if such be all the gratification' received after the fatigue of the ascent.

The mind, however, will soon be relieved at the recollection of the great command given by the elevation; and the eye, leaving the immediate scenery, will wander with delight round the whole circumference of the horizon. . . . All the objects on the plain below are, in fact, dwindled away to the eye of the spectator into littleness and insignificance. . . . The shrubbery on the sandy isthmus looks like dots, and the farms and their enclosures as so many lines, and the more-finished parts of a plan drawn on paper.[18]

In Barrow's account, the exhausted body doubts the worth of a short excursion because of the dullness of the immediate surroundings; on the other hand, for the mind, the value of the ascent is established by the panorama it affords, the fact that the traveller can experience the surrounding world as a picture. The association of the mind, the larger view, and information prompts an opposed series of implications, of curiosity and a kind of vision that responds to proximate surroundings and is overwhelmed by the condition of the body, rather than delighted by the larger scene. This overdetermination of intellect by corporeality is of course expressed in the vocabulary of curiosity, which like hunger and lust is not governed by the mind, but is 'aroused', 'gratified', and so on; this is hardly specific to the period, but it is notable that the aim of a desire 'more laudable' than curiosity is the subsumption of other lands to the form of representation, over which one possesses a 'great command'. It is as if picturing, understood immediately and explicitly as an operation of power, somehow establishes the legitimacy of a kind of knowledge or interest that is otherwise problematic, otherwise anxious and giddy. This is highly suggestive, so far as the imaging of the objectifications of curiosity, of ethnographic specimens, is concerned, and this is a point I shall return to.

Before doing so, however, it is worth examining in more detail the perspective from which curiosity did not need to be disavowed. Mungo Park, a contemporary of Barrow's, whose martyrdom in the course of later exploration no doubt accounts for his greater reputation, did not divorce inquisitiveness and reason in the manner of Burke and Barrow, but, more like Alexander von Humboldt, traced his motives in travelling to 'a passionate desire to examine into the productions of a country so little known; and to become experimentally acquainted with the modes of life, and character of the natives'.[19] While curiosity is again unambiguously understood as a form of passion, there was no effort to differentiate some higher kind of legitimate knowledge from it; it was rather proportionate with, and a proper response to, a state of ignorance; as the editor of a later digest of Park's writings observed, Africa was 'esteemed an object of curiosity, chiefly, because it is unknown'.[20] On his journey into what is now Senegal and Gambia, Park was obliged to explain his motivation to a number of indigenous rulers, and experienced some difficulty in conveying the disinterested character of his pursuit of knowledge:

I repeated what I had before told him concerning the object of my journey, and my reasons for passing through his country. He seemed, however, but half satisfied. The notion of travelling for curiosity was quite new to him. He thought it impossible, he said, that any man in his senses would undertake so dangerous and long a journey, merely to look at the country, and its inhabitants.[21]

The suspicion, 'that every white man must of necessity be a trader', caused Park considerable difficulties: in another case a local monarch 'seemed to doubt the truth of what I asserted; thinking, I believe, that I secretly meditated some project which I was afraid to avow'. It is not clear to me that the confusion was entirely in the minds of the Africans. Park stated at several points that he hoped that his geographical discoveries would open new sources of wealth and new channels of commerce for his countrymen, whom he saw as 'men of honour who would not fail to bestow that remuneration which my successful services should appear to them to merit'.[22] Just as the interior of Africa was constituted as an epistemic lack, it was also a commercial one: the sad fact was that 'a country so abundantly gifted and favoured by nature, should remain in its present savage and neglected state', but Park's investigations had revealed that there were many 'circumstances favourable to colonization and agriculture'; all that the natives needed was 'instruction, to enable them to direct their industry to proper objects.'[23] Park himself defined his interest through contrast with the activity of the trader, but affirmed at the same time a metonymic continuity with trade and colonization; his passion to see, and the activity of commerce, were clearly separate, but the latter would follow naturally from the former.

The definition of knowledge on the basis of what it is not – as a kind of evacuated desire, or a base one transposed to noble objects – recurs in eighteenth- and early nineteenth-century travel writing, and was extended in a remarkable manner by the artists Thomas and William Daniell in their introduction to a published series of aquatint views of the voyage out to India via China that they had made in 1785–6:

Curiosity has penetrated the veil of mystery that so long enveloped [Asiatic] civil and religious systems; and their pompous pretensions to antiquity, their venerable laws and institutions, are now exposed to the sacrilegious scrutiny of strangers. It was an honourable feature in the late century, that the passion for discovery, originally kindled by the thirst for gold, was excited to higher and nobler aims than commercial speculations. Since this new era of civilization, a liberal spirit of curiosity has prompted undertakings to which avarice lent no incentive, and fortune annexed no reward: associations have been formed, not for piracy, but humanity; science has had her adventurers, and philanthropy her achievements: the shores of Asia have been invaded by a race of students with no rapacity but for lettered relics; by naturalists, whose cruelty extends not to one human inhabitant; by philosophers, ambitious only for the extirpation of error, and the diffusion of truth. It remains for the artist to claim his part in these guiltless spoliations. . . .[24]

This highly rhetorical passage is consistent with Park's formulations, in the sense that curiosity is defined only in relation to what it is not; it is invasive and acquisitive, but is dissociated from exploitation or profit, having only the immaterial objects of vision and knowledge, rather than the material one of gain; knowledge and inspection are ends in themselves, prompted only by the fix of the novel, by passionate curiosity, the motive you have when you don't have a motive. While this could be seen to evoke only a kind of vacuity, it rests upon the deeper congruence between knowledge and trade to which I have already referred.

A suggestion that curiosity, a kind of interest that fetishized novel objects, actually entailed some 'risk' to the knowing subject, may seem itself to fetishize some textual ambiguities and unduly amplify their significance for any concrete, historical, knower. In the case of the Cook voyages, however, and with particular reference to collecting, the identity and authority of scientists and others arguably *was* open to being mocked and disfigured, both in the experimental context of contact with islanders, and in the theatre of British public debate, within which the self-presentations and motivations of scientists were not always represented in the terms they themselves projected.

On a number of occasions, Pacific islanders who came into contact with the British, who were for most of them the first white men they had ever encountered, mistook either groups of sailors or individuals for women; in the far south of New Zealand, friendly relations were established, despite the barrier to communication, with a small, apparently nomadic, family, who paid no attention when the captain gave orders for the fife, bagpipe and drum to be played for their amusement. 'However, the young woman shewed a great partiality to a young seaman, and from her gestures it was supposed that she took him for one of her own sex; but whether he had taken some improper liberties, or whether she had any other reason to be disgusted, she would never suffer him to come near her afterwards.'[25] It is apparent from the original diary that there was no real obscurity: the woman, who also took 'two Gentlemen & two Sailors' to be of her own sex, saw the man urinating.[26] A week or so later, in the same vicinity, the dignities of both Cook and the painter Hodges were threatened in a distinct but not entirely unrelated fashion: an older man, on board the vessel with the same girl, attempted to adorn Cook:

The man now pulled out a little leather bag, probably of seals skin, and having, with a good deal of ceremony, put in his fingers, which he pulled out covered with oil, offered to anoint captain Cook's hair; this honour was however declined, because the unguent, though perhaps held as a delicious perfume, and as the most precious thing the man could bestow, yet seemed to our nostrils not a little offensive; and the very squalid appearances of the bag in which it was contained, contributed to make it still more disgustful. Mr. Hodges did not escape so well; for the girl, having a tuft of feathers, dipt in oil, on a string round her neck, insisted upon dressing him out with it, and he was forced to wear the odoriferous present, in pure civility.[27]

It would perhaps be wrong to suggest that there is much here other than the embarrassment and awkward cultural compromise that is so often imposed on tourists, migrants or anyone else making a conscious attempt to make themself acceptable or 'purely civil' in an exotic cultural context. It is revealing, however, that it was necessary for Cook, rather than for the artist, to resist this particular treatment, which suggests the extent to which authority and dignity had to subordinate, rather than be subordinated by, the novel, asserting the subject's will and reason over the object's fix on curiosity. Cook's voyage was of course dedicated to the disclosure of the novel, and shifted restlessly from one discovery to the next, in a fashion reminiscent of Burke's giddy curiosity, but affected a 'great command' through its assertiveness with respect to novelties, expressed graphically in charts and coastal profiles; all this, however, was perhaps sensibly jeopardized by feminizing adornment; Cook himself was never mistaken for a woman.

A form of ambiguity and risk that is of more direct relevance here relates to the status of the natural scientists – Banks, on the first voyage, and Forster on the second. The editor of Cook's account, John Hawkesworth, was less circumspect than he might have been in alluding to the sexual contacts between the sailors and Tahitian women, and the prominence of Banks in his account suggested to many readers that Banks's botany was fraudulent, 'that he was more interested in exotic women than exotic plants'.[28] This was the theme of a number of satirical verses, such as *Transmigration* (1788):

> ATTEND, ye swarms of MODERN TOURISTS,
> Yclept, or Botanists or Florists:
> Ye who ascend the cloud-capt Hills,
> Or creep along their tinkling Rills;
> Who scientifically tell
> The Wonders of each COCKLE-SHELL;
> And load the Press with Publications,
> With *useless, learned* DISSERTATIONS.
> Ye who o'er Southern Oceans wander
> With simpling B——ks or sly S——r;
> Who so familiarly describe
> The Frolicks of the wanton Tribe,
> And think that simple Fornication
> Requires no sort of Palliation.
> Let wanton Dames and Demireps,
> To *Otaheite* guide their Steps;
> There Love's delicious Feasts are found;
> There Joys *so innocent* abound!
> Behold, a Queen her Gul o'er reaches;
> First steals, and then she wears his Breeches.
> Such luscious Feats, when told with Ease,
> Must Widows, Matrons, Maidens please;
> Nor can they blush at having read
> What ye so modestly have said:
> Yet though ye strive to dress your Story,
> And make (what is your Shame) your Glory,
> With us this makes no Variation;
> Still is it simple FORNICATION,
> Whether in DRURY'S ROUNDS ye sport,
> Or frisk in OBEREA'S COURT.[29]

Here, the ambiguity of licensed or licentious authority is most conspicuously at issue; science is not only a cover for fornication, but even in its public character is shown to privilege trivial objects such as cockle-shells, and to express itself in works that are equally effusive and useless. While Banks could hardly respond to such a categorical rejection of natural history, he could dispute the extent to which his interests were professed rather than genuine, and he effected this by presenting himself – in a portrait that was published as a mezzotint – not only with curiosities, but with a folio of botanical drawings that together mark the accomplishments of the voyage. If this picture is ambiguous, if it suggests vanity and personal acquisitiveness with respect to the curiosities that surround the subject, this implication is counterbalanced by the presence of the strictly scientific image of the plant, which is obviously a specimen, not an ornament. This is, I suggest, the point at which the diverse and problematic meanings of 'curiosity' enable us to understand the engraved artefacts with which I began. They can be seen to do – albeit more comprehensively and unambiguously – the same work as the sketch of the plant beside Banks; they struggle to licence collecting – and particular collectors – by abstracting the objects of their desire from licentious associations, from desire itself.

The question of the origins of the representation of artefacts in a dehumanized, abstract fashion might be traced back through a variety of earlier modes of depicting medallions, agricultural implements and classical antiquities, although I do not propose to do so here. But it appears that the immediate model for the Cook voyage productions derived from the conventions of natural history illustration, and that most of the images published with the account of the first voyage were drawn by Banks's own draughtsmen, who treated the objects in the same way that they approached natural specimens. Artificial and natural could even be placed together, as in a plate in another work from the 1770s, Forster's translation of Osbeck's *Voyage to China*. If there is nothing striking or remarkable about this, that fact itself attests to the extent to which we are now accustomed to the idea that artefacts are specimens; it requires a certain defamiliarization to see this identification as contingent and historical, as something that has a genealogy, that had to be struggled for at a particular time. The effort to make this identification in the field of vision must be seen as a difficult one, not only because it entailed a struggle with private and unscientific interests in curiosities, but also because it was internally duplicitous and dishonest. In fact, artefacts were not specimens in any meaningful sense: they were not the objects of any theoretical discourse or systematic inquiry; there was nothing akin to Linnaean classification that could be applied to ethnographic objects; they were not drawn into any comparative study of technology or craft; they played no significant part in the ethnological project of discriminating and assessing the advancement of the various peoples encountered,

J. R. Smith's mezzotint after Benjamin West, *Joseph Banks*, c. 1772.
Dixson Library, State Library of New South Wales, Sydney.

Marine life and Chinese implements illustrated in Pehr Osbeck's
Voyage to China and the East Indies (London, 1771).

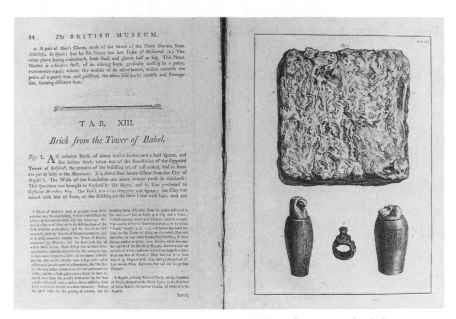

John and Andrew van Rymsdyk, 'Brick from the Tower of Babel',
from their *Museum Britannicum*, 2nd edn (London, 1792).

which instead turned on distinctions in political forms and the condition
of women. They were specimens because they were treated as such, and
their display in the space of the specimens, which abstracted them from
any immediate human interest (in ornament, for instance), was part of an
expressive work that evoked and licensed the science of men like Banks
and Forster. Once somewhat older, Banks did in fact find his status
legitimized and endorsed, even if with gentle irony:

Sir Joseph was so exceedingly shy that we made no sort of acquaintance at all. If
instead of going around the world he had only fallen from the moon, he could not
appear less-versed in the usual modes of a tea-drinking party. But what, you will
say, has a tea-drinking party to do with a botanist, a man of science, a president
of the Royal Society?[30]

And he has since, of course, become part of national pantheons,
particularly in Britain, Australia and New Zealand. From this vantage
point, the effort to discredit natural history as trite and promiscuous
seems merely an evangelical irrelevancy, a misconstruction of real
scientists whose work participated in a wider, highly consequential,
expansive project; but the suggestion that I have advanced, that licentiousness was an ambivalence internal to curiosity rather than merely an
external deprecation of it, is directly expressed by some others who
claimed a scientific interest in the rarities of the British Museum.

In 1788 John and Andrew van Rymsdyk, 'pictors', published their
Museum Britannicum, a set of plates of curiosities in the British Museum;
this unusual work made much of its precise mimesis, true imitation being
the 'solemn Law' guiding the artist, who declared 'himself an enemy to
Nature-Menders, Mannerists, &c.', and the plates are indeed fetishistic
in their attention to the appearances and details of particular antiquities
and natural curiosities. To say that the volume was a work of entertainment rather than science is to understate its flagrant disinterest in any
classificatory systematization and the corresponding extremity of its
enthusiasm for the singular and bizarre:

Now, in a Work of this kind, some Objects will always be found more *pleasing*
than others, according to the different *Tastes*, Studies, and Geniuses of particular
Men: – this I was soon made sensible of, for when I began to shew my Designs to
the Ladies and Gentlemen, some wished my Work had consisted of BOTANY;
others of BIRDS, BUTTERFLIES, or QUADRUPEDS; some again of FISH, SHELLS,
and FOSSILS; a few wanted them all ARTIFICIAL &c. . . . Therefore I came to a
Resolution to chuse an Intermixture, which will be found to consist of some
things fine, others but middling, and a few perhaps quite indifferent.[31]

The giddy and random vision that this eclecticism prompted is distinctly Borgesian; the plates included Taylor-birds' and wasps' nests; the Oculus Mundi, or eye of the world, a Chinese pebble that becomes transparent in water; a penknife with a gold tip, employed in an alchemist's sleight-of-hand; a brick from the Tower of Babel; 'A very curious *Coral*, modeled by Nature, in the form of a Hand or Glove'; Governor Pitt's brilliant diamond; and some weapons, including the Flagello, an unlawful instrument said to have been extensively used 'in the *Irish* massacre of King *Charles*'s time; though far be it from me to advance any thing that is not true'. Lest these oddities testify insufficiently to the perversity of interest, we also find stones from the urinary tract, one 'with a Silver Bodkin': '. . . it is generally supposed that the lady had an obstruction in the urinary passage; she made use of the Bodkin (to remove it), which by some accident slipt and remained in the bladder; the stony substance forming itself gradually *Stratum Super-stratum* round it – The same case happened to a woman, who made use of a large nail; the stone and nail may be seen at a friend's of mine.'[32] Another illustration showed 'One of the *Horns* of Mrs. *French*', who was exhibited at shows; this caption detailed a number of other cases of women who grew horns like rams, cast them, and grew further pairs; despite the sex of the ram, this proclivity was evidently unknown among male humans. The Rymsdyk responsible for the preface to the *Museum Britannicum* hardly excluded improper constructions of licence when he noted that 'Drawing and Studying these Curiosities' was 'like a luxurious Banquet, to me indeed the most voluptuous Entertainment'.[33]

For the natural historians, the abstraction of artefacts into a scientific enclave was a double operation that both legitimized the status of the natural philosopher and made the particular claim that a curiosity was a philosopher's specimen, something in a scientific enclave rather than an object of fashion or mere commodity, which those lacking scientific authorization might traffic in and profit from. The difficulty of the first aspect of this project, displayed in the *Museum Britannicum* and in the absurdities of societies of antiquaries,[34] was that it was readily imitated and appropriated in a fashion that at once deployed a scientific cover for licentious, trivial or fetishistic pursuits, and parodically suggested the licence and ambivalence internal to proper forms of inquiry, manifested subsequently in the well-known prurience of various forms of colonial science. In this sense, the conflicted character of the interest in curiosities is not simply a peculiar response to a particular – though not particularly important – set of novel things, but is also emblematic of the whole project of expansive curiosity, which sought to abstract, generalize and dehumanize particular and contingent forms of knowledge that in fact, as Park acknowledged, did spring quite directly from passion and private interest.

The difficulty of the second part of the project arose from the conflicts between those scientists who asserted their right to control specimens, and the interests of others who sought to deal in them or use them. There is not much direct information concerning the purchasing and display of curiosities in the late eighteenth century, but there are suggestive allusions, such as Keate's observation that the hatchets of the Pelew Islanders 'were not unlike those of the South Sea islands, of which so many have been seen in England';[35] it is clear, however, from the voyages themselves, that many common sailors acquired substantial collections, often with a view to sale at home. Forster noted that 'the Ship's-Crew are mad after Curiosities; & buy them preferably to fresh Fish'; this thirst conflicted directly with his own interest, especially when common sailors sought to resell items (here natural rather than artificial specimens) to him at exorbitant prices:

Today a Saylor offered me 6 Shells to sale, all of which were not quite compleat, & he asked half a Gallon brandy for them, which is now worth more than half a Guinea. This shews however what these people think to get for their Curiosities when they come home, & how difficult it must be for a Man like me, sent out on purpose by the Government to collect Natural Curiosities, to get these things from the Natives in the Isles, as every Sailor whatsoever buys vast Quantities of Shells, birds, Fish, etc. so that the things are dearer & scarcer than one would believe, & often they go to such people, who have made vast Collections, especially of Shells viz. the Gunner & Carpenter, who have several 1000 . . . some of these Curiosities are neglected, broke, thrown over board, or lost.[36]

In another context Forster complained that sailors did not make available a boat that would have permitted him to go ashore 'to collect more new things. . . . I am the object of their Envy & they hinder me in the pursuit of Natural History, where they can, from base & mean, dirty principles . . . the public looses by it, who pays & whose chief views are thus defeated. . . . But it cannot be otherwise expected from the people who have not sense enough to think reasonably & beyond the Sphere of their mean grovelling Passions.'[37] Forster thus associated his own interest with that of the Government and the public, while representing the sailors as acting from a mercenary greed that directly conflicted with 'the common cause'. Forster sought to illustrate his own publication from the voyage – a work of geographical and ethnological exposition, rather than the standard narrative – with plates 'of Natural History, Utensils, Implements of War, etc.', while the official history would have included the views, landing scenes and portraits of islanders; Forster would have supervised the drawing and engraving of the weapons and utensils, but in the course of protracted negotiations, he quarrelled with Cook and the Admiralty, and finally published separately with none of the plates.[38] Given the extent to which Forster's status had been at issue, both on the voyage itself and in the course of later disputes that need not be entered into here, it becomes increasingly clear, I suggest, that what the images of curiosities depicted was rather less important than what they evoked. As objects of reason, they could be dissociated from passion, commerce and luxury, from the base avarice of the common sailors who were so readily mistaken for women.

Krzysztof Pomian's discussion of the seventeenth- and eighteenth-century discourses around collecting reveals that those who were curious were contrasted, at various times, with those who were scientists and with true connoisseurs. Curiosity was almost constantly extruded, as an other, all too similar to more legitimate interests in inquiry or in objects, yet necessarily disavowed by them. The shifting and uncertain significance of these terms in late eighteenth-century British scientific travel reinforces the sense that authority was constantly claimed through distinctions and modes of representation of the kind I have reviewed; though curiosity could, in contrast to commerce, take its turn as the more legitimate of two contrasted interests in travel and knowledge. The effort to privilege scientific interests in curiosities hardly seems, however, to have been coherent or efficacious. Because legitimate collecting was often constructed only in terms of what it was not, and because its legitimating devices were readily simulated by those like the Rymsdyks who were plainly licentious, curiosity remained a deeply contentious field. Even the triumph of capitalism did not enable this shadow of commerce to transcend the ambiguous licence of an endless, rapacious, unstable and competitive pursuit of novel objects.

7

From Treasury to Museum:
The Collections of the Austrian Habsburgs

THOMAS DACOSTA KAUFMANN

Because of their status as Holy Roman emperors (later, emperors of Austria), whose rule extended across many realms of Central Europe, and their personal interest and involvement, the Austrian Habsburgs hold a significant position in the history of collecting. Although they do not always offer the first, or the most striking, examples for every development in collecting, in many instances the Habsburgs introduced important innovations; they also constitute one of the longest surviving traditions. Members of the Habsburg dynasty established or enlarged a variety of collections from as early as the thirteenth century right through until the dissolution of Austria-Hungary as a result of the settlement of the First World War. Moreover, they amassed collections that are outstanding for the quality, as well as quantity, of objects they contained. The Habsburgs thus illuminate many salient aspects in the history of collecting, from the treasury to the modern museum. The story of Habsburg collecting also provides a useful point of reference to other approaches to the phenomenon of collecting.

While the outlines of this story can be traced more easily from the *Kunstkammer* of the Renaissance to the Kunsthistorisches Museum that was established in Vienna in the nineteenth century, the origins of Habsburg collecting are to be found in the medieval *Schatz*. The definition of the *Schatz*, or treasury, at times called *Schatzkammer* (but distinct from the later entity known by the same name in the seventeenth century), as it existed in the Middle Ages is, however, amorphous: an impression of the earliest Habsburg collections must be teased from disparate documents, in which no one distinctive term seems to have been employed. From these sources and from the objects that have survived, it can nevertheless be established that the collections amassed by the Habsburgs in the Middle Ages mainly involved their personal goods. For example, one of the earliest pieces of evidence regarding a Habsburg ruler in this respect mentions the family jewels that belonged to Albrecht II, the second member of the dynasty to reign as Holy Roman Emperor (ruled 1298–1308). The direct association with the dynasty also accounts for statements repeated at various times since the reign of Duke Rudolf IV Habsburg in the four-teenth century, to the effect that the holdings of the dynasty constituted family property that was to be kept together, undivided by bequests.[1]

Hence heterogeneity marks the earliest Habsburg collections, as indeed it does those new forms that emerged from them in the sixteenth century. In addition to jewels, ornaments and the silver plate that could be used at banquets, the treasury might, as its name implies, contain treasure in the forms of minted and unminted metal. A treasury could also contain documents, symbols and insignia as well as other items that supported the dynasty's claims, such as regalia, including the Archduke's hat (*Erzherzogenhut*, a kind of crown), other crowns, sceptres and orbs, that belonged to members of the House of Austria, when these symbols of rule were not actually in use.

Objects that might be considered to have had either a curious or even a sacral value also found their way into the *Schatz*. For example, although they are evinced only from the sixteenth century, the unicorn (really narwhal) horn, or the dish allegedly used at the Last Supper, in which the Saviour's name was believed to be discernible, were long-prized Habs-burg possessions: they came in time to be regarded as permanent possessions of the House of Habsburg itself. From an early date a further assortment of items, among them books and reliquaries, including objects that might be called works of art, also entered the collections of the Habsburgs, as they did those of other princes.[2]

A treasure hoard may carry connotations of secrecy as well as security, and in this connection it is worth noting where treasuries were kept in the Austrian lands. The holdings of the Habsburgs' predecessors, the Babenbergs, were already housed in a *Gewölbe*, a cellar or vault, in the sense of a bank vault, to which the medieval *Schatz* was certainly comparable.[3] Keeping objects secure from theft or fire may also account for the location of later collections, such as the famed *Grünes Gewölbe*, the 'Green Vaults': this collection was kept in cellars in the Dresden *Schloss* behind secure doors – rooms so secure that, for the most part, they even survived twentieth-century fire-bombing.[4] In the fifteenth century, when Emperor Frederick III Habsburg (ruled 1440–93) set about reorganizing his family's collections, those of Ladislas Postumus were located in a *Turmlein auf dem purckchtor zu Wienn*, that is, a keep or dungeon. It was also said that while Frederick's own collections were not secret, they were not on open display either.[5]

The location, and the attitude towards display, are significant, for they established patterns that were certainly continued by Habsburg rulers in the sixteenth century, although the interpretation of the limited accessibility to collections at this time is disputed. Before the eighteenth century, public contact with the collections was limited to a select few; access to what were, after all, private possessions in a private residence was by and large severely restricted.[6] Some recent interpretations have likened modern museums to (albeit panoptic) prisons.[7] In view of the location and relative seclusion of earlier forms of collections, it would rather seem that the transformation of Habsburg collections from the dungeon vault to the public museum can more appropriately be described as a transition from a prison-like space to a relatively open, less policed one.

Transformations in Habsburg collecting and patronage began to come about in the late fifteenth century, during the reign of Frederick III's successor, Maximilian I (1493–1519), through new impulses transmitted from Burgundy and Italy. On the one hand, the dukes of Berri and of Burgundy had gathered together formidable collections that included precious gilt vessels, exquisite manuscripts and impressive tapestries. Through these ensembles, the dukes, and the French kings to whom they were related, made collecting into a prestigious activity.

Through Maximilian's marriage in 1477 to Maria, daughter of the last duke of Burgundy, the Habsburgs inherited the rich *Burgunderschatz*, the surviving treasure of the dukes of Burgundy, which was added to the Habsburgs' own treasury. Maximilian also lived for a while in the Low Countries, and it was there that his son and grandson, Charles V and Ferdinand I, were brought up; there they would have had direct contact with Burgundian culture. Maximilian also patronized some of the same rich sources of art in the Low Countries that the dukes of Burgundy had favoured, among them panel painters, and manuscript and book illuminators of the Ghent–Bruges School. After Maria of Burgundy's death, Maximilian married Bianca Maria Sforza; as a result, he became embroiled in political conflicts in northern Italy, but he also became familiar with its culture. In the course of his military campaigns in Italy Maximilian could have seen at first hand manifestations of princely patronage and collecting at those north Italian courts that flowered during the Quattrocento. Familiarity with humanist doctrine must also have been furthered in the aftermath of the marriage of Philip the Handsome, Maximilian and Maria's son, to Joanna the Mad, the daughter of Ferdinand of Aragon and Isabella of Castile.[8]

Fifteenth-century humanists in Italy had provided a justification for collecting and patronage in articulating a doctrine of magnificence that ultimately was derived from Aristotle's *Ethics*. In Medicean Florence and Aragonese Naples, for example, teachings were propounded that justified expenditure on objects bought not for their use but for their splendour, rarity or expense. This theory not only rationalized collecting that which might be called works of art, but also inherently implied that collecting such objects enhanced the reputation of a prince. According to Jacopo Pontano, one of the promulgators in Naples of this doctrine, magnificence is demonstrated through collecting objects such as bronzes, paintings, tapestries, furniture, carpets, carved ivory saddles, precious boxes, books, and vessels made of rock crystal, gold, onyx and other precious stones. Similar items came to be found in Habsburg collections.[9]

During Maximilian's reign Burgundian and Italian ideas may have provided more of an inspiration for patronage than for collecting, however. Maximilian became a great patron of contemporary artists, commissioning works from famous figures, such as Albrecht Dürer and Albrecht Altdorfer, among others. Illustrations and descriptions indicate that Maximilian also possessed personal collections, which seem not to have been too different from the medieval *Schatzkammer*. But the Emperor's peripatetic life hardly allowed for the establishment of a lasting fixed residence, so whatever items he collected were by necessity dispersed throughout his numerous dwellings.

Thus, not until the era of Maximilian I's grandson, Ferdinand I, did new currents redirect the course of collecting. During the reign as Holy Roman Emperor (from 1519) of his brother Charles V, Ferdinand ruled over the Habsburgs' hereditary domains in Central Europe (including Austria), before succeeding to the Imperial title in 1558; in 1526 Ferdinand had become King of Hungary and Bohemia. For Ferdinand I, the Berri and Burgundian heritage seems to have been quite important. When Ferdinand established his own court at a permanent residence in Vienna, he changed its ceremonial customs to conform to Burgundian ones. And, in Burgundy's wake, he collected early fourteenth-century French and fifteenth-century Burgundian manuscripts, and patronized manuscript illuminators from the regions once ruled by Burgundy.

Ferdinand also demonstrated that his patronage was informed by a newer understanding of art, one that had also been inspired by Italy as well as by Burgundy. The story of the *Ehrenpild*, a statue made in 1525, suggests something of the change in attitude that took place. In order to cover a wager that the ruler had made, a nude was stipulated, but the subject was not further specified. All that was demanded for the piece was a clever pose, which was supposed to demonstrate diligence, the sculptor's skills, and be well-made (with *Artlichkeit*).[10] In calling for a demonstration of mastery of composition and execution, the *Ehrenpild* required some of those elements that can be regarded as pertaining to a notion of art as a form of skill or mastery, as it was defined in Latin as *ars*, in Greek *techne*, and in German *Kunst*.

The formation of an appreciation for *Kunst* provides the background for the foundation of a new sort of collection that appeared during Ferdinand's reign. Ferdinand was especially interested in coins and antiquities. He also had precious objects and paintings gathered together in Vienna from the residences where they had been dispersed, and placed in their own special location. For this space a new word came into circulation in the 1550s: *Kunstkammer*.[11] While it is not clear if the use of this term means that a thorough-going change in the conception of collecting had occurred by this time, some aspects of Ferdinand's collections can nevertheless be distinguished from those of the medieval *Schatzkammer*. Documents had already been removed from the *Schatzkammer*; a separate library seems to have been established in the mid-sixteenth century; and objects like paintings that were evidently regarded as works of art were added to the *Schatzkammer*, turning it into what might thus be called a *Kunstkammer*, in the sense of a chamber for art.

While Ferdinand I's *Kunstkammer* was one of the very first Central European institutions to be so designated, an impression of what, in reality, a *Kunstkammer* might comprise can be better established from the collections of his sons. Ferdinand I's successor, Emperor Maximilian II (ruled 1564–76), Archduke Ferdinand II (of the Tyrol), and Archduke Karl (Charles) II (of Inner Austria) all formed important collections. Probably because its inventories survived and were published in the late nineteenth century, its contents remained at least in part intact (and *in situ*), until the twentieth century, its setting has not been so drastically altered as have those of other collections, and it has been partially reconstructed in its original location, the collections of Ferdinand II 'of the Tyrol' have gained the most attention.[12]

Ferdinand II's collections were displayed in chambers built for the purpose in his castle at Ambras near Innsbruck. In addition to a *Kunstkammer* proper, they consisted of a small antiquarium, with niches in which were placed statues of emperors and Habsburg ancestors, a library, and an important collection of arms and armour. This last accumulation, the *Rustkammer*, was formed around suits of armour that

had belonged to famous men, and also included *Turcica*. It seems
especially to have interested the Archduke, because in 1593 Jacob
Schrenk von Nötzing's catalogue of it was printed, the first such work
published at the instigation of a collector (as distinct from descriptions of
collections by others). Ferdinand's *Kunstkammer* was, like his other
collections, composed of heirlooms, gifts and acquisitions. In it, objects
were grouped according to materials in differently coloured cases, a
display that was meant to set off the contents. It contained scientific
objects, natural specimens, exotica from overseas, and *artificialia*, that is,
things made by man, in other words objects that could be described as
exhibiting *Kunst*.

Although earlier historians had difficulty fathoming what principle, if
any, may have determined the creation of such a heterogenous collection,[13] the Ambras assemblage is now frequently taken to typify the
'universal' quality of the sixteenth-century *Kunstkammer*. In such a
collection, the works of man – products of artifice – may be regarded as
complementing works of nature, especially samples of the rare or
supposedly unique. In many such milieux, menageries and gardens also
provided a supplement to the illustrations, skeletons and the stuffed, or
otherwise preserved, specimens found in the *Kunstkammer*. Altogether,
such gatherings represented the world *in toto*. In containing both man-
made and natural objects, the Habsburg collections of the second part of
the sixteenth century, like other *Kunstkammern*, thus reflected the
contents of the universe in all its variety.

Other aspects of the inventory, display and systematic acquisition of
certain objects suggest that the *Kunstkammern* of this time possessed a
further symbolic dimension. For example, in their universal aspiration
the *Kunstkammern* could be regarded as an embodiment of an encyclopaedic ideal, such as had been enunciated in antiquity and the Middle
Ages. In containing samples of all that was to be found in the macrocosm,
the greater world, the *Kunstkammer* can be thought to represent the
world in microcosm. In this respect it was not merely a curio cabinet, but
encompassed a vision of the world broader even than that implied by
more recent museums, which, even while they may attempt to present a
complete vision of the history of art, in most instances lack examples of
other aspects of human and natural creation, and cannot therefore be
said to offer a truly encyclopaedic vision.[14]

While they are less well known, the collections of Maximilian II also
possessed notable features. In Vienna, the Emperor's collections were
housed on the upper floors of newly constructed stables, the *Stallburg*;

this is a frequently repeated arrangement, one that may have arisen from the need for large spaces. Whereas the Ambras collections were more accessible, there is evidence that foreign rulers who visited Maximilian in Vienna saw his collections, which thus came to be regarded as something special: this provides part of the background for the seeming exclusiveness of the collections of Maximilian's son Rudolf. Another aspect of diplomacy that affected the growth of collections from ancient times was gift-giving: the famous salt-cellar made by Benvenuto Cellini, for example, came into the hands of the Habsburgs because it was given to Archduke Ferdinand for having served as a proxy at the marriage of the King of France to a Habsburg archduchess.[15]

But the symbolism of some of the objects contained in Maximilian's collections carried a specific charge. Their imagery turns on the notion that the macrocosm, the greater world and time, were linked by a system of correspondences to the microcosm, the world of man. This notion underlay the construction of a collection that had objects which corresponded to all the aspects of the greater world. Accordingly, a fountain made by Wenzel Jamnitzer for Maximilian in the shape of an Imperial crown combined the year (*annus*), personified by the figures of the Seasons that constituted its base, and the world of matter (*mundus*), whose various figures related to the four figures, with the world of man (*homo*), the body politic, that adorned the whole. The universe was thereby shown to be under the control of the Emperor, whose portrait statue stood at the fountain's summit. The series of paintings of the *Elements* and *Seasons* presented to Maximilian II by the court artist Giuseppe Arcimboldo also participated in this vision. Arcimboldo's portrait heads, painted assemblages of items pertaining to the subject represented, simulate the contents of a *Kunstkammer*. Indeed, his pictures have even been interpreted as introductions to Maximilian's *Kunstkammer*.[16] Whether this was so, a presentation poem that accompanied the paintings indicates that they offered a message that the world abided in harmony under the beneficent, eternal rule of the Habsburgs, whose devices and initials accordingly adorn them.[17]

The famed collections of Maximilian's son, the Emperor Rudolf II (reigned 1576–1612), represent the high point of Habsburg collecting in the form of the *Kunstkammer*, much as Arcimboldo's portrait of Rudolf in the guise of the god Vertumnus culminates his series of the *Seasons* and *Elements*. After Rudolf established his residence in Prague in the 1580s, he gradually had the Hradčany Palace and its grounds redesigned, redecorated and extended to house what became one of the largest and most important collections in European history. The grounds included a lions' den, an aviary, a drained moat to contain the deer, and formal gardens. The Belvedere at one end of the gardens housed the instruments of the renowned astronomer Tycho Brahe, whom Rudolf brought to Prague along with many other instrument-makers and scientists, such as Johann Kepler.

The Palace itself was given a new stables wing, with rooms upstairs containing antiquities and contemporary sculptures in formally designed spaces. In corridors on an upper floor of a wing connecting the stables to the so-called Summer House in the older body of the Palace were some of the thousands of paintings the Emperor owned. They included works by earlier masters, such as Peter Brueghel and Dürer, and various Italians, among them Parmigianino, Leonardo da Vinci and Correggio, along with pictures by contemporaries, many of whom were court painters. The bottom floor of this connecting wing may have contained the workshops of the many artisans who flocked to Prague to enrich the collection. Their products, made from rock crystal, gold, silver and various precious stones, remain esteemed objects in today's European and American museums. The *Kunstkammer* proper was located on the first floor.

While Rudolf's interest has been deemed idiosyncratic, and the seemingly unusual congeries of works of art, books, *naturalia* and scientific instruments present in his *Kunstkammer* for a long time struck sceptical critics as an unsystematic cabinet of curiosities that represented a frivolous pastime or refuge from matters of political importance, recent investigations have corrected these impressions. Rudolf's taste has been related to that of several other, earlier Habsburgs. Not only did he inherit his father's collections and the appointed court artists, but Maximilian II's predilection for artists such as Titian and Giambologna seems to be reflected in Rudolf's patronage of Venetian painters and the Netherlandish sculptor Adriaen de Vries, a sculptor trained by Giambologna, who became Rudolf's court artist. In his amassing a huge collection of paintings, Rudolf seems to have sought to emulate the impressive collections of his uncle, cousin and brother-in-law Philip II of Spain, at whose court he was raised, and whose love for Venetian and Netherlandish paintings he shared. And many of the objects in the *Kunstkammer*, as well as the works of art there, specifically echo those of his uncle Ferdinand of the Tyrol, whose collection he took pains to acquire and preserve for the House of Habsburg.[18]

It may even be argued that by assembling the greatest collection of his time, Rudolf was not avoiding affairs of state, but making a political statement. In a world of rulers who were also collectors, the arts could become a locus for diplomatic activity, in which the exchange and commissioning of works of art played a central role. Rudolf, in fact, had an impact not only on contemporary rulers, for whom collections were necessary signs of status, but more generally on noblemen. While his collections, like those of most contemporary Central European rulers, were secluded, this does not mean that they were entirely inaccessible. The *Kunstkammer* was shown to visiting dignitaries; ambassadors were taken to the collections as a sign of favour, or when they departed from court; court artists also seem to have had regular access to the collections, as the impact of earlier works on their own suggests. Furthermore, artists' friends or associates were also able to see the collections, as is revealed by a number of documented visits by commoners, early copies made after paintings in the collections, and even in the advice to visit Prague given in his *Schilderboeck* by the Netherlandish artist and art historian Karel van Mander.

Rudolf's possession of a universal collection could symbolically represent his Imperial majesty, his control over a microcosm, that reflected his claims to mastery of the macrocosm of the greater world, and over the body politic of which he was sovereign. In the atmosphere provided by the interest in the occult that was also fostered in Prague, this interest may have assumed another guise. It is possible that Rudolf's *Kunstkammer* was a magic memory theatre, through which he may have thought he might grasp and control the larger world through some sort of occult power. Certainly a similar quasi-occult view of collecting as contributing to the completion of a Hermetic project is what Francis Bacon, Rudolf's contemporary, proposed as the end result for the establishment of workshops, laboratories and collections by a ruler.[19]

In any event, the Emperor's holdings aided the intellectual and artistic pursuits of his court scholars and artists. The latter frequently copied or emulated Rudolf's prized items in their own works of art; the holdings also provided raw material, as well as examples, for scientific investigation.[20] They were, therefore, far more than just materials for recreation or contemplation, although they were no doubt that too.

Rudolf's collections overshadow those of his immediate successors. The troubles of the first half of the seventeenth century – most notably the Thirty Years War – were bound to have had a negative effect on collecting, just as they did on many other aspects of cultural endeavour in Central Europe. In particular, the Prague collections were diminished by sales and gifts, starting with the assumption of power by the Bohemian estates in 1619, and continuing with sales and gifts in 1635. As one of the last acts of armed conflict, in 1648 Swedish armies sacked the Hradčany, carrying away much of what remained of Rudolf's treasures.

Nevertheless, a significant redirection of collecting occurred during the reigns of Matthias (to 1619), Ferdinand II (to 1637) and Ferdinand III (to 1657). Although later events were to prove Matthias's efforts fruitless, he sought to keep intact the collections of Rudolf II, those of his other siblings, Archdukes Albrecht VII and Maximilian III, and those in Ambras. Emperor Ferdinand II established the principle of primogeniture, which determined that the Habsburg collections were inalienable family possessions, to pass always to the eldest son. When certain items were moved, for example from Prague to Vienna, they were, moreover, absorbed into different sorts of collections.

These were the library and the *Schatzkammer* proper. The library contained not only books, but also the Emperor's coin collection. And while the Habsburg's *Schatzkammer* of the seventeenth century contained works of art along with *naturalia* and *mirabilia*, much as the *Kunstkammer* had done, most of the scientific instruments present in the earlier *Kunstkammer* were lacking. Instead, as in the medieval *Schatzkammer*, the centrepieces of this collection became the Habsburgs' regalia and other items inalienably associated with the archducal house. Thus the revival of the term *Schatzkammer* betokens a turn from the idea of the universal *Kunstkammer* of the Rudolfine era.

By the later seventeenth century, another new foundation within the *Schatzkammer* suggests a further evolution in Habsburg collections. This was the sacred or ecclesiastical *Schatzkammer*, an institution that survives within the Vienna *Schatzkammer* to this day. In this collection, liturgical vessels, reliquaries and textiles were kept with other objects from the sacred realm. While not new – the *Reiche Kapelle* of the Munich Residenz anticipates it – the foundation of this collection again suggests the increasingly 'Holy Roman' aspirations of the Habsburg emperor toward 1700.[21] The glorification of the ruler as a divinely favoured being received expression not only in small works, such as the ivory monuments Matthias Steinl made for the *Schatzkammer*, but in the large *Pestsäule*, the plague column on the Vienna *Graben*. These works are directly connected with the initiation of artistic activity that constituted the bloom of Vienna *gloriosa* towards 1700.[22]

During the reign of Emperor Leopold I (1658–1705), another collection was established in Vienna that points towards the later transformations of the eighteenth century. As stadholder of the Spanish king in the southern Netherlands from 1647 to 1656, Archduke Leopold Wilhelm (1614–62) had already begun collecting many of the Italian and Netherlandish paintings and sculptures that came to constitute his distinguished collection. This collection, which in part compensated for the losses of Rudolf II's holdings, was later taken to Vienna and set up in the *Stallburg*, where Maximilian II's *Kunstkammer* had been. The Flemish painter David Teniers made small copies of many of the pictures in the collection, and in addition published reproductions of many of them in a pictorial theatre, a *Theatrum Pictorum*, which was intended to spread its fame. Leopold Wilhelm's collection was designated a *Kunstkammer*, and in it an interest in art does seem to predominate. While the representational interest continues, since many other aspects of the earlier *Kunstkammer* were not present in Leopold Wilhelm's collection (most notably, its emphasis on *naturalia* and scientific objects), it thereby represents a more strictly aesthetic definition of this entity.[23]

Where the organization of Leopold Wilhelm's collection foreshadows the developments that were to take place in the following century, certain changes in the collections of Emperor Leopold I parallel the increase in specialization that was to be found in Leopold Wilhelm's *Kunstkammer*. These include the growth and reorganization of the Imperial library and coin cabinet under the direction of expert personnel, among them Peter Lambeck. During Leopold I's reign, objects of historical, as opposed to artistic or naturalistic, interest were also increasingly separated from the *Kunstkammer* proper.[24]

The tendencies prefigured in the later seventeenth century came to fruition in the eighteenth. During the course of the eighteenth century the Habsburg collections were transformed in a manner that is homologous, and indeed in some instances the result of the revaluation and reconceptualization of the nature and history of the visual arts that occurred in the German-speaking world. Early in the century the Imperial court architect Johann Bernhard Fischer von Erlach had adumbrated an independent history of architecture based on a succession of images. By mid-century Alexander Gottlieb Baumgarten had developed a philosophical aesthetics, in which beauty became part of an independent science, and Gotthold Ephraim Lessing had laid the ground for an independent criticism of the visual arts that was equal to that of the better-known French writers. Johann Joachim Winckelmann was also to establish an independent history of art. In addition to Fischer von Erlach, several of these figures were also associated with the Imperial court: Lessing made efforts to establish an academy in Vienna, and Winckelmann died on his return from a triumphant visit to Vienna, where the first *Gesamtausgabe* of his writings was later published.

Of course, historical connections cannot be so neatly established with the Habsburg collections, for in Vienna at least it took a while for some of the newer tendencies, tendencies more broadly associated with the Enlightenment in its Germanic form of *Aufklärung*, to exert an impact on collecting. During the reign of Charles VI (*d.* 1740), the successor of the relatively short-lived Joseph I (1678–1711), who had been Fischer's pupil, a rationalized and orderly approach continued to be applied to the collections. Scholars such as C. G. Heraeus took charge of the collection of coins and medals, and an inventory of the picture gallery was drawn up. Several publications accompanied the efforts that were directed at making catalogues of the collections. Some of the collections, including the *Schatzkammer*, were even made accessible to the public. The Imperial library received special attention: its reorganized holdings were housed in an impressive new structure attached to the Imperial palace, an edifice designed by Fischer von Erlach and completed by his son, Joseph Emanuel; this publicly accessible building contained allegorical frescoes by Daniel Gran, glorifying Imperial patronage.[25]

The construction and decoration of the new building suggest that during the early eighteenth century the collections were still treated as part of a grander Imperial scheme. They remained an interest and an expression of an absolutist court, another mark of that representational style sometimes called the *Kaiserstil*.[26] A painting by Solimena of Gundaker, Count Althan, presenting the inventory of the Imperial picture collections to the Emperor communicates this idea quite well, as it dresses up in the trappings of Baroque allegory in a large picture the medieval tradition of the dedication page.

Moreover, at a time when in Dresden the old *Kunstkammer* was split into separate parts, the Imperial art collections, while placed in different rooms, were kept together in the *Stallburg*.[27] Pictures, medals, coins, sculptures and goldsmiths' works were incorporated into overall decorative schemes. These followed formal principles of design rather than other notions of display.

Fundamental transformation in the organization of the collection had to wait until the reigns of Maria Theresa (*d.* 1780; her husband, known as Franz I, served as Emperor 1745–65) and Joseph II (*d.* 1790). After the Imperial collections had been significantly enriched by the addition of the collection of Prince Eugene of Savoy – a particular boon for the library

Francesco Solimena, *Gundaker, Count Althan, Presenting the Inventory of the Imperial Painting Collection to Charles VI*, 1730s. Kunsthistorisches Museum, Vienna.

and the Imperial collection of graphic arts – new administrative positions were introduced. These included a *Schatzmeister*, a gallery inspector, and various curators (Intendants) for the other collections.[28]

The creation of new positions correspond to the establishment of new institutions. At the beginning of Maria Theresa's reign, around 1740, a *Münz-* and *Medaillenkabinett* joined the *Hofbibliothek* and *Schatzkammer* as independent entities within the Imperial structure of collections. Soon after, in 1748, *naturalia* were separated from the

Schatzkammer or *Kunstkammer*; which led to the constitution of a *Naturalienkabinett*. Similarly, that same year a *Physikalischeskabinett*, later known as the '*Mechanisch-physikalisches Kunstkabinett*' was founded. In this collection, mechanical and scientific instruments and devices of various kinds were preserved. As a result of the new foundations, the *Schatzkammer* itself gradually came to resemble its present condition, that is, a treasury of objects associated with the House of Austria. Here, too, objects came to be appreciated more for their historical than their numinous associations.

In Vienna as earlier in Dresden, then, the old universal *Kunstkammer* yielded to newer principles of organization, which in turn led to its dissolution into constituent elements. In mid- and late-eighteenth-century Vienna the break with earlier forms of collecting resulted not only from the imposition of what could be called modern, rational principles of organization. Educational or didactic goals, rather than a quest for rarity or a desire for splendour, also came to determine both the internal display and selection of items for the collection of *naturalia*.

Another development that occurred during the reigns of Maria Theresa and Joseph II also had an important impact on the history of art. This was the foundation of an independent public picture gallery. This foundation was one in a sequence of changes that affected the Imperial collections of paintings. Those in Prague and Ambras were reorganized; paintings were selected and brought to Vienna. Acting as gallery inspector, the painter Joseph Roos (Rosa) also reorganized the collections that were still kept in the Vienna *Stallburg*, and began to assemble paintings for a separate picture gallery. From 1776 these began to be displayed in Prince Eugene's suburban Vienna residence, the Belvedere.

The ultimate aim behind the establishment of this collection was that of educating the public. Joseph II had dedicated the Vienna Augarten and Prater as parks for public relaxation and amusement. The new Gemälde-galerie in the upper Belvedere was also opened, free of charge, to the public. By facilitating access to the picture collections, a contribution was to be made not only to their enjoyment, but to the general education of the populace, by providing an opportunity for instruction in the visual arts.

In a more specific way, instruction in drawing, an activity that was introduced to schools throughout the Empire during the reign of Maria Theresa, would gain from the study of original works of art. The initial stages of drawing were taught from copying other works of art.[29] For a more general public, whose numbers were expanding, information about the paintings in the Imperial collections and an introduction to them were provided by the compilation and subsequent publication of inventories and catalogues, including those made by J. B. Primisser in 1773 for the paintings in Ambras, and by Christian Mechel in 1781 for the newly opened Belvedere. These publications were responses to a public interest that, at the same time, they had to form.

Mechel's catalogue articulated principles that had determined the reorganization and display of the paintings carried out by him in the Belvedere. Mechel suggested that the only sure way to knowledge was through looking and comparing; this was a process, moreover, that was not only made possible but directed through the way in which the pictures were hung in the Belvedere. Through systematic arrangements, a *dépôt de l'histoire visible de l'art* (a deposit of the visible history of art) was created. This arrangement ordered paintings according to school and to period. Art-historical principles thereby replaced the formal and aesthetic determinants that had governed earlier arrangements. When Mechel suggested didactic aims for the arts, to replace what he called merely 'passing distraction', he was, of course, not presenting an entirely new approach. Since antiquity, instruction as well as delight had been claimed as aims for art. Mechel's specific system of organization into schools also has its precedents, since in the eighteenth century several collections and curators, including Roos in Vienna, had already divided collections into schools.[30] In Dresden, Carl Heinrich von Heinecken, who had earlier illustrated the Saxon paintings collections in prints, was also to present collections according to period.

But none of these circumstances should diminish the significance of the innovations revealed in the Vienna Gemäldegalerie. Before the Musée Napoléon, the British Museum or the Altes Museum in Berlin, a public museum was created in Vienna that was devoted to the presentation of a separate category of visual art. This category was classified according to clearly enunciated historical principles.

The importance of these innovations may be insufficiently appreciated, perhaps because their further consequences for both the museum and academic milieux were somewhat slow to be realized. While far-reaching changes in the ethos of Habsburg collections could be effected during the reigns of such enlightened monarchs as Joseph II and his successor Leopold II (1790–2), the Habsburgs' involvement – during the reign of Franz II (until 1835) – in the French Revolutionary and Napoleonic Wars, when works from Austrian collections were in fact seized for the Musée Napoléon, decelerated the pace of change. One of the most significant developments for the future history of the collections was the relocation in 1800 of the great graphic collection of Albert of Sachsen-Teschen, the basis of the present Albertina, in housing adjacent to the Imperial court complex.[31] Otherwise, the era of reaction that set in under Prince Metternich's direction after 1815 was not propitious for the collections. The continuing growth of a professional curatorial staff seems the most remarkable phenomenon of the time, something that may be related to the growth of a class of officials in Vienna.[32]

It was from this quarter that suggestions were in fact again made to employ the collections for the public good. In the *Vormärz* atmosphere of the 1840s, Josef Calasanz Arneth, director of the *Münzkabinett*, proposed that the collections be reunited, and used as a means for instruction and general *Bildung*.[33] Although these suggestions were not immediately taken up, they formed the background for the transformations that occurred during the reign of Franz Joseph. As one result of the Imperial response to the revolutionary upheavals of 1848, the collections eventually were almost all turned into public museums.

From 1857 the collections were included in general plans for the expansion of Vienna. The destruction of the old city walls during the Napoleonic War led to a programme that included their removal. In their place, and that of the surrounding glacis, the Ringstrasse was laid out as a tree-lined thoroughfare.[34] For the centre, opposite the Hofburg, of this new system, plans were made for Imperial museums. From 1868 to 1880 proposals were debated; finally, a plan was approved by Gottfried Semper, a renowned architect whose opinion had been sought. By 1891 a new Kunsthistorisches Museum had been erected to face a Naturhistorisches Museum, forming an Imperial forum of the arts and sciences.[35]

Situated near to the Hofburg, the arts and sciences were presented to the public in a grand neo-baroque building, replete with symbolism. The arts were housed in their own building opposite, and thus separated from the *naturalia* and objects of anthropological interest contained in the Naturhistorisches Museum. The arts were presented by media, school and historical sequence. This organization corresponded to a comparable ordering of natural objects. Craft objects were given their own museum elsewhere, while the personal treasures of the Imperial house were confined to the Hofburg. Placed thus, in grand, accessible buildings, the Imperial collections were incorporated as public museums in modern Vienna's life.

They were still called the 'collections of the loftiest Imperial house', however, and so the museums founded in the later nineteenth century

Gottfried Semper's and Karl von Hagenauer's new home
for the Kunsthistorisches Museum, Vienna,
built in the 1870s.

under the Habsburg double aegis obviously belong to a world that was to vanish after the First World War. Yet their legacy survives. Not only do institutions like the Kunsthistorisches Museum remain as active centres of display, exhibitions and scholarship, but the links established between the collections and other intellectual foundations in the nineteenth century have greatly affected the growth and direction of art history as an academic and intellectual discipline.

From their beginnings, the directors and curators of the Vienna museums were also professors of the fledgling discipline of the history of art, starting with Rudolf Eitelberger, *extraordinarius* professor of art history and first director of the Austrian museum of *Angewandte Kunst*. Famous scholars, from Alois Riegl to Julius von Schlosser, served as curators before becoming professors, while the graduates of the art-history faculty of Vienna University became great museum men, such as Wilhelm von Bode. The collections also served as a regular part of academic instruction. Beginning in 1882, the *Jahrbuch* of the Vienna collections set a standard for museum-related publications; from an early date it published archival materials, demonstrating the link between objects and written documents.[36] This symbiosis of collecting, publishing and teaching has done much to shape the continuing course of art history.

Since the recent plans for a new museum of contemporary art and a library are currently an issue, that physical place has even become a subject for heated public debate. The collections of the Austrian Habsburgs have in the end thus metamorphosed from private, princely matters to professional and professorial preoccupations, with an important place in the public sphere.[37]

8

A Collector's Model of Desire:
The House and Museum of Sir John Soane

JOHN ELSNER

Collecting is the desire of the Museum. The museum seeks to be a static hold-all, largely a finished piece (although with blurry edges caused by de-accessioning and new aquisitions), a mausoleum of previous collections; collecting is the dynamic that brought it into being. While the museum is a kind of entombment, a display of once lived activity (the activity whereby real people collected objects associated with other real people or living beings), collecting is the process of the museum's creation, the living act that the museum embalms.[1]

On those curatorial labels that celebrate an object's acquisition, a particular series of past owners, the process of an item entering its final resting place, there is not only a rhetorical pride (and a scholarly bravado) but also a kind of nostalgia.[2] The very historiography of museums (all those articles about collectors) and the now burgeoning discourse of museology are themselves nostalgic evocations of an origin – that dynamic process in which the particular accumulation of things that is the identity of any museum came into being.

This essay has two aims. First, to explore the process of transition from collection to museum, from the living and changing body of collected artefacts to that pivotal moment when, on some fundamental level, change is arrested and the museum begins. I shall do this by focusing on a nineteenth-century collection still *in situ* in its original ambience, now frozen into a permanent museum. Second, while collecting, obviously, is a movement of desire and acquisition (not least the desire to become valorized as The Collection of a Museum), I want to examine the way it is also a process of nostalgia.

Just as the museum looks back to the 'real' life, the activity, of the desire that brought it into being, so that desire, that very process of collecting, itself looks back to an origin. Collecting is inherently a cult of fragments, a sticking together of material bits that stand as metonyms and metaphors for the world they may refer to but *are not*.[3] Its desire,

then, the inspiration for its enlivening and obsessional dynamic, is for the
plenitude of objects that once – in some imaginary world – were all
together and so did not need to be collected. But (and here we may move
from general observations to something more specific) that imaginary
world *did* exist, at least for those collectors from the Middle Ages
through the Renaissance and on to the Getty people – as well as for the
protagonist of this essay, Sir John Soane – who have been obsessed with
the idea of the classical. For Antiquity, and especially Roman Italy, has
always been that endlessly bounteous mother-earth out of which the
fragments now housed in museums from St Petersburg to Texas were
once extracted.[4]

In suggesting that Roman Italy was constructed as the all-plentiful
provider and the Ur-collection, I wish to address a dream lying wistfully
behind the collecting impulse: namely, the urge to evoke, even sometimes
to fulfil, that myth of a completion, a complete ancient world, which was
once itself *collected* in the imperial splendour of Rome. For ancient Rome is
more than just the supreme paradigm of collectors (its collections were and
are our canon) and the ultimate exemplar for empires. It was these things
not just because of its priority in the past of Europe but because (in the myth
that it told to glorify itself) it *succeeded*. That myth, which brought
fulfilment in the act of accumulation together with supremacy in the arts of
government, may only have been propagated by the Romans and without
total faith, but it was believed (and needed to be believed) by the myth-
making collectors from the Renaissance to the Enlightenment whose
activities have generated our cultural institutions, above all the museum.

'A MODEL-HOUSE'

The material body of evidence to which I want to turn in an exploration
of these questions is the house and museum of Sir John Soane. In his
private town-house (whose current postal address is 13 Lincoln's Inn
Fields, London WC2 3BP, but which in fact occupies most of numbers 12
and 14 as well), Soane (1753–1837), the architect to the Bank of England
and Professor of Architecture at the Royal Academy, collected and
displayed an extraordinary number of books, paintings, architectural
models, drawings, prints, plaster-casts and sculptural fragments.[5] Sir
John Soane's Museum is (like the Isabella Stewart Gardner Museum in
Boston) a very special case of the private house that, with its collection
intact, is memorized *in situ* as museum. It thus embodies and freezes for
posterity the moment at which collecting (and redeploying a collection)
ceases, the moment when the museum begins.

By an Act of Parliament of 1833, the Soane collection was donated to the nation with the stipulation that the 'Trustees and their successors shall not (except in Cases of absolute Necessity) suffer the arrangement in which the said Museum or Collection or Library respectively shall be left by the said Sir John Soane at the time of his decease to be altered'.[6] Much might be said about this remarkable testament, which Soane included as an appendix in his *Description of the House and Museum on the North Side of Lincoln's Inn Fields*, privately printed in London in 1835.[7] But suffice it to comment here on the way the Act attempted to transform what in the 1820s and 1830s was consistently described as Soane's 'house and museum' into a Museum pure and simple.[8] By its particular terms the Act avoided both the dispersal of a great collection and its assimilation within a greater whole, such as the British Museum,[9] as happened to several other major collections kept in private houses in eighteenth- and early nineteenth-century London.[10] On the contrary, it preserved a collection – characterized by its changes and dynamics – in a fixed final state (final only at a particular moment by the fortuitous 'decease' of its owner) as a museum. Moreover, what was preserved was not just the collection in its entirety, but its very specific manner and context of display.

Soane himself had orchestrated the transformation of his house into an institution, of his collection into a museum.[11] In 1827 *The Gentleman's Magazine* had described the house as 'an edifice intended solely for his own domestic uses, private tastes, and particular attachments'.[12] But in the 1830s Soane published three consecutive versions of the *Description* of his house, each incrementally enshrining the permanence and significance of the collection.[13] The *Description* of 1830 (itself a late progeny of Soane's manuscript attempt of 1812 at 'Crude Hints towards a History of my House') represented a tour through the house emphasizing the most important objects on display. Already here, that part of the collection under the dome at the back is described as the Museum, while the picture room is a mini-gallery in its own right. None the less these gestures towards institutional or official space remain within the broader ambit of domestic space: all the *Descriptions* are subtitled *the residence of John Soane*. The *Description* of 1832 reprints the text of 1830, but with significantly greater pretensions: dedicated to Augustus Frederick, Duke of Sussex, it included a French translation of the text as well. It also added to the Introduction the sense that the collections had a national rather than merely personal significance – 'to evince the desire of the Possessor of the Collection to promote to the utmost of his power the

interests of British Artists'. By 1835, however, the emphasis had
profoundly changed. Not only had the, by now elderly, architect
established the independence and perpetuity of the collection as a
Museum by the Act of Parliament of 1833, he now incorporated the Act
into the *Description* as an appendix. The text was rewritten, significantly
changing the order of progress through the house, and a series of
evocative ekphrases of the various rooms by Soane's friend Barbara
Hofland (described as 'a lady' and signed 'B.H.') supplemented Soane's
own description. Once again the text was repeated in French.

These descriptions are not catalogues, although part of their purpose is
to enumerate the most prestigious contents of Soane's rooms. In
describing the house, they enact an itinerary through it, taking the reader
on a carefully orchestrated journey that is itself also an argument for the
significance of Soane's collection as a distinctive entity. This literary
journey through the spaces and contents of a house, at once a private
house and a publicly accessible collection, is punctuated by plates – visual
representations of the objects *in situ* or of particular pieces or groupings
of pieces. Not only does the development of the text and illustrations over
successive editions imitate the dynamic of an expanding collection at the
height of its collector's zeal, but the appearance of new editions is itself an
important act in the establishment of the collection as publicly significant
enough to become a Museum. In Soane's case, the process of classification and inventory was itself analogous to that of collecting and
rearranging the collection; and all these efforts were themselves designed
to elevate the pretentions of the fragments he owned into a coherent
whole worthy of being a model Museum.

The exercise of translating the private into the public, the personal
collection into a museum for the nation, is thus to be seen as a peculiarly
textual act.[14] It lies in the creation of the handbook, in legal formulae
(such as the Act of Parliament) and in the paraphernalia of the official
language with which Soane came increasingly to frame the description of
his collections. None the less, on Soane's death in January 1837, there
was still a certain ambiguity about quite *what* the house and collection he
had bequeathed to the nation actually meant. In November of that year,
*The Penny Magazine of the Society for the Diffusion of Useful Know-
ledge* published an issue devoted to the new museum:[15]

In visiting the house and museum of Sir John Soane, it must not be forgotten
what his object was in thus leaving them for the use and inspection of the public.
The house was a private house; *as* a private house it is intended to remain. To
admit the public indiscriminately into a small private house, in the same way as

they are admitted into the British Museum, or any other national depository of art, would not only be incurring risk of loss or damage, or at least of great deterioration, but would be defeating the very *uses* of the property.[16]

Yet, as much as the anonymous author of the *Penny Magazine* article insists on 'domestic character and privacy' (p. 458) as defining qualities of the collection he visits, the comparison with 'the British Museum or any other national depository of art' gives the game away as to the desire for the Soane collection to be a museum. The author divides his description between the 'domestic portion' (p. 458) or 'what is strictly the house of Sir John Soane' (p. 460) and 'the museum, or collection generally', including the picture-room (pp. 460–4). Of course, the division is artificial, since physical access to the one could only be through the other. The problem in a sense is one of definition, the result of a private collection talked up, as it were, into a museum. But the vacillation between house and museum, never quite resolved in Soane's own attempts to redescribe his collection, is still apparent in the modern state of the house, where the upper storeys are nowadays reserved for office space and for the resident-warder's flat. Perhaps the *Penny Magazine* got it about right when its author wrote (p. 458) that

It is a model-house, intended for architects, artists and persons of taste. Let them dissent as much as they please; still it furnishes hints and suggestions, which they may profit by and improve upon.

A HOUSE OF MODELS

Perhaps the most curious, and certainly one of the more copious, components of the Soane Collection is the large group of architectural models. Soane possessed over one hundred scale models of his own buildings (made, of course, by hands other than his own), some twenty plaster models of antique buildings in their 'original' (i.e. restored) state and fourteen cork models of ancient buildings in their current (i.e. ruined) state.[17] Apart from these classical and classicizing models, Soane also owned a cork model of Stonehenge.[18] The majority of the models were displayed in a designated Model Room, whose centrepiece was a pedestal specially designed to show one of Soane's proudest possessions, a massive cork model of the ruins of Pompeii as they were *c.* 1820. The rest, including the cork models of Stonehenge, the Temple of Fortuna Virilis in Rome and four Etruscan tombs,[19] were displayed in other parts of the house, especially in the New Chamber of the Crypt.[20]

The Model Room, more than any other aspect of the collection, bore witness to the collector's relentless dissatisfaction with a final display, his continuous urge to try again.[21] In the 1820s Soane had a Model Room made in the basement in which the major antique models were displayed. In 1829 the Model Room was moved to the attic, and in 1835 was moved again to the second (or Chamber) floor.[22] The models not only formed a direct link between Soane's profession as architect and his persona as collector, but this search for a right place for them reflects most directly Soane's constant discomfort with the finality towards which his collection was moving. For although the Model Room was the most peripatetic of Soane's collectables, it was also in some sense the centre – the very heart – of the collection.[23]

One striking feature of the three editions of the *Description* of Soane's collection that he published between 1830 and 1835 is the fact that he chooses to travel through the house by different routes. The editions of 1830 and 1832 take the reader through the ground floor of the house in a clockwise direction, while the version of 1835 reverses this and leads the visitor in an anti-clockwise passage. However, all three take the visitor upstairs after the tour of the ground floor and basement (a tour that erases the distinctions of 'museum' and 'domestic . . . privacy' established by the description of 1837 in the *Penny Magazine*). In all three versions of Soane's own *Description*, the apogee of the entire experience of the house is the Model Room. In 1830 and 1832 this stood in the attic, so that the journey through Soane's house climaxed in the twin spectacles of the real city displayed by a series of spectacular views of London through the windows, and a fantasy world comprising a cornucopia of antiquity's proudest buildings in little models arranged on a pedestal in the centre of the room.[24] The last plate of the editions of 1830 and 1832 – plate 16 – illustrated this topmost room, the pedestal and its models bathed in sunlight from the lantern and the windows. By 1835 Soane had moved the Model Room down from the top of the house to the Chamber Floor, the front room on the second floor of 13 Lincoln's Inn Fields (the room that, until she died in 1815, had been Mrs Soane's bedchamber).[25] His last *Description* also culminates with the Model Room in its new position, this time with the addition of Barbara Hofland's commentary.[26] Again, the last plate of this edition – plate 38 – shows 'the view in the Model Room', now a more cluttered and interior space with further models arranged on little tables around the room as well as on the pedestal.

Let us look at the presentation of the Model Room in Soane's final *Description* (1835, pp. 87–8):

The attic Model Room, plate 16 of Soane's *Description of the House and Museum on the North Side of Lincoln's Inn Fields* of 1830 and 1832.

'View in the Model Room' on the Chamber Floor, plate 38 of the *Description* of 1835.

On the pedestal is a large model in cork of the Ruins of Pompeii, shewing the excavations round the two theatres, the Temple of Isis, and the other portions of the buried city, as they appeared about the year 1820. Surrounding these ruins are Models, also in cork, shewing, on a large scale, the relative proportions of the Columns in the three Temples at Paestum; a Model of the Temple at Tivoli; of the Arch of Constantine; and of the three columns in the Campo Vaccino. Upon the pedestal is raised an Architectural composition, decorated with bronze columns, on which are placed cork Models of the hypaethral Temple at Paestum, of the Remains of the Temple of Jupiter Tonans; and of the Monument of the Horatii and Curiatii, near Albano. Raised above these, on pedestals, are Models, also in cork, of each of the three Temples at Paestum.

Interspersed with the above enumerated are eleven highly finished Models in plaster of Paris, of the Propylaea, at Athens; the Tower of the Winds; the Temple of Minerva, in the Acropolis of Athens; the Pantheon, in Rome; the Temple on the Ilissus, near Athens; the hexastyle peripteral Temple at Paestum; the Temple at Pola in Istria; the Temple of Minerva Polias, Erechtheus and Pandrosus, at Athens; and the Portico of Diocletian: opposite the chimney, on the pedestal, are restorations of the Tomb at Mylasa, and of the Temple at Tivoli, sometimes called the Temple of Vesta.

Around the room are nine other plaster Models, six of which are on pedestals, and three on the chimney-piece, consisting of the Lantern of Demosthenes (as copied at St. Cloud); the Arch of Theseus, at Athens; the Pedestal supporting Four Columns, at Palmyra, forming a square composition, with a Pedestal in the centre for a statue; the Temple of Neptune, at Palmyra; the Mausoleum of Mausolus; the Temples of Antoninus and Faustina, at Rome; and of Venus, at Baalbec; a Tomb at Palmyra; and the Temple of Fortuna Virilis, in Rome.

This nigh-exhaustive inventory of the most prestigious surviving buildings of antiquity is conceived within a single space. This one room incorporates in their complete, three-dimensional, if miniature, form all the buildings from which many of Soane's most prized architectural fragments (exhibited in the other rooms of his museum) had been gathered. Elsewhere in his *Descriptions*, Soane points out his 'marble capitals from the Villa Adriana' (at Tivoli), his fragments from the Temple of Jupiter Tonans, his pilasters from the Pantheon.[27] Here the synecdochic strategy of the museum, thanks to which architectural fragments are able to *evoke* the grandeur of the actual buildings (the wholes of which the fragments are parts), is replaced by a microcosmic method in which the scientifically measured and scaled-down model *represents* the real building. The models, by being slotted into a line or series of models of prestigious buildings, thus place their prototypes not only into a nineteenth-century Neoclassical context in Soane's house, but into a newly recreated architectural history of antiquity.[28] As a model,

Cork model, probably made by Domenico Padiglione in Naples after 1804, of the 'Etruscan' tomb excavated at Canosa, southern Italy.

THE PORTICO, OR EXCHANGE AT PALMYRA.
(RESTORATION)

Plaster model by François Fouquet of Paris, of 'the Portico, or Exchange, at Palmyra', purchased by Soane in 1834.

the building acquires its place in history by its position on, or relation to, the great pedestal on which Soane displayed the models.

But the act of defining these ancient buildings as a kind of history is also a destruction of their geographical distinction. Greek and Roman buildings from Italy (centuries apart in their origins) are juxtaposed with classical monuments from Greece, Istria and Syria. By confining diverse spaces and the line of historical time to one room and largely to one architectural contraption (the pedestal), which dominates the room, Soane concocts a Neoclassical myth of antiquity's architecture, an imaginative evocation, rather than any kind of reality. The models come in two types: cork models representing monuments in their ruined, i.e. current or archaeological, state, and plaster models that recreate their originals in an ideal, pristine state. In his practice of display, Soane 'intersperses' cork models of ruined buildings with plaster models of finished monuments in their 'original' form. Two ideals of romanticism – the ruin and the original masterpiece – collide ('interspersed') on the pedestal. Strangest of all is the repetition of buildings in both ruined and 'original' form – not only one of the Paestum temples and the Temple of Vesta at Tivoli, but also the Temple of Fortuna Virilis at Rome (whose cork model was in the Crypt).[29] In effect, the models in this room conspire to evoke an entirely unreal mystique of the classical, although they do so under the guise of the most practical and utilitarian of architectural tools, the scale model.

Yet, while display might unite the brown cork models with the pure white of plaster, the ruined with the perfect, Soane's rhetoric is careful to separate them. His paragraphs divide the models into a classification of cork followed by plaster. In his *Lectures on Architecture* Soane had written in 1815 (some years, in fact, before he purchased the bulk of his collection of models):

It is much to be lamented that of the remains of the great structures, once the pride of Greece and Italy, and of the Gothic Buildings, we should possess so few Models, and even those, so far as I have seen, are insufficient to explain their different modes of Construction.[30]

This professional lament on the part of Soane the architect was swiftly followed by a more idealist and antiquarian paean:

Large Models, faithful to the Originals, not only in Form and Construction, but likewise to the various colours of the Materials, would produce sensations and impressions of the highest kind, far beyond the powers of description and surpassed only by the contemplation of the Buildings themselves. . . .[31]

The rhetorical taxonomy that divides cork from plaster, the contemporary and ruined from the past and pristine, is itself embedded in the collector's nostalgia for more than merely the prototype imitated by his copy, the ruined temple at Athens or Rome represented by his model. It looks beyond this yearning to those 'sensations and impressions of the highest kind' in which the original as it originally was can be imagined. The small step in discourse, mirrored in the material shift from cork to plaster, is emblematic of the imaginative leap from actual to ideal, on the edge of which the whole Soane collection conspicuously teeters and which the Model Room certainly transgresses.

The key that unites these two exemplary images of the classical – the present ruin and the past perfection – is the great cork model of Pompeii situated on the pedestal's heart. Here, in the fruitful earth of Italy, archaeology could uncover not just ruins but perfectly preserved classical monuments. Take John Britton's description of the Pompeii model, 'the chief' of Soane's models:

By this model, which occupies a space of about eight feet square, we are presented with the appearance of the streets, houses, temples, theatres, &c., which, after having been buried in the volcanic lava of Vesuvius for nearly two thousand years, are exposed to view and examination, as fresh and vivid as if they had been concealed only a few years. A cursory survey of this desolated city awakens both awful and interesting reflections: for we naturally and imperceptibly wish to ascertain the condition, manners, customs, arts, &c., of the people who were busily engaged in their worldly occupations, when the whole was suddenly engulfed in death and destruction.[32]

The models of antiquity's buildings cluster around this ur-model of the very process of unearthing the ancient world. Pompeii, itself a ruin, an archaeological site, exposes to view remains 'as fresh and vivid as if they had been concealed only a few years'. Soane's model of Pompeii figures not just the highly contemporary dynamic by which antiquity was revealed in the early nineteenth century, but also the very genesis, the ground, of collecting itself.[33] In the Model Room Soane deploys three modes of collecting: antiquity as it currently *was* in literal terms (the discourse of the ruin, of the cork model), antiquity as it was in its perfection *imagined to be* (the discourse of restoration, of the plaster model) and antiquity as *source*, as the copious plenitude out of which objects could be unearthed and collected. Pompeii, centre of the room, is a focal metaphor for the nostalgia, and also for the endless potential, of collecting.

In this sense, the Pompeii model can be seen as something rather more than a representation of a set of ancient monuments; it is in fact an extraordinarily modern site. Indeed, the Model Room itself is far from being the preserve of antiquity. Beneath the pedestal's exhibition of antiquity's finest buildings is a bravura display of Soane's own major works in miniature:

Under the pedestal are Models in wood of the south-east angle of the Bank of England and the Three per Cent Reduced Office; the Bank Stock Office; the original Design for the New Board of Trade and Privy Council Offices, at Whitehall; a Model of the national Debt Redemption Office, in which is a bronze statue of William Pitt, by Westmacott; of a Machine for driving piles; of a design in Gothic style for the Exterior of the buildings connected with the Court of King's Bench, next New Palace Yard; and a Model in Plaster of part of the New State Paper Office, as originally designed.[34]

By their very placement, these Soanean buildings claim descent from the antique. Soane's house in Lincoln's Inn Fields, itself an architect's 'model-house', a spectacular performance of virtuoso architectural feats in the (relative) miniature of what the *Penny Magazine* insisted was 'a very limited space . . . (of) domestic character and privacy',[35] serves as the frame for the models of Soane's own buildings, which themselves rest on the base of antiquity's pedestal. By invoking famous British architects, such as Sir Christopher Wren (p. 88) – some of whose collection of models Soane claimed to possess – and Sir William Chambers (p. 87) – whose original designs fill the drawers of the pedestal – Soane paints an evolutionary picture of the progress of British architecture from the influences of Greek and Roman antiquity, through some of Britain's finest architects, and finally *to himself!*

But the assertions of the Model Room are even more flagrant than this. By their form as models, the models of Soane's own buildings marry with the classical models to form a single collection, a single set. This is an outrageous parallelism, of course. It implies, with little space for modesty, not only that Soane's buildings may dwell on equal terms with all that is classic in architecture, but that together (together in miniature on the pedestal) Soane's buildings and ancient architecture constitute a single new entity. As the author of the article in the *Penny Magazine* noticed, the siting of the Model Room high in the house is hardly accidental. The conflation of ancient and Soanic buildings in miniature is deliberately juxtaposed against 'the rather extensive view of London to be obtained from the gallery, or loggia, of the second floor' (p. 459). To invoke a pun of which Soane was not unconscious, the Model Room serves as a model, a set of criteria, against which the actual architecture of London is to be judged.

In effect, these actual buildings now become items in the same set as those in the Model Room. They are 'miniaturized' as distant views, or at least presented as a series of specimens viewed from the panopticon of Soane's Chamber floor windows, as it were, under glass. Just as Soane's own buildings underlie the pedestal, so the panorama of real London rooftops all about – as seen from the vantage point of the Model Room – seems to underlie the space occupied by Soane's house. While the classical models are cast as a paradigm for architecture, so London itself – and especially Soane's own buildings (both as models and as the house that houses those models) – are cast as reflections of the classical ideal most perfectly evoked in this room. . . .

Soane did not himself make these suggestions in this text. On the contrary, his account is a rather dry enumeration, although it has moments when the owner's desire for his model to be the prototype pushes through the prose – for instance in the slide from a model of the National Debt Redemption Office to the actual Office in which stands Sir Richard Westmacott's statue of William Pitt (p. 88). However, Soane included as a supplement to his own account the rather more vivid descriptions of Barbara Hofland. This makes the final version (1835) of his *Description* a richly layered text, for it juxtaposes the enumeration of the named male owner – a catalogue for posterity – with (in smaller print) the effusive and poetic comments of the anonymous 'Lady', B.H. The Lady, Soane's female voice as it were (the voice that can, if necessary, be disowned but which speaks with a certain passion that the sober male must aver) can speak the sins that Soane's own narrative dare not name. Whatever Hofland's actual thoughts, B.H., as Soane's ventriloquist doll, is the *Description*'s literary device for framing, upholding and at the same time standing back from a series of desires unseemly in the professional architect, the gentleman professor, but irrepressible in the megalomaniac collector. The equivocation within Soane as to his collection being a private house or a public museum is now enacted in a literary schizophrenia between the sober man enumerating his possessions and the feminized initials, B.H., dreaming what those possessions might mean.

Here is B.H. approaching the Model Room (p. 92):

In a short time we become sensible that our situation in this gallery [the morning room] enhances the pleasure and importance of the view by the classical impressions it communicates. Without, on either hand, are the fine statues from the Temple of Pandrosus [the caryatids Soane built into the exterior face of the house]; within, are casts from beautiful sculptures, and pictures of ruins in Palermo and Syracuse. Conscious that our imaginations have received an impetus from the many objects of grandeur and beauty we have lately beheld, and which are still floating in the 'mind's eye', and perhaps adding ideal ornament to the surrounding buildings, we turn gratefully to the source from whence the sensation was derived, and look eagerly around the Model-room.

The experience of all 'we have lately beheld' (which is to say, the whole house and museum), itself summarized as 'adding ideal ornament to the surrounding buildings' (which is to say, to London seen through the windows), turns out to have its *source* in the Model Room.

Here is B.H. on entering the room (p. 92):

Our first attention is fixed perforce upon Pompeii; for what subject so powerful and terrible in its general character – so affecting in its details, could arrest the mind of man, or employ his faculties, either in actual research or ideal supposition? – The excavations made when this model was finished shew us a Temple of Isis, which must have been very splendid, an amphitheatre capable of containing fifteen thousand persons, and a theatre for tragedy which could accommodate five thousand. A large portion of the excavation is made in that part considered to be the soldiers' quarters, which appears to have been adorned with columns. There is also a basilica where justice was administered, a forum, numerous shops, and private houses, each proving, from its situation with regard to culinary utensils and food preparing for use, how sudden as well as terrible was the destruction which overwhelmed the inhabitants, and rendered its site unknown for ages, blotting out its very existence from the earth.

Where Soane's voice exercised restraint in leaping from representation to reality, that of B.H. barely allows the reader to remember that it is a *model* she is describing. Our attention fixes upon Pompeii itself – we get about a sentence before we are reminded it is a model of Pompeii. The story she tells is of actualities – of theatres, temples, the administration of justice, shops, private houses, cooking. It is a tale of identification with antiquity and emotion at Pompeii's fate. The paragraph that follows this quotation is a hyperbolic revelling in the horrors of Vesuvian disaster, filled with 'appalling objects of terror', 'lingering misery', 'utter hopelessness' (pp. 92–3). In effect, the plenitude of the *source* has caused B.H. to excavate not merely objects but a whole archaeology of emotion.

From this remarkable description, remarkable above all for how far behind it leaves the sculpted cork of its object,

Turn we, then, to these more beautiful and less affecting objects – these exquisite representations of those ancient, magnificent, and far-distant edifices, which we can never hope to behold through any other medium than that which Art bestows. . . (p. 93).

It is as if the text must remind itself (and us) very firmly that it is *representation* (the 'medium . . . which Art bestows') and not reality with which it is dealing. But on the level of representation, B.H.'s poetic voice can enact many of the shifts that Soane could only suggest:

From Pompeii to Paestum appears a natural transition . . . (p. 93).

Only natural because the models are adjacent.

Near them [the Paestum temples] is the little temple of Tivoli . . . (p. 93).

Near only in representation and in discourse, for very far in miles.

Three gigantic pillars alone remain of the Temple of Jupiter Tonans, and three in the Campo Vaccino; but what glorious relics do we find them! Here, too, are the remains of Palmyra . . . (p. 93).

In a spectacular fusion of both reality-effects and an insistence on representation as no more than representation, B.H. can see the miniature pillars of a model as 'gigantic' and at the same time compress the distance from Rome to Palmyra (in Syria) into the words 'here, too'. What, we must ask, *are* the 'glorious relics' we are invited to find? The original buildings or the models themselves? The relic-models evoke history as reverie, identification through fantasy as real experience:

Whilst we wander in imagination amongst the once splendid edifices of this City of the Wilderness, our memory recalls the history . . . (p. 93).

The brilliant achievement of B.H.'s description is gradually to transform the models, mere resemblances of real buildings, into charged objects in their own right. As a collection, they become more than collector's items, they become an imaginative world that never existed, a world which collectively they represent and which through imagination they come to embody. The models become identified with the buildings they imitate, and in doing so they become models in the sense of paradigms:

Every model offered to our eye has probably been derived from the Greeks, whose original genius, assisted by their intercourse with Egypt, had attained perfection in the Arts of Architecture and Sculpture, while Rome was still in her infancy. To the happy facility with which the Romans adopted the arts and arms of surrounding nations may be imputed the power over them which they eventually obtained – a fact that should never be lost sight of by the student, since it may animate the languid to new exertion, and teach the enthusiastic and eccentric spirit to weigh the worth of old examples before he relinquishes them for the crude visions of a brilliant but untamed imagination. (p. 94)

By a questionable train of logic (itself the result of a brilliant and untamable imagination), B.H. moves from the models as architectural paradigms to the models as eloquent teachers in the art of empire.

By the end of her spectacular series of ekphrases, it is impossible to identify the referent of B.H.'s own writing:

Every observer, more especially . . . the traveller in Italy . . . may here retrace his own emotions whilst beholding a majestic ruin or a still surviving temple, fraught with glorious recollections as to its origin, and proud of the triumphs of Art in its erection, and with the noble poet may say of this idolised country –
'Thou art the garden of the world – the home
Of all Art yields and Nature can decree
E'en in thy desert what is like to thee?
Thy very weeds are beautiful; thy waste
More rich than other climes' fertility;
Thy wreck a glory, and thy ruin graced
With an immaculate charm that cannot be defaced.'

Are these majestic ruins and still surviving temples those seen in Italy or in Lincoln's Inn Fields? Are the glorious recollections on the origin any more than B.H.'s own thoughts prompted by the 'source'? Are the triumphs of Art in the erection of buildings those of the ancients or of the builders of Soane's own models? Finally, is the 'idolised' country not closer to England, indeed to Soane's own Model Room, than to antiquity? The loss of a clear referent in this prose, the ambiguity of which is designed to enhance the status of the models, is a textual mimesis of the way the models themselves elide their referents and assume a power of their own.

A MODEL WORLD

As an interior at the summit of the visitor's ascent through the museum (and at the culmination of each *Description*), the Model Room recapitulates the lessons of the house. It affirms the collection as above all offering an *architectural* dispensation for experiencing antiquity through modernity, the antique building as the contemporary architect's model, the modern world as a pastiche of ancient remains. It re-presents the clutter of the house through the ordered placing of the models on and around the pedestal. It reinvents the collection not just as a *synecdochic* cult of the fragment (where the parts, and the casts of parts, evoke the wholes from whence they derive), but also as a series of *representations*, whereby antiquity is imagined and grasped as an ideal realm of miniatures.[36]

The collection of models in Sir John Soane's Museum evokes a world. Although each has its own referent, its own real building that it reflects through scale mensuration, as a *group* the models abandon that direct reference altogether. Instead they imagine an ideal Neoclassical world, a model for the real world. They are a complete summary of the knowledge and the artefacts within the Soane Museum, for they *are* the three-dimensional fullness that the fragments and the casts are merely part of, which the images and the books can only describe.

In effect, Soane's model world provides a remarkable example of the theme of the miniature and of the miniature as site of desire.[37] First, unlike other miniatures, architectural models belong to that pragmatic stage in a building's evolution when the model, or maquette, evokes the not-yet-constructed edifice, an ideal edifice one day to be completed (pending the patron's approval of the model itself). Yet models are more than mere drawings, more than the two-dimensional blueprints from which buildings may be constructed by the expert but can hardly be imagined by the layman. Architectural models are already a significant step towards the *realization* of the final product, a step in the process of desire beyond the drawing and into a more than conceptual space. Many of the models of Soane's own buildings had their origins in this process. The model, as is normal in architectural practice, was thus the material articulation of a desire (on the part of the patron and the architect) for there to be, one day, a final building.

Second, models memorialize famous monuments. This is, of course, the function of the models of antique buildings – whether cork ruins or pristine plaster-casts. They freeze in material form in the here and now the desire for a lost or distant grandeur. In this sense they are nostalgic, although – in spurring on travellers to visit the originals – they may also evoke a yearning for the not-yet-seen, the past that will be future. The models of Soane's buildings, by their being placed adjacent to the models of antiquity's most lauded constructions, acquire also this quality of prized memorial, so that in them the desire-to-construct becomes blurred with the desire-for-the-previously-constructed. In a wonderful example of romantic idealism, the buildings of the present (the product of so many reinterpretations of the past) are collapsed into the mythic time of the past and so themselves become memorialized as classic.

As a *collection*, the models come to figure their collector's desire. Their yearning (and his yearning for them) is to be a complete series (even a series that may repeat some of its members). And so they commemorate the famous objects in which Soane traces his architectural ancestry not

Plate illustrating a cork model, probably made by Padiglione
after 1804, of an 'Etruscan' tomb excavated at Paestum;
from Soane's *Description* of 1835.

only item by item, but also as a totality, a paradigmatic classical heritage.
The supreme model, however, the great cork model of Pompeii, goes
beyond this. It commemorates not only its object (an archaeological site)
but also the archaeological *act* of disinterring ancient objects (like the
other objects in the museum), and thus the act of collecting them (and
even that of collecting at large). The Pompeii model, symbol of that ever
fruitful soil from which archaeology may unearth the past, stands for and
glorifies the antique provenance of the whole collection and thus
authenticates the value of the collection institutionalized as Museum. It
represents, by metonymy, that great collection for which all archaeological museums must dream, the earth's own archaeological plenitude.

The Pompeii model is not the only one to celebrate the collection's
privileged origins in archaeological discovery. In the crypt of his
Museum, Soane kept 'four Cork Models of ancient sepulchres', probably made in Naples in the early nineteenth century.[38] These depict the
tombs in painstakingly accurate detail, recording the items discovered
during excavation. Not only are the tomb walls decorated with paintings of 'Etruscan' warriors or stuccoes of animals, but around the
miniature skeleton are arranged small-scale reproductions of the vases
found in the sepulchre. These vases are extraordinarily exact reproductions of originals known to have entered the collection of Sir
William Hamilton.[39] Here is Soane's description of these tomb models:

The walls of these models are decorated with painting and sculpture; and in the body of the chamber are deposited the skeleton, a variety of Etruscan vases, and implements of sacrifice. They are, therefore, very interesting, as explaining the method of sepulture in use amongst the ancients, and accounting for the high state of preservation in which are found, from time to time, so many Etruscan vases, pateras, and other utensils of remote antiquity.[40]

The tomb models figure the origins of Soanean objects such as the Etruscan vases displayed on brackets and shelves in the Library, which were represented as a privileged group in his Museum. Moreover, they represent such objects in their ancient context 'of remote antiquity', as themselves items in an Etruscan collection. The emphasis on the life of the ancient context is still more marked in the drawings Soane commissioned of them. While the tomb model, for all its accuracy, is always a model, the drawing – with just a little artistic embellishment to place it in a landscape – *could* represent the real thing. The miniature objects within Soane's tomb models are displayed as items in a real collection that (like Soane's) was to celebrate its owner's memory for posterity and even to be memorialized in these nineteenth-century miniatures and the drawings made of them. Above all, the tomb models portray their vases as items to be collected and redisplayed in a new context, like Soane's Museum. Metaphorically, the tomb models point to the self-enshrinement of their collector in the museum-mausoleum of his own house.

While the Pompeii model celebrates the *anticipation* of archaeology – that fruitful earth which *will* yield ever more copious relics of the past – the Etruscan tombs show the triumph of archaeology in uncovering an ur-collection of items to be re-collected in the wake of their nineteenth-century disinterment. The models of the tombs figure the nostalgia of Soane's own collection to be a classical collection, and hence its desire for valorization as an accumulation worthy of those made by the ancients. What is remarkable about these models is that they not only materialize that desire as miniatures, but they then incorporate it, commemorate it, as a further item in the series Soane collects. What is now obvious is that his models are not a collection of equivalent objects. They form a sequence of disparate modalities that present an archaeological recession from modern buildings to ancient buildings in their current (ruined) state, to ancient buildings in their ideal (pristine) state, to the site of Pompeii as figure for the unearthing of yet more (new) ancient remains, to the Etruscan tombs as ancient interiors that were themselves the museums of collected antiquity. . . . So, in miniature and material form Soane's models trace the ancestry of Soane's desire as architect, as archaeologist and as collector.

Joseph Michael Gandy, *Public and Private Buildings, Executed by Sir J. Soane
between 1780 & 1815*, 1818. Sir John Soane's Museum, London.

'Vases in Mr Soane's Collection', title-page plate of J. Britton's
Union of Architecture, Sculpture and Painting (London, 1827),
and afterwards reproduced in Soane's *Description* of 1835.

This archaeological recession is not the only mode by which the models figure Soanean desire. For, through their display, Soane placed them in an interior space that implied the potential for a spatial recession of ever-increasing interiority. In placing the models together (at least those gathered in the Model Room), Soane created a strange Neoclassical world in which these very distinct figurations of desire could coexist in an ideal space. This space, the Model Room, was the three-dimensional realization of a vision Soane had experienced even before he formally constructed a room for the models. In a wonderful pen-and-watercolour drawing, made for an exhibition of Soane's buildings at the Royal Academy in 1818, Joseph Michael Gandy, the architect's perspectivist, drew a compendium of his master's executed works as if they were models in a room vaulted by one of Soane's characteristic canopied saucer-domes.[41] Just as the Model Room was later to reinvent Soane's 'real-life' buildings together with their ancient heritage within a Soanean interior, so here Gandy prefigured that three-dimensional effort with a drawing in two dimensions. The real buildings become models imagined in the mind – in the mind of the miniature figure in the lower right of the picture holding dividers and designing a ground plan for a new building. Unlike the Model Room itself, Gandy's drawing could represent not only buildings re-imagined as models but also the key figure in the genesis of the Soanean fantasy world – Soane himself as architectural demiurge.[42]

In Gandy's drawing, as in Soane's Model Room, the monuments are displayed without any relation to their particular time or place. All are jumbled in the Neoclassical interior of a dominating, ordered space (the dome, columns and entablature of the drawing, the pedestal in the room), a space organized in relation to the architect himself. Like the imaginary world created by the Soane collection as a whole, the models and this drawing of models, while constantly parading their formal and stylistic reference to the past, ignore real chronology. They evoke a visionary and imaginative world where ideal, transhistorical, orders and forms may not only characterize buildings but may incorporate those buildings within other buildings. The models, both Gandy's and Soane's, are interiors within an interior (an interior that replays their own forms). They gesture, in ever decreasing miniature, to an infinite series of centres within centres.[43]

While a real building can never be fully surveyed or controlled – for it always contains its viewer – the model is the building reduced to a toy. It is architecture the owner *can* survey.[44] Just as all the models may be surveyed in the panopticon of the dome's interior space (or that of the 'lantern light' in the Model Room of 1830 and 1832),[45] which encloses all these models of buildings, so (by being contained within an interior) each model hints that it may itself contain secrets not visible in the controlling space of the Model Room or the architect's mind. Even as the Soane Museum evokes the myth of the owner's control through its offer of miniatures exposed to view, so it figures (especially in Gandy's drawing) the possibility of an endless recession that denies control through the hint of a receding secret hidden away in one of the model interiors.

The models of the Etruscan tombs are the key to the double recession of desire we have been tracing here – a spatial recession into ever more interior space and an archaeological recession into ever more 'remote antiquity'. In a wonderfully self-reflexive Soanean joke, the tombs reveal the hidden contents of a miniature interior space and of a distant archaeological time. These objects, the hidden contents of the fruitful earth, are themselves *collectables*, choice pieces to be picked up by the magpie collector from the collection of their former owner enshrined as mausoleum. . . . In the logic of Soane's models, the secret that denies control can always, infinitely, be added as a further item to the catalogue that seeks control. But as mausoleum, as an institution frozen only on its owner's 'decease', Soane's Museum is figured by these models as a tomb that is itself liable to future plunder.

9
Cabinets of Transgression: Renaissance Collections and the Incorporation of the New World

ANTHONY ALAN SHELTON

Opinion is divided over the extent to which the medieval world-view was replaced by new sets of attitudes and interpretative frameworks during the Renaissance. Hodgen, Keen and Laurencich-Minelli clearly identify medieval attitudes and modes of thought persisting through the Renaissance; Le Goff even suggests that the 'Middle Ages' be extended to cover the phase of European history that stretches from the 3rd century AD to the mid-nineteenth century.[1] Change, of course, is never a uniform process simultaneously affecting all of a society's institutions, and the gradual shift from a medieval to a Renaissance world-view saw attempts both to reconcile contending views and tolerate their mutually exclusive coexistence. Neither the European attitude to collecting nor interpretations of the significance of the New World were uniform, but certain categories and rhetorical devices stand out as more commonly employed than others, and it is these that are my subject here. Nowhere do these various world-views appear in more striking relief than when Europeans attempted to explain and so come to terms with the existence of a fourth continent – the New World – and decide on the significance of its inhabitants, flora, fauna and artificial curiosities. Cosmological uncertainty shadows the different motivations behind, and organization of, Renaissance collections that attempted to incorporate representations of the fourth continent. To understand the commerce in, and significance of, natural and artificial curiosities from the New World it is necessary first to describe the broad set of philosophical speculations and attitudes inherited from the Middle Ages that lay behind the culture of collecting between the sixteenth and eighteenth centuries.

THE MEDIEVAL INTELLECTUAL STRUCTURE OF
RENAISSANCE COLLECTIONS

In *The Waning of the Middle Ages* (1924), the Dutch historian Johan Huizinga argued that the Medievals subsumed aesthetics under the sense of wonderment, which, as Eco has been quick to remind us, was tightly integrated within scholastic philosophy to provide a means of achieving communion with God.[2] Eco cites the example of Abbot Suger of St Denis, who was responsible for many of the artistic and architectural projects undertaken by the ecclesiastic authorities in the Ile de France. Taking his cue from King Solomon, Suger believed that churches should be the repositories of all beautiful objects: he described the Treasury of St Denis as including 'a big golden chalice of 140 ounces of gold adorned with precious gems, viz., hyacinths and topazes, as a substitute for another one which had been lost as a pawn in the time of our predecessor . . . [and] a porphyry vase, made admirable by the hand of the sculptor and polisher, after it had lain idly in a chest for many years, converting it from a flagon into the shape of an eagle'.[3] Other offerings protected in churches included altars, chalices, ciboria, chasubles, candelabras and tapestries, not to mention funerary monuments, stained-glass windows and *jubés*.[4] Some medieval churches also contained relics – remnants of the Apostles and martyrs – or objects that were said to have been in contact with them.[5] These were protected in bejewelled reliquaries made of precious metals. The possession of relics had political implications. The bodily remains of sacred persons were believed to retain some of the individual's qualities and authority, and were of sufficient value to sanctify a place and encourage the foundation of new ecclesiastical establishments.[6] Important relics inspired large pilgrimages and increased the importance and prosperity of settlements. Consequently, throughout the Renaissance, cities competed to possess the bones of the Church Fathers as well as the remains of classical thinkers and the founders of eminent institutions.[7] During the Middle Ages and the Renaissance, therefore, artefacts were valued for their marvellous or miraculous qualities – their magical reputations – manifested through the use of precious materials and the quality of craftsmanship.

In the Middle Ages the arts were subordinate to a didactic function, much of which was intended to serve the Church. Honorius of Autun justified the art of painting by its three objectives: to beautify the house of God, to recall to mind the lives of the saints, and to provide 'the literature of the laity'.[8] This view was reiterated in the Synod of Arras:

'Unlettered people, who cannot appreciate this through reading Scripture, can grasp it in the contemplation of pictures.'[9] This didactic function was meant to transport admirers from contemplation of material phenomena to a higher spiritual plane, a plane that permitted communion with the Divine. For the medieval mind, the beauty to be found in the material world was only a reflection of a transcendent ideal beauty whose source was God.

Medieval aesthetics consisted of a theory of ideal proportion,[10] together with an appreciation of light (*lux, lumen* and *splendor*) and colour. Theirs was a world of intense visual culture, and they were able to synthesize and represent phenomena by a highly developed language of symbol and allegory: 'The Medievals inhabited a world filled with references, reminders and overtones of Divinity, manifestations of God in things. Nature spoke to them heraldically: lions or nut-trees were more than they seemed; griffins were just as real as lions because, like them, they were signs of higher truth.'[11] Beauty and virtue were conflated, which led to art being above all a tracing of a higher order decreed by God. According to Eco:

At best, art could produce beautiful images, arrangements of material that were superficial only. But it had to preserve a kind of ontological humility before the primacy of nature. The objects produced by art did not introduce a new order, but remained within the limits of their substance. They were simply 'reductions to images by means of measurement'. They existed by means of the material which sustained them, whereas natural objects existed by virtue of divine participation.[12]

Le Goff[13] has drawn attention to the close connection that exists between visual images and the idea of the marvellous, for *mir*, the root of *mirabilis* (marvellous, wonderful) and *mirari* (to wonder at), is from where our word 'mirror' derives. Acknowledging Pierre Mabille's *Le Miroir du merveilleux* (1965), Le Goff agrees that 'the men of the Middle Ages drew a parallel between mirari, mirabilia (marvel) and mirror . . . thus linking the marvel to the complex of images and ideology associated with the mirror'.[14]

These earlier notions concerning art, nature and Divinity, and their relationship with the marvellous and miraculous, hold two important implications for the understanding of collections. First, they explain the medieval origin of the rationalization that lay behind the reduction in the Renaissance of the relations between natural and artificial phenomena to the terms and juxtapositions of objects arranged in a collection. The collection came to provide the mirror of nature as it was formulated by

Divine agency. Symbol and allegory permitted the miniature representation of the universe, while a theory of the innate meaning of objects determined their relationship.

The second implication concerns the meaning the Medievals attributed to the sense of the marvellous. At a general level, the marvellous could be interpreted as a painting or a valuable piece of the lapidary's or metalworker's art, work that invited communion with the Divine. In this sense, assemblages of objects, when they conformed to the ideal relations between phenomena, might be said to have pointed to the divinely sanctioned ideal order of the world. But the medieval world also saw the marvellous as including contingent and altogether exceptional events. This view found its most eloquent exponent in William of Ockham, who denied the existence of any cosmic order or chain of being that linked phenomena or events. According to Ockham, objects had only a nominal existence, and were unregulated by the mind of God. Collections could, therefore, be arranged without any apparent order between their constituent items. For collectors of a nominalist persuasion, what was important were curiosities, rare or near-unique phenomena that were thought to have resulted from some exceptional condition or circumstance. It is curious that other than the judgmental criteria affecting taste, such ideas do not appear to have influenced the accumulation of collections or the classification of objects during much of the medieval period. It was left to Renaissance collectors to define their objectives, and to justify their activities and the presentation of the components of their collections using the intellectual views of the previous age.

COLLECTIONS OF CURIOSITIES

Collections of curiosities, succinctly described by Pomian as hoardings of 'rare, exceptional, extraordinary, exotic and monstruous things',[15] had their heyday after the end of the Middle Ages: collections of this kind flourished from c. 1550, began to wane during the seventeenth century, and by 1750 were very rare indeed.[16] Pomian notes that between 1556 and 1560 the Netherlandish collector Hubert Goltzius listed 968 collections that were to be found in the Low Countries, Germany, Austria, Switzerland, France and Italy.[17] Another collector, Pierre Borel (1620–71), personally knew of 63 collections in France, while the Venetian Republic could boast at least 70.[18] Not all these collections were motivated by identical desires, nor did they follow the same model of organization. Pomian judiciously reminds us that differences in the wealth, education and social rank of individuals, as well as the various degrees of receptivity to new ideas to be found in the cities, all helped determine different types of collections.[19]

Encyclopaedic collectors in France were known as *curieux* because of their passion for, and commitment to, seeking deeper knowledge of the workings and nature of the universe, and a fuller, perhaps grander, picture of the totality of creation. Pomian defines curiosity in terms of desire and passion – 'a desire to see, learn or possess rare, new, secret or remarkable things, in other words those things which have a special relationship with totality and consequently provide a means for attaining it'.[20] A large part of the justification for collections in the Renaissance was borrowed from medieval scholasticism, its ideas concerning the innate meaning of things and the nature of revelation, and its vision of the relationship between the microcosm and macrocosm. Following the advice contained in Samuel Quiccheberg's *Inscriptiones vel tituli theatri amplissimi* (1565), some cabinets were provided with annexes to house a library, laboratory or forge, which were put to use for experiments whose ambiguous significance lay somewhere between medieval magic and enlightened scientific demonstration.[21] Some Churchmen expressed their unease, even opposition, concerning 'curiosity'. Both St Augustine, writing in Late Antiquity, and St Thomas Aquinas in the Middle Ages were afraid that curiosity might transgress the approved boundaries set for knowledge and the methods for its attainment, and had sought to circumscribe enquiry in order to block the road that led to mortal danger. Nevertheless, the numbers of *curieux* expanded considerably, and attracted a diverse following. Goltzius himself, an engraver by profession, testified to the diverse types of people who accumulated collections in his day: they included the Pope, cardinals, emperors, kings, princes, theologians, lawyers, doctors, scholars, poets, priests, monks, officers and artists.[22] And like the great medieval churches that were filled with sacred remains, Renaissance collections contributed to the fame and reputation of Europe's towns and cities; there were, however, strong personal motivations underlying the enthusiasms of their creators.

Pomian has provided five relatively detailed profiles of collectors obsessed with the encyclopaedic ideal: Pierre Borel, who lived in Paris, and Andrea Vendramin (1554–1629), Federigo Contarini (1538–?1613), Girolamo Gualdo (1496–1566) and Ludovico Moscardo (?1611–81) in Venice.[23] Vendramin's own catalogue listed the contents of his collection under a variety of headings, which included the following:

Pictures; sculptures of divinities, oracles and ancient idols; costumes of different lands; ancient instruments of sacrifice including urns and lamps; medals of ancient Romans and famous Venetians; Egyptian rings and seals decorated with scarabs, emblems and other signs engraved in stones and gems; pure, mixed and composite natural substances; whelks, shells and conches from various parts of the world, both east and west; illustrated books on chronology, prints, animals, fish and birds; plants and flowers.[24]

The inventory of the Contarini collection, drawn up after its owner's death, contained a similar miscellany of objects: corals, crystals, petrifications, minerals, oysters with two pearls, horns, teeth and claws, statues, medals, cameos, antiquities and paintings.[25] After it was inherited by Carlo Ruzzini (1554–1644) and subsequently enlarged, the collection became one of the most important cabinets in Venice. A Veronese collector of the time, Mapheus Cusanus, appears to have had a particular predilection for 'Egyptian Idols taken out of the Mummies, divers sorts of petrified shells, petrified cheese, cinnamon, spunge, and Mushromes'.[26] Clearly, although written guides and disquisitions on classifications had been in circulation since antiquity, there still remained plenty of room for personal preferences and idiosyncratic expressions. Ludovico Moscardo divided his collections according to the three broad groupings that had been taken from Pliny the Elder's *Historia naturalis*: antiquities; stones, minerals and earths; and corals, shells, animals, fruits, etc. This meant that 'giants' bones' were considered to be antiquities, while mummies, musical instruments, paintings, clocks and Indian shoes qualified as minerals or earths.[27] In Bologna, the Marchese Ferdinando Cospi (1619–86) assembled another notable collection of the bizarre and extraordinary, with the original intention, so he claimed, of providing 'a youthful pastime', although he later used it to more pragmatic effect.[28]

The earlier cabinets, including the renowned collections of Ulisse Aldrovandi (1527–1605), Antonio Giganti (1535–1598) and the University of Leiden, did not even distinguish between objects found in nature (natural curiosities) and those made by exceptional craftsmen (artificial curiosities),[29] though by the mid-sixteenth century, such a division was often used as a minimum classificatory principle. Pierre Borel, Ferdinando Cospi, Ole Worm (1588–1654) and the collections in the Copenhagen Museum and Bodleian Library were divided into natural and artificial curiosities.[30] In the Worm collection, artificial curiosities were subdivided according to the materials from which they were made (clay, amber, gold, silver, bronze, iron, glass and wood).[31] One room of

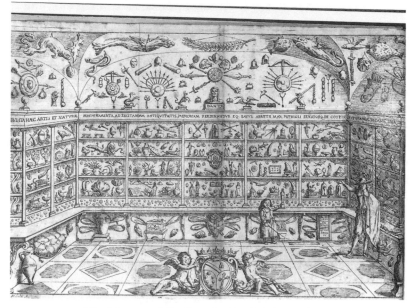

The Museum of Ferdinando Cospi, Bologna, from
L. Legati, *Museo Cospiano* (Bologna, 1677).

The Museum of Ole Worm, Copenhagen, from Worm's *Museum Wormianum seu
Historia Rerum Rariorum* (Amsterdam, 1655).

the Copenhagen Museum was devoted solely to diverse clothing and
Indian, Inuit and Turkish arms and utensils.[32] Some cabinets, such as
those belonging to Cospi and the Milanese nobleman Manfreda Settala,
juxtaposed objects to exemplify similarities believed to exist between
different cultures.[33] One of the leading exponents of this method was
Lorenzo Pignoria, whose appendix to Vincenzo Cartari's *Le vere e nove
imagini dei delli antichi*, first published in 1615 and regularly
reissued, encouraged a comparative approach to Mexican, Japanese and
Chinese mythology in order to illustrate the many different permutations
of paganism. Heikamp and Ryan concur that Pre-Columbian items were
few, and included chiefly for comparison with classical or Christian
religion.[34] The cultural origins of these items seem to have been of less
importance than their broad geographical provenances. Frequently, the
civilizations of the New World – Aztec, Toltec, Mixtec, Maya – were
conflated, and the inhabitants of distinct city states and regions were
subsumed under general rubrics. Paganism provided a primary category,
and material examples and cultural practices had importance only in so
far as they imparted evidence of its distribution.

The Renaissance initially accepted the significance of collections as
expressed through medieval thought, but later the theological reasoning
of the Middle Ages was slowly transformed into secular rationalization.
The two central, undisputed axioms that underlay the Renaissance
collection and classification of artefacts were the belief that by using the
devices of symbolism and allegory inherited from the Middle Ages,
creation could be replicated in miniature and represented by the careful
and deliberate assemblage of signifying objects, and that the juxtaposition of the constituent items and parts of the collection could no more be
fortuitous than the universe it was said to mirror. According to the
influential seventeenth-century museographer Emanuele Tesauro, all
natural objects contained their own particular allusion to specific ideas.
Meaning was innate to nature, thereby permitting Tesauro to argue that
'if nature speaks through such metaphors, then the encyclopaedic
collection, which is the sum of all possible metaphors, logically becomes
the great metaphor of the world'.[35] Nevertheless, the order of nature was
not envisaged as repetitive, or shackled to coherent sets of laws, but was
subject to unlimited variability and novelty. The Renaissance still
believed in a world in which God could intervene to perform the
miraculous. Writers like Pierre Boaistuau and Conrad Wolffhart kept
alive ideas about monsters and unnatural occurrences by concurring with
the medieval belief that God possessed the power to alter the course of

nature and create grotesque deformations and monstrosities that served as ill augurs.[36] What the collector sought, therefore, were not common or typical items, but rare, exotic and extraordinary testaments to a world subject to Divine caprice.

Among clerics, such as Stefano Borgia (1731–1804), Athanasius Kircher (1601–1680) or Antonio Giganti, the encyclopaedic ideal was pursued in order to illustrate the authority of God, whose design gave reason to all creation. Church collections benefited greatly from the ecclesiastical humanism heralded by the Council of Trent (1545–63), which encouraged missionary work abroad that often led to the exchange of exotic gifts among Churchmen. Borgia's position, first as secretary and then as prefect of the Congregation of the Sacred Propagation of the Faith, brought him into close contact with missionaries all over the world, and allowed him considerably to enlarge his collections of exotica.[37] Giganti was secretary to the cleric Lodovico Beccadelli, whose collection Giganti eventually inherited, and later to the Bishop of Bologna, Cardinal Gabriele Paleotti.[38] These positions provided Giganti with the kinds of contacts that allowed him to enlarge his collections, just as the Medici used their close ties with the Habsburgs to pursue similar objectives. Giganti's universal metaphor juxtaposed like with unlike items, which meant that groups of objects were arranged together in his collections in accordance with particular themes. The symmetry by which he arranged and grouped objects was conceived as inherent in nature: it mirrored the harmonious unity of the world.[39]

Ulisse Aldrovandi had a very different background and reason for assembling his cabinet. By profession an academic at the University of Bologna, he used his collection for teaching and research. The purpose behind the assemblage was not to celebrate the symmetry and harmony of the divine order, but to help verify Hippocratese opinion that environment, because of its influence on production and the availability and use of raw materials, conditioned different customs. Aldrovandi examined the material technologies of exotic and ancient peoples in order to ascertain what practical help they might be able to give to Europe, and thereby pioneered the scientific uses of collections that were to supplant medieval encyclopaedism after 1750.

Cabinets of curiosities became the allegorical mirror reflecting a perfect and completed picture of the world. As Susan Stewart has commented, 'the collection presents a hermetic world: to have a representative collection is to have both the minimum and the complete number of elements necessary for an autonomous world – a world which is both full and singular, which has banished repetition and achieved authority'.[40]

If the image of the reflected world was originally drawn from Christian cosmology, in the later Renaissance, under the patronage of the aristocracy, merchants and statesmen, it assumed a secular turn. Cultivating gardens, gathering antiquity's remnants, and completing the full metaphorical extension of the collection was, among these influential groups, undertaken to demonstrate personal worth and to legitimate their social positions.[41] While collections may formerly have been assembled in ways that allowed for some caprice on the part of their instigators, after wider access was allowed, or once they became public property, a tendency to catalogue and perfect the encyclopaedic image gradually increased. The published catalogue became synonymous with the high point of achievement: it announced that the collector had reached his objective – completion; it was an attempt to ensure the collection would be preserved from depredations; and it was a means by which the identity of the collector was fused with the collection.[42] After Cospi donated his collection to the city of Bologna in 1667, he arranged for it to be catalogued by Lorenzo Legati. Settala catalogued his own collection in five illustrated codexes with accompanying manuscript notes.[43] Clerics, on the other hand, who had fewer political exigencies, waited much longer for their catalogues to appear. Aldrovandi's catalogue – the *Musæum metallicum* (1648) – of the collection he donated to the Senate of Bologna in 1603, remained unpublished until 43 years after his death.[44] Athanasius Kircher wrote a description – the 'Kircheriana domus naturae artisque theatrum' – of his Amsterdam collection in 1678, which was followed by a published catalogue by Filippo Bonanni only in 1709 – 29 years after Kircher's death.

The perfection of the secularized model of the encyclopaedic ideal was achieved by the Medici when Francesco I became Grand Duke of Tuscany in 1574. Francesco dissolved his studio, which had been constructed in the 1570s, and put his collections on public display in the newly built Uffizi Palace in Florence. The ideals that had motivated his endeavours, however, no longer envisaged a model of the universe with God at its centre, but instead a representation of creation that allowed each princely ruler symbolically to claim his dominion over the world as a means of glorifying and celebrating a family's influence, and legitimating its titles and position. In sixteenth-century Milan, all but two of the sixteen leading galleries of pictures belonged to members of the Milanese government.[45] This transfer to the public gallery of sumptuous private

The Kircher Museum in Rome, from Athanasius Kircher, *Romani Colegii
Societati Jesu Musæum Celeberimmum* (Amsterdam, 1678).

property, paralleling a change in its perception from souvenirs to the
'great world' metaphor, consecrated collecting as an expression of the
worthiness of an individual life. Private biography was thereby magnified
and projected through public exhibition.

Objects of curiosity were widely exchanged within the nobility. Gifts
made between such families were a means of reinforcing the sense of self-
worth they enjoyed as a class, just as the degree of comprehensiveness of a
collection could be reflected in the degree of esteem a collector enjoyed
among his peers. Conversely, the limited availability of certain types of
exotic items encouraged competition between collectors. The quality of

even the best collections could by turns be enhanced or tarnished, depending on whether the community of *curieux* chose to assist or frustrate a collector.

Natural history collections, allegorical gardens, antiquities and libraries all had scientific implications that went beyond their immediate inspirations. Ferdinando I de' Medici, for example, reorganized the botanical gardens at Pisa and constructed a museum of natural history which became a centre for teaching and research. His father, Cosimo I, founded the Accademia del Cimento,[46] encouraged the cultivation of Mexican plants and their uses in medicine, and imported rare animals from Africa and America for his menageries.[47]

Every collector is faced with the dilemma of the eventual completion and closure of his or her collection. But nowhere was this problem more pronounced than in the grand project collectors of the sixteenth to eighteenth centuries set themselves. The use of collections to evoke publicly the worthiness of their owners led to the patronage of scholars who exerted themselves to expand and complete the encyclopaedic metaphor. Painting and illustration offered another partial aid by providing substitute representations of rare, unobtainable, non-preservable or intangible subjects. Aldrovandi included in his collection ten illustrated volumes of accurately drawn and coloured plants and six of 'birds, beasts and fishes',[48] while written compilations of ethnographic, geographical, zoological or botanical knowledge became very popular in the period. More ambitious still were the picture series intended to represent the totality of a subject. Etienne Delaune (1519–95), Jost Amman (1539–91) and Giovanni Battista Tiepolo, to mention but three artists, contributed to the exhaustive attempt at allegorical representation of the Four Continents that included their native people, characteristic flora and fauna, minerals and artefacts. The most outstanding example of this genre is probably Jan van Kessel's *Amerika* (1664–6), painted in oil on copper, now in Munich's Alte Pinakothek. The central panel shows two groups of Brazilian Indians in a Baroque-style room surrounded by examples of America's characteristic animals, while smaller, adjacent panels contain paintings of landscapes inhabited by mammals, reptiles and birds.[49] Other examples, worth mentioning because they treat America and adorn the building of that arch-pragmatist and perfecter of the universalist ideal, Ferdinando I de' Medici, are the Armoury frescos. The ceiling in the Uffizi's Armoury was painted by the Florentine Mannerist Ludovico Buti in 1588. The central scene shows an Indian nobleman seated on a litter carried by various

Jan van Kessel, *Amerika*, 1664–6. Alte Pinakothek, Munich.

bearers. The party is surrounded by an idealized landscape full of exuberant tropical and semi-tropical vegetation and exotic birds, while smaller frescos illustrate scenes from the conquest of Mexico and battles between pagans and Christians. The Armoury originally served to house the Medici's collections of exotic costumes, weapons and items of natural history, including art and artefacts from the New World; and frescos provided an appropriate encapsulating context.[50] Artistic and scientific types of patronage were greatly expanded by the encyclopaedic passions of those among the *curieux* who attempted to complete the world metaphor, not only through collecting, but through demonstrations of natural processes and even topographical depictions and schemes of the heavens.

EUROPEAN RECEPTIVITY TO NEW WORLD TREASURES

As Greenblatt has argued, the category of the marvellous provided an important means of incorporating knowledge of the new phenomena found in America.[51] In the beginning, far from creating any crisis of interpretation by threatening firmly-held cosmographic principles, Europeans treated the discovery of the new continent and its people as a marvel, and responded to the accounts with tolerant curiosity. The European reaction to the inhabitants of America has been thoroughly treated by a number of writers,[52] while its impact on certain medieval categories – geography, botany and zoology – has also been discussed elsewhere.[53] What I wish to concentrate on here is the European attitude towards the New World's *material* culture, and its selective availability to European collectors.

The European understanding of the New World was mediated through medieval categories that included the marvellous, paganism, ideas about divine revelation, and the discourse of origins.[54] Exploration itself offered more than just pleasure, or amusement, escape, terror or even the simple satisfaction of curiosity. Journeys could themselves partake of the marvellous, and were expected to provide a more comprehensive explanation of the world.[55] The circumstances of Hernando Cortéz's early sixteenth-century explorations and campaigns caused Bernal Díaz, one of Cortéz's fellow conquistadors and, subsequently, a chronicler of Cortéz's conquest of Mexico, to 'marvel' on seeing the treasure of Axayacatl that was concealed in a palace in Tenochtitlan, just as he did when confronted by Aztec gardens, while the sight of Tenochtitlan more than amazed him, for he was actually unable to decide whether what he was seeing was real or illusory.[56]

The New World's material products that most attracted the Spaniards were items that closely corresponded with the canons of taste they had inherited from medieval thought; indigenous concepts of worth, often based on materials or artefacts not valued in Europe, were of limited interest. Consequently, the cargoes of Aztec treasure dispatched to Europe to exemplify Amerindian products and wares, and win political favour for the explorers, were adjudicated by European criteria of rarity, and hence value, and by the ability of New World's craftsmen realistically to copy natural phenomena. This emphasis is clearly to be seen in Díaz's descriptions of the perfection of Aztec gold and silverwork and the best of their painters, which he favourably compared with those of Greece, Italy and Spain:

There are three Indians now living in the city of Mexico, named Marcos de Aquino, Juan de la Cruz and El Crespillo, who are such magnificent painters and carvers that, had they lived in the age of the famous Apelles of old, or of Michelangelo or Berruguete in our day, they would be counted in the same rank.[57]

Aztec material culture and technology also made a great impression on the religious chroniclers and defenders of the native population. Diego Durán and Bernardino de Sahagún included detailed descriptions of indigenous arts and crafts, while Las Casas, in his *Apologetica historia*, described the technical knowledge and creative abilities of the native inhabitants as a way of indicating their intellectual attainments. Like other observers, Las Casas was also struck by the ability of the featherworkers:

The activity in which they seem to excel over all other intellects and which makes them appear unique among the nations of the earth is the craft they have perfected of representing with real feathers, in all their natural colours, all the things that they and other excellent painters can paint with brushes. They used to make many things of feathers, including animals, birds, men, cloaks or mantles, apparel for the priests, crowns or mitres, shields and flyswatters, and a thousand other things. . . . Before the coming of the Spaniards they used this art and craft to make marvellously perfect things . . . all so natural or lifelike that if they represented a living thing the work seemed alive, and if they represented an inanimate thing the copy seemed natural. . . . One of the greatest beauties of their featherwork, especially in an object of large size, is the placing of the feathers in such a way that, viewed from one direction, the object looks golden though there is no gold in it; viewed from another direction it is iridescent, though green is not its principal colour, and so on, all with marvellous luster and grace.[58]

Las Casas judged these works by the fundamental categories inherited from medieval aesthetics – light, colour and the correct positioning of each element of the composition – which are evaluated by their fidelity to the 'real'. It is not surprising that pre-Hispanic examples of featherwork were included in the shipments of treasure Cortéz sent to the court of the Spanish monarch, or that missionaries and priests had Indian craftsmen create religious images, regalia and retablos from this material. An undated tribute list, believed to refer to the period 1523–8, notes that 117 items of featherwork, including 68 shields, capes, garments, head-dresses, fans and figures, were given to various churches, convents and individuals in Spain.[59] Like the medieval justification for painting, the featherworkers' art provided a means for communion with God, and involved the Church doing no more than redirecting the subject and changing the patronage and organization of its exponents. Examples of featherwork were one of the most sought-after commodities from the Americas. In 1539 it was reported that Cosimo de' Medici owned a rich collection of feather costumes and other objects, while his son Ferdinando owned two feather pictures that he later passed on to his brother's second wife, Bianca Capello. According to a document dated 1571, Ferdinando also possessed fans made of parrot feathers and two bishop's mitres. In 1587, when Ferdinando succeeded his brother Francesco I as Grand Duke, both mitres were sent to Florence; within ten years one of them had been lost, although the other survives today in the city's Museo degli Argenti. Another six mitres have also been preserved. One is now in the Escorial, to where it was transferred in 1576 by Philip II, while another, in the treasury of the Cathedral of Milan, is by tradition thought to have been given to Pius IV by converted Mexican Indians in 1559 when he was crowned pontiff. The third, in the Museum für Völkerkunde, Vienna, originally came from Ferdinando's *Kunstkammer* at Ambras Castle. Like the majority of surviving Pre-Columbian pieces that were brought to Europe at an early date, the other mitres – at the Musée Historique des Tissus in Lyon, the Cathedral of Toledo and one formerly belonging to a private collection in Hohentwiel in Germany (and which now belongs to the Hispanic Society of America, New York) – have uncertain provenances, although the subject-matter of the first is similar to those in Florence and the Escorial. Feather pictures were included in a number of early collections. Aldrovandi had a picture representing St Jerome, but, like the two presented by Ferdinando to Bianca Capello, neither can be firmly identified with contemporary surviving examples. Four feather pictures, representing St Jerome, St Ambrose, St Augustine and St Gregory, are still preserved in the Santa Casa of Loreto, a gift from the Augustinian monk Pietro Lanfranconi in 1668. Another, representing the Madonna, and reportedly given to the same institution, has since been lost. The Museum für Völkerkunde in Vienna contains pictures representing both St Jerome and the Madonna, while further examples of the featherworkers' art can still be found in the Armeriá Real and the Museo de las Americas in Madrid.[60] Other examples of featherwork in Vienna, including the feather crown reputed to have belonged to Motecuhzoma II and a decorated shield, are said to have been part of the original treasure sent by Cortéz to Charles V.[61] Brazilian featherwork was also much sought after, and even though never used to produce Christian religious images and cult objects it was classified alongside Mexican works. The Tupinamba cloak now in the Musées Royaux d'Art et d'Histoire, Brussels, first appears in an inventory of material in the royal arsenal in 1781, while two earlier ones recorded from the *kunstkammer* of the Danish Royal household, now in Copenhagen's Nationalmuseet, can be traced back to 1689. The example in Brussels is telling because it was formerly identified as belonging to

Motecuhzoma II, and provides a good illustration of how specific cultural attributions were ignored by a discourse that subsumed difference under the general categories of the pagan and the marvellous.

Sumptuous objects, chosen because of colour, natural fidelity or craftsmanship, were dispatched to the Spanish court by Cortéz to furnish exotic evidence of his accomplishments. The first shipment, made in 1519, consisted of the treasures that Motecuhzoma II had sent Cortéz in the hope of halting his advance from the coast. According to Bernardino de Sahagún, the first gifts given by Motecuhzoma II to Cortéz consisted of mosaic masks and precious regalia of the gods Quetzalcoatl, Tezcatlipoca and Tlaloc.[62] These were all gods associated with Aztec royal succession and kingship, and the regalia may have been intended to symbolize Motecuhzoma's acquiescence to foreign authority. Díaz's documentation of the conquest provides information on at least thirteen occasions when Cortéz received gifts from the ambassadors of Motecuhzoma or from representatives of local communities. In Tabasco, for example, Cortéz received a 'present of gold, consisting of four diadems and some gold lizards, and two (ornaments) like little dogs, and ear-rings and five ducks, and two masks with Indian faces and two gold soles for sandals, and some other things of little value'.[63] Later, at San Juan de Ulua, one of Motecuhzoma's subordinate governors, Pitalpitoque, brought the Spaniards gold jewellery.[64] The following day another governor, Tendile, arrived with more valuables: 'he took out of a petaca, which is a sort of chest, many articles of gold beautifully and richly worked and ordered ten loads of white cloth made of cotton and feathers to be brought, wonderful things to see, besides quantities of food'.[65] At the next meeting Tendile was accompanied by another governor, Quintalbor, who brought further presents. According to Díaz:

The first article presented was a wheel like a sun, as big as a cartwheel, with many sorts of pictures on it, the whole of fine gold, and a wonderful thing to behold, which those who afterwards weighed it said was worth more than ten thousand dollars. Then another wheel was presented of greater size made of silver of great brilliancy in imitation of the moon with other figures shown on it, and this was of great value as it was very heavy – and the chief brought back the helmet full of fine grains of gold, just as they are got out of the mines, and this was worth three thousand dollars. . . . Then were brought twenty golden ducks, beautifully worked and very natural looking, and some (ornaments) like dogs, and many articles of gold worked in the shape of tigers and lions and monkeys, and ten collars beautifully worked and other necklaces; and twelve arrows and a bow with its string, and two rods like staffs of justice, five palms long, all in beautiful hollow work of fine gold. Then there were presented crests of gold and plumes of rich green feathers, and others of silver, and fans of the same materials, and deer copied in hollow gold and many other things that I cannot remember for it all happened so many years ago. And then over thirty loads of beautiful cotton cloth were brought worked with many patterns and decorated with many coloured feathers, and so many other things were there that it is useless my trying to describe them for I know not how to do it.[66]

After Tendile returned from Tenochtitlan with news that Motecuhzoma had refused to meet Cortéz, Tendile offered the Spaniards a new consignment of gifts:

Ten loads of fine rich feather cloth, and four chalchihuites, which are green stones of very great value, and held in the greatest esteem among the Indians, more than emeralds are by us, and certain other gold articles. Not counting the chalchihuites, the gold alone was said to be worth three thousand dollars.[67]

Another large consignment of gold and precious cloth was sent by Motecuhzoma shortly after Cortéz had persuaded the Totonac to refuse further tribute to the Aztec emperor.[68] And on their first meeting, Motecuhzoma presented Cortéz with a 'very rich necklace of golden crabs'.[69] Cortéz was not himself blind to the quality of Aztec craftsmanship, which prompted him to ask:

What greater grandeur can there be than that a barbarian monarch such as Motecuhzoma should have imitations in gold, silver, stones, and featherwork of all the things existing in his dominion? The gold and silver things are so like to nature that there is not a silversmith in all the world who could do better; and as for the stones, there is no imagination which can divine the instruments with which they were so perfectly executed.[70]

In addition to these formal presentations of precious materials, Díaz also recounts the bartering that occurred between Cortéz's men and the Indians so that the former might obtain gold and food. The gold from Motecuhzoma's treasury was melted down and some of it used to make long heavy chains that the conquistadors conspicuously wore. According to Díaz, 'some of our soldiers had their hands so full, that many ingots of gold, marked and unmarked, and jewels of a great diversity of patterns were openly in circulation. Heavy gaming was always going on with some playing cards . . .'.[71] Early in 1520 part of the consignments of treasure accumulated by Cortéz arrived in Spain and was placed on public display in Toledo. That spring they were taken to Valladolid, then late in the summer they arrived in Flanders, where they were seen and admired by Albrecht Dürer. A second shipment was sent in 1522, and another in September 1526. The third shipment of treasure Cortéz dispatched to Spain included Christian images, crucifixes and medallions that had been copied by the Aztec metalworkers at his request.[72]

The arrival in Europe of Aztec valuables astounded those who beheld them, and wealthy collectors were smitten by desires to renew their efforts to complete 'comprehensive' collections. Peter Martyr could not hide his amazement:

I am at a loss to describe the aigrettes, the plumes and the feather fans. If ever artists of this kind have touched genius, then surely these natives are they. It is not so much the gold or the precious stones that I admire, as the cleverness of the artist and the workmanship, which must exceed the value of the material and excite my amazement. I have examined a thousand figures which it is impossible to describe. In my opinion, I have never seen anything which for beauty could more delight the human eye.[73]

Similar statements of admiration and marvel at the workmanship were voiced by renowned European craftsmen, among them Benvenuto Cellini and Dürer. In 1522 Martyr invited members of the diplomatic corps to view the second shipment of treasures sent to Charles V, which the Venetian ambassador, Contarini, described to his Senate three years later. After extolling the qualities of the gold and silverwork and the obsidian mirrors, he reserved his greatest praise for the featherwork, which he thought 'miraculous' – 'Never have I seen embroidery so lovely and delicate as some examples of this work'.[74]

Apart from the vast quantities of booty taken by the Spaniards, gold, silver and 'chalchihuites' (jade, and related stones of a green-blue colour) were also discovered under the foundations of temples, and in at least one case were the subject of a lawsuit between a settler and the Crown.[75]

Although inventories might not even begin to give an accurate idea of the amount of material sent back from the New World, they do clearly reveal the tastes and interests of the Spaniards at the time of the conquest. It would be surprising if other members of the expedition had not also brought back, or sent home, various objects, and Heikamp confidently believes 'numerous shiploads of treasures reached Europe'.[76]

In addition to the treasures from Mexico, the conquest of Peru in 1533 yielded further quantities of Indian booty. The objects obtained by Pizarro from the ransom of Atahualpa alone were said to be sufficient to fill a room 25 feet long and 15 feet wide even when piled higher than the upraised arms of a tall man.[77] Francisco de Xeres, writing of some of the articles sent to Spain, recounted the following:

The ship brought, for his Majesty, thirty-eight vases of gold and forty-eight of silver, among which there was an eagle of silver. In its body were fitted two water

The Museum of Ferrante Imperato, Naples, from Imperato's
Historia naturale (Naples, 1599).

jars and (or?) two large pots, one of gold and the other of silver, each of which
was capable of containing a cow cut in pieces. There were also two sacks of gold,
each capable of holding two fanegas of wheat, an idol of gold the size of a child
four years old, and two small drums. The other vases were of gold and silver,
each one capable of holding two arrobas and more. In the same ship passengers
brought home forty-four vases of silver and four of gold.[78]

The tribute destined for the King reached Seville on 25 April 1538.[79]
According to the Peruvian historian Medina:

There were recorded with it three golden sheep, of 118 or 119 marcs; 20 statues
of women with their tapaderas [fine clothing], whose weight ranged from 124 to
95 marcs; a male dwarf with an artificial bonnet and crown. The workmanship
of these feminine figures must have been very faultless, since on the inventory it
appears one of them lacked a finger.

As for the objects of silver, it appears they were more artistic, if one may say so,
since they included three sheep and a shepherd; twelve statues of women, large
and small, which, like the former, had 'tapaderas' to fit them, according to the
phrasing of the inventory; and finally, 29 jars, all with two handles, a dog's head
and two pick-axes.[80]

What, then, was the fate of all these unique objects once they reached
Europe's shores? Unlike the Mexican artefacts that had arrived, none of

the Peruvian antiquities from this period are thought to have survived.[81] Much of the state treasure formerly belonging to Axayacatl was melted down and cast into ingots, while the jewellery was 'undone and taken to pieces'. Axayacatl's was probably the largest hoard taken by Cortéz, and is repeatedly referred to by Díaz:

I say there was so much, that after it was taken to pieces there were three heaps of gold, and they weighed more than six hundred thousand pesos . . . without the silver and other rich things, and not counting in this the ingots and slabs of gold, and the gold in grains from the mines.[82]

Little, apparently, of this treasure remained intact, although some additional fine chalchihuites and 'three blowguns with their pellet moulds, and their coverings of jewels and pearls, and pictures in feathers of little birds covered with pearlshells and other birds' may have reached Spain.[83] One document mentioning a personal treasure of precious jewellery given to Cortéz by the Indian population before his return to Spain in 1532 recorded a similar fate before it left Mexico:[84] much of the gold was melted down in Mexico and part of it was then used to pay for supplies for the military campaigns, or circulated in order to bribe various Spanish factions, thus sealing alliances. Such practical constraints and considerations clearly overrode any views that collectors might have expressed, and had the effect of rationing what was available to them. Another large quantity of treasure, accumulated by Cortéz in 1519–20, was lost in Lake Texcoco during the Spanish retreat from Tenochtitlan, while during the same campaigns Cortéz's Tlaxcalan allies carried off more from plundered Aztec cities. Part of the bundles of precious cloth were also used as payment to his Indian allies, and thus may never have left Mexico's shores. Chalchihuites was similarly used by the Spaniards to bribe Indians for information. After the Spanish rout at Tenochtitlan, precious materials, including chalchihuites, vastly deflated in the hands of the desperate and hungry Spaniards, were even exchanged for food.

Even many of the gold ornaments and ritual objects that Cortéz and others sent to Europe on account of their fine craftsmanship were probably eventually melted down and thereby converted into monetary worth. As for the jewels, some exceptionally exotic items were reworked and converted into more appealing and usable adornment. European craftsmen inlaid Pre-Columbian gold animals with precious stones and converted them into pendants. Even jewellery was not sacrosanct, and could either be reworked again in accordance with fashion or else be melted down to provide finance when needed.[85] Mexican mosaic works were also taken apart and their precious and semi-precious stones reused for European decorations.

There is no doubt that the material from the New World was not thought, in the formal sense, to constitute a collection, and much of it, in one form or another, was re-distributed. The Spanish Crown had no formal policy towards the collection and preservation of antiquities until 1716,[86] and what had survived in the royal palace had probably done so because it had been regarded as furnishings and decorative art. Many more items were probably given to members of the aristocracy, and thus have been added to collections. It is not uncommon to find Pre-Columbian objects listed in the inventories of private individuals. Moran y Checa mentions Diego Hurtado de Mendoza and the Count of Guimera, for example, as collectors who possessed numerous gold 'idols' and antiquities from the New World.[87] Nevertheless, the fate of most New World artefacts ended in the foundries, jewellers' workshops and banks, or fell victim to the general carnage of everyday life. European collectors were left with a severely limited choice of objects, further restricted by Spain's indifference to the fate of New World artefacts and its quick willingness to convert the cultural spoils of conquest into financial gain.

NOVELTY, GENEALOGY AND DOMESTICATION

Having reviewed the ontological and aesthetic categories that provided the criteria by which New World objects were evaluated, and described the kind of objects that filtered into Europe, it yet remains to be seen how such categories and classifications facilitated the incorporation of potentially transgressive objects into the existing European order.

It is difficult to correlate the greater part of the inventories I have mentioned with existing artefacts in museums or private collections. Part of the treasure sent to Charles V, which included gold butterflies, a snail's head, an eagle with pendants, a 'monster' and various animals made from low-value gold, were inherited by his son Philip II.[88] The Peruvian viceroy, Francisco de Toledo, suggested in 1572 that Philip create a museum of the Americas in the royal palace. This seems to have born fruit, for in 1667 an attaché at the French embassy in Madrid reported that in the Palacio del Buen Retiro he had seen,

a treasure house of all that was most precious ever produced in the Indies. I mean the hangings of cloth made from the bark of trees, the costumes of Motecuhzoma and of the Incas of Peru, the strangely-wrought cases, the stone mirrors, the bed curtains made of feathers . . . one would have to spend a whole day there to be able to claim to have seen it all closely.[89]

Sadly, after surviving so many upheavals, most of these items appear to have been destroyed in fires that gutted different parts of the Buen Retiro in the seventeenth and eighteenth centuries.[90] It was not, however, until 1716, when Philip V established the Royal Library (which included a cabinet of curiosities containing mathematical instruments, medallions and other antiquities), that the Crown adopted any firm policy towards the preservation and collection of antiquities.[91]

After the late sixteenth century, far fewer articles reached Spain from the New World. As a result of the Royal Cedula of 1577, the clergy were forbidden to make further compilations of Indian customs, and the export of material culture was officially discouraged.[92] Nevertheless, items continued to arrive in Europe via a clandestine trade through the Italian ports, and found ready homes among the great Italian collectors. Studies of the inventories of the collections of Cospi, Giganti, Aldrovandi and the Medici have disclosed part of their former Pre-Columbian holdings.[93] Equally important are the descriptions and drawings of Pre-Columbian objects contained in the catalogues and inventories of collections. In many cases, the preoccupation with valuable materials – based on rarity, chromatic qualities and fidelity to natural forms – is strongly reflected in the objects collected. A familiarity and appreciation of monetary value, however, was far from absent, and appears to have increased later in the period. Even Suger in the twelfth century was conscious of the worth of Church collections, but Cortéz and his men were interminably engaged in translating indigenous symbolic values of artefacts into their European mercantile worth. The ability of such collections to dazzle, amaze and provide a conspicuous badge of wealth, status, taste and learning was never lost. Having said this, the Mexican heads and figurines illustrated in Aldrovandi's *Musæum metallicum* cannot be considered exceptional when judged by contemporary knowledge of pre-Hispanic art. Similarly, many of the small heads and figurines identified by Heikamp as formerly belonging to the Medici are not outstanding.[94] More revealing still is that a substantial number of these and other Mexican artefacts formerly belonging to these collections are not Aztec at all. This raises the possibility that they were shipped by subsequent looters, who robbed graves to satisfy the European market, or that they had been for some time in the care of the former Aztec collectors, who we know revered antique works and reused them in rituals.[95]

Other objects, however, were by all accounts spectacular, and would wholly have satisfied the period's taste for the unique and marvellous. I have already mentioned featherwork. But in addition, the Medici family, for example, possessed manuscripts, including codexes, such as the Vindobonensis, Magliabecchiano, and Sahagún's *Historia general de los cosas de Nueva España*, two Teotihuacan-style stone masks and various turquoise mosaic masks, only two of which survive.[96] Another mosaic mask, together with a sacrificial knife formerly belonged to Aldrovandi. Two other inlaid handles belonging to sacrificial knives are illustrated in Legati's catalogue of the Cospi collection.[97] These were given to the city of Bologna in 1667, where they were both preserved in the University's archaeological museum until one was transferred to the Pigorini Museum in Rome in 1878. Giganti had succeeded in acquiring two feather head-dresses from Florida, a sacrificial knife, a stone axe, bows and arrows, an obsidian razor, nine stone idols, two parts of a Mexican codex and a Pre-Columbian map, as well as a Tarascan feather-mosaic picture, a mitre and other objects of indigenous manufacture.[98] The Cospi and Borgia collections also included Mexican codexes. By far the largest surviving collection of turquoise mosaics is preserved in the British Museum,[99] although the Pigorini Museum, the Nationalmuseet in Copenhagen, Berlin's Museum für Völkerkunde,[100] and the Dallas Museum of Fine Art also possess important examples. In the case of the pieces in the British Museum, as with much other Pre-Columbian art that reached Europe early, it is difficult to date their arrival or trace their subsequent history prior to their acquisition in the nineteenth century. Most of the pieces are believed to come from former Italian collections.[101] A cedar mask covered with turquoise mosaic thought to represent the sun god Tona-tiuh, or Quetzalcoatl, and a knife with a mosaic handle are thought to have been part of the same collection that had remained in Florence until 1830. Another mosaic mask, probably representing the rain god Tlaloc, purchased at the Demidoff sale in Paris in 1870, was then believed by Lehmann to have formerly belonged to the Medici, and two other mosaic items – a circular shield and an animal head acquired in 1866 and 1868 respectively – were purchased from the dealer William Adams, who claimed to have obtained them from northern Italy. The extraordinary double-headed serpent pendant acquired for the British Museum by A. W. Franks in 1894 also had an Italian provenance. The remaining mosaic works in the British Museum have a still more uncertain history.[102] A mosaic-encrusted skull has only been traced as far back as 1847, when it was in Bruges; a helmet to 1854 when it belonged to a certain W.

Chaffers in Paris; and a small seated figure of a jaguar to 1877, the year it was acquired by the Museum. Another turquoise mosaic mask, which I have identified with Xiuhtecuhtli, now in the Pigorini Museum, apparently has a more detailed history, which can be traced back to Cosimo de' Medici. It remained in the Medici collections until 1783, when it was transferred to Florence's Museo di Fisica e Storia Naturale. The piece was rediscovered by Luigi Pigorini in 1823 in a workshop, the 'Opificio delle Pietre Dure'. It has been claimed that a number of these surviving examples of mosaic work, including the mask at the Pigorini Museum and various of the pieces in the British Museum, were part of the 1519 shipment of treasures that Cortéz sent to Charles V, but the evidence for this is far from conclusive; such claims must be considered to be part of the mythology of these objects of 'marvellous origin'.

There is what at first appears to be a paradox in the motivation and organization of cabinets of curiosity. As we have seen, cabinets alluded to the marvellous and represented the examples of random novelty. American artefacts were easily incorporated into such collections and assimilated in accordance with the same terms, that is to say, as yet further marvels. The sum of novelties and extraordinary occurrences did, however, have its own reason and significance in terms of its allusion to a divine plan. The marvellous had its own order. America could, therefore, not only be incorporated into the existing world-view, but used to demonstrate that order's value and correctness.

Michael Ryan has argued that Europe had an easily adjustable category – the 'pagan' – within which to categorize the inhabitants of new worlds.[103] 'Paganism' both allowed the admittance of cultural diversity and provided it with a biblical pedigree. It incorporated the people and customs of the fourth continent into the same class as the inhabitants and religions of the classical world and barbarian Europe. The standard compendiums of mythology of the period, by Lilio Giraldi, Natale Conti and Vincenzo Cartari, all classified classical, Asian and American customs under the rubric 'pagan',[104] which, as we have seen, also provided the basis for a comparative classification of the material culture from these regions. Paganism had a common origin with Christianity: a kind of parallel development, perceived as a history of error and folly perpetrated by Satan. The virtues and values of the Christian world are almost confirmed through their juxtaposition with their opposites found in pagan countries. They are almost inverted mirror images. Time after time, whether in defence or in condemnation of the Indies, the missionary chroniclers of Mexico (Oviedo, Las Casas, Durán,

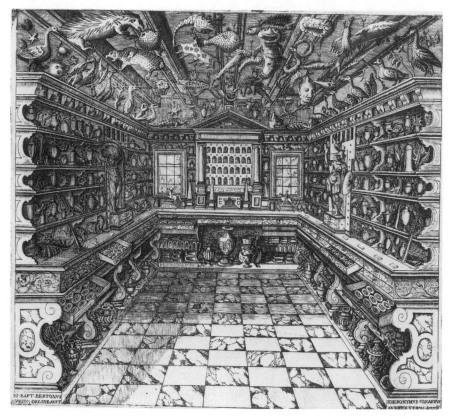

The Museum of Francesco Calzolari, Verona, from B. Ceruti & A. Chiocco,
Museum Calceolarium (Verona, 1622).

Sahagún, Acosta, Torquemada) drew comparisons between indigenous
and classical customs, not simply to make them intelligible, but to
consciously substitute the terms of the indigenous discourse to those
commensurate with sixteenth-century Europe, and thereby affect the
colonization of the American imagination. The subordination of accurate cultural data to the vastly more important need to demonstrate the
inclusiveness of paganism created an apparent homogeneity between the
different high civilizations of the Americas, as well as blurring their
distinctions from other 'pagan' cultures. This is only subtly suggested in
the classification of collections, where inaccurate attributes and provenances – far from suggesting important and conscious errors in Renaissance and post-Renaissance knowledge – indicate a relative lack of
concern with exact provenance. What was important was an object's

testimonial quality as a pagan attribute. When the turquoise-encrusted cedar mask that is now in the British Museum was earlier identified as Egyptian,[105] or the Mixtec-Puebla stone head originally in the Sloane collection and now also in the British Museum was described as an 'Egyptian head of the Sun',[106] it should be recalled that such objects functioned not within an ethnographic discourse but in a theological discourse that had as its objective the establishment and legitimation of paganism as a category.

The date and circumstances of the divergence of the pagan races from the Christian world in the remote past greatly occupied the minds of the chroniclers who endlessly hypothesised on the origins of the Aztec and Inca, who they usually related to an obscure offspring of Noah or a lost tribe of Israel. Cortéz even sent what he took to be a huge human leg-bone to Charles V, in order to confirm that the indigenous population had indeed descended from the giants whom their histories claimed had inhabited the pre-diluvial world.[107] Small wonder, then, that racial genealogies and conjectural histories partly informed written compendiums of customs and arrangements of material culture.

Between the sixteenth and eighteenth centuries, the heyday of the cabinet of curiosity, examples and testaments to the marvellous, the bizarre and the uniqueness of the universe were collected, but collections were usually far from being random or capricious. Cabinets of curiosity, initially informed by medieval concepts of aesthetics and allegory, were later sometimes challenged by particularly pragmatic and politically expedient motivations that led to their public display and the substitution of a mercantile over a metaphysical value. Whether they mirrored the God-centred universe inherited by the Renaissance, or the emergent man-centred, pragmatic world manipulated by merchant princes and aristocrats, cabinets expressed a visual image of the inclusiveness of the European view of the world and its facile ability to incorporate and domesticate potentially transgressive worlds and customs. The truly marvellous and extraordinary accomplishment of medieval thought was that it made marvellousness itself a category of the mundane.

Death and Life, in that Order, in the Works of Charles Willson Peale

SUSAN STEWART

Any collection promises totality. The appearance of that totality is made possible by the face-to-face experience of display, the state of all-at-onceness under which the collection might be apprehended by an observer. This display marks, of course, the defeat of time, the triumph over the particularity of contexts in which the individual objects were first collected. In the arrested life of the display, the collected objects are held together by the dual processes of temporal diremption and the imposition of a frame. The displayed collection finds its unity in memory and narrative. From the toys of the dead in Egyptian tombs to the animated statues of Daedalus described in Plato's *Meno* and Aristotle's *De anima*, to the terror of infinite motion expressed in the fairy tale of the red shoes that will not stop, animation reverses the stasis of display and suggests that the collection might speak or come to life. Through animation, all-at-onceness becomes extension, movement, consequence and reciprocity.[1] This dream of animation has thereby a kind of socio-political claim, for it posits the collection as an intervention or act of significance, and it compels the consciousness of the observer to enter into the consciousness of the collector: the opaqueness and fixity of the collection on display is transformed into the utopian republic that is fantasy, where individual desire finds its fellow dreamer and recognizes itself.

In this essay I want to explore the interrelations of display, arrested life, the attribution or erasure of cause and context, and absolute or totalized knowledge – the sense of completion that is the key for the collection and for the recollection it promises. Although the given qualities of animated objects allow them to endure beyond flux and history, this very transcendence and permanence also links them to the world of the dead, to the end of organic growth and the onset of inaccessibility to the living. It is not surprising that mechanical toys and objects such as those I have mentioned express a repetition and infinite action that the everyday world finds impossible: mechanisms do not feel or tire, they simply work or do not work. As part of the general inversion that the world of the dead represents, the inanimate comes to life in the service of the dead awakened. The theme of animation is itself a kind of allegory of memory, and of the role willed memory plays in re-awakening the obdurate material world given the passage of time. I am also interested in the link between the collection and the portrait as devices for recollection – gestures of *countenance* designed to stay oblivion.[2] But rather than continuing in such general terms, I prefer to focus on a particular historical moment, the end of the Enlightenment, and a set of aesthetic practices in which these issues appear – the painting and collecting activities of Charles Willson Peale – in order to continue, with some vividness, our metaphor. Further, Peale's practices take place in a context of changing religious and political thought that provides a suggestive supplement to any universal theory of collecting.

Peale was born on the eastern shore of Maryland in 1741, the son of a schoolteacher who had been convicted of a felony in England. The family moved from one small Maryland town to another until it settled in Annapolis when Peale was nine. Having been apprenticed as a saddler when young, Peale went on to practice various professions throughout his long life: repairer of bells, watches and saddles, sculptor, painter of miniatures and portraits, Revolutionary soldier, propagandist and civic official, mezzotint engraver, museum keeper, zoologist and botanist, and the inventor of various mechanisms, including a portable steam-bath, a fan chair, a velocipede, a physiognotrace for making silhouettes, a polygraph for making multiple copies of documents, a windmill, a stove, a bridge and false teeth. He studied painting in London with Benjamin West for two years (1767–8). When he returned he moved his family to Philadelphia; it was there, at the height of the Revolution, that he served as a soldier and made banners and posters for the war effort.[3]

In the eighteenth century most established artists had a studio-cum-gallery in which to display works for sale or works in the artist's personal collection. In Peale's case the exhibition gallery he maintained eventually became the first American museum, embracing both cultural and natural history. During the War for Independence Peale expanded his display to include an exhibition of portraits of Revolutionary heroes. Beginning with his first portrait of George Washington in 1772, by 1782 Peale had established a tall and long skylit chamber for showing both head-and-shoulders and full-length portraits. He arranged the portraits high on the wall in order to represent the world's primates, while lower forms of life

Titian Ramsay Peale II after Charles Willson Peale, *The Long Room*, 1822.
Detroit Institute of Art.

that he had collected filled the cases and the floor. A watercolour of 1822
by his son Titian Ramsay Peale II after an outline by Peale, records
Peale's museum after it had been relocated in the Long Room of
Philadelphia's Statehouse. Cases of birds line the left wall; the portraits
hang above. To the right are display cases containing insects, minerals
and fossils. On them rest busts of Washington, Benjamin Rush and
others. What cannot be seen here are the additional rooms and the table
for exhibiting experiments involving electricity and perpetual motion.

In addition to the vertical, hierarchical arrangement of the Long Room
on the principles of evolution, the materials were organized according to
what Peale knew of the Linnaean system. Peale explained that in

an extensive collection should be found, the various inhabitants of every element,
not only of the animal, but also specimens of the vegetable tribe, – and all the
brilliant and precious stones, down to the common grit, – all the minerals in their
virgin state. – Petrefactions [sic] of the human body, of which two instances are
known, and through that immense variety which should grace every well stored
Museum. Here should be seen no duplicates, and only the varieties of each
species, all placed in the most conspicuous point of light, to be seen to advantage,
without being handled.[4]

Peale proposed that the 'gentle intelligent Oran Outang', lacking speech, should be placed nearer to the monkey tribe than to that of humans, and that the flying-squirrel, ostrich, cassowary and bat provided the connecting links between quadrupeds and birds. Peale was an innovator in museum display techniques. Finding that ordinary taxidermy did not produce a lifelike effect, he stretched skins over wooden cores he had carved in order to indicate musculature,[5] and he provided a painted contextual background for each specimen. The museum displayed both live and dead animals. When a live grizzly bear escaped, Peale was forced to shoot it.[6]

By 1794 Peale's collections were so enormous that his museum had to be moved to Philadelphia's Philosophical Hall. Following Rousseau's ideas concerning nature as the proper teacher of mankind and his own deeply-held Deist beliefs in a non-intervening God, Peale saw this enterprise as a 'School of Wisdom' designed to teach the public to follow the example of nature. It is clearly the case that Peale's activities as a painter and collector served the interests of post-war American society – his portraits memorialized the heroes and patrons of the War for Independence, his collections of cultural and natural objects provided in miniature a synopsis of the New World, linking recent historical events to the grand context of nature and providing evidence of a natural providence legitimating those events. To this extent Peale's collecting activity parallels those of British antiquaries in the late Renaissance, such as John Leyland and William Camden, both of whom provided secular and nationalist narratives that were designed to supplant the older forms of religious authority. Yet, if we turn to the particular details of Peale's aesthetic practices at large – his paintings and inventions as well as his collections – we find other interpretations are possible, which are linked to Peale's own psychological history and to the religious and intellectual climate of his day.

Peale's Deism can be discerned in the very names he gave to his children. He refused to give them either family names or biblical names; rather, he took their names from his copy of Matthew Pilkington's *Dictionary of Painters*: Raphaelle, Angelica Kauffman, Rembrandt, Titian, Rubens, Sybilla (after, obviously, the Sybils). And later he expanded to Franklin (after Benjamin), Aldrovand (after Ulisse Aldrovandi, the Renaissance museum-keeper of Bologna) and Linnaeus. Moreover, he recorded their births, not in the traditional family Bible, but on the fly-leaf of his Pilkington. Like Washington, Jefferson and Franklin, Peale was attracted to British Deism, with its tenet of God as inventor and first cause, without any particular justification for institutional religion and clericism, its interpretation of Christianity as a moral system akin to civic virtue, and its picture of nature as regular and predictable.[7] Yet there are two aspects of Deism as it was debated in Britain and also in America that are of particular relevance here. As a legacy of Newtonian physics, Deism – at least before Hume's *Treatise* of 1739, with its critique of causality, had gained popular currency – held the external world to be material and composed of objects now moving, now at rest. Rest, not motion, is their natural state; and when objects move, it is because an active force is moving them. Motion that seems to be initiated by purely material objects is simply transmitted motion, like billiard balls colliding with one another. True autokinesis is found only in human beings. This motion is initiated by the will, and the *feeling* of causing motion is enough to give evidence that one causes it. If all motion originates in the will, then the motion studied by scientists must also originate in the will, and eventually one must reach a first cause of motion, which is God.[8] Second, among Deists there was an ongoing conflict regarding life after death. Throughout the eighteenth century some contended that this world is the *only* world, while others believed in an after-life, one in which moral virtue would be rewarded. Many argued against Calvinist notions of election, yet Franklin, for example, came at the end of his life to hold that the soul was immortal.[9] What remained basic tenets of Deist thought were the denial of miracles, of supernatural revelation and of any special redemptive interposition of God in history. These central theological arguments were very influential regarding the formal choices Peale made in his art: the material, knowable world can be organized by an empirical and reasoned science; human will is the source of all motion in the physical world, while human motion is caused by divine agency; death is a material fact and the categories 'life' and 'death' are mutually exclusive; biblical and mythological narrative cannot represent reality.

Peale's only true apprenticeship as a painter came during his time in London with Benjamin West in 1767–8. But West's influence is remarkable only for its absence in Peale's subsequent work: Peale rarely chose to imitate the style of history and mythological painting that West practised once he was no longer able to get commissions for religious paintings from the Church of England.[10] This fact might best be explored by turning to Peale's copy of West's *Elisha Restoring the Shunamite's Son*. This copy was one of the first works he completed after arriving at West's London studio; Peale made a small (16 x 24 inches) watercolour copy of this biblical composition, which he took with him when he returned to Maryland, and eventually included it in his exhibition gallery. The biblical story (2 Kings 4:8–37) tells of a wealthy, childless woman who provided the prophet Elisha with food and rest; in return Elisha predicted the birth of a son to her. The prediction comes true, but the child later dies, even though Elisha's servant Gehazi tries to revive it. Elisha then appears, and putting his mouth on the boy's mouth, and his hands on his hands, miraculously makes the flesh of the child become warm. The child sneezes seven times and opens his eyes. West, and Peale after him, shows the moment of the revival: the mother is seen from behind as she bends over the child. The child's limbs – still limp – complete the triangular composition, with both mother and child held within the trajectory of the prophet's open hands. Gehazi is recognizable – holding the staff that failed to revive the boy – to the right.

Peale made very few copies of paintings by others during his career, and this is the only original painting of West's that he copied during his apprenticeship.[11] He preferred to paint 'from life', a tenet clearly allied to his Deism, with its rejection of bibliolatry and textual evidence and its turn to nature and the authority of sensory experience. (There is a passage underlined in a copy of Rousseau's *Emile* that was once owned by Peale, which urges teachers never to substitute representation for reality, or shadow for substance, but to teach only from actual objects, and the underlining is probably in Peale's hand.[12]) Further, Peale's museum was made up of actual samples, not replicas or models. Yet just as Peale had subjected himself to West's technical authority when making his copy of *Elisha*, so he chose for his borrowed subject one that – ordinarily – would have been an anathema, that is, a belief in the evidence of miracles and divine interposition.

The early *Elisha* by Peale that is so distant from his personal religious and aesthetic principles might be contrasted profitably to *Rachel Weeping*, an oil painting that he worked on intermittently between 1772 and 1776.[13] Unlike the remote event that is the miracle of Elisha, the subject of this work stems directly from an immediate, personal tragedy. Charles and Rachel Peale lost their first four children in infancy; this particular picture records the death of the fourth, Margaret, the victim of a smallpox epidemic in Annapolis in 1772. Moved by a request from Rachel that he make a memorial portrait of the child, Peale first painted the infant alone, with the arms and chin bound down by white satin ribbons, as can be seen here in the foreground. He later added his wife and a table of medicines in order to symbolize the family's futile attempts

Charles Willson Peale, *Rachel Weeping*, 1772–6. Philadelphia Museum of Art.

to save the child's life. Although this is one of the few non-commissioned, and therefore personal, works in Peale's collection, he nevertheless hung it in his painting room. Because Rachel could not bear to look at it, he eventually placed it behind a green curtain, and for a time a note was pinned up too: 'Before you draw this curtain / Consider whether you will affect a Mother or Father who has lost a child.'[14] The story of Peale's *Rachel* is the opposite of West's *Elisha*, for the former is an account of the stubborn material truth of death itself. Rachel holds herself in a gesture of containment, and the one irruption to such stillness – the tears that seem to bead on the surface of the paint – become material both there and in the biblical title that the family later gave the picture.

Rachel Weeping is only the first example of Peale working through, via his painting and collecting activities, an anxiety regarding death. Mastery over anxiety is aided by the establishment of an empirical referent, a bringing to consciousness of the latent understanding, and a transformation of that referent into experienced understanding. For Peale, the creation of new knowledge was a stay against death. And taxonomy, the structural organization of knowledge, served as an antidote to surplus meaning and emotion. His practices are reflected in a well-known passage in Freud's essay of 1916 on mourning and transience:

We only see that libido clings to its objects and will not renounce those that are lost even when a substitute lies ready to hand. Such then is mourning . . . when it has renounced everything that has been lost, then it has consumed itself, and our libido is once more free . . . to replace the lost objects. . . . It is to be hoped that the same will be true of the losses caused by this war. . . . We shall build up again all that war has destroyed.[15]

Peale certainly lived at a time and place when infant mortality, epidemics and war were all commonplace. But the question for him was the meaning of suffering if divine interposition was not possible, and the meaning of nature's lessons when such lessons were clearly unnatural, even monstrous. *Rachel Weeping* is a painting about the limits of nature and about science's limited capacity to intervene in nature. The other side of the Rousseauist doctrine of natural virtue is nature's indifference, ambivalence and capacity for anachronism and disorder. The material representation of death helps recollect the referent and bring it to the attention of knowledge.

Of all the facts science could provide, one that continued to escape verifiability and remained at the centre of much scientific debate at the time was the one concerning death. Benjamin Rush, for example, Peale's family doctor during his Philadelphia years, had in his library two pamphlets on the problem of suspended animation. The first, 'An Essay on Vital Suspension: Being an Attempt to Investigate and to Ascertain Those Diseases, in which the Principles of Life are Apparently Extinguished, by a Medical Practitioner', which had been published in London in 1741, explains that the best way to investigate the nature of death was to consider the 'inherent properties of life'. When this project of delineating properties results only in ambiguity, the author concludes that in nature 'all bodies in nature are *aut viva aut mortua*, there being no intermediate state. The second is that it must be a work of supernatural human art to recall to vital existence that which is dead'. After the expression of further doubts and hesitations, the author suggests that stimulants be applied to denudated muscle, and if any contraction follows, life remains: 'It is proof of the temerity and imbecility of human judgement; that we have too many instances on record, wherein even the most skilful physicians have erred in the decisions they have pronounced, respecting the extinction of life, this should incite the practitioner never to be deterred.'[16] A later pamphet, 'An Enquiry into the Causes of Suspended Animation from Drowning with the Means of Restoring Life', by a New York physician, David Hosack, recommends the application of heat to the body's system much in the style of Elisha reviving the Shunamite's son.[17]

Given the ambivalent status of signs of life and death, and their capacity for misrepresentation, certain eighteenth-century folkloric practices are of particular relevance. Often in the houses of the dead, clocks were stopped at the hour of decease, mirrors were turned to the wall and black cloth was thrown over pictures – and over any beehives in the garden.[18] These performances made to apprehend time and the motion of representation can be connected to the imperative of viewing the corpse. Death is signified in these instances by a halting of motion and a stilling of context and multiplication, and by attention to the empirical reality of sense impression regardless of the physician's doubts concerning the validity of such impressions. In *Rachel Weeping* the mother's gaze does not enter the frame of the picture-portrait of the dead child. By placing the work behind a curtain, Peale made permanent his mourning, and by showing the child and mother withheld from gesture and motion, he painted the end of human will and autokinesis. This presentation made the gallery visitor's experience of viewing the painting continuous with the mourner's experience of viewing the corpse. When Rachel herself died (April 1790), either from a lung disorder or from the complications of her eleventh pregnancy, Peale refused to have her buried for three or four days because of his fears about premature burial. Her death was made much more difficult for Peale by the concurrent death of his friend Benjamin Franklin.

A year and a half later Peale added a series of remarks to his initial address to the Board of Visitors appointed for his new museum. In them he explained that he intended to follow the Linnaean system, and added a startling point. Explaining that 'good and faithful painting' can make the likeness of man available to posterity, he nevertheless wished to find a way to use 'powerful antisepticks' to preserve the remains of great men, thereby keeping their bodies from becoming 'the food of worms' and making them available for memorial reverence. He was sorry he had not preserved Franklin's remains in this way, he added.[19] According to Lillian Miller:

Although [Peale] never exhibited embalmed people in the museum, his proposal was serious and follows from two central tenets: that as a species in the order of natural history, human beings should be treated like other species, and that moral values could be transmitted to posterity by the physical representations of exemplary men. For Peale death was an event in the economy of nature and no special sanctity was attached to the corpse.[20]

Despite Miller's claim regarding the typicality of Peale's Enlightenment attitude toward death, there remains in his work a persistent theme of anxiety concerning the death of children and the possibility of war as a cause of human extinction. Although natural death is reconcilable to Enlightenment values, the death of a child is in a profound sense *unnatural*, a death that most radically arrests the progress of time. In March 1806 Peale attempted to obtain an embalmed child from a New York church,[21] a request that was made many years after the deaths of his first children, but it does echo another moment of trauma in his life. In the chaotic aftermath of the Revolutionary defeat at the Battle of Trenton – 'the most hellish scene I have ever beheld', he told Jefferson – Peale was unable to recognize his brother James. A man walked out of the line of soldiers toward him: 'He had lost all his clothes. He was in an old, dirty, blanket jacket, his beard long and his face so full of sores he could not clean it, which disfigured him in such a manner that he was not known to me at first sight.' What war had destroyed – clothes, face, recognizable identity – are exactly those qualities that make portraiture intelligible.[22] James's disfigurement shattered Peale's ideals regarding knowledge and recollection, key ideals to aesthetic and epistemological values.

After the War for Independence was over, and so too Peale's brief period of further public service, he suffered a kind of breakdown – the symptoms were his inability to move or to remember. This memory loss was centred on the order and number of his children and an inability to recall whether members of his family were alive or dead. Toward the close of 1782 Peale had decided to re-hang *Rachel Weeping* in his gallery behind the curtain with the accompanying message. He also added some verses, which he said were anonymous, but which are to be found on the last page of his Letterbook for 1782–95. They warn that death is 'no more than moulded clay', but that the adjacent display might nevertheless evoke an excessive response in anyone who cares to view a mother's unceasing mourning:

> Draw not the Curtain, if a Tear
> just trembling in a Parent's eye
> Can fill your awful soul with fear,
> or cause your tender Breast to sigh
>
> A child lays dead before your eyes
> and seems no more than moulded clay
> While the affected Mother crys
> and constant mourns from day to day.[23]

It was a month or so later that Peale experienced the breakdown, writing on 15 January 1783 that for more than two years he had been in a kind of lethargy marked by dramatic memory loss:

Some short time past I was sitting by the fireside musing within myself when a thought struck my fancy, i.e. how many children have I. Four, I answers as if it were by Instinct, four! Let me see if I am right and looking round (and) began to name them as they appeared before me, as my not seeing Raphaelle, I was puzzled for a some moments to make out my number.

He then recounted an instance the day before, when he 'chanced to be looking at the picture of my mother-in-law'; he instantly remembered her person, but could not recollect whether she were dead, nor the circumstances of her will.[24]

It is significant that it is a painting, that of his mother-in-law, that in this case induced the state of confusion concerning life, death and his mother-in-law. The painting is a kind of presence, a bringing to mind if not to sense, but what kind of presence is it? One of the ways in which a painter can explore the cognitive boundary between displays of death and displays of life is through the art of *trompe l'oeil* – tricks of the eye that suspended animation, or an exaggeration of the conventions of realistic art, can perform. Following eighteenth-century aesthetic conventions, Peale ranked the various forms of *nature morte*, which he referred to as 'deceptions', very low in his hierarchy of painting because they teach no moral values. Yet he sees such work as potentially crowd-pleasing or, more charitably perhaps, as being attractive to *afficionadi* of painterly technique. Yet *trompe l'oeil*, itself a kind of material and secular miracle of animation, appealed to Peale in various ways throughout his career, and it was to be a painterly device that was particularly favoured by Raphaelle, his most troubled child. For example, the lifesize painting that is most often called *The Staircase Group: Raphaelle and*

Charles Willson Peale, *The Staircase Group*, 1795.
Philadelphia Museum of Art.

Titian Ramsay Peale I, was finished for the 'Columbianum, or American Academy of Painting, Sculpture, Architecture, and Engraving', a temporary exhibition held at the Philadelphia Statehouse in 1795. It shows Peale's two sons on a winding stairway. The deception was designed to fool the viewer into believing in its reality. Peale insisted that the picture be hung in a doorway rather than on the wall, and he had an actual step built into the room at the base of the painted step. According to Rembrandt Peale, George Washington, on a later visit to the Museum, bowed politely to the figures, mistaking them for 'living persons'.[25] As far back as 1787 Peale had placed a life-size wax figure of himself in his Museum as a way of fooling the public into assuming he was present. And there are other accounts of Peale travelling through Maryland in a carriage harnessed simultaneously with living horses and stuffed fawns, as well as several other taxidermic specimens.[26]

Peale's 'deceptions' may be seen in classic psychoanalytic terms as 'derealizations'. They serve, like all derealizations, as means of defence, of keeping at bay the irreducible fact that a boundary exists between life and death. The second characteristic of derealizations – their dependence on the past, on the ego's store of memories and earlier painful experiences – is also evident here. The theme of animation centres on issues of the preservation of meaning in the face of its traumatic disturbance.[27] As Peale began to recover from his post-war breakdown, his first project was to create an exhibition of moving pictures. He decided to invent a spectacle similar to Philippe de Loutherbourg's miniature theatre of sound and light in London. Peale made six pictures, which he advertised in 1785 as 'perspective views, with changeable effects, of nature delineated in motion'. His scenes included dawn rising over a rural landscape, night sinking on Market Street in Philadelphia, a Roman temple battered by a thunderstorm that ended in a rainbow, a view of Satan's fiery palace as described by Milton in *Paradise Lost*, and a representation of the famous sea battle that took place between the *Bonhomme Richard* and the *Serapis* during the War for Independence.[28]

In these works Peale experimented with light, painting, sculpture and the use of natural objects. Carved waves were worked by means of cranks, while real spray spurted from concealed pipes. Painted transparencies were passed across one another before candles in order to produce airy effects. Foreground objects were either flat cut-outs or three-dimensional props, and Peale sustained the phantasmagoric mood with music he played on a specially built organ. He soon discovered, however, that the public wanted perpetually new works – all of which cost a great

deal in time, labour and materials. In a letter written in 1788 Peale told
Benjamin West that for two or three years he had studied and laboured to
create this exhibition of moving pictures, and in doing so he had 'injured
his health and straitened his circumstances'.[29]

It was at this time that Peale turned fully toward his project for a
museum, or, as he called it, a world in miniature. He began by building a
landscape on the gallery floor comprising a thicket, turf, trees and a pond.
On a mound he placed those birds that commonly walk on the ground, as
well as a stuffed bear, deer, leopard, tiger, wildcat, fox, raccoon, rabbit
and squirrel. Boughs were loaded with birds, while the thicket was full of
snakes. On the banks of the pond he placed shells, turtles, frogs, lizards
and watersnakes, while in it swam stuffed fishes between the legs of
stuffed waterfowl. A hole in the mound displayed minerals and rare
earths.

Peale's major contributions for his collection were either gifts, largely
curiosities or other items that were in some way souvenirs of historical
events and famous persons, or things he and his sons gathered as they
travelled in search of specimens. In his search for varieties of every species
– with no duplicates – he promulgated Linnaeus's system in the interest
of universal laws.[30] Although later, as his own dynasty grew, he began to
imagine his museum's world as one of paired specimens for reproduction,
his wish that there be 'no duplicates' is connected to the concepts of
uniqueness, individuality and character that inform his portraiture: the
republic of the New World was to be built from the singular actions of
singular individuals.

Peale's *Discourse Introductory to a Course of Lectures* of 1800 is
perhaps the fullest statement of his philosophy of collecting. He links
himself in a great chain of largely unrecognized founders of national
museums, from the Alexandrian library and repository of Ptolemy
Philadelphus (a kind of historical pun on his own name and location) to
contemporary British and Continental museums. By 1800 Peale's collections were overflowing Philosophical Hall, while Raphael's and Rembrandt's Museum in Baltimore, begun in 1797, was continued by
Rubens. Peale's *Discourse* is in fact a somewhat hysterical document, full
of elevated scientific claims and sudden plunges toward dark lyrical
effects. In recounting the history of museums, he includes a dirge to
Aldrovandi before he goes on to tell of the British Museum and how hard
it is for the public to view it. A recurring theme in the *Discourse* is the idea
that science is a cure for war. Peale records that 'the chiefs of several
nations of Indians', who had previously been bitter enemies, met by

chance when visiting the Museum and were inspired to resolve their differences.[31] But most jarringly, as Peale presents his philosophical and political rationale for the museum, he weaves into the lecture the story of the death of his son Titian in 1798. This had occurred in September of that year, and two months later Raphaelle Peale's first child died in infancy. In 1799 Peale named a son by his second wife after Titian. Thus he connects the rebirth of the museum with the rebirth of his son. The *Discourse* includes the performance of two musical interludes, with words by Rembrandt Peale, the first of which is the 'Beauties of Creation':

> Mark the beauties of Creation,
> Mark the harmony that reigns!
> Each, supported in its station,
> Age to age unchang'd remains.

The second is an 'Ode on the Death of Titian Peale':

> His early loss let Science mourn
> Responsive with our frequent sighs, –
> Sweet flower of genius! That had borne
> The fairest fruit beneath the skies![32]

Again, taxonomy is seen as an antidote to emotion and surplus meaning. Peale attached a note to his *Discourse* explaining that

This early devoted and much lamented youth, died with the Yellow Fever in New York in 1798. It might be excused if the fondness of a parent indulged in the eulogium of his son; yet the testimony of numerous friends and acquaintances confirm his worth . . . and the plans which he had commenced, to the prosecution of which his whole soul was devoted, far beyond his years, raised the greatest expectation of his becoming the Linnaeus of America. . . .'[33]

In ensuing years, with yellow fever making periodic reappearances, Peale advertised the Museum in the *Philadelphia Repository and Weekly Register* as a place where lost children could be kept until called for.[34]

In 1801 Peale heard of the discovery of huge bones on a farm near Newburgh, New York. He and Rembrandt quickly travelled to the farm, examined the bones and purchased rights to dig further in the marl-pit where they had been found.[35] Peale recorded that 'the pleasure which I felt at seeing the place where I supposed my great treasure lay almost tempted me to strip off my clothes and dive to the bottom to feel for bones'.[36] Cuvier had earlier published details of the mastodon, an example of an extinct species. The discovery of this specimen was further dramatic evidence that a species could become extinct. The American

Philosophical Society made the Peales a loan towards the cost of the excavation, and the family eventually put together two mastodon skeletons that went on to a wide and varied career as exhibitions – from Peale's Museum to P. T. Barnum's exhibitions to the American Museum of Natural History in New York to the Peale Museum in Baltimore, where one set is currently on display. In 1807 Peale wrote to West of his progress in making a painting of the site: 'Although I have introduced upwards of 50 figures, yet the number of spectators in fine weather amounted to hundreds. Eighteen of my figures are portraits, having taken the advantage of taking most of this number of my family.'[37]

The Exhumation is a summa of Peale's career, offering a counterpoint to a copy he made in 1819 of Charles Catton's *Noah and his Ark*, just as the realism of *Rachel Weeping* was in counterpoint to the copy of *Elisha*. Peale's copy of Catton's *Noah and his Ark* and his own picture of the exhumation provide a number of insights into the relations between mourning and taxonomy, memory and animation I have been pursuing. As Peale continued through 1808 to work on his depiction of the exhumation, he added portraits of more and more family members and friends, all of whom he wished to include in the glory of his momentous discovery. Just as Noah's sons, in the face of extinction, would help their father gather members of each species and begin a new world, so would Peale's aesthetic dynasty continue his scientific project. Rembrandt's pamphlet of 1803 on the mastodon proclaims that 'The bones exist – the animals do not!' He goes on to explain in this pamphlet that science has awakened this buried fact of 'stupendous creation'.[38] Science's triumph over death is demonstrated quite literally, for Peale includes in his painting both the living and the dead. It dramatizes a critical moment in the excavation when a violent thunderstorm threatened to flood the pit and so end the search, and thus forms a complement to, and inversion of, the Noah's Ark theme. Here the dead – extinct species *and* those of Peale's family and friends who are gone – are awakened and brought back into the light. Yet, just as in *Noah and his Ark*, flooding threatens, and the family is once again the focus for regeneration and recollection. Peale wrote that he admired very much the innocence of the venerable old man in *Noah and his Ark*, also the sweet idea of parental love, the peacock and the other birds whose lines of beauty are so richly tinted. 'I can only say', he added, 'that it is a Museum in itself and a subject in the line of the fine arts and that although I have never liked the copying of pictures, yet should I wish to make a copy of it'.[39]

It has long been a convention of the conversation piece, a genre Peale

Charles Willson Peale, *The Exhumation of the Mastodon*, 1806–8.
The Peale Museum, Baltimore.

Charles Willson Peale, *Noah and his Ark*, 1819. Pennsylvania Academy
of the Fine Arts, Philadelphia.

knew well and often practised, to evoke mourning in a scene by including allusions to, or representations of, the dead in a picture of the living. Mario Praz has pointed out that these conventions frequently rely on portraits accompanied by busts, as is the case in Peale's play on such conventions in *The Peale Family*, which he worked on from 1770 to 1776 and again in 1808.[40] Here the family is gathered around a scene in which Charles, stopping at his easel with face lowered from view, and James, pointing with a maulstick, are giving their brother St George advice, as St George tries to draw a portrait of their mother holding Charles's daughter Eleanor. The family is flanked by busts of Benjamin West, Peale himself, and his early patron Edmund Jennings, and by an oil sketch, on the easel, of the Muses: those in the customary place of the dead are, here, (living) immortals. And the children, who in conversation pieces of this kind are usually those who receive whatever lessons the dead have to teach, are here infants who died in their first year. This aspect of death that is pushed to the front is underscored by the still-life in the foreground of the picture and by the non-reciprocity of the gazes depicted. One of Peale's last additions to the painting was the dog, Argus, that also appears in the foreground. It was then that Peale painted *out* the words 'Concordis Anima' (Harmony embodied) previously inscribed. He told Rembrandt that he had erased these words because 'the design was sufficient to explain the theme'.[41]

But we can also see that it is time that has erased the truth of the legend. Once more the lesson nature has to teach is an unnatural one. By the time the picture was finished, in 1808, only Charles and James Peale remained alive.[42] And we cannot help but remember that the dog is named 'bright-eyed' after the giant who was put to death by Hermes and whose eyes were then set in a peacock's tail. Nature's lesson is the production and reproduction of nature, not the production of order and sequence, and nature calls for vigilant observation, not the construction of moral aphorisms.[43]

Peale recognized that he was himself pressed to complete works such as *The Family Group* in preparation for death.[44] Among his last works are his portrait of 1822 of James studying a portrait miniature by lamplight, and his self-portrait of the same year, *The Artist in his Museum*. Peale had been asked by the Museum trustees to paint a life-size, full-length portrait of himself, and he told Rembrandt:

I think it is important that I should not only make it a lasting ornament to my art as a painter, but also that the design should be expressive that I bring forth into public view the beauties of nature and art, the rise and progress of the Museum.[45]

Charles Willson Peale, *The Artist in his Museum*, 1822.
Pennsylvania Academy of the Fine Arts, Philadelphia.

Peale holds back the curtain so that the collections might be seen, and places in the foreground the giant jaw and tibia of the mastodon – the mounted skeleton can be discerned to the right just above the set-aside palette. A Quaker woman holds up her hands in astonishment at the mastodon, while a father talks with his son, who is holding an open book; another figure looks at the birds. At the age of 81, Peale here conducts an experiment in the relation between artificial and natural light, the latter coming from behind, the former from a mirror that reflects a secondary light onto Peale's head. The light of painting thus turns back from the foreground of the picture, while the light of nature travels forward from the back, with Peale silhouetted by their interaction. Yet the curtain reminds us of the collected and staged qualities of this nature, and also of the curtain that hides the scene of death and extinction in *Rachel Weeping*. And the life-size 'deception' of Peale's figure appears realistically on the most artificial side of the curtain.[46]

This work, admittedly, does little to resolve for us the status of the animated taxonomy, and even less, perhaps, to define the boundary where life ends and art begins. There are few pictures of knowledge farther from Platonism than the Enlightenment's sceptical empiricism on the one hand and psychoanalytic concepts of latency and the unconscious on the other. Yet in the case of Peale we see the limit of Enlightenment taxonomy as the threshold of inarticulate emotion. Peale frequently referred to himself as a 'memorialist', meaning by this that he painted the dead in the service of a future memory. Further, just as Freud's theory of mourning stems from the traumatic consequences of war, so does Peale develop his museum as an antidote to war's losses and as a gesture against disorder and the extinction of knowledge. In this nexus of motion and emotion, arrested life and animation, loss and memory, that Peale has bequeathed to us we can begin to recollect, with both a sense of difference and sense of urgency, a central issue regarding representation.

'Mille e tre': Freud and Collecting

JOHN FORRESTER

Even when one is no longer attached to things, it's still something to have been attached to them; because it was always for reasons which other people didn't grasp. . . . Well, now that I'm a little too weary to live with other people, those old feelings, so personal and individual, that I had in the past, seem to me – it's the mania of all collectors – very precious. I open my heart to myself like a sort of showcase, and examine one by one all those love affairs of which the rest of the world can have known nothing. And of this collection to which I'm now even more attached than to my others, I say to myself, rather as Mazarin said of his books, but in fact without the least distress, that it will be very tiresome to have to leave it all. (Swann, in *Remembrance of Things Past*)[1]

Imagine you are lying on Freud's couch. What can you see? Directly above you on the wall to your left hangs a colour print of the rock-cut temple at Abu Simbel in Egypt. To its left is an Egyptian mummy portrait, in tempera on wood, of a balding, middle-aged man wearing a white tunic decorated with two embroidered bands, dating from the Roman period c. 250–300 AD. Further along the wall, so you can look at it if you raise your eyes from your feet and glance up and left, is a copy of a Roman frieze depicting the woman Gradiva, with her characteristic raised instep. On the wall facing you, above your feet, is a picture of Oedipus contemplating the question the Sphinx has put to him.

You are surrounded by objects from the ancient world. And the voice behind you tells you that these objects are a decaying reflection of equally ancient objects within you. Listen to what Freud records himself as having said to the patient known as the 'Rat Man':

I then made some short observations upon *the psychological differences between the conscious and the unconscious*, and upon the fact that everything conscious was subject to a process of wearing-away, while what was unconscious was relatively unchangeable; and I illustrated my remarks by pointing to the antiques standing about in my room. They were, in fact, I said, only objects found in a tomb, and their burial had been their preservation: the destruction of Pompeii was only beginning now that it had been dug up.[2]

Egyptian mummy portrait, *c.* 250–300 AD,
in Freud's collection (no. 4946).

This characterization of the mind's contents as being like the objects in his collection of antiquities is given the virtuoso touch in a famous depiction of Rome, the city that Freud loved above all others:

Now let us, by a flight of imagination, suppose that Rome is not a human habitation but a psychical entity with a similarly long and copious past – an entity, that is to say, in which nothing that has once come into existence will have passed away and all the earlier phases of development continue to exist alongside the latest one. This would mean that in Rome the palaces of the Caesars and the Septizonium of Septimius Severus would still be rising to their old height on the Palatinate and that the castle of S. Angelo would still be carrying on its battlements the beautiful statues which graced it until the siege by the Goths, and so on. But more than this. In the place occupied by the Palazzo Caffarelli would once more stand – without the Palazzo having to be removed – the Temple of Jupiter Capitolinus; and this not only in its latest shape, as the Romans of the Empire saw it, but also in its earliest one, when it still showed Etruscan forms and was ornamented with terracotta antefixes. Where the Coliseum now stands we could at the same time admire Nero's vanished Golden House. On the Piazza of the Pantheon we should find not only the Pantheon of to-day, as it was bequeathed to us by Hadrian, but, on the same site, the original edifice erected by Agrippa; indeed, the same piece of ground would be supporting the church of Santa Maria sopra Minerva and the ancient temple over which it was built.

This devoted evocation of history is imbued with the tender familiarity of the lover for all the parts and secret places of the loved one, a knowledge that is the fruit of long years of study and visiting. But Freud's effort to bring all of history together in one picture is doomed to fail, as he himself immediately recognizes:

There is clearly no point in spinning our phantasy any further, for it leads to things that are unimaginable and even absurd. If we want to represent historical sequence in spatial terms we can only do it by juxtaposition in space: the same space cannot have two different contents. Our attempt seems to be an idle game. It has only one justification. It shows us how far we are from mastering the characteristics of mental life by representing them in pictorial terms.[3]

The tender familiarity with the history and topography of all the Romes, ancient, medieval and modern, is only a prelude to the realization of how inadequate an analogy the archaeological, the antique analogy, is. It is as if Freud has collected all these objects, has acquired all this knowledge of the classical past, only to find that it has all been 'an idle game'.

Freud's desire to be an archaeologist of the mind was a long-standing feature of his inner life. Stones talk to archaeologists, he asserted in 1896 in one of his first psychoanalytic papers, 'The Aetiology of Hysteria', and in exactly the same way so do forgotten, buried memories talk to the psychoanalyst armed with the technique of free association – 'the procedure of clearing away, layer by layer, the pathogenic psychical material, which we like to compare with the technique of excavating a buried city'.[4] Perpetual student of the 'prehistoric' – one of his favourite terms for the forgotten, infantile past of his patients – Freud the archaeologist of the mind was entirely committed to the archaeological analogy in looking to the contents of the mind as so many objects to be uncovered, pieced together, dated, placed back in their original contexts, or treated as so many false leads planted by later grave-robbers. In 1896, one of his first models of the mind bore the unmistakeable stamp of his enthusiasm for the prehistoric, couched in the evolutionary and philological dialect of the time:

I am working on the assumption that our psychic mechanism has come into being by a process of stratification: the material present in the form of memory traces being subjected from time to time to a *rearrangement* in accordance with fresh circumstances – to a *retranscription* . . . the successive registrations represent the psychic achievement of successive epochs of life. At the boundary between two such epochs a translation of the psychic material must take place. . . . If a later transcript is lacking, the excitation is dealt with in accordance with the psychological laws in force in the earlier psychic period. . . . Thus an anachronism persists: in a particular province, *fueros* are still in force; we are in the presence of 'survivals'.[5]

And about the same time he wrote this, Freud began to collect antiquities.

By the time he died, in September 1939, Freud's collection was a considerable one: something over 3000 pieces, including hundreds of rings, scarabs and statuettes. He kept them in the two rooms he worked in, making a distinct separation from the other family rooms, which were decorated in ordinary turn-of-the-century style, with heavy, contemporary furniture and lots of family photos. This is a clear indication that his collection was both something private for him, to be kept separate from his familial existence, and that it was something bound up with his work, both as writer and analyst.

He started collecting sometime in the 1890s and from the start most of the objects were sculptural. Having started with copies of Renaissance masterpieces, Freud quickly found the main theme of his collection: nonfragmentary pieces from ancient Rome, Greece and Egypt. In the 1920s he widened his compass somewhat to include Chinese pieces. The *Anschluss* of 1938 forced the Freud family to leave Vienna for London; Freud feared that his large collection of antiquities would be confiscated. With help from Princess Marie Bonaparte, the official valuer from the Kunsthistorisches Museum, and others, he managed to take all of them with him – in contrast to his books, a large portion of which were, whether by necessity or because of their bulk, sold before departure.[6] Fearing the worst, Freud had confided one piece to Marie Bonaparte for her to smuggle out of the country in case the whole collection was confiscated: a four-inches-high Roman copy of a 5th-century BC Athena that sat in pride of place on his desk at Berggasse 19. While they were packing to leave Vienna, the family attempted to record the position of each piece of his formidable collection; when they finally settled into their new house in Maresfield Gardens, Hampstead, the maid, Paula Fichtl, arranged the collection accordingly, lining the walls and cabinets of the large pair of ground-floor rooms that became Freud's study and consulting-room.[7] As Freud afterwards wrote to his ex-analysand and friend Jeanne Lampl de Groot: 'All the Egyptians, Chinese and Greeks have arrived, have stood up to the journey with very little damage, and look more impressive here than in Berggasse. There is just one thing: a collection to which there are no new additions is really dead.'[8] Freud himself died a few months later.

Freud's collection of antiquities had always been confined to his study

Freud's desk and chair at Maresfield Gardens, London.

and consulting room, which had originally been, until 1907, on a different floor of Berggasse 19 from the family apartments, and which was always a separate space from the family rooms. As Bettelheim noted,

all these many, many objects were crowded into his treatment room and study; none of them spilled over into the many rooms next door which formed the family living quarters. What more definite statement could Freud have made that his collection was part and parcel of his psychoanalytic interests, and not at all of his life as paterfamilias? It is a contrast that seems to declare: 'Unique though my life as the discoverer of the unconscious is, my life with my family is ordinary.'[9]

The unremarkable, bourgeois style of the family rooms was therefore a considerable contrast to the amassed figures of Egyptian, Greek and Roman gods that lined the wall and swarmed over the desks and tables in Freud's professional space. When Stefan Zweig included a study of Freud in his *Die Heilung durch den Geist* (Leipzig, 1931), it rankled with Freud that Zweig had not sufficiently appreciated this contrast between the private and the professional. Freud wrote to him, noting how Zweig had placed an 'emphasis on the element of *petit-bourgeois* correctness in my person', and attempted to deflect this imputation as follows:

despite my much vaunted frugality I have sacrificed a great deal for my collection of Greek, Roman and Egyptian antiquities, have actually read more archaeology than psychology, and that before the war and once after its end I felt compelled to spend every year at least several days or weeks in Rome, and so on.[10]

One is reminded of the reaction of the Comtesse Anna de Noailles, the French poetess, on meeting Freud: 'Surely', she exclaimed, '*he* never wrote his "sexy" books. What a terrible man! I am sure he has never been unfaithful to his wife. It's quite abnormal and scandalous!'[11] To outsiders, the strict habits and familial dutifulness of Freud's life irremediably condemned him as a mediocre bourgeois professional, whereas Freud himself felt that his antiquities, his archaeology and his psychoanalytic theories at least blunted, if not entirely exculpated him from, such a charge.

Freud's interest in his collection was, as we might expect, overdetermined. One feature is clear: his interest in his objects was historical rather than aesthetic, and partook of a late nineteenth-century museum culture.[12] As Spector remarks:

Except for the bookcases, the interior resembles those old-fashioned provincial museums housing collections of local specimens, both geological and historical (collected for their cultural and historical rather than for their aesthetic value), such as one can see in parts of Austria even today.[13]

Yet it was not a public collection – although I will modify this judgement somewhat later in this essay – and it was essentially for the personal enjoyment of the owner. Nor was it a systematic collection: it was acquired in a slow and steady fashion over some 40 years, but each newly acquired acquisition depended primarily on the virtues of the piece, on its particular contingencies, rather than its place within a predestined order. As Freud's letter to Lampl de Groot indicates, the vitality of his collection did not stem from its embodying some ideal of completeness or universality; its vitality depended on new acquisitions, and Freud continually rang the changes on the arrangement in his rooms of the pieces. When he died, the collection stopped growing, and turned into the curious entity it now is: a museum within a museum, a collection of antiquities within a museum devoted to the founder of psychoanalysis. His daughter Anna fostered the transformation from living collection into dead museum by preserving Freud's study, with his collection, intact and untouched for over four decades, while she continued to live in the remainder of the house, which was decorated with less anxious attention to the preservation of the family's past, although it does house its fair share of turn-of-the-century Austrian stoves and stuffed armchairs, promiscuously rubbing shoulders with more modern, functional furniture. She probably imagined her father regarded only his psychoanalytic work as worthy of such preservation; the maternally dominated side of the house deserved no such sepulchral devotions. While Anna was alive, the living museum of Freud's consulting room was occasionally opened up and used for seminars. Now, following her death in 1982, the Freud Museum is a properly functioning public space, with opening hours, a visitors' book, staff, people running things backstage, and its quota of Youth Training Scheme attendants and trainees.

If the collection was only alive as it was being added to, it was also characteristic of Freud's attitude to his pieces that he was ready to surrender them, give them away, or swap them for others. For instance, an Egyptian mummy-mask of the Roman period that eventually found itself beside Freud's armchair behind the couch was acquired from one of his regular dealers, who would bring objects for him to consider buying. Freud was quite taken with the mask, but found its cost prohibitive. Unwilling to let it go he did a deal, saying he would pay something like a third of the sum in cash, and the rest in antique rings from his collection. He showed the dealer the drawer in which the rings were kept, and asked him to choose the ones he wanted that would make up the price. Such an easy come, easy go attitude to his pieces indicates that Freud's initial collecting impulse was not the systematic miser's refusal of differentiation, but was more akin to the hobbyist's welcoming of the individuality of each acquired item. Freud had no difficulty in desacralizing – in de-accessioning, one might say – the gods in his collection.[14] Such an attitude was, it should also be said, entirely characteristic of Freud's generosity: not only did he support his own large family of six children, wife, and sister-in-law, but a steady flow of gifts, sometimes akin to grants, went out to a wider circle of young friends and the children of hard-up families. 'My psychic constitution urgently requires the acquisition and the spending of money for my family as fulfilment of my father complex that I know so well', he wrote to a colleague during the First World War.[15] This may well have been true, but the father complex also insisted that Freud spent money on an ever-widening circle of friends and disciples. And the father complex had an important say in the founding and development of his collection of antiques.

Freud started acquiring artistic objects just after his father's death in October 1896, and almost explicitly in response to that event, since he

Display cases and shelves of books at Maresfield Gardens, London.

Egyptian coffin mask of the Roman period
in Freud's collection (no. 4823).

found them a 'source of exceptional renewal and comfort'.[16] The
majority of historians have agreed with Freud himself that this death was
a major turning-point in his life and work, precipitating him into a
neurotic crisis of self-doubt and obliging him to undertake his self-
analysis. The eventual product of this period of self-doubt was the
mature Freud and his masterpiece, *The Interpretation of Dreams*,
finished in 1899. Looking back at that work in 1908, when he was
writing the preface to its second edition, Freud declared that 'it was, I
found, a portion of my own self-analysis, my reaction to my father's
death – that is to say, to the most important event, the most poignant
loss, of a man's life'.[17] Beginning with the father's death, and only kept
from death as long as it was growing, Freud's collection of antiquities
elegantly demonstrates how a collection can symbolize the battle of life
within death, of life being infiltrated by death, of a space cleared for the
expression of this battle by the objects the collector has chosen as his
personal representatives.

In what sense was Freud's collecting a response to this most poignant
of all losses? In early 1895 he had offered an explanation of such
behaviour:

When an old maid keeps a dog or an old bachelor collects snuffboxes, the former
is finding a substitute for her need for a companion in marriage and the latter for

Greek terracotta statuette of a sphinx, 5th/4th century BC,
in Freud's collection (no. 4387).

his need for – a multitude of conquests. Every collector is a substitute for a Don Juan Tenerio, and so too is the mountaineer, the sportsman, and such people. These are erotic equivalents.[18]

The idea of cultural activity – keeping domestic animals, collecting snuffboxes – as a substitute for the libidinal tie to an idealized object is already implicit in this account. The absence of the phallic object, both for old maids and bachelors, is the source of their eccentric habits. Yet there is a difference between men and women, which Freud pursues:

Women know them too. Gynaecological treatment falls into this category. There are two kinds of women patients: one kind who are as loyal to their doctor as to their husband, and the other kind who change their doctors as often as their lovers. This normally operating mechanism of substitution is abused in obsessional ideas – once again for purposes of *defense*.[19]

The women collect doctors, symbolic substitutes for the lovers they refuse themselves, just as the men collect substitutes for the conquests they never had, or no longer, have. Freud's own thesis about collectors will thus easily apply to himself: but for him, it is his father who is the Don Juan – the father whose three wives cast him somewhat in the light of a ladies' man[20] – and Freud's collecting is both a substitution for the father's conquests and an act of homage to the dead father he is tempted to idealize. Indeed, it is in Freud's consulting room that we see take shape the collection that is the response to his father's death: not only the antiquities, but also the case histories of women, the legitimate scientific collection that is distinctively Freud's, the mark of his own, as opposed to his father's, or anyone else's, originality and sublimated 'sexual megalomania'.[21]

I have already noted how the location of Freud's collection of antiquities exclusively in his working-space signals its intimate connection with his psychoanalytic work. However, we should not let the impressive and visible weight of Freud's collection, its sepulchral resonance with the museum, obscure the fact that this was not the only sort of collecting he engaged in. The case histories of patients were, to be sure, a seemingly conventional enough form of medical writing, in which he followed in the footsteps of teachers such as Charcot and the other clinical neurologists who influenced him, Hughlings Jackson for example. Yet the work of Richard von Krafft-Ebing, one of the founders of sexology, and the professor of psychiatry in Freud's Vienna, consisted precisely in the pedantic form of collecting and naming of sexual perversions – for example sadism and masochism, the best known of his many categories;[22] as one of Krafft-Ebing's contemporary Viennese critics put it, he was 'an untiring collector who has acquired the false reputation of an expert'.[23] When it came to collecting and naming sexual perversions and characteristics, Freud was remarkably orthodox and unadventurous; his expertise in scientific collecting lay elsewhere.

Freud found his true métier as a scientific collector in the late 1890s, in a series of unprecedented collections he started at that time. The first collection was his set of cases; but even within each case, the work consisted in collecting 'scenes', collecting 'memories', and establishing the links between these discrete items and thus making overall sense of them. The second collection was of dream texts and their analyses, begun in 1895, but turned into a substantial segment of his working activity in the late 1890s. The third such collection followed shortly after, in June 1897: 'I must confess that for some time past I have been putting together a collection of Jewish anecdotes of deep significance'.[24] The last two collections intertwined – in one dream-analysis published in 1900, Freud noted that the 'material out of which the dream was woven included at this point two of those facetious Jewish anecdotes which contain so much profound and often bitter worldly wisdom and which we so greatly enjoy quoting in our talk and letters'.[25] And then there was the third collection, perhaps the most unusual, but one that was marginally less eccentric for a neurologist who necessarily paid great attention to the minute details of sensory and motor disturbances: slips of the tongue, misreadings, mistakes, misnomers, mislayings, misprints, faulty actions – all those failures of action that are signalled in German by the prefix 'Ver-'.[26] Freud's first paper on these 'parapraxes', as they were eventually termed in English, was published in 1898: the example he selected from his collection was an instance of forgetting that he himself had suffered. The following year he published another paper, this time on his earliest childhood memory, noting that 'before dealing with the psychological problems attaching to the earliest memories of childhood, it would of course be essential to make a collection of material by circularizing a fairly large number of normal adults and discovering what kind of recollections they are able to produce from these early years'.[27]

Freud described his 'Egyptian dream-book' (as he jocularly referred to *The Interpretation of Dreams*)[28] just before its publication in 1900 in the following endearing way: 'No other work of mine has been so completely my own, my own dung heap, my seedling and a *nova species mihi* on top of it'.[29] With these three ways of characterizing his dream collection, he returned to the botanical interests of his youth, when he 'was an enthusiastic walker and nature lover, and would roam the forest and woods near Vienna with his friends, bringing back rare plants and flower specimens'.[30] In these crucial years, then, Freud opened up a whole set of related fields of phenomena, whose scientific study would require assiduous and painstaking collections: dreams, jokes, parapraxes, early memories. It is alongside these distinctively Freudian collections that we should place his contemporaneous collection of antiquities.

If the late 1890s was the most significant period in Freud's development of psychoanalysis, which was founded upon the idiosyncratic collections he established at that time, it was also, he later claimed, his period of splendid isolation, when his ties of collegial friendship were loosened, with the exception of his dependence on Wilhelm Fliess. When he did re-establish strong and many-sided relations with others – if he ever did – it was in a new mould, as he drew around him a steadily growing band of followers, disciples and admirers. This movement of withdrawal and detachment from the world followed by a re-attachment in a different modality is reminiscent of, maybe even formed the model for, his later theory of narcissism, and in particular its application to the processes underlying paranoia: 'the process of repression proper consists in a detachment of the libido from people – and things – that were previously loved. It happens silently. . . . What forces itself so noisily upon our attention is the process of recovery, which undoes the work of repression and brings back the libido again on to the people it had abandoned'.[31] In the period when he was developing his thesis concerning the mechanism of paranoia and its relationship to narcissism, he offered an account of the paranoiac and the artistic creator, in whose illness occurs 'the detachment of the libido from the objects (a reverse course is taken by the collector who directs his surplus libido onto the inanimate objective: love of things)'.[32] Whereas the paranoiac fails to re-establish libidinal relations, enlarging his own ego at their expense, the collector restores ties with the world – but only in the form of loved things, rather than loved people. He has found a balance between the newly pressing needs of narcissism and the requirements of the world. The collector thus rediscovers his narcissism in the charm of the objects, each of which reflects back a portion of his lost libidinal objects. The refrain of the charm of the object that is out of reach, contained and self-sufficient – either because of its own nature or perhaps because this object is dead, only the shadow of an object – is continued in Freud's famous portrait of the narcissistic woman: 'another person's narcissism has a great attraction for those who have renounced part of their own narcissism and are in search of object-love. The charm of a child lies to a great extent in his narcissism, his self-contentment and inaccessibility, just as does the charm of certain animals which seem not to concern themselves about us, such as cats and the large beasts of prey'.[33] In his friend and follower Lou Andreas-Salomé, Freud had found the model for such a woman. And she had noted in her diary a telling story Freud told her, of a cat that would climb into his study at Berggasse 19 every day through an open window and 'inspect in passing the antique objects which he had placed for the time being on the floor. But when the cat proceeded to make known its archaeological satisfaction by purring and with its lithe grace did not cause the slightest damage, Freud's heart melted and he ordered milk for it. From then on the cat claimed its rights daily to take a place on the sofa, inspect the antiques, and get its bowl of milk'. Freud may have now warmed to the cat, but 'the cat paid him not a bit of attention and coldly turned its green eyes with their slanting pupils toward him as toward any other object'.[34]

Baudrillard sees the object in a collection as 'the perfect domestic animal',[35] and there may be a grain of truth in the crude view that after his self-analysis Freud's 'libidinal' relations turned towards narcissistic women – women he could admire and who would not threaten to overwhelm him – domestic animals, and the objects in his collections.[36] The collector may be using his collection to express relatively simply his attachment to his ideal objects: collectors talk to their collections, just as dog-owners talk to their dogs. Freud would commune in silence with a newly acquired piece over lunch.

At first sight, there are two features of Freud's collection of antiquities that make it quite different from the collections of dreams and jokes. First, the antiquities are material objects, whereas dreams and jokes are purely verbal or mental phenomena. Second, the antiquities have a cultural sanction of respectability, whereas Freud was under no illusion that the accusation that dreams, jokes and slips were phenomena of no cultural or psychological significance would be rebutted either by common sense or scientific authority. Consideration of both these seemingly divergent characteristics will help us understand more about how all of these collections functioned within Freud's psychoanalytic work.

The first distinction – that antiquities are material, whereas dreams are non-material and mental – is where we started from, with Freud's attempt to draw an analogy between the historical topography of Rome and the simultaneous coexistence within the mind of psychic events from different epochs. Freud's conclusion, we should remind ourselves, was that the mind preserved its past better than the city of Rome ever could: 'the destruction of Pompeii was only beginning now that it had been dug up'.[37] In a curious way, the blurred, fragmentary and inscrutable characteristics of so many of the objects in Freud's collection of antiquities – the scarabs, the funerary urns – serve to remind us that the material survivals from the past are less loquacious than the psychic survivals from infancy that Freud's psychoanalytic method could decipher with confidence. In Freud's world-view, when it came down to it, psychic reality was more real than material reality. Dreams were more stable objects than sepulchres.

H.D., the most eloquent of Freud's former patients, captured his vacillation between the reality of the psyche and the reality of the material past in her description of her first meeting with Freud in his consulting-room:

Automatically, I walk through the door. It closes. Sigmund Freud does not speak. . . . I look around the room. A lover of Greek art, I am automatically taking stock of the room's contents. Pricelessly lovely objects are displayed here on the shelves to right, to left of me . . . no one had told me that this room was lined with treasures. I was to greet the Old Man of the Sea, but no one had told me of the treasures he had salvaged from the sea-depth . . . waiting and finding that I would not or could not speak, he uttered. What he said – and I thought a little sadly – was, 'You are the only person who has ever come into this room and looked at the things in the room before looking at me.'[38]

Yet this poet's enormous interest in his things did not prevent her from seeing very clearly the interplay between the mental and the material in his method:

Thoughts were things, to be collected, collated, analysed, shelved or resolved. Fragmentary ideas, apparently unrelated, were often found to be part of a special layer or stratum of thought and memory, therefore to belong together; these were sometimes skilfully pieced together like the exquisite Greek tear-jars and iridescent glass bowls and vases that gleamed in the dusk from the shelves of the cabinet that faced me where I stretched, propped up on the couch in the room in Berggasse 19, Wien IX. The dead were living in so far as they lived in memory or were recalled in dream.[39]

Their journeys into the past and future together – 'a present that was in the past or a past that was in the future'[40] – allowed them to share objects. H.D. had been to the Temple at Karnak, displayed above the couch; they could both share in reminiscences of the flowers of Rome, he the gardenias he so loved to wear and she the almond. And H.D.'s recollection of her analysis points us back to the second of the superficial differences between a collection of antiquities and a collection of jokes.

The transience of a flower may commune with an Artemis of the 2nd-century AD through the beauty that they have in common. But it is not just ephemera that are the objects of analysis: an analysis will look to farts as much as to flowers for its truth. Freud became, in all seriousness, an archaeologist of farts:

> while, as they lie in the grass of our neglect,
> so many long-forgotten objects
> revealed by his undiscouraged shining
>
> are returned to us and made precious again;
> games we had thought we must drop as we grew up,
> little noises we dared not laugh at,
> faces we made when no one was looking.[41]

Freud is a collector of farts and grimaces, an archaeologist of rubbish *avant la lettre*, as well as a collector of the fading, yet precious detritus of Western civilization. The public Freud, with his reputation for shocking, distasteful and immoral claims about all human beings; the private Freud, with his well-ordered life and his bourgeois collection of culturally respectable art objects. These dichotomies are also familiar in the Janus-faced character of psychoanalytic aesthetics: How could the founder of the quintessentially modernist movement that is psychoanalysis have had such unimpeachably conservative taste in art?

The lack of an account of form in his personal aesthetic has often been the answer that critics have given to the deficiencies of psychoanalytic aesthetics, and this criticism has often been illustrated by referring to Freud's own confessions of his inability to appreciate beauty in art in any other way than by analysing and understanding it.[42] One thing is clear: for Freud, the only skill he felt he could bring to bear in any sphere was that of analysis. Synthesis, he would say, was a function of the ego, and the ego, as the enemy of the unconscious, would and should always take care of itself without the aid of the psychoanalyst. Hence the formal characteristics of art were something he would turn away from as essentially uninterpretable; he would turn instead to detail. It is in the preoccupation with detail that the radical innovations of psychoanalysis are to be found. Traces, signs, small things, overlooked singularities: the science of clues whose genealogy Carlo Ginzburg sketches for us in linking Holmes the detective, Freud the analyst and Morelli the art historian.[43] Certainly the unsystematic character of Freud's collection is also an indication of his disinclination for the formal; his statues were precious as individuals, with histories and distinctive peculiarities. Freud's inclinations, even in science, were never toward counting; he never needed a Leporello to enumerate his conquests. No catalogue of his collection was compiled in his lifetime.

To illustrate how everyday objects are transformed by Freud's principles of interpretation, and thus how a new theory of objects (including collectables) in general becomes possible, I shall examine a long footnote from the analysis of one of Freud's own dreams in *The Interpretation of Dreams*. The 'Count Thun' dream included the following passage:

It was as though thinking and experiencing were one and the same thing. He [an elderly gentleman] appeared to be blind, at all events with one eye, and I handed him a male glass urinal. . . . Here the man's attitude and his micturating penis appeared in plastic form.

In a long, complex, but by no means complete analysis of this lengthy dream, Freud disclosed how when he was seven or eight, he had urinated in his parents' bedroom and his father had reprimanded him, saying 'The boy will come to nothing.' As did so many of Freud's dreams, this dream represented a reversal and a refutation of the father's crushing of the boy: now it was his elderly father, the man in the dream, who was urinating in front of the son – the father had come to nothing (having died some months before). And it was the son who had become 'something' – in particular, he had made profound discoveries about the theory of hysteria. Freud concluded a long and ill-organized footnote (to which he had consigned a number of unassimilated associations that had come up in the course of the lengthy dream analysis) with the following explanation:

The phrase *'thinking and experiencing were one and the same thing'* had a reference to the explanation of hysterical symptoms, and the *'male urinal'* belonged in the same connection. I need not explain to a Viennese the principle of the *'Gschnas'*. It consists in constructing what appear to be rare and precious objects out of trivial and preferably comic and worthless materials (for instance, in making armour out of saucepans, wisps of straw and dinner rolls) – a favourite pastime at bohemian parties here in Vienna. I had observed that this is precisely what hysterical subjects do: alongside what has really happened to them, they unconsciously build up frightful or perverse imaginary events which they construct out of the most innocent and everyday material of their experience. It is to these phantasies that their symptoms are in the first instance attached and not to their recollections of real events, whether serious or equally innocent. This revelation had helped me over a number of difficulties and had given me particular pleasure. What made it possible for me to refer to this by means of the dream-element of the 'male urinal' was as follows. I had been told that at the latest *'Gschnas'*-night a poisoned chalice belonging to Lucrezia Borgia had been exhibited; its central and principal constituent had been a *male urinal* of the type used in hospitals.[44]

The dreamer is thus offering his father a male urinal that is also a poisoned chalice: an Oedipal act, to be sure. But this 'poisoned chalice' includes within itself its own inner principle of transformation: this rare object, Lucrezia Borgia's own chalice, an object any museum curator would give his eye-teeth for, is constructed 'out of trivial and preferably comic and worthless materials (for instance, in making armour out of saucepans, wisps of straw and dinner rolls)', or male urinals. The Viennese principle of the *Gschnas* becomes the underlying principle for mental objects in general: what is rare and precious is constructed out of the worthless and trivial – and vice versa. And the dream itself becomes such a carnival, Freud's own *Gschnas*-night, in which worthless objects – such as a male urinal – are transformed into a celebration of filial triumph over the father.

This attention to the trivial detail of the life of everyday objects is typical of Freud's analysis of dreams. The mechanisms of displacement and condensation entail that such everyday objects are veritable philosopher's stones, becoming infinitely displaceable, perpetually unstable. In the lability of Freud's night-time celebrations and the analyses that accompany them we encounter the typical modernist objects – the ready-made, the found object, the bit of detritus; the god is a shout in the street, the surrealist celebration of the transvaluation of all values. We are a long way from those musty archaeological objects infected with 'chronic necrophilia', as an Italian Futurist call to arms damned them. Yet the interpreter of dreams, the celebrant of the principle of the *Gschnas*, would never have dreamt of adding a Picabia or a Duchamp to his collection of antiquities. Where he outdid anything that Duchamp or the Dadaists would ever achieve was in turning his collections of dreams, jokes and slips into the serious stuff of science. Each dream, each slip, each joke is a urinal that unconscious mechanisms transform into a grail worthy of inclusion in any museum of modern science.

Thus Freud's psychoanalysis did transform despised and neglected objects into precious things, it did bring ubiquitously covert objects of shame into a public world of objects. These collections of his started off as very individual and idiosyncratic examples of the genre: collections of jokes and dream texts must, without the benefit of hindsight, rank with stamp and bottle-top collecting as narrowly conceived and singlemindedly eccentric. But the antiquities Freud also collected give the lie to one aspect of this view of him as an eccentric. These antiquities represent the first appearance of Freud's vision of his work as embodying essential elements of the cultural traditions to which he was selfconsciously heir.[45] Winckelmann the archaeologist; Goethe the worshipper of Italy; Akhnaten the founder of monotheism; Moses the Egyptian; Aeschylus the teller of ancient family tragedies; and Athena, representative of justice, mercy and wisdom: all these are embodied in the collection of objects, and it is their possession that realizes Freud's desire to be a universal and public citizen of this world, walking through the Museum of history and culture.[46] Collectors are often extremely private, especially when they collect such strange objects as dreams. In contrast, all of Freud's collections were permeated by a public and enlightenment ideal.

The power of this ideal informing his collection can be gauged from his own sceptical analysis of it, when, like all other ideals, it was revealed as an illusion by the First World War. The idea of European civilization had been based on universal moral standards that made each participant in that civilization a citizen in a 'new and wider fatherland', of both south and north, sea and mountain.

Roman statuette of Athena, 1st/2nd century AD,
after a Greek bronze, in Freud's collection (no. 3007).

This new fatherland was a museum for him, too, filled with all the treasures which the artists of civilized humanity had in the successive centuries created and left behind. . . . each of these citizens of the civilized world had created for himself a 'Parnassus' and a 'School of Athens' of his own.[47]

Freud's collection of antiquities, and the very idea of psychoanalysis itself, as embodied in his collection of jokes and dream texts, was his own museum of these treasures come down to us from Parnassus. To paraphrase Marx's description of money as 'general wealth in the form of a concise compendium, as opposed to its diffusion and fragmentation in the world of commodities',[48] one could say that Freud's collection of antiquities was a concise compendium of his version of civilization, as opposed to its diffusion and fragmentation in the world of everyday life – a world that none the less could be measured and weighed in the scales of the analytic method. All this was lost in the descent into war's barbarism, with its blood, its complete disregard of law and ethical requirements, and its liberation of the hate and loathing with which all these universal citizens now mutually regarded one another: the war 'tramples in blind fury on all that comes in its way, as though there were to be no future and no peace among men after it is over'.[49]

Freud's collecting, then, always aspired to a public and social function, even when the civic context of the Great War undermined the untroubled sense of participation in 'this common civilization'. His private collection never became a furtive, private vice. The impulse to give friends and followers pieces from the collection came to him often. Even though his collection was a personal affair, it was not a hoard, not a sequestered treasure, jealously guarded. Baudrillard depicts this mode of relation to the hoarded object in the following way:

The reason why you don't lend your car, your pen, your woman is that these objects are, within jealousy, the narcissistic equivalent of the ego: if this object is lost, or is damaged, that's castration. You don't lend your phallus, that's the basic thing.[50]

Freud's involuntary giving of precious antiques to his friends and disciples showed he was not afraid to lose the phallic element located in his collection. Perhaps this urge to generosity was like his public collection of dreams: in so far as he gave to these disciples various rings and statuettes, they became Freudians, part of his international movement, part of his political/scientific collection.

Freud's use of his collection indicates a further feature that contrasts with the mode of pure accumulation. His collection of antiquities was itself already public and fully integrated with the public functions of psychoanalysis: as symbol, as pedagogic device, as seductive gadget. The (private) impulse to acquire, derivative from one aspect of the father-complex, the desire to have all the women, was overshadowed and overtaken by another aspect of that same complex, the (public) impulse to spend, to dispense largesse to his family, followers and readers. In this sense Freud's collections were a natural history of civilization, constructed in the same spirit of self-serving public service that other nineteenth-century scientific collectors envisaged. In Britain in the mid-nineteenth century, one or two individuals would act as centralized exchanges, correspondence-network organizers, for collections of objects, such as butterflies, flowers, orchids, sea-fish.[51] Participants would send in specimens collected locally, and would receive in return, via the central communication system, excess specimens from other collectors in other parts of the country. In order to acquire, one had to give. And the scientific fruit or product of this market was the map of the flora and fauna of the British Isles. Freud's collections functioned like that. Potential followers instinctively knew that items for the collection, whether dreams, jokes or antiquities, were the appropriate gift for Professor Freud: the later editions of both *The Interpretation of Dreams* and *The Psychopathology of Everyday Life* are greatly expanded versions, filled out with these additional contributions to his scientific collections. The product of this centralized system of dream-specimen collection would be the cartography, the completed natural history of the mind.

Following Susan Stewart's fine analysis in her book *On Longing* (1984), we can see that Freud's objects (the antiques and texts) served both the functions of evoking the past, of entering into the nostalgic dimension of the souvenir, and of effacing the past, of building a new timeless world of the collection. Freud's collections embodied the principle of the souvenir and that of the collection, that is both the aesthetic of origin and presence, of restoration and provenance, and the aesthetic of collection, accumulation and exchange, with its indefinite seriality. His were souvenirs precisely because they did confer authenticity on the past and served the primary function of remembering – they were postcards from the past; they were souvenirs in the sense that they involved adventure and the danger and risk of discovery: think of Freud's identification with Heinrich Schliemann, the risk-loving entrepreneurial discoverer of the souvenir of all of Western culture, or of his identification with the conquistadors. Freud's objects were also souvenirs in that they infected him and his patients with the scenes they depicted, just as Stewart describes the souvenir magically bringing us back to the scene of its origin.

In a scrapbook, Stewart argues, 'the whole dissolves into parts, each of which refers metonymically to a context of origin or acquisition. . . . In contrast, each element within the collection is representative and works in combination toward the creation of a new whole that is the context of the collection itself. The spatial whole of the collection supersedes the individual narratives that "lie behind it".'[52] One might think that, in as much as Freud's collections were committed to the rediscovery of the past, they were more like a scrapbook than a museum gallery. But they were also items in a collection that denied history, that found a non-historical principle of ordering and classification: the theory of desire, libido and the drives, the inner logic of the passions – the ultimate time of the collection is the a-temporality of the unconscious.

Yet the model of the dream consistently subverts the model of permanence offered by the ancient statues in their cases, standing guard over desk and couch. Freud's analysis of the collection of screen memories revealed how memories are tendentious, how their function as witnesses is a false function, a false form of remembering instead of desiring. Where the souvenir exhorts memory, Freud's collections also exhort forgetting, the forgetting that will do away with repression, which is an inexpedient form of remembering. Freud's collections encourage us finally to forget the effects of the murder of Akhnaten, and of Moses, of Clytemnestra and of Laius. But whereas Winckelmann's pilgrimage to Rome, repeated so faithfully by Freud his epigone, would eventually lead to the 'tyranny of Greece over Germany', so well captured by Freud's collection of antiques and palpable in museum collections throughout the world, the aim of Freud's other collecting activities, in his psychoanalytic practice, was to render palpable, so as to *dissipate*, the tyranny of each individual's forgotten past. You enter the analyst's consulting room, and you bring a collection whose internal structure is then made visible as inherently tyrannical. And Freud's collectables, whether Athena or absurd dream, are not only derisory remnants of past cultures, but also objects beyond price, standing simultaneously outside monetary exchange systems and ready to enter into them. The dream will be revealed to be both what is most singular, eccentric and peculiar to you, and also as what is most ineluctably your heritage, your place in the exchange systems that presided over your birth and destiny and your value to others.

Freud offered his patients two different models of remembering and forgetting:[53] remembering as a means of disinterring the past so as to destroy it by finally releasing it into oblivion, and remembering as a means of preservation, a lucky chance amid the processes through which the past inexorably vanishes. In the language of the oldest instincts, there is forgetting as spitting out, as rendering utterly alien, an absolute form of forgetting; and then there is forgetting as digesting, incorporating, in which one remembers by becoming the thing remembered.[54] Freud's collection of antiques was used to tack between these two senses of remembering. The objects retrieved from the wreckage of Pompeii were only glimpses of a past irretrievably lost, although Freud and others like him – connoisseurs, antiquarians, museum curators – made every effort to preserve these objects, as they inevitably crumble into dust. They remind us that psychoanalysis is a cure made possible by means of the kind of remembering that makes forgetting possible.

But could not this process of preservation, Freud's patients would ask him, be in the end as destructive as the forgetting from which the torment of their neurotic symptoms arose? Might it not be more dangerous to dig up these forgotten objects than to let the sleeping dogs of Pompeii lie? No, Freud assured them: remembering would never result in their being overwhelmed by the evil impulses and desires from the past. The desire to be rid of present tormenting ideas would always mean that a victory over the past was assured. Digging up Pompeii, Freud implied, did not risk causing another eruption of Vesuvius.

Yet this answer is fundamentally disingenuous; the transference was the permanent reminder of the vitality of the volcanic forces slumbering in the patient's symptomatic forgetfulness. 'In view of the kind of matter we work with, it will never be possible to avoid little laboratory explosions',[55] he wrote to Jung when the erotic passions of both analyst and analysand were clearly getting out of hand; it is the word 'laboratory' that is consolatory here – the reassurance that psychoanalysis is only an experiment, not real life, and that the dark forces that are released in the course of psychoanalysis can be left behind, forgotten forever, when one leaves the couch. Yet the ambiguity, the ambivalence about forgetting and the permanence of the cultural achievement of remembering is left behind, with the 'exquisite Greek tear-jars and iridescent glass bowls and vases that gleamed in the dusk from the shelves of the cabinet'.

Freud's collection was undoubtedly his treasure. While he was alive, adding to it, it too remained alive; when he died it became a museum piece, with labels and attributions, and became subject to rules not applied to the other objects that had belonged to Freud. Yet it still remains true that the collection's principle of unity stems from its being a part of a larger museum, of memorabilia, of souvenirs, rather than of authentic antiquities. The collection has become a museum within a museum: a museum of precious ancient objects, within an ordinary house in Hampstead, full of ordinary *fin de siècle* Viennese objects, where a great man died. The contrast with the Sigmund Freud Haus at Berggasse 19 in Vienna clearly illustrates the peculiarity of this overlapping of two different styles of museum. In 1975, the time of my first visit, it was an apartment with bare walls, no furniture and a few glass cases with manuscripts and other minor memorabilia. It was dominated visually by blown-up-to-life-size photographs of how it once had been, photographs that stood in for all the objects that had been removed to London when the Freuds escaped from the Nazis. It had a derisible atmosphere, perhaps one deliberately induced to remind visitors of yet one more loss that the war had visited on Vienna; but it still prompted the thought that a museum of fake souvenirs is a fake museum – a screen museum, the Freudian might say. In London, however, we find a meticulously conserved milieu: the real furniture, the books, the little objects useful in everyday life and useless anywhere else, Freud's couch, his pen, the photographs of his dogs – yes, in his old age, after his cancer operations, he even began to collect dogs; and to remind us that this is truly the world of souvenirs, locked away in a cupboard upstairs there are his dentures and the dreadful prosthesis that served him for an upper jaw in his later years, visited and scrutinized by Professors of Dentistry and Cancer, writing histories of Freud's illness, operations and death, or histories of early twentieth-century treatments of the particular carcinoma Freud had been forced to live with. Yet within this perfect souvenir-world is a 'living' collection of antiques, ready to tour the world as Freud's collection, ready to be loaned to other museums for exhibitions on Umbrian bronzes, or early terracotta statuettes.

H.D. knew better than anyone what sort of collector Freud was. Once he had settled into his house in Hampstead in November 1938, she anonymously sought out and sent him those flowers that she alone knew were his favourites – gardenias, which reminded him of being in Rome. On the accompanying card she scribbled 'To greet the return of the Gods'. This meant, in their private language, the settling in of his collection of antiques. Freud wrote her the following note:

Dear H.D.,
   I got to-day some flowers. By chance or intention they are my favourite flowers, those I most admire. Some words 'to greet the return of the Gods' (other people read: Goods). No name. I suspect you to be responsible for the gift. If I have guessed right don't answer but accept my hearty thanks for so charming a gesture. In any case,

affectionately yours,
Sigm. Freud[56]

Flowers were the quintessential gift. Freud's favourite flowers were the quintessential gift that this intimately attuned patient of his could give him. And she and he had already remarked on the closeness in English between the words 'Gods' and 'Goods'. Goods meant to them what is exchanged, and also what is highest, most ethical, and aesthetically pure. And this anonymous gift then provoked an elegant thankyou that pretended to preserve her anonymity. In other words, he will never know for sure whether she was the giver or not. But in assuming it, and thanking her, he continued the exchange that the play on words between Gods and Goods opened up. For Freud, if for no one else, the treasures were continuous with the everyday life of analysis, were potentially exchangeable as gifts or for money; they were something more than goods, but not quite gods. They did not strive for a timelessness beyond the world of goods. In 1938 in Vienna Freud did not utter one cry of despair or complaint at the prospect of losing his whole collection; it never occurred to him that he might die with his treasure rather than part from it. It was not a *priceless* collection in the sense of being beyond financial calculation – which makes of the economic the only possible measure of value – but priceless in the sense that it did not matter very much whether a monetary value was attached to it or not. Yet again, Freud would have appreciated Marx's description of money as 'the god among commodities . . . it represents the divine existence of commodities, while they represent its earthly form'.[57] But he also knew that if certain objects, certain 'commodities', become gods, they can only do so by retaining their dynamic relationship to more earthly objects. Without the presence of measure and exchange, Marx wrote, 'accumulating [treasure] is nothing more than the accumulation of gold and silver, not of money'.[58] We might apply this dictum to Freud in the following way: without the dynamic relationship between his collection of antiquities and his psychoanalytical work, the antiquities would simply have been a collection of old objects, things neither of historical nor personal value.

The amicably intimate wordplay between 'gods' and 'goods' by Freud and his gifted patient reminds us of one further dimension of Freud's collecting activities: the manner in which the collections mediated between the Jewish and non-Jewish cultural heritage. By definition, or rather by biblical edict, Freud's gods could not be Jewish gods. No Jew can make a collection of material objects without knowing that these are profanities, false gods, marks of the alien cultures outside the mental and physical space granted to the Chosen People. Quite selfconsciously, in 1897 Freud began a collection of Jewish anecdotes, almost as a deliberate counterpart to his collection of pagan and Gentile antiquities; there certainly could be no collection of Jewish antiquities. The Jew and his goods – this is the cultural image that neither H.D. nor Freud could, in 1938, readily forget; instead H.D. welcomed the arrival of the Jew and his gods. Freud did not pass up the opportunity to underline the ambiguous function of his collection of pagan and Gentile art, the symbol of his participation in the non-Jewish universal history of Enlightenment. And his refusal to forget allows us to underline, finally, that his collection of jokes, alongside the equally textual, some have said Talmudic,[59] collections of dreams and slips, allowed yet one more assimilation of the Jewish culture of the immaterial word.

Many men who have devoted their lives to making money have ended up wishing for the form of immortality that a public collection of priceless goods confers. Freud was neither a man who devoted his life to making money nor someone whose artistic collection would earn him immortality. But he may well have had the desire for immortality that the act of collecting so often embodies – and Freud's collection of dreams is certainly his guarantee of immortality. For some, like the mythical figure who buys the only extant second example of his first edition in order to burn it, recognizing the necessary incompleteness of every collection is the kiss of death to their fantasy of mastery; for others, to complete a collection is the end of a life's work, so they continually postpone acquiring that 'final' object. Many different collectors, wealthy or not, find in their collections a means of jousting with death. Yet Freud and the Annenbergs, the Mellons, the Thyssens of our age might share something in common: the desire to free a space in which money, while not excluded, does not rule. We know that psychoanalysis obeys the law of the market. And it is possible that regulating dreams according to that market may pull them away entirely from their function as souvenirs towards their function as items in a collection. Yet Freud wished to establish dreams, jokes, symptoms, and their material symbol, his collection of antiquities, as emblematic of a shared and universal humanity, neither economic, nor quite aesthetic or ethical. For many of these rich men mentioned above, collecting functions as a nostalgic vestige of a pre-abstract, pre-monetary relation to the object. The collection is an attempt to restore such a non-arbitrary, non-accidental relation, although the means by which this is achieved, through money, defeats precisely this aim. Yet the objects, the items in the collection, represent this hope through their not being money, through their being objects organized in a classification that is not that of number and abstract exchange, whether the principle of unification and distribution is that of Impressionist paintings, Egyptian scarabs, stamps or women. Each of these collections represents an attempt at withdrawal from the public discourse of the market, and an attempt to find a local shelter from that discourse in the scent of the harem, whose charm is always that of intimacy restrained by seriality, and seriality infused with intimacy.[60]

Freud's collection certainly partakes of this ideal, yet it appeals to science – whether archaeology or psychology – as the ground of this ideal. This does not mean that discovering the particular eccentricities of a collection – whether it be the sensual avarice of Don Juan or the ascetic moderation and imperial completeness of Darwin's collection of barnacles – reveals the ideal as hollow or self-deceiving. Rather, it shows us the genealogy of the scientific or analytic ideal. Clearing the space, the space of analysis, for dreams and jokes was for Freud first and foremost a scientific task: his collection was to rank alongside that of Linnaeus or of Darwin. And it may well be the spirit of 'scientific' acquisition pervading Freud's collections that will continue to dissuade us from aligning Freud more closely to ethical naturalists such as Montaigne and Nietzsche, as we are often tempted to do, than with those empirical scientists who always remained his models. In the end, his collection of antiquities was clearly more commonplace, despite its personal and private character, than his public collections of cases, dreams and jokes.

There was one personal dream that, throughout his adult life, Freud said resisted all his attempts at analysis: Freud

was standing before the gates of a beer garden, supported in some way by statues, but he could not get in and had to turn back. Freud told the princess [Marie Bonaparte] that actually he had once visited Padua with his brother and had been unable to enter the grottos behind a very similar gateway. Years later, when he returned to Padua, he had recognized the place as the one in his dream, and this time he had managed to see the grottos. Now, he added, every time he found himself unable to unriddle an enigma, he would dream this dream again.[61]

The superficially wishfulfilling meaning of the dream appears clear, whatever the enigma of its depths: Freud would dream of the locked gates because he had, by a fortunate accident, gained access to the grottoes guarded by the statues. The wish was surely that a similar fortunate accident would once again grant him such access. Being granted access to a place that we have visited before, but do not recognize in our dreams: this is the scene of the uncanny, as Freud himself analysed it in his paper on that theme. And the place that we have visited before but will not allow ourselves to recognize on this second visit is the mother's womb. There is a clear resonance with the only dream, a nightmare, that Freud recorded from his own childhood:

I saw *my beloved mother, with a peculiarly peaceful, sleeping expression on her features, being carried into the room by two (or three) people with birds' beaks and laid upon the bed.* I awoke in tears and screaming, and interrupted my parents' sleep.[62]

The figures with birds' beaks were recognized by Freud as taken from a book his family owned, the Philippson Bible, pictures of gods from an ancient Egyptian funerary relief. The dream, he decided, fulfilled the wish that he might make his mother his own. Every problem that Freud confronted, then, took on the same character: a riddle of the Egyptian Sphinx that this new Oedipus must answer, whose solution would allow him to take possession of the mysterious space over which, like the gods

Falcon-headed 'Egyptian' wooden figure, a 19th-century fake
in Freud's collection (no. 3124).

in his collection arrayed silently on his desk, the statues stood guard. Every piece or item in each of his collections thus represented a paternal figure standing guard over the mysterious feminine. And every successful act of analysis of them represented an Oedipal victory. Perhaps Freud regarded this dream as resisting analysis because it hinted that successful analysis was only a matter of good luck, just as many collectors regard their most precious piece as the one that came to them by way of the most fortuitous, casual and unlikely encounter.

Collecting Paris

NAOMI SCHOR

The body of postcards that I want to explore in this essay constitutes what we might call the *discourse of the metropolis,* understood here both as the urban centre of a country (France) where the opposition between the capital and the so-called provinces is particularly marked, and as the seat of a colonizing power in full expansion. I want to examine how in the early part of this century Paris produced an iconography that was abundant, systematic and cheap, and offered its citizens (and proffered to the world) a representation of itself that served to legitimate in a euphoric mode its nationalistic and imperialist ambitions.

But before going on to consider these cards – many of which are culled from my own collection – I want to contextualize them: first, by considering the very act of collecting, and second, by considering some information about the postcard itself, with special reference to France.

COLLECTING

Among the nineteenth-century social types studied by Walter Benjamin, the collector occupies a privileged place: collecting, rather more than *flânerie,* is the activity that most closely approximates that of the author in that collecting and especially (though not exclusively) book-collecting involves the retrieval and ordering of things past; collecting provides the link between the bourgeois childhood evoked in *Berlin Childhood* and the adult project of *Das Passagen-Werk.*[1] In one of his most charming texts, a public lecture entitled 'Unpacking my Library', and subtitled 'A Talk about Book Collecting', Benjamin wrote: 'Every passion borders on the chaotic, but the collector's passion borders on the chaos of memories'.[2] Books, or any other objects collected by what Benjamin calls a 'genuine' or a 'real' collector ('U', pp. 59, 62), are treasure-houses of memories because each book-object evokes the precise memory of where it was acquired and under what conditions; further, each book evokes the original context in which it was housed. Unpacking his books as day fades into night, Benjamin is overcome by a Proustian rush of memories of places and people, many now lost to him forever:

Memories of the cities in which I found so many things: Riga, Naples, Munich, Danzig, Moscow, Florence, Basel, Paris; memories of Rosenthal's sumptuous rooms in Munich, of the Danzig Stockturm where the late Hans Rhaue was domiciled, of Sussengut's musty book cellar in North Berlin; memories of the rooms where those books had been housed, of my student's den in Munich, of my room in Bern, of the solitude of Iseltwald on the lake of Brienz, and finally of my boyhood room, the former location of only four or five of the several thousand volumes that are piled around me. ('U', p. 67)

Inevitably for Benjamin the memories evoked by his books return him to childhood, indeed to his mother. As he reaches the end of this addictive activity, unpacking, he comes to what is in fact the matrix of his entire collection, though as he admits they did not 'strictly speaking. . .belong in a book case at all: two albums with stick-in pictures which my mother had pasted in as a child and which I inherited. They are the seeds of a collection of children's books which is growing steadily even today, though no longer in my garden' ('U', p. 66). The mother's albums, the boy's room, these are the privileged originary instances Benjamin recovers on unpacking his library.[3]

Collecting, when it is not unpacking, is for Benjamin a form of psychotherapy, a healing anamnesis, a means of re-membering his fragmented past, of re-collecting a lost maternal presence, the plenitude of childhood — his mother's, his own. There is, in fact, a strong Oedipal motif at work in this seemingly light piece: just before he comes upon the maternal albums, Benjamin describes at some length two diametrically opposite experiences in the auction house, a positive one where he, an impecunious student, snaps up a bargain ignored by the more affluent bidders, and one he qualifies as negative. Yet here, too, Benjamin outsmarts the experts, so it is not his failure to acquire the desired book that marks the experience as negative; rather, it is the light it sheds on the workings of homosocial rivalry, on the mechanisms of mediated desire. In this second auction scene, worthy of Dostoyevski, the coveted book occupies the space of the female (maternal) object desired by two males, one clearly more powerful because better-off:

The collection of books that was offered was a miscellany in quality and subject matter, and only a number of rare works on occultism and natural philosophy were worthy of note. I bid for a number of them, but each time noticed a gentleman in the front row who seemed only to have waited for my bid to counter with his own, evidently prepared to top any offer. After this had been repeated several times, I gave up all hope of acquiring the book which I was most interested in that day. . . . Just as the item came up I had a brain wave. It was simple enough: since my bid was bound to give the item to *the other man*, I must not bid at all. I controlled myself and remained silent. What I had hoped for came about: no interest, no bid, and the book was put aside. I deemed it wise to let several days go by, and when I appeared on the premise after a week, I found the book in the secondhand department and benefited by the lack of interest when I acquired it. ('U', pp. 65–6)

Through self-control and cunning – 'collectors', he observes, 'are people with a tactical instinct' ('U', p. 63) – Benjamin wrests the object away from the threatening rival, but the Oedipal triangle has invaded the world of the book collector. That the book is feminine as well as maternal in Benjamin's theory of book collecting – and, as we shall see in a moment, collection-theory, such as it is, is shot through with sexual, indeed sexist metaphors – is confirmed by a striking orientalist analogy Benjamin employs to describe the collector's gesture of releasing a book from captivity:

One of the finest memories of a collector is the moment when he rescued a book to which he might never have given a thought, much less a wishful look, because he found it lonely and abandoned on the market place and bought it to give it its freedom – the way the prince bought a beautiful girl in *The Arabian Nights*. ('U', p. 64)

Whatever the memories evoked by his books, for Benjamin the activity of collecting is bound up with the act of rememoration, and that act is figured as profoundly magical. Thus in the envoi of this extended prose-poem Benjamin once more evokes the supernatural world of *The Arabian Nights*, except that in this teasingly obscure instance the container of the captive spirits, of the genii, is none other than the collector himself:

For inside him [the collector] there are spirits, or at least little genii, which have seen to it that for a collector – and I mean a real collector, a collector as he ought to be – ownership is the most intimate relationship one can have to objects. Not that they come alive in him; it is he who lives in them. So I have erected one of his dwellings, with books as the building stones, before you, and now he is going to disappear inside, as is only fitting. ('U', p. 67)

But does Benjamin's theory of collecting apply to all collections? Do all objects possess the same mnemonic properties as those with which Benjamin endows his beloved books? Are books a typical or a special case?

For the past few years I have collected postcards: I have purchased them at specialized postcard fairs, from private dealers, at flea markets; a few have been given to me as gifts. Unlike other objects I collect, for example a brightly coloured turn-of-the-century porcelain known as majolica, my postcards are not possessed of the magical mnemonic properties Benjamin attributes to his books. With the exception of one or two real finds in my collection – whose acquisition was marked by a particular feeling of triumph – I would be hard pressed to say how I came by a particular card. When I open my album or my storage boxes, time is not recaptured. How then am I to account for these cards' failure to produce memories, their mnemonic sterility? The answer is seemingly simple: postcards are organized in series, and their very seriality negates their individual mnemonic properties; what matters in the case of my postcard collection is not the contiguity between an individual card and the environment from which it was detached; rather it is the contiguity I restore between a single card and its immediate predecessor and follower in a series I am attempting to reconstitute, or the contiguity I create between cards linked by some common theme. The metonymy of origin is displaced here by a secondary metonymy, the artificial metonymy of the collection.

Benjamin was not entirely unaware of this secondary metonymy; it constitutes for him the antithesis of the chaos of memories in the dialectics of collecting: 'there is in the life of a collector a dialectical tension between the poles of disorder and order', he notes ('U', p. 60). The pole of order is represented for Benjamin by the catalogue, which imposes seriality on the random purchases of the book collector.

Benjamin's dialectical scheme points to a possible explanation for the inapplicability of Benjamin's theory to my postcard collection: his confusion or failure to distinguish between what Susan Stewart has described as the souvenir and the collection, two closely linked but radically different assemblages of objects. According to Stewart, then, Benjamin's books function more as souvenirs than as parts of a collection. The souvenir 'speaks to a context of origin through a language of longing, for it is not an object arising out of need or use value; it is an object arising out of the necessarily insatiable demands of nostalgia'.[4] The souvenir serves to 'authenticate a past or otherwise remote experience' (*OL*, p. 139). There are, of course, important differences between Benjamin's books and the typical souvenirs Stewart has in mind – antiques, exotic objects, replicas of the Eiffel Tower or the Liberty Bell – and yet there is an interesting convergence in a sub-category of the souvenir, 'souvenirs of individual experience', which include 'scrapbooks, memory quilts, photo albums, and baby books' (*OL*, p. 139). The childhood albums of Benjamin's mother, while not composed of personal memorabilia, hover on the limit, and as the original books in Benjamin's library, the books of origins, decisively inflect his collection in the direction of the personal, the originary, the unique, the auratic. They serve as the authenticating, naturalizing ground for his later acquisitions; they draw his collection like a vortex into the past, into a nostalgic longing for a missing maternal presence.

According to Stewart's paradigmatic opposition, Benjamin's collection is not in fact a collection, but a collection of souvenirs. His library *qua* souvenir overrides and very nearly cancels out its nature as a collection. What then defines the collection? It is, as we have already seen, seriality. What distinguishes the collection from the souvenir is that a collection is composed of objects wrenched out of their contexts of origins and reconfigured into the self-contained, self-referential context of the collection itself, and 'this context destroys the context of origin' (*OL*, p. 165). In a parallel opposition of re-presentation and collecting, Dean MacCannell observes: 'The idea behind a *collection* is to bring together and catalogue diverse examples of a type of object: Eskimo snowshoes, oil paintings, African masks. There is no effort to rebuild a natural, cultural or historical totality. Order is superimposed by an arbitrary scheme like the Dewey decimal system. Whereas re-presentations demand identification, collections require an esthetic.'[5]

Clearly, in both MacCannell's and Stewart's shared system of values, the collection is far more reprehensible than the souvenir, hence Stewart's eloquent title heading: 'The Collection, Paradise of Consumption'. For in her terms, the collection not only represents the destruction of an originary context connoted as natural; by the same gesture, the erasure of all traces of the process of production, it wipes out both labour and history: 'In the souvenir, the object is made magical; in the collection, the mode of production is made magical' (*OL*, p. 165).

Stewart shares with Jean Baudrillard, on whom she draws, a judgemental discourse on collecting; for both, collection is a degraded form of consumption, but whereas Stewart's collector is a possessive bourgeois subject of late capitalism, Baudrillard's is a misfit who would be at home in Freud's Vienna, perhaps even in Freud's cabinet of antiquities. Whereas Stewart's analysis of the collection is predominantly Marxist, Baudrillard's analysis of the collection passion is heavily psychoanalytic: collecting is a regressive (anal) activity with strong narcissistic and fetishistic traits; in this discourse, to collect is to deny not so much labour and history as death and castration. Unlike Benjamin's collector, who is merely childlike, and Stewart's, who is a late capitalist consumer,

Baudrillard's is a neurotic: unable to cope with the struggles of intersubjectivity, Baudrillard's collector prefers to seek out instead the specular satisfactions afforded by inert objects (or domesticated animals); unable to deal with the irreversibility of time and the death it inevitably entails, the collector conjures them by living in a sort of collector's time, a time out of time; unable to desire others in their totality, the collector – and collecting here is viewed as a sort of poor, or rather rich, man's fetishism – invests part objects with a largely sexual desire.

Before coming to what I consider most valuable in Baudrillard's psychology of collecting, I must comment on the extraordinary sexism of his analysis. In fact the two aspects of his argument are intimately linked. For Baudrillard the collector – like the fetishist or the anal compulsive with whom he shares certain traits – is unquestionably male: thus Baudrillard compares the particular pleasure the collector experiences with the pleasures of the harem: 'Master of a secret seraglio, man is never more so than when surrounded by his objects.'[6] The paradigmatic collector – as in the novel by the same name – is a man whose extreme castration anxiety leads him to a pathological need to sequester the love object or loved objects: 'What does the sequestered object represent? . . . If one lends neither one's car, nor one's pen, nor one's wife, it is because from the perspective of jealousy these objects are narcissistic equivalents of the ego: if this object is lost, if it is damaged, it's castration. One does not lend one's phallus, that's the heart of the matter' (*SO*, p. 139). Lacking the phallus, women, at least implicitly, cannot in Baudrillard's analysis collect.

Both Stewart's genderless and Baudrillard's insistently phallocentric theorization of collecting point up the need to think through the incidence of gender on collection and its theories. To do so it would be necessary to open up once again the vexed question of female fetishism, for as Emily Apter has recently argued, in the nineteenth-century French novel, collecting is the feminine form of fetishism par excellence;[7] furthermore, as she also demonstrates, in the extreme case of erotomania, the secure boundary between the male collector and the female collectible is dislocated, as the prostitute-collectable and the collector-client change places.[8]

And yet, for all their offensive phallocentrism, Baudrillard's sexual analogies do yield a crucial insight into the psychology of the collector, whether male or female: cast as an insatiable Don Juan or a master of the harem, Baudrillard's collector values objects only in that they can be inscribed into a series. Seriality is the crucial motivating factor of the true collector; even those collectors who are driven by the quest for the rare object are motivated by an intense awareness of the series. In this insistence on seriality Baudrillard remains of course profoundly structuralist; the pleasure of collecting is the pleasure of difference, as much as it is of an illusory completion and reassuring lack. To give pleasure, the collector's object of desire must implicitly refer to a series. At the same time, to perform its other psychic regulatory functions – and for Baudrillard collecting performs the same homeostatic functions as dreaming – the series must always remain open, for lack is the guarantor of life: to complete the series is to die.

Denied, forgotten, destroyed, [or] potential, the series is always there. In the humblest of everyday objects just as in the most transcendent of rare objects, it feeds the sense of ownership or the game of passion. Without it no game would be possible, thus no possession either and properly speaking, no object. The truly unique object, one that is absolute, without antecedent, without dispersion in a series – whatever series – is unthinkable. No more than a pure sound, it does not exist. (*SO*, p. 131)

TOPOGRAPHICALS

A frequent theme in books about postcard collecting is the bewilderment of the novice when confronted with the multiplicity of categories into which postcards are by convention divided. 'Newcomers to the postcard collecting scene are always puzzled about what to collect and how to go about starting . . .', writes one author.[9] The lists of categories arrayed before the fledgling collector read like some Borgesian encyclopaedia entry gone wild, because, in the words of one of its historians, 'Postcards have shown, and continue to show it all. . . . In a sense . . . this world of ours is a mosaic with each piece of the puzzle having its postcard representation.'[10]

Clearly, part of the pleasure of the postcard collector consists in the crisscrossing of categorical boundaries, the revelling in the jarring juxtapositions characteristic of the postcard album:

North, south, east, or west. Brown skin, yellow skin, red, or white. Rich, poor. Laborer, president, king. Bedouin tribesman. Sunshine, snow, hurricane, volcanic activity. Beaches, palaces, grass huts. Politics, war, social history. Holidays and humor. Street scenes and pastures. And always, always more. (*PC*, p. 137)

The problem posed by the endless proliferation of categories – the postcard world awaits its Linnaeus – is further complicated by the existence of multicategorical cards:

Many a dealer has been faced with the poser of where to put what when confronted with a postcard with a post office in the foreground, a railway station which can just be glimpsed in back, and a reasonable view of a train travelling down the middle. So a choice has to be made between three different classifications. (*CP*, p. 27)

The new collector is generally advised that the only way to orient him- or herself in this categorial or thematic maze is to zero in on a single theme or category, preferably topographicals or view cards – the largest and most popular category of postcards – representing familiar places: 'The soundest advice to beginners is to concentrate on collecting views relating to the areas in which they live and work. From this modest base there will soon emerge a very wide choice of themes to suit individual tastes' (*CP*, p. 28). One's place of origin or the sites of one's daily life provide, then, the best foundation on which to build a postcard collection. Postcard collecting implies, at least at the outset, a sense of identity strongly rooted in a specific place, a home. When postcard vendors exhibit their wares at different locations they tend to cater to local collectors' interests and tastes: trays and trays of postcards of New England villages at New England fairs and flea markets; trays and trays of postcards of Paris by *arrondissement* in Paris. Indeed, as one postcard historian notes, the craze for collecting hometown topographicals is particularly pronounced in France, where the topographical is the dominant category, a situation deeply bound up with the French sense of the *terroir*, of a national identity rooted in a specific place of origin. Some French collectors, especially of Parisian postcards, are even said to push their sense of the local so far as to specialize in a single street, no doubt their own.[11]

Had I, as a new collector, followed this advice I should have begun by collecting cards of Providence, Rhode Island, where I worked and lived at the time I began my collection, or perhaps of New York, where I was born, raised, educated and employed until my mid-thirties. In truth neither possibility ever occurred to me; from the outset I was drawn to postcards of a place where I neither live nor work, France, and very quickly within France, Paris. This choice suggests the inadequacy of a model based strictly on an unexamined notion of one's place of birth, work, or daily life as grounding one's identity, what Biddy Martin and Chandra Talpade Mohanty call the 'unproblematic geographic location of home'.[12] This model cannot account for the possibility of a dislocation as constituting the foundation of one's being, or at any rate one's collecting, but as we have seen – for the collector – being and collecting are intimately related. In Martin and Mohanty's text, the 'illusion of home', or of at-homeness, is shattered by the realization that 'these buildings and streets witnessed and obscured particular race, class, and gender struggles'.[13] This is the postmodern, postcolonialist condition: what is at first experienced as a secure, identity-giving and sheltering space is revealed to be a place of bloody struggle and exclusion.

For me that uncanny home that is not home is Paris: but what is hidden there is a form of violence and racial struggle not generally understood today when the trinity of race, class and gender is invoked. I am speaking of anti-semitism, theirs not mine. Paris is the place that would have been my home but for the Holocaust. My parents, Polish Jews, left Poland in the late Thirties with the intention of settling in Paris. In June 1940, they and thousands of others fleeing Hitler's impending arrival left Paris and headed south. They were among the lucky ones: unlike Benjamin and the countless others who did not make it, they eventually crossed the border between France and Spain and finally settled in New York. French was my first language, and the language in which I was educated. In 1958 I visited Europe and Paris for the first time. Since then, as a professional student of the French language and culture I have been back often. Perhaps someday, I fantasize, I shall retire to Paris. For now I have chosen to write on Paris, in order to come to terms with a longing, a fascination, an ambivalence, unfinished business.

In Martin and Mohanty's superb reading of Minnie Bruce Pratt's autobiography, her sense of at-homeness is exploded by the realization that it is founded on the exclusion of others: blacks, Jews, members of the working classes. It is this realization that makes of her text an exemplary political narrative. But what if one discovers that one's sense of never being at home, one's sense of exile, is founded on a quite different disillusion: the realization that the longed-for home (that is, Paris) was in fact the place where those that were excluded were one's parents? My idealization of Paris (and France), fostered by my education and confirmed by my career, has for years blinded me to the realization not of my, or my family's, guilty participation in mechanisms of exclusion based on race – of course, being excluded does not prevent one from excluding – but – and this realization is equally devastating – of my wilful denial of the hideous historical realities of French collaboration in the genocide of my 'race'. Let me be quite clear on this point: my realization was not of the Holocaust in general, but of the fact that some of the same people who sell me baguettes and croissants today, or their parents, would 50 years ago have happily shipped my parents off to Drancy. Today they vote for Le Pen. And I collect postcards of belle époque Paris.

As predicted in the how-to books, my collection of French, then Parisian, postcards eventually took shape, became more focused, more specialized. As I sifted through box after box of cards, I began to notice one particular series of view-cards of Paris that stood out from the rest: those bearing the mark 'LL'. Writing of 'the enigmatic Frenchman who merely describes himself as L.L.', Dûval notes:

L.L. was a bit of a 'Scarlet Pimpernel'. His globe-trotting activities took him and his camera to many places foreign to his native shores with no one quite knowing where or when he would turn up next. But such is the clarity and sparkling animation of his work, it is instantly recognizable even before those tell-tale initials have been sighted. And how those initials have tantalized the devotees of the work of L.L. So frustrated was one collector he dubbed them to mean 'Little and Large' and so ended the speculation as far as he was concerned. (*CP*, p. 31)

The information about LL is sketchy at best. What appears established today is that LL stands for the Lévy brothers, Lucien and Ernest, sons of J. Georges Lévy, and that the Maison Lévy et Ses Fils was winning gold medals for its photographs as far back as the Exposition Universelle of 1855.[14] It is also known that sometime around 1919 LL merged with one of, if not *the* major producer of postcards of Paris and LL's chief competitor, Neurdein Frères (ND), which means that between them Lévy-Neurdein produced several thousands of views of Paris. LL advertisements, printed in professional journals or on promotional postcards, boast of the exhaustiveness as well as the quality of their views, not only of France but of major international cities. And indeed those distinctive initials, which function as a sort of modernist logo, turn up on all manner of cards, including many of those included in Malek Alloula's *The Colonial Harem*.[15]

However far one may pursue this line of research, it is unlikely that one would ever completely clear up the enigma of those initials, because manifestly, as in any large-scale documentary project, LL stands less for a personal signature than for a protocol that can be carried out repeatedly and everywhere by any number of anonymous executants. The initials LL guarantee a certain uniformity of the products that bear its trademark. There is an LL look, and it is precisely this distinctive look, the LL way of framing and segmenting turn-of-the-century Parisian urban reality, that interests me rather than the promotion of LL as *auteur(s)*.[16]

INVENTING THE POSTCARD

Though the first official postcard was printed by the Austrian Government in 1869, and the postcard industry continued to grow steadily throughout the late nineteenth century, it is not really until the turn of the century that the postcard developed into the mass means of communication and object of enthusiastic and cross-class collection it was to become in the period up to and including the First World War, generally considered the postcard's golden age. Not surprisingly, and for a number of reasons, the new mode of communication is associated with the feminine. Thus James Douglas affirms peremptorily in 1907: 'The Postcard has always been a feminine vice. Men do not write Postcards to each other. When a woman has time to waste, she writes a letter, when she has no time to waste, she writes a postcard.'[17] The association of femininity with postcard writing lends weight to the continuist school of postcard historians (Staff, for example), for what we have here is a transfer of the traditional association of femininity with letter-writing to a new mode of written communication, further reinforced by the association of the feminine with the trivial, the picturesque, the ephemeral. But the association of the feminine and the postcard exceeds the traditional link between women and letters, for unlike the letter, the postcard is not just a means of communication; it is also an object of collection, and this collecting activity secures the feminization of the postcard in the mind of its early commentators, such as the author of an article of 1899 in *The Standard*:

The illustrated postcard craze, like the influenza, has spread to these islands from the Continent, where it has been raging with considerable severity. Sporadic cases have even occurred in Britain. Young ladies who have escaped the philatelic infection or wearied of collecting Christmas cards, have been known to fill albums with missives of this kind received from friends abroad. (quoted in *PP*, p. 60)

Nor is this gendering of the postcard collection mania uniquely British. In 1900 we find the following observations in the advice column of *La Femme chez elle*: 'A very feminine collection which has grown enormously in recent years is that of illustrated postcards. . . . Recently a veritable commerce of polite remarks and courtesies between young men and women has been established due to postcards. This pastime does not lack charm; for a well brought up young lady with a staunch heart and a cultivated mind, it provides thousands of ways of demonstrating her tact and savoir-faire.'[18] If, as we saw earlier, collection is generally theorized as a masculine activity, the postcard constitutes an interesting exception to these laws of gendering: it is the very example of the feminine collectable.

Throughout the formative stage of the postcard industry, which by the turn of the century had developed into a major economic sector employing some 30,000 people in France alone,[19] various changes took place that were to contribute to its immense popularity. These include the legislation of private as opposed to government-controlled production (1894), the lowering of postage rates, and the widespread dissemination of new reproductive techniques (notably *phototypie*). Perhaps no change was more momentous in its consequences than the crucial move to divide the postcard's back, which occurred in 1902 in Britain and 1903 in France. With the division of the card's back the hierarchic relationship between the two sides of the card was inverted; the recto became the verso: 'from 1904 on, the address side, which was still called recto, will be authorized to carry a message on half its surface. Little by little, it is no longer what one writes which is primary but the illustration, and following common practice it is this side which will henceforth be referred to as the recto, the message side coming to occupy second place and to be called verso'.[20] The gradual promotion of the iconic face of the illustrated postcard to primacy can be considered a sign of the rise of the culture of the image; it does not, however, signify that the message side of the card is of any lesser interest.[21]

In Europe no single event contributed more to popularizing the picture postcard than the series of World's Fairs and Expositions that were such landmark events during the latter half of the nineteenth century. The real beginnings of the picture postcard in France are generally thought to be the centennial exhibit of 1889 in Paris, where the Figaro-produced postcards (known as 'Libonis') of the Eiffel Tower could be purchased and mailed on the spot. It is really the World's Fair of 1900 that inaugurates the age of the postcard in France.

One can scarcely exaggerate the significance of the Universal Exposition of 1900 in providing a catalyst for the development of an indigenous French postcard industry. What needs to be considered here is the significance of the link between this event and the mass production and dissemination of the pictorial postcard, especially as it represented Paris. What many historians of the postcard neglect to bring out is that the coupling of the popularization of the picture postcard and these spectacular events confirms not only the postcard's democratic vocation but also its less attractive penchant for propaganda and nationalistic self-promotion. And more so than in any other country, to promote the nation in France is to promote its capital, and vice versa. For it is impossible to speak of this Exposition without taking account of a simple, but crucial fact: beyond the numerous exhibits of exotic foreign and regional native cultures and artefacts, what people came to see – and they came in their millions (51 million visitors is the number now cited) from all parts of France and the world – was Paris itself. The chief display of the Expo of 1900 was Paris, a Paris fully recovered from the three traumatic events that had blighted earlier fairs: the triple traumas of Haussmannization, the Siege of Paris and the Commune, and in a different way, the Dreyfus Affair, which had seriously weakened France's self-aggrandizing claim to being a world-class fount of justice and human rights.

Visitors to the Expo of 1900 were greeted at the main gate by an immense piece of kitsch statuary: a controversial piece called *La Parisienne*, which broke with the tradition of allegorical female statuary: 'The City of Paris welcoming its guests has been personified not by a Greek or Roman lady in classical drapery but by a Parisian woman dressed in the latest fashion.'[22] Continuing this emphasis on Paris, the Exposition grounds boasted (in addition to the building representing contemporary Paris) a reconstituted medieval Paris, as though the Paris of Hugo's *Notre-Dame de Paris* had to be placed *en abyme* as a sort of foil for the new Paris that was being displayed and celebrated all around it. And finally, there was the high point of the fair, the Rue de Paris, extending from the Invalides bridge to the Alma bridge, a street representing the entertainments available in the city of light.

To celebrate Paris was to assert French national identity, to the exclusion of France's other cities, as well as to reaffirm its claim to being not just the capital of France but of the so-called civilized world. As Paul Greenhalgh points out, what distinguished the French exhibitions and perhaps especially the event of 1900 was their nationalistic emphasis, in contrast with the more commercial character of the British and American productions. And this emphasis on Frenchness was inseparable from, indeed conveyed by, the emphasis on Paris: 'The obsession with the civilizing aspects of "Frenchness" led to a concentration of resources on events in Paris. . . . Paris was the show-piece which drained resources in order to tell the world what it was to be French, much to the annoyance of many other French cities and areas.'[23] The potent link between the rise of the postcard industry and the promotion of the nation and its capital are expressed with naïve enthusiasm by a contemporary journalist:

The triumph of the Post Card is once again the 1900 Exhibition. It was reproduced a thousand ways, embellished, overloaded with all the fantastic luxury of the most perfect bad taste: sites, types, unknown corners, overviews, costumes, perspectives, architecture, all topics, all points of view on the huge international exhibition were exhausted. Even the lightwork was imitated by sewing star-shaped beads onto the images. Despite the infantile aspect of these illustrations destined to dazzle simple souls, there is something touching about these processes. It is France they celebrate, that they make known and loved. . . . For my part I love these multicoloured paint-daubed squares of paper which naively radiate the childlike glory of the fatherland.[24]

THE POSTCARDING OF PARIS

As many commentators have pointed out, throughout the nineteenth century, but especially during its latter half, artists, writers, journalists and photographers were seized with the obsession to submit the entire social body to exhaustive scrutiny and record. It was, in Philippe Hamon's apt phrase, the 'age of the exposition': 'a panoptic and democratic obsession with transparency, display, openness, lighting, and free-flowing traffic (i.e. everyone can see everyone else) was thus established'.[25] As Dean MacCannell points out, this ideal of transparency is the essence of modernization, which he defines as 'the opening up and dramatization of every important social institution'.[26] And nowhere was this obsessive desire to expose and classify the real more active than in Paris, because as Daniel Oster and Jean Goulemot observe, the city's very heterogeneity inspires taxonomies: 'Diversity gives rise to inventories'; and further, 'Paris is a city one numbers [*numère*] and ennumerates [*énumère*].'[27] These inventories take the form of the famous *physiologies*, the equally famous *guides* (especially the *Paris-Guide* assembled for the 1867 World's Fair with contributions from the greatest contemporary writers), much of the works that comprise Balzac's 'Comédie Humaine' and Zola's 'Rougon-Macquart', Maxime Du Camp's multi-volume *Paris*, and many, many more. In fact, as Hamon acutely notes, in the case of Paris the taxonomic urge to systematically articulate and classify does not operate on a completely inchoate referent, for Paris is itself 'previously structured by authority' (*pouvoir*) – in the form of 'quarters', 'districts', 'aligned' streets or 'registered' landmarks.[28] There are, notes Hamon, twenty volumes in Zola's Rougon-Macquart series, just as there are twenty *arrondissements* in Paris! What we have, then, in the case of Paris is a layering effect, grid upon grid.

Haussmannization enhanced this 'pre-articulation' of the urban fabric by 'segmenting' the city into increasingly discrete and socio-economically homogeneous *quartiers*, whose express function it was to separate the classes, and whose perhaps unintended effect was to confine the working classes to isolated districts, cut off from the flow of urban life.[29]

Haussmannization widened not only the gulf between the *beaux quartiers* and the teeming ghettoes of the dangerous classes, but also, and this is of particular interest to me, the gap between the bourgeois spectator-*flâneur* and both the bourgeois woman and the worker whose access to metropolitan life was severely limited: 'It was the bourgeois who was most likely to be able to move from scene to scene; the worker whose lesser economic circumstances were more likely to confine him to a locale', writes Richard Sennett.[30] The ability to move from *quartier* to *quartier*, hence to adopt the all-seeing perspective of the taxonomist, was throughout much of the nineteenth century a privilege of class and gender, since as all agree there was no female equivalent to the *flâneur*; in Janet Wolff's apt phrase, the 'flâneuse' was 'invisible', unthinkable.[31] Whatever it is that the LL initials hide, I would be most surprised to discover that any member of the LL team was a woman or a worker. The postcarding of Paris then participates in, indeed spectacularly carries forward into the twentieth century, the nineteenth-century representation of Paris as made up of ever more finely fragmented coequal visual units, and that representation is bound up with the marking of differences along class and gender lines. Yet, at the same time, it must be noted, some of these postcards also attest to the breakdown of these systems of segregation inherent in modernity: several highly popular series of postcards are devoted to a small group of women (often fallen aristocrats) who symbolize the coming of a new age of female urban mobility: the women coach-drivers, the secular goddesses of *nouveau* Paris.

The postcarding of Paris was an immense enterprise: the chief series on Paris (Tout Paris, Gondry, ND, LL, FF, CM) produced, as far as I can make out, something like 10,000 views of the city, and to this we must add many smaller series, such as those on the *petits métiers* or on sports. There are cards covering every aspect of Parisian life: its small crafts (ragpicker, umbrella salesman, dog-shaver, mattress-maker), its markets (Halles) and slaughterhouses (Villette), its bizarre characters (Bibi *la purée*, the shoe-shiner; E. Guenon, the human telegraph; MacNorton, the human aquarium; G. Ménart, the ratcatcher; M. Rémond, the walker on water in the Bois de Boulogne), its fires and floods (notably that of 1910), its strikes and demonstrations, on the one hand; its glitzy social events (the races, visiting royalty), beautifully manicured gardens, fine shops, and spectacular public monuments, on the other. In the most extensive series each number corresponds to a particular view, and major sites are photographed from every conceivable angle: the Madeleine is viewed frontally at close range, from midway down the rue Royale, and

Paris Nouveau – nos jolies cochères.

L'Arc-de-Triomphe et les Champs-Elysées.

from as far as the Place de la Concorde; each gargoyle on Notre-Dame's towers has its slot.[32]

Produced during what was clearly experienced by contemporaries as a transitional moment, the postcards record both the vanishing *vieux* Paris and the emerging *nouveau* Paris, or Paris *moderne*.[33] And yet I would argue that despite the great diversity of *belle époque* Paris postcards, which defy easy generalizations, the LL series most accurately represents the dominant discourse on Paris produced by Paris in the first decade of the twentieth century, a discourse clearly inflected by a politics of class, civic and national privilege. When subjected to close scrutiny, the series is in fact highly selective in its representation of the city. And this selectivity, or lack of exhaustiveness, is typical of Paris postcards in general even to this day. The *arrondissements*, for example, are not all equally well represented. Gérard Neudin, in his authoritative guide, lists among the well-represented *arrondissements* the first, fifth, sixth, seventh, eighth and ninth, which means that all the others, which include both the high-bourgeois sixteenth and seventeenth as well as the more working-class eighteenth and nineteenth – residential areas unlikely to be visited by tourists – are under-represented.

The vision produced by many of these cards is that of a prosperous city bustling with commercial and leisure activities, a remarkably beautiful city miraculously free of unsightly slums and disfiguring poverty, a place where people throng the broad avenues and boulevards, or are strangely absent from museum interiors, but a city where no one is ever caught working. In short, the Paris of the postcard of 1900 is a highly idealized Paris, the home of a triumphant middle class, and in this it is no different from its Edwardian counterparts, for, as Dûval notes, 'it is difficult to find postcards showing views of the less salubrious areas in which the majority of people lived. Professional photographers tended to concentrate on the more aesthetic aspects of what was fashionable and picturesque rather than record the grimy drear of the back streets' (*CP*, p. 33).

Not surprisingly, given this decidedly bourgeois emphasis, the very centre of LL's Paris has shifted away from the traditional centre of the Ile de la Cité. As against Notre-Dame, the ground zero of an earlier Parisian self-representation and panoramic totalization – Hugo's famous circular sweep from the towers of Notre-Dame – the inaugural card in the series ratifies the shift to the west and the upper-class neighbourhoods brought about by Haussmann: it represents l'Arc de Triomphe. An overwhelming number of cards represent the great sights of the right bank: the Arch, the

Champs-Elysées, the Bois, the Madeleine, the Parc Monceau, the Opéra. For though LL is primarily a recorder of facades, certain cards record in great detail the interiors of such monuments as Notre-Dame, the Opéra, the Panthéon and, most uncannily, the Louvre and other museums.

If what fascinates in the colonies, as well as in the more exotic regions of France, is the quaintness of dying traditional societies with their beautiful costumes, strange rituals and other emblems of auratic cultures, what is conveyed by views of Paris *c.* 1900 is the thrill of modernization. The Paris of LL is not the Paris of Eugène Atget (the author of the 80-card series 'Petits Métiers de Paris'), a Paris of eerily deserted back streets and melancholic fountains. Rather, it is a Paris proud of its glorious past but enamoured of the present. Everywhere are the icons of modernization: trains, buses, passenger cars, and even planes flying incongrously low. It is not unusual in these resolutely modernist cards to find the emblems of progress piled one on top of the other: a flotilla of omnibuses parked near the Métro entrance in front of a train station, a plane flying over the Eiffel Tower while a *péniche* sails by, and so on.

Perspective is crucial to the effect produced by these artfully constructed views. The camera is almost never positioned at ground level; rather, it hovers somewhere slightly above, so that the viewer dominates the scene. Major monuments often serve as vanishing points, which has the effect of diminishing their intrinsic interest – they are at best hazy vertical forms in the distance – while heightening the sense of rational urban planning. Symmetry further contributes to a reassuring sense of balance and harmony, even when, as is sometimes the case, all the people seem to be walking down one side of the avenue or street.

Here and there a detail of street life arrests one's glance in the manner of the Barthesian *punctum*, and the street scene is the universe of the *punctum*: a man checks his fly as he leaves a public urinal, a dapper walker lifts his cane in the air as he prepares to cross the street, two coachmen chat during a traffic jam in the Bois, a man seated on a bench in front of the Grand Palais tips his straw hat to an invisible person beyond the borders of the card, a horse-drawn cart piled high with hay crosses a tram while a man – perhaps suffering from hay-fever – passes by blowing his nose.

Above all, LL's Paris, more so than that of any of LL's competitors, is a Paris suffused with a warm and radiant light: in contrast with other series, which often go in for Monet-like variations on Paris in the rain, Paris in the snow, Paris at dusk and Paris by night, it is – or at least it seems to be – always high noon in LL's views of Paris. This euphoric

Gare de l'Est – Entrée du Métropolitain.

Rue Jean-François Lépine.

777 PARIS. — La Tour Eiffel. — LL.

La Tour Eiffel.

luminosity is, of course, an effect produced by technical advances in the field of photographic reproduction, notably the process invented by one Tessié du Motay, known as *phototypie*, which enables the cheap reproduction of photographs with, in the words of one historian, their 'values of shadow and light, going from deep black to pure white and including all the shades of grey'.[34] But it is also a key element in LL's grammar of representation.

And this brings us to what is finally for me a central issue, since it is precisely what is almost always left unaccounted for, namely the extraordinary pleasure produced by viewing these cards, *le plaisir de la carte*. Unquestionably that pleasure is complex: part visual (these cards are very beautiful), part cognitive (these cards contain a great deal of

Le Théâtre du Gymnase et le Boulevard Bonne-Nouvelle.

Le Faubourg du Temple.

information), above all, the *plaisir de la carte* is nostalgic. As Staff observes, there is something essentially Proustian about early picture postcards:

Today, when an Edwardian picture postcard is held in the hand, time for the moment is captured; for the picture is not just a reproduction or copy such as can be seen in a book, but is an actual representation of that time, and is something belonging to those years. (*PP*, p. 71)

This is a crucial insight: what we have here is not simply a representation of Paris, but a fragment of past Parisian life. The postcards we hold in our hands and file away in our albums are the same cards as those we can see represented on postcards of postcard displays; they create, however tenuously, a direct link between the viewer and the viewed. The complex and shifting reality that was Paris at the turn of the century is here reduced to a series of discrete units that can be easily manipulated and readily consumed.

CODA: BENJAMIN'S PARIS

After the golden age of the postcard came its decadence. The quality of the images declined, the craze for postcard collecting waned, and albums formerly displayed on the living-room were relegated to the attic. The comparison between the sparkling, richly detailed view-cards of the first decade of the century and the muddy sepia-coloured view-cards of the Thirties provides striking and highly legible information about the shift in urban self-representation from the pre-war period to the Depression years. There is more going on here than a mere decline in the quality of reproduction; the discourse produced by these cards is shot through and through with a melancholic nostalgia that the future-oriented World's Fair of 1937 and its multifarious glossy black-and-white postcards cannot offset. And that is not all: if we turn over the cards produced by the editor Yvon – who is to the Paris of the Thirties what LL was to that *belle époque* – we find that many of them are part of a series called 'Paris . . . en flânant'.

Though the *flâneur* as such is a nineteenth-century type whose modern avatars are, according to Benjamin, the reporter and the sandwich-man,[35] his own reflections on the *flâneur* must be seen against the background of a Paris packaged as a series of *passéistes* tableaux arrayed before a regressive twentieth-century *flâneur*. Even as Benjamin is promoting the *flâneur* as artist of modernity, the mass media (notably in the form of the ubiquitous postcard) is engaged in making *flânerie*

Postale Galerie – 186, rue de Rivoli.

synonymous with a rejection of modernity, a bittersweet quest for a fleeting past, a way of life about to be engulfed in apocalypse, the very same one that engulfed Benjamin. The next chapter in the *discourse of the metropolis* will be written by its new occupants, and notably by that paradigmatic hurried modern tourist, Adolf Hitler. Here, even the promiscuous postcard industry falters, and there are as yet in the immense and constantly expanding bank of Paris view-cards (at least to my knowledge) no postcards of the famous photographs that show Hitler in front of the great monuments of Paris. But perhaps it's only a matter of time.

References

Introduction

1 In R. Wolff Purcell and S. J. Gould, *Illuminations: A Bestiary* (London, 1986), p. 14. Classic accounts of classification include J. Goody, *The Domestication of the Savage Mind* (Cambridge, 1978) and M. Foucault, *The Order of Things: An Archaeology of the Human Sciences* (London, 1970). Reflections on classification and nomenclature are the basis of several chapters of Italo Calvino's whimsical novel *Mr Palomar* (London, 1985).

2 M. Kundera, *The Unbearable Lightness of Being* (London, 1984), p. 248.

1 Jean Baudrillard: The System of Collecting

This essay first appeared under the heading 'Le Système marginal: la collection' as a chapter in Jean Baudrillard's book *Le Système des objets*, which was published in Paris by Gallimard in 1968.

1 Maurice Rheims, *La Vie étrange des objets* (Paris, 1956), p. 28.

2 Ibid., p. 33.

3 As witness the remarks of Monsieur Fauron, president of the Society of Cigar Band Collectors, in the magazine *Liens*, Club Français du Livre, May 1964.

4 Rheims, op. cit., p. 50.

5 In almost all cases, the series is a kind of game that allows one to prioritize one of the two terms and institute it as the standard. A child rolls marbles along the ground: which one will go farthest? It is no accident that it is invariably the same one that wins: this is because the child has invested a preference in it. This standard, this hierarchy he has dreamt up, rests on nothing but himself: he doesn't so much identify with a given marble as with the fact that it wins every time. Yet he is simultaneously present in every marble in so far as he represents their hidden corollary: in rolling them one by one, he plays the game of constituting himself as a serial progression, at the same time as he constitutes himself as the ultimate term of the series – the one that wins. Here we find an explanation of the psychology of the collector: in collecting privileged objects, he constantly confirms himself as the one that wins.

6 Any given term in the series could turn out to be this final term: any given engraving by Callot might be the one to 'round off Callot'.

7 At once the object becomes the locus of a network of habits, the focal point round which routine behaviour patterns crystallize. It may well be that, conversely, every habit is anchored in an object. In our daily lives, objects and habits are inextricably entwined.

8 It may be noted – and the demise of the grandfather clock may not be irrelevant – that the wrist-watch signals an irreversible trend among modern artefacts towards

miniaturization and individualization. It is moreover the tiniest, the most loyal, the most precious of private machines. An intimate mechanical talisman, crammed full with invested emotion, it is the object of daily complicities, of fascination (especially in children), of envy.

9 Here it is exactitude that corresponds to velocity in space: one is compelled to devour time in measured bites.

10 Rheims, op. cit., p. 42.

11 The notion that collecting represents a game with death (a passionate game, moreover), and is in this respect symbolically more powerful than death itself, is illustrated in an amusing tale told by Tristan Bernard. A man sets out to make a collection of children – legitimate, illegitimate, adopted, the fruit of a first, then of a second marriage, the foundling, the bastard and so forth. One day he throws a party to which they are all invited, whereat a cynical friend observes that one of the children is missing. 'Which one?', the collector anxiously asks. 'Your posthumous child', is the answer. Upon which the impassioned collector impregnates his wife and commits suicide.

The same system can be detected in its pure state, free of thematic colouring, within any game of chance, which explains the superior fascination exerted by the latter. What is signalled here is an absolute beyond mortal experience, as the pure subjectivity projects its supposed mastery over the pure series, facing all the vicissitudes of the game in the confident knowledge that no-one has the right to invoke the true conditions of life and death within the context of the game.

12 The same of course applies to pets and, by extension, to the 'object' of the sexual impulse, which gets exactly the same treatment within the jealousy system.

13 One should take care to differentiate between *disappointment*, a built-in reaction within the regressive system or series, and *lack*, of which I spoke earlier, and which, on the contrary, is a sign that the confining system is beginning to relax its grip. Disappointment means that the subject is still trapped within the system, whereas lack points the way toward contact with the world outside.

14 Ultimately the woman is reduced to her hair, then her feet, then, in the logic of regression, to even less personal features or attributes, until the fetish finally crystallizes, at the very opposite extreme from the living person, in the form of the suspender-belt or the brassière. In this way we come back to the material object, the possession of which implies the final evacuation of the presence of the other.

15 Hence the tendency of desire to have recourse to that radically simplified version of the living sexual object, the fetish, a penis-substitute and consequently a locus of high affective investment.

16 Similarly, possessive identification tends to occur where a living being is deemed to be a-sexual, as in the case of babies: 'Oh, *I*'ve got a headache, have *I*?', we might say to a baby. Or even: 'Oh, *we*'ve got a headache, have *we*?' Such misleading identification gets blocked off by castration anxiety once one faces a sexed person.

17 This distinction between serial satisfaction and genuine pleasure is a fundamental one. In the latter case, there is a sort of pleasure in pleasure, thanks to which satisfaction transcends itself as such and merges into a proper relationship. Whereas, in the case of serial satisfaction, this secondary aspect of pleasure, the dimension within which it might fulfil itself, simply lapses, goes begging, or is blocked. Whereupon satisfaction gets sidetracked into succession, compensating through quantity and repetition for a totality beyond its reach. This explains why some people stop reading the books they have purchased, yet still carry on buying more and more books. This is also why some people repeat the sexual act, or multiply their partners, in a project of indefinite compensation for the loss of love. Any pleasure in their pleasure has evaporated. All that is left is satisfaction. The one necessarily rules out the other.

18 However, even when a collector takes steps to invite other people to look at his collection, it is on the understanding that, when they enter the relationship previously restricted to subject and object, they remain non-participants.

19 The same would not be true, however, of scientific knowledge or of memory, which are equally forms of collecting, albeit of facts and information rather than objects.

3 *John Windsor: Identity Parades*

1 My articles on this conference appeared in *The Independent* (9 May and 20 June 1992). The following notes identify further articles by me in the same newspaper.

2 Gibbs: *The Independent* (3 October 1992).

3 Tat: *The Independent* (13 March 1993).

4 Opie: *The Independent* (4 April 1992).

5 TGI Friday: *The Independent* (13 March 1993).

6 The Elvis cult: *The Independent* (15 August 1992).

7 D. Stanley, *Life with Elvis* (Old Tappan, NJ, 1986), p. 116.

8 G. Marcus, *Dead Elvis: A Chronicle of a Cultural Obsession* (Harmondsworth, 1992), pp. 136–7.

9 Mabe: see Marcus, op. cit. [p. xviii].

10 Winter's cottages: *The Independent* (22 August 1992).

11 Swatch: *The Independent* (21 November 1992).

12 Romanies: *The Independent* (1 April 1989).

4 *Roger Cardinal. Collecting and Collage-making: The Case of Kurt Schwitters*

1 M. Proust, *Du Côté de chez Swann* (Paris: Gallimard / Collection Folio, 1976), p. 13.

2 See Baudrillard, 'The System of Collecting', above: pp. 7–24; and W. Benjamin, 'Unpacking my Library', in *Illuminations* (London, 1973), p. 62.

3 See K. Pomian, *Collectors and Curiosities* (Cambridge, 1990), p. 5, 30.

4 The estimate is given by J. Elderfield in *Kurt Schwitters* (London 1985), p. 76. I am deeply indebted for my information about Schwitters to this work, as well as to W. Schmalenbach's *Kurt Schwitters* (Munich, 1984). Both monographs include generous illustrations. See also S. Gohr, *Kurt Schwitters. Die späten Werke* (Cologne, 1985), and the Tate Gallery exhibition catalogue *Kurt Schwitters* (London, 1985).

5 I can only hint here at the wider evolution of the collage, which has such a central role in the history of modern art. In this context it is customary to date the practice back to the Cubist *papiers collés* of 1912–14 made by Picasso, Braque and Gris. Subsequent developments, encompassing Dada and surrealist paper collage and extending to the curiosity boxes of a Joseph Cornell and the junk configurations of a Tony Cragg, and covering such variants as photomontage, the readymade, the assemblage and the installation, are charted in D. Waldman's *Collage, Assemblage and the Found Object* (London, 1992), and are addressed theoretically and analytically in *Collage: Critical Views*, ed. K. Hoffman (Ann Arbor, 1989). If, in more general terms, we identify collage as a principle of composition based on the arrangement of readymade components on a flat, bounded surface, its ancestry could be traced back to Victorian scrapbooks, pasted screens and patchworks; or, further still, to medieval stained glass or Byzantine mosaics. Of course, to stretch a concept too far is to lessen its effectiveness, but I would hope that these references might alert the reader of this book to the many other arenas of human activity in which are re-enacted the fundamental impulses of gathering in and singling out, of juxtaposing and displaying, of coaxing

many small things to form one large, expressive thing.

6 Krzysztof Pomian defines a collection as 'a set of natural or artificial objects, kept temporarily or permanently out of the economic circuit, afforded special protection in enclosed places adapted specifically for that purpose and put on display' (op. cit., p. 9). This definition holds good, as I hope my discussion will show, for the three types of artefact that Schwitters pioneered (collage, assemblage and environmental work), though his concept of 'enclosed spaces' needs to be stretched in order to appertain both to picture-frame and exhibition area.

7 Conversely, if indeed there are secret collections, so there is also clandestine collage-making. I have a friend who, for several years, has made small collages on a daily basis, storing them almost stealthily in dated albums. Such a private and serial activity partakes doubly of the collecting impulse, for the accumulation of collages itself modulates into a concerted collection, while each fresh collage is a constellation fished up from the large box wherein the collage-maker hoards his precious store of magazine cuttings and other scraps.

8 Schwitters, *Das literarische Werk*, v (Cologne, 1981), p. 335; quoted in Gohr, op. cit., p. 21.

9 Susan Stewart summarizes James's observations of the wood-rat's collecting impulse (made in his *Principles of Psychology*) in her *On Longing* (London, 1984), pp. 153–4. James's comparison of the rat's hoards with the senseless collections made by the inmates of lunatic asylums reminds me of the 'schizophrenic box' in André Breton's private collection. This artless conglomeration of broken scissors, nibs, buttons, and the like, may have been the prototype for Breton's surrealist object-poems. See R. Cardinal, 'Surrealism and the Paradigm of the Creative Subject', in *Parallel Visions: Modern Artists and Outsider Art*, ed. M. Tuchman and C. S. Eliel (Los Angeles, 1992), p. 100.

10 B. O'Doherty, *Inside the White Cube: The Ideology of the Gallery Space*, (San Francisco, 1986), p. 45. O'Doherty offers a further instance of the transfigurative use of space in the anecdote about Schwitters organizing a living area underneath a wooden table during the weeks he spent in 1940 in an internment camp on the Isle of Wight (see ibid., p. 46). Such 'lowliness', ironically yet ritually assumed, reflects the effort of the prisoner to defy the reductionism of his captors, and the self-abasement of the shaman who knows that to plunge into the underworld is the precondition of illumination. The tale epitomizes the general philosophy of Schwitters's collage-making as, in effect, a dialectical grappling with *that which lies underfoot*.

11 A partial replica of the first *Merzbau*, based on old photographs, has been built within the Sprengel Museum in Hanover. A second *Merzbau* was begun at Lysaker in Norway in 1937 during the artist's exile, but burned down in 1951. Schwitters began his third and last such work, known as the *Merzbarn*, in a barn in Westmorland in England in 1947, only a few months before his death. Its remains, consisting of a partly decorated stone wall, were later rescued and installed in the Hatton Gallery in Newcastle upon Tyne. The sparseness of this work is in touching contrast to the lost complexity of the first *Merzbau*.

12 See H. Richter, *Dada: Art and Anti-art* (London, 1965).

13 For a fuller account of Schwitters's aesthetic alignments, see Elderfield, op. cit., especially pp. 120–8, 230–1. See also Annely Juda Fine Art, *Dada-Constructivism: The Janus Face of the Twenties* (London, 1984). Werner Schmalenbach insists that it is the *Merzbau* which most strongly resists assimilation to the Constructivist ideal (see op. cit., p. 144).

14 'Holland Dada' (1923), quoted in Elderfield, op. cit., p. 88.

15 R. Hausmann, *Courrier Dada*, quoted in Richter, op. cit., p. 151.

16 See Elderfield, op. cit., p. 85.

17 See, for example, *Black Dots and Square* (1927) or *Mz 30, 35* (1930), both reproduced by Schmalenbach in op. cit., p. 172 and 175. The most unequivocal proof of Schwitters's Constructivist leanings would be the clean, bold geometric lithographs issued in 1923 as the *Merz Portfolio*.

18 See *Windswept* (1946), reproduced in Schmalenbach, op. cit., p. 233.

19 Another striking instance of how mute objects can be used to evoke drudgery and poverty is James Agee's classic documentary book about Alabama sharecroppers in the Depression, *Let Us Now Praise Famous Men* (Boston, 1941). Agee achieves pathos through understatement, baldly inventorizing the contents of poverty-stricken homes, citing such things as threadbare clothes, broken buttons and cracked crockery, as well as quoting directly from the montage of calendars, magazine ads and newspaper cuttings stuck to the walls. The emotive impact of the writing is amplified by an accompanying portfolio of untitled photographs by Walker Evans.

20 See the colour reproduction in Gohr, op. cit., p. 56. This piece, made in London shortly after Schwitters's release from internment, carries some sombre overpainting, yet would be very hard to contemplate purely as an abstract colour design.

21 In France one can still buy cheap industrial bottle-racks identical to Duchamp's notorious *readymade*. A colleague of mine recently acquired one, and is now faced with the interesting quandary as to whether to cherish it as a cultural trophy or collector's curio (the aesthetic function) or to actually dry bottles on it (restoring the use function, but in a spirit of irony that complicates matters!). For a discussion of the aesthetic career to which banal objects may or may not aspire, see chapter 4 of A. C. Danto's *The Transfiguration of the Commonplace: A Philosophy of Art* (London, 1981). As for Cubism, it is instructive to note that news clippings in *papiers collés* by Picasso have recently been probed for clues to his political leanings, an approach that obviously ruins the modernist paradigm of the autotelic artwork. See P. Leighten, *Re-Ordering the Universe: Picasso and Anarchism, 1897–1914* (Princeton, 1989).

22 R. Harbison, *Eccentric Spaces* (New York, 1977), p. 158.

23 See Ellen Dissanayake's examination of art as 'a behavior of making special' in 'Art for Life's Sake', *Art Therapy*, IX/4 (1992), pp. 169–75.

24 I am reminded of Antoine Roquentin, the anti-hero of Sartre's novel *Nausea*, with his perverse habit of fiddling with sodden newsprint in puddles, as if to revive a child's ecstasy of messiness.

25 Stewart, op. cit., p. 135.

26 See the hieratic opening of 'Die Lehrlinge zu Sais', in Novalis, *Werke*, ed. G. Schulz (Munich, 1969), p. 95.

5 *Mieke Bal: Telling Objects: A Narrative Perspective on Collecting*

1 *Capital*, 1, p. 72, cited in W.J.T. Mitchell, *Iconology: Language, Text, Ideology* (Chicago, 1986), p. 189.

2 'The Age of the World View', *Measure*, 2, pp. 269–84, cited in E. Hooper-Greenhill, *Museums and the Shaping of Knowledge* (London, 1992), p. 82.

3 *Framing the Sign: Criticism and Its Institutions* (London, 1988), p. 203.

4 Speech-act theory considers language from the angle of its effectivity. It was first developed by J. L. Austin, and set out in his posthumously published *How to Do Things With Words* (1962). Austin proposes a distinction between utterances that are constative, informative, and those that are performative – that have no meaning other than the act they, in fact, *are* (like promising). When you say 'I promise', you *do* it; that is the only meaning the verb has.

5 My theory of narrative can be found in M. Bal, *Narratology: Introduction to the*

Theory of Narrative (Toronto, 1992). For discussions with other narrative theories, see M. Bal, *On Story-telling: Essays in Narratology* (Sonoma, CA, 1991).

6 This conclusion is reached through different routes by historiographers like Hayden White, *Metahistory: The Historical Imagination in Nineteenth-century Europe* (Baltimore, 1973); idem, 'Interpretation in History', *Tropics of Discourse* (Baltimore, 1978), pp. 51–80.

7 S.M. Pearce, *Museums, Objects and Collections: A Cultural Study* (Leicester and London, 1992).

8 P. Brooks, *Reading for the Plot: Design and Intention in Narrative* (New York, 1984).

9 Pearce, op. cit., p. 47.

10 Represented primarily by Melanie Klein, *The Psycho-analysis of Children* (New York, 1975), and by D.W. Winnicott, *Playing and Reality* (London, 1980).

11 But for the persistent carry-over between explicating articulation and explanations of origin in psychoanalysis, see T. Pavel, 'Origin and Articulation: Comments on the Papers by Peter Brooks and Lucienne Frappier-Mazur', *Style*, XVIII (1984), pp. 355–68.

12 Pearce, op. cit., p. 47.

13 Bourdieu, *Distinction: A Social Critique of the Judgement of Taste* (Cambridge, Mass., 1984), p. 54, cited in Pearce, op. cit., p. 50.

14 Clifford, 'On Collecting Art and Culture', *The Predicament of Culture: Twentieth-Century Ethnography, Literature and Art.* (Cambridge, Mass., 1988), pp. 215–51.

15 Clifford, op. cit., p. 218.

16 This was the purpose of my analysis of a few rooms of the American Museum of Natural History, published as 'Telling, Showing, Showing Off', *Critical Inquiry*, XVIII/3 (1992), pp. 556–94.

17 For a good, succinct discussion of this concept of interest, see R. Geuss, *The Idea of a Critical Theory: Habermas and the Frankfurt School* (Cambridge, 1981), pp. 45–54, and, of course, Habermas's own seminal book *Knowledge and Human Interest* (London, 1972).

18 To clarify the issue, I am radicalizing Clifford's argument slightly.

19 Jean Baudrillard, *Le Système des objets* (Paris, 1968), p. 135; Clifford, op. cit., p. 220.

20 Sigmund Freud, 'Some Psychological Consequences of the Anatomical Distinction Between the Sexes' (1925), in J. Strachey, ed., *The Standard Edition of the Complete Psychological Works*, XXI (London, 1963), pp. 149–57; Otto Fenichel, 'Fetishism', in *The Psychoanalytic Theory of Neurosis* (London, 1936), pp. 341–51.

21 For a feminist critique of fetishism, see Naomi Schor, 'Salammbô Bound', in *Breaking the Chain: Women, Theory and French Realist Fiction* (New York, 1985), pp. 111–26; and for a feminist reflection on female fetishism, idem, 'Female Fetishism: The Case of George Sand', in *The Female Body in Western Culture: Contemporary Perspectives*, ed. S. Rubin Suleiman (Cambridge, Mass., 1985), pp. 363–72.

22 For a more extensive analysis of the intimate – and narrative – connections between psychoanalysis and visuality, see 'Blindness or Insight? Psychoanalysis and Visual Art' in M. Bal, *Reading Rembrandt: Beyond the Word-Image Opposition* (New York, 1991), pp. 286–325.

23 Mitchell, op. cit., pp. 160–208, esp. p. 191.

24 Mitchell, op. cit., p. 191.

25 Ibid.

26 Slavoj Žižek, *The Sublime Object of Ideology* (London, 1989), p. 32.

27 Žižek, op. cit., p. 34.

28 Ibid.

29 Ibid., p. 45.

30 Mitchell, op. cit., p. 176.

31 Ibid., p. 188.

32 Schor, 'Salammbô Bound', p. 119.

33 W. Durost, *Children's Collecting Activity Related to Social Factors* (New York, 1932), p. 10; cited in Pearce, op. cit., p. 48.

34 D. J. Meijers, *Kunst als natuur: De Habsburgse schilderijengalerij in Wenen omstreeks 1780* (Amsterdam, 1991).

35 Brooks, op. cit., *passim*.

36 C. Bremond, *Logique du récit* (Paris, 1973); idem, 'The Logic of Narrative Possibilities', *New Literary History*, XI (1980), pp. 398–411.

6 *Nicholas Thomas: Licensed Curiosity: Cook's Pacific Voyages*

I am grateful to Stephen Bann and Norman Bryson for their suggestions concerning an earlier draft of this essay.

1 See Roland Barthes, 'The Plates of the *Encyclopaedia*' in his *New Critical Essays*, trans. R. Howard (New York, 1980), pp. 23–39, and A. Arber, *Herbals: Their Origin and Evolution; A Chapter in the History of Botany* (1938, reprinted Cambridge, 1986).

2 R. Joppien and B. Smith, *The Art of Captain Cook's Voyages* (New Haven, 1985–7), II, pp. 71–73.

3 N. Bryson, 'Chardin and the Text of Still Life', *Critical Inquiry*, XV (1989), pp. 228–34; see also ibid, *Looking at the Overlooked: Four Essays on Still Life Painting* (London, 1990).

4 *The 'Endeavour' Journal of Joseph Banks*, ed. J. C. Beaglehole (Sydney, 1962), I, p. 288.

5 The development of these interests are discussed in my book *Entangled Objects: Exchange, Material Culture and Colonialism in the Pacific* (Cambridge, Mass., 1991).

6 K. Pomian, *Collectors and Curiosities: Paris and Venice, 1500–1800* (Cambridge, 1990), especially pp. 53–61.

7 *The Journals of Captain James Cook*, ed. J. C. Beaglehole (Cambridge, 1955–67), II, p. 272, 375; *The 'Resolution' Journal of Johann Reinhold Forster*, ed. M. E. Hoare (London, 1982), p. 300, 360, 491; [John Marra], *Journal of the Resolution's Voyage in 1772–1775* (London, 1775), p. 163; some of these are quoted and discussed in Thomas, *Entangled Objects*, pp. 130–32, and in B. Smith, *European Vision and the South Pacific*, 2nd edn (New Haven, 1985), p. 124.

8 *Journals*, II, p. 532.

9 Ibid., p. 254.

10 George Keate, *An Account of the Pelew Islands*, 3rd edn (London, 1789), p. vii.

11 Edmund Burke, *A Philosophical Enquiry into the Origin of our Ideas of the Sublime and Beautiful*, ed. J.T. Boulton (Oxford, 1958), p. 31.

12 Henry Home, Lord Kames, *Elements of Criticism* (London, 1762, 6th edn 1785), I, p. 269.

13 Adam Smith, *The Theory of Moral Sentiments* (1759), IV.1.8–10; David Hume, 'Of Commerce', in *Essays, Moral, Political, and Literary*, ed. T. H. Green and T. H. Grose (London, 1898), I, pp. 295–6. Cf. the discussion in J. G. A. Pocock, *The Machiavellian Moment: Florentine Political Thought and the Atlantic Republican Tradition* (Princeton, 1975), pp. 494–8.

14 Fanny Burney, *Cecilia*, ed. P. Sabor and M. A. Doody (Oxford, 1988), p. 106.

15 Samuel Richardson, *Clarissa* (Oxford, 1930), I, p. 101.

16 Edward Gibbon, *Memoirs of My Life*, ed. B. Radice (Harmondsworth, 1984), p. 134; cf. N. Wraxall, *Cursory Remarks made in a Tour Through some of the Northern Parts of Europe* (London, 1775), p. 27, 38–9.

17 Johnson, *A Journey to the Western Isles of Scotland* (1775), in *Selected Writings*, ed. P. Cruttwell (Harmondsworth, 1968), p. 307.

18 John Barrow, *An Account of Travels into the Interior of Southern Africa, in the Years 1797 and 1798* (London, 1801), pp. 37–8.

19 Mungo Park, *Travels in the Interior Districts of Africa . . . in the Years 1795, 1796, and 1797* (London, 1799), I, p. 2.

20 Anon., *Travels in the Interior of Africa, by Mungo Park, and in Southern Africa, by John Barrow, Interspersed with Notes and Observations, Geographical, Commercial, and Philosophical* (Glasgow, 1815), p. 1.

21 Park, *Travels*, p. 54.

22 Ibid., p. 75, 95–6.

23 Ibid., pp. 311–12.

24 Thomas and William Daniell, *A Picturesque Voyage to India, by way of China* (London, 1810), pp. 1–2.

25 George Forster, *A Voyage Round the World*, ed. R. L. Kahn (Berlin, 1968), pp. 99–100.

26 *The 'Resolution' Journal of Johann Reinhold Forster*, p. 254. This text was the basis for the published narrative by George Forster, Johann Reinhold's son, referred to in the previous note (25).

27 George Forster, *Voyage*, p. 107.

28 Smith, op. cit., p. 46.

29 Cited in Smith, op. cit., p. 47.

30 *The Diary and Letters of Madame d'Arblay* (Fanny Burney), ed. C. Barrett and A. Dobson (London, 1905), III, p. 481 (entry dated March 1788).

31 John and Andrew van Rymsdyk, *Museum Britannicum: or, a Display in Thirty Two Plates, of Antiquities and Natural Curiosities, in that Noble and Magnificent Cabinet, the British Museum*, 2nd edn (London, 1791), p. iv.

32 Ibid., p. 49 (caption to pl. XIX).

33 Ibid., p. iii.

34 See Samuel Johnson's essay, 'A Club of Antiquaries', in *The Rambler*, no. 177 (26 November 1751).

35 Keate, *Account*, p. 312.

36 *The 'Resolution' Journal of Johann Reinhold Forster*, pp. 555–7.

37 Ibid., p. 647.

38 Michael Hoare, 'Introduction', *The 'Resolution' Journal*, pp. 117–8.

7 *Thomas DaCosta Kaufmann: From Treasury to Museum:*
The Collections of the Austrian Habsburgs

1 A. Lhotsky, *Die Geschichte der Sammlungen*, in *Festschrift des Kunsthistorischen Museums zur Feier des Fünfzigjährigen Bestandes* (Vienna, 1941–5); pt. II provides a detailed overview that remains fundamental for the history of the Habsburg collect-ions, and is especially unsurpassed for the earlier periods. The information cited here is taken from pt. II, I, pp. 1ff, 17, 21.

2 Ibid., p. 21ff; see p. 155 for the unicorn horn and *Achatschale*.

3 Ibid., p. 3f.

4 A recent summary of the history of the Dresden *Schloss* and its various rooms, with further bibliography, is provided in *Das Dresdener Schloss: Monument sächsischer Geschichte und Kultur*, exhibition catalogue, Dresden Schloss, Grünes Gewölbe (Dresden, 1989).

5 Lhotsky, op. cit., p. 53, 62.

6 The terms of this debate are summarized and responded to in my *The Mastery of Nature: Aspects of Art, Science and Humanism in the Renaissance* (Princeton, 1993), p. 176ff.

7 See D. Preziosi, 'The Question of Art History', *Critical Inquiry*, XVIII (1992), p. 380, and his recent *Rethinking Art History: Meditations on a Coy Science* (London, 1989).

8 Although not specifically about art, J.-D. Muller, *Gedächtnis: Literatur und Hofgesellschaft um Maximilian I* (Munich, 1982), is to be recommended for its treatment of the culture of Maximilian's court. E. Scheicher's excellent *Die Kunst- und Wunderkammern der Habsburger* (Vienna, 1979) traces the relation of the collections of Maximilian I and Ferdinand I to their antecedents and sources. For the relation of Maximilian I to the court of Spain, especially in regard to patronage and collecting, see *Reyes y Mecenas: Loy Reyes Católicos, Maximiliano I y los Inicios de la Casa de Austria en España*, exhibition catalogue, Toledo, Museo de Santa Cruz (Elemond, 1992).

9 This passage follows the argument set out in my *The School of Prague: Painting at the Court of Rudolf II* (London, 1988), p. 15, with references at p. 119, n. 25.

10 See G. van der Osten and H. Vey, *Painting and Sculpture in Germany and the Netherlands, 1500–1600* (Harmondsworth, 1969), pp. 254–5.

11 Ferdinand's patronage and collections merit more attention: see, in the meantime, Lhotsky, op. cit., p. 145, and Scheicher, op. cit., p. 62ff.

12 For the collections of Ferdinand II of the Tyrol see Scheicher, op. cit., p. 73ff, with references to earlier sources; *eadem*, in *Die Kunstkammer (Führer durch das Kunsthistorisches Museum*, no. 24) (Innsbruck, 1977), pp. 13–23; *eadem*, 'The Collection of Archduke Ferdinand II at Schloss Ambras: Its Purpose, Composition and Evolution', in *The Origins of Museums: The Cabinet of Curiosities in Sixteenth- and Seventeenth-century Europe*, ed. O. R. Impey and A. G. MacGregor (Oxford, 1985), pp. 29–38; also *eadem*, 'Zur Entstehung des Museums im 16. Jahrhundert. Ordnungsprinzipien und Erschliessung der Ambraser Sammlung Erzherzog Ferdinands II.', in *Der Zugang zum Kunstwerk: Schatzkammer, Salon, Ausstellung, 'Museum' (Akten des XXV. Internationalen Kongresses für Kunstgeschichte, Wien, 1983, 4)* (Vienna 1986), pp. 43–52.

13 For example, the famous work by Julius von Schlosser, *Die Kunst- und Wunderkammer der Spätrenaissance* (Leipzig, 1908).

14 For more on this, and in answer to Preziosi, 'The Question of Museums', see *The Mastery of Nature*, p. 174ff.

15 The issue of diplomacy and the *Kunstkammer* is discussed in my 'Remarks on the Collections of Rudolf II: The *Kunstkammer* as a Form of *Representatio*', *Art Journal*, XXXVIII (1978), pp. 22–8. For the gifts to Ferdinand of the Tyrol see M. Leithe-Jasper, 'Der Bergkristallpokal Herzog Philipps des Guten von Burgund', *Jahrbuch der Kunsthistorischen Sammlungen in Wien*, n.s. 30, LXVI (1970), pp. 227–41.

16 For this hypothesis, and the relation of Jamnitzer's fountain to the *Kunstkammer*, see S. Alfons, 'The Museum as Image of the World', in *The Arcimboldo Effect: Transformations of the Human Face from the Sixteenth to the Twentieth Century*, exhibition catalogue, ed. P. Hulten: Venice, Palazzo Grassi (Milan, 1987), pp. 67–88.

17 For this interpretation of Arcimboldo's paintings of the Seasons, Elements and Rudolf II, see most recently (and completely) *The Mastery of Nature*, pp. 100–35; the poems are reprinted there on pp. 197–205.

18 Recent revisionist treatments of Rudolf's *Kunstkammer*, with much new information, are offered by E. Fučíková, 'Zur Konzeption der rudolfinischen Sammlungen', in *Prag um 1600: Beiträge zur Kunst und Kultur am Hofe Rudolfs II*, ed. Fučíková (Freren, 1988), pp. 59–62; *eadem*, 'Die Sammlungen Rudolfs II', in Fučíková *et al.*, *Die Kunst am Hofe Rudolfs II* (Hanau, 1988), pp. 209–46. For a view of the collection, see *Prag*

um 1600: Kunst und Kultur am Hofe Rudolfs II, exhibition catalogue; Kulturstiftung Ruhr, Essen (Villa Hügel), and Kunsthistorisches Museum, Vienna (Freren, 1988–89).

19 The interpretation in these two paragraphs summarizes my *The Mastery of Nature*, pp. 176–85.

20 For these aspects of Rudolf's collections see Beket Bukovinská, 'Die Kunst- und Schatzkammer Rudolfs II: Der Weg vom Rohmaterial zum Sammlungsobjekt als ein Erkenntnisprozess', in *Der Zugang zum Kunstwerk*, pp. 59–63; E. Fučíková, 'The Collection of Rudolf II at Prague: Cabinet of Curiosities or Scientific Museum?', in *The Origins of Museums*, pp. 47–53; and *eadem*, 'Die Kunstkammer und Galerie Kaiser Rudolfs II als eine Studiensammlung', in *Der Zugang zum Kunstwerk*, pp. 53–8.

21 The discussion in these paragraphs draws on R. Distelberger, 'The Habsburg Collections in Vienna during the Seventeenth Century', in *The Origins of Museums*, pp. 39–46.

22 For this point, which in part diverges from Distelberger's interpretation, see the discussion in my forthcoming book on 'Central Europe in the Making: Art, Culture, and Society from the Renaissance to the End of the Old Régime'.

23 See Distelberger, 'The Habsburg Collections', pp. 45–6, with further references.

24 See Lhotsky, op. cit., esp. p. 376ff.

25 The best source for the history of the collections under Karl (Charles) VI remains Lhotsky, op. cit., pp. 387–409. For the imperial library (*Hofbibliothek*), see most recently H. Lorenz, *Johann Bernhard Fischer von Erlach* (London, 1992), pp. 40–41, 166–71.

26 See F. Matsche, *Die Kunst im Dienst der Staatsidee Kaisers Karl VI: Ikonographie, Ikonologie und Programmatik des 'Kaiserstils'* (Berlin, 1981).

27 For eighteenth-century developments in the Dresden collections, to which reference is made here and below, see G. Heres, *Dresdener Kunstsammlungen im 18. Jahrhundert* (Leipzig, 1991).

28 In addition to the primary sources cited, this discussion of the transformation of the collections under Maria Theresa and Joseph II draws largely from Lhotsky, op. cit., pt. 2, II, pp. 413–66.

29 See in general W. Kemp, '. . . *einen wahrhaft bildenden Zeichenunterricht überall einzuführen': Zeichnen und Zeichenunterricht der Laien 1500–1870. Ein Handbuch* (Frankfurt, 1979); and J. van Horn Melton, *Absolutism and the Eighteenth-century Origins of Compulsory Schooling in Prussia and Austria* (New York, 1988).

30 A recent study by D. J. Meijers, *Kunst als natuur: De Habsburgse schilderijengalerij in Wenen omstreeks 1780* (Amsterdam, 1991), adduces these examples and argues for seeing this change as an outgrowth rather than metamorphosis from the earlier court collections; she also points to parallels in the treatment of natural history, as was evinced in the simultaneous reorganization of the *Naturalienkabinett*.

31 An accessible history of this collection and its fate is given by W. Koschatzky, 'The Albertina in Vienna', in *Old Master Drawings from the Albertina*, exhibition catalogue, ed. Koschatzky: National Gallery of Art, Washington, D.C., and the Pierpont Morgan Library, New York, (Washington D.C., 1984), pp. 13–20.

32 Lhotsky, op. cit., pt. 2, II, p. 468ff.

33 For Arneth's efforts, see especially Lhotsky, op. cit., p. 541ff.

34 The most complete study of this phenomenon is the series of books begun under the editorial direction of Renate Wagner-Rieger, *Die Wiener Ringstrasse, Bild einer Epoche: Die Erweiterung der Inneren Stadt Wien unter Kaiser Franz Joseph* (Wiesbaden, 1980). See also C. E. Schorske, *Fin-de-siècle Vienna: Politics and Culture* (New York, 1980), p. 24ff.

35 In addition to Lhotsky's *Geschichte der Sammlungen*, see his *Die Baugeschichte der Museen und der Neuen Burg (Festschrift des Kunsthistorischen Museums zur Feier des*

Fünzigjährigen Bestandes), pt. 1 (Vienna, 1941), for the pre-history and history of the building of the Kunsthistorisches and the Naturhistorisches Museum.

36 See J. Białostocki, 'Museum Work and History in the Development of the Vienna School', in *Wien und die Entwicklung der kunsthistorischen Methode (XXV. Internationaler Kongress fuer Kunstgeschichte CIHA Wien 4.–10. 1983)* (Vienna, 1984), ed. H. Fillitz and M. Pippal, 1, pp. 9–15.

37 For the notion of the change in the nature of the public sphere, see the by now classic study by Jürgen Habermas, *Strukturwandel der Öffentlichkeit* (Frankfurt, 1962).

8 *John Elsner: A Collector's Model of Desire: The House and Museum of Sir John Soane*

1 This paper is for Mary Beard, who first convinced me of the value of studying the phenomena of collecting and the museum. For their comments and discussion, I am most grateful to Caroline Arscot, John House and especially Roger Cardinal.

2 On nostalgia and artefacts, see especially S. Stewart, *On Longing: Narratives of the Miniature, the Gigantic, the Souvenir, the Collection* (London, 1984), pp. 23–4, 138–46.

3 In this sense, collecting is a kind of 'science of the concrete' or 'bricolage' in the sense used by Claude Lévi-Strauss in his *The Savage Mind* (London, 1966), pp. 1–33. On the theme of 'bricolage' in relation to Soane's Museum, see J. Summerson, 'Union of the Arts: Sir John Soane's Museum-House', *Lotus International*, XXXV (1982), pp. 64–74, esp. p. 69.

4 For an account of the taste for classical sculpture, especially antique works from Italy, from the Renaissance through to the Enlightenment and beyond, see F. Haskell and N. Penny, *Taste and the Antique: The Lure of Classical Sculpture, 1500–1900* (London, 1981); on collecting and antiquities, see K. Pomian, *Collectors and Curiosities: Paris and Venice, 1500–1800* (Cambridge, 1990), pp. 34–6, 78–99; on the British and the antique in the time of Soane see, for example, N. Penny, 'Collecting, Interpreting and Imitating Ancient Art', in M. Clarke and N. Penny, eds., *The Arrogant Connoisseur: Richard Payne Knight (1751–1824)* (Manchester, 1982), pp. 65–81.

5 On Soane as a collector, see S. G. Feinberg, *Sir John Soane's Museum: An Analysis of the Architect's House-Museum in Lincoln's Inn Fields, London*, University of Michigan PhD thesis, 1979 (University Microfilms International, 1980); S. G. Feinberg Millenson, *Sir John Soane's Museum* (Michigan, 1987); and H. Dorey, 'Soane as a Collector', in P. Thornton and H. Dorey, eds., *A Miscellany of Objects from Sir John Soane's Museum* (London, 1992), pp. 122–6.

6 On Soane's bequest, see Feinberg, op. cit., pp. 289–93; J. Summerson, *A New Description of Sir John Soane's Museum* (9th edn, London, 1991), p. 81 (Appx 2). For the Act, see J. Soane, *Description of the House and Museum on the North Side of Lincoln's Inn Fields* (London, 1835), pp. 101–9 (citation from section 1, p. 102).

7 Soane, 1835, pp. 101–9.

8 Soane himself published three separate descriptions of his house – in 1830, 1832 and 1835 – each entitled *Description of the House and Museum on the North Side of Lincoln's Inn Fields*. His friend, the publisher John Britton, issued *The Union of Architecture, Sculpture and Painting: Exemplified by a Series of Illustrations, with Descriptive Accounts of the House and Galleries of John Soane* (London, 1827). The posthumous (and anonymous) account of his bequest published in *The Penny Magazine of the Society for the Diffusion of Useful Knowledge*, no. 363 (31 October–30 November 1837), pp. 457–64, was entitled 'The House and Museum of Sir John Soane'. Soane's earlier attempt (in 1812) to describe his collection (an unpublished manuscript in the Library of Soane's Museum) was entitled 'Crude Hints towards a

History of My House in L. I. Fields', implying that at that time the Museum was still firmly, and only, a 'house'. In the same year *The European Magazine* (vol. LXII, July–December 1812, pp. 381–7) published an account of the collection entitled 'Observations on the House of John Soane Esq., Holborn-Row, Lincoln's Inn Fields'; here again the term 'museum' describes only one part of the building and collection (p. 382) while the house is again firmly a 'house'. On 'The Genesis of Sir John Soane's Museum idea, 1801–1810', see S. G. Feinberg, *Journal of the Society of Architectural Historians*, XLIII (1984), pp. 225–37.

9 Although, in section xviii of the Act, Soane left open the possibility that he might bequeath the collection to the Trustees of the British Museum 'for the purpose of being by them separately and distinctly preserved at the British Museum, and there to be called "The Soane Collection" '; See Soane, 1835, p. 108. For a contemporary attack on the Soane donation as a 'mere mockery' that was 'dictated solely by selfish vanity', see 'The Soanean Museum', *The Civil Engineer and Architect's Journal* (November 1837), p. 44.

10 For instance, the first collection of vases of Sir William Hamilton, acquired by the British Museum in 1772, or the collection of Roman sculptures belonging to Charles Townley, acquired in 1805; see B. F. Cook, *The Townley Marbles* (London, 1985) and I. D. Jenkins, *Archaeologists and Aesthetes* (London, 1992), esp. pp. 102–39. See also I. D. Jenkins, ' "Athens Rising Near the Pole": London, Athens and the Idea of Freedom', in C. Fox, ed., *London – World City* (London, 1992), pp. 143–53.

11 For a detailed account see Feinberg, 1979, and Feinberg Millenson, op. cit.

12 *The Gentleman's Magazine*, XCVII 2, 1827, p. 129.

13 For these editions see Feinberg, 1979, pp. 293–7.

14 On Soane's Museum as a 'house of verbiage', see R. Harbison, *Eccentric Spaces* (London, 1977), pp. 31–2.

15 'The House and Museum of Sir John Soane', *Penny Magazine of the Society for the Diffusion of Useful Knowledge*, no. 363 (31 October–30 November 1837), pp. 457–64.

16 Ibid, p. 458. The élitism of this account is interestingly in tension with the target readership of the *Penny Magazine*. It had been launched in 1832 as a cheap and improving family paper with a lower-middle-class and upper-working-class readership; it claimed a circulation of 200,000 in the mid-1830s: see R. Altick, *The English Common Reader* (Chicago, 1957), pp. 332–9. Readers of the *Penny Magazine* were specifically the indiscriminate public to whom this article was giving a certain voyeuristic access to the House, but which it was firmly suggesting should remain outside its doors.

17 See Summerson, 1991, p. 85; M. Richardson, 'Model Architecture', *Country Life*, CLXXXIII (September 1989), pp. 224–7. There has been little discussion of the classical models so far as I am aware – although on the makers of the plaster models see G. Cuisset, 'Jean-Pierre et François Fouquet, artistes modeleurs', *Gazette des Beaux-Arts*, CXV (May-June 1990), pp. 227–40, but for the models of Soane's own buildings see J. Wilton-Ely, 'The Architectural Models of Sir John Soane: A Catalogue', *Architectural History*, XII (1969), pp. 5–38.

18 This is discussed in Thornton and Dorey, op. cit., p. 68.

19 See Thornton and Dorey, op. cit., pp. 66–7. As Barbara Hofland put it (Soane, 1835, p. 39): 'the fine model of the Roman temple contrasted with the rude erection of shapeless pillars congregated by the Druids'.

20 See Soane, 1835, pp. 34–5.

21 Even before he began the house-museum at Lincoln's Inn Fields, Soane had plans for a 'Gallery of Plaister Casts and Models' at his country house, Pitshanger Abbey, Ealing, west of London; See Feinberg-Millenson, op. cit., pp. 5–13.

22 See Feinberg, 1979, pp. 91–2; Richardson, op. cit., pp. 224–5.

23 The history of the Model Room after Soane's death is a sad one. Against the spirit of the Act of Parliament, if not the strictest interpretation of its terms, the models were later dispersed throughout the house. The final Model Room (of 1835) on the second floor of 13 Lincoln's Inn Fields became the Curator's office. The attic room where they had temporarily been displayed in 1829–35 is now part of the resident-warder's flat. Only after 1969, when the Trustees of Sir John Soane's Museum took possession of 12 Lincoln's Inn Fields, was a Model Room re-established, this time on the second floor of no. 12. For all this see Richardson, op. cit., p. 227. The current Model Room (which may only be seen on request) is thus an academic reconstruction (or a postmodern reconstitution) of that key feature of the Museum which – unlike the rest – has been lost, at least in respect of the various situations chosen for it by Soane. The deep insignificance attributed to the models by posterity is evidenced in A. T. Bolton's edition (1911) of Hofland's descriptions of Soane's house (originally published in the *Description* of 1835): Bolton entirely omits Hofland's lengthy and enthusiastic account of the Model Room, choosing to replace it with the following footnote: 'The Editor has passed over the description of the Model Room as too long for these pages and mainly interesting to professed students of Architecture. The Models are of two kinds, Antique and Soanic, the latter of great value to architects interested in the work of Sir John Soane.' See B. Hofland, *Popular Description of Sir John Soane's House, Museum and Library*, ed. A. T. Bolton (London, 1911), p. 54.

24 Soane, 1830, p. 25 and 1832, p. 25: 'This room is lighted from a lantern light, and by two windows in the south front, which afford a panoramic effect of some of the magnificent structures of the metropolis, and extensive views of the environs.' For further comments on the views from the Model Room (this time the room as restructured after 1835), see the articles on the Soane Museum in *The Illustrated London News* (25 June 1864), p. 622, and *The Graphic* (1 November 1884), pp. 466–7.

25 See Summerson, 1991, pp. 64–9.

26 Soane, 1835, pp. 87–94.

27 For example, in Soane, 1835, p. 12 (Jupiter Tonans), p. 35 (Villa Adriana); Soane, 1830, p. 12 (Pantheon and Jupiter Tonans).

28 On nineteenth-century views of the chain of art, see Jenkins, op. cit., pp. 56–74.

29 Soane, 1835, p. 34.

30 J. Soane, *Lectures on Architecture*, ed. A. T. Bolton (London, 1929, lecture xii (delivered 1815), p. 191. Soane began to collect models of classical buildings in 1804, but made the bulk of his purchases in the 1820s and 1830s (see Richardson, op. cit., p. 224).

31 Soane, 1929, p. 192.

32 Britton, op. cit., p. 45.

33 Britton continues his narrative of the Pompeii model (p. 45) with an account of the history of its archaeology.

34 Soane, 1835, p. 88.

35 See p. 458. The whole passage is revealing: 'Sir John Soane's object was to show how much could be done in a very limited space; how a dwelling-house, without losing its domestic character and privacy, could be made to combine, at almost every turning, much of those varied and fanciful effects which constitute the poetry of architecture and painting. In fact, if the expression may be permitted, the house, though consisting only of very few rooms of but limited extent, is an architectural kaleidoscope, presenting a great variety of combinations within a very small space.'

36 On 'collections as microcosms' see Pomian, op. cit., pp. 69–77.

37 For a discussion of a miniature see Stewart, op. cit., pp. 37–69, and (as souvenir) pp. 132–51.

38 See Soane, 1835, pp. 34–5; Summerson, 1991, p. 40; Thornton and Dorey, op. cit., p. 66.
39 On the value of these models as excavation records for the modern archaeologist, see M. Mazzei, 'L'ipogeo Monterisi Rossignoli di Canosa', *Archeologia e Storia Antica*, XII (1990), pp. 123–67, esp. p. 130 and figs. 42.1 and 42.4.
40 Soane, 1835, pp. 34–5.
41 See the discussion in B. Lukacher, 'John Soane and his Draughtsman Joseph Michael Gandy', *Daidalos*, XXV (15 September 1987), pp. 51–64, esp. pp. 54–7.
42 Here I disagree with Lukacher, op. cit., p. 56, who suggests that the figure must represent Gandy. I think the dividers and plan tell in favour of the architect, but the ambivalence as to whether the models in the drawing are Soane's buildings or Gandy's (the architect's or the draughtsman's) must remain in play.
43 Cf. Stewart, op. cit., p. 61, on the implications of the doll's house.
44 Here the models partake of what Pomian, op. cit., calls the collector's 'desire to miniaturize the constituent parts of the world in such a way as to allow the eye to take them all in at the same time, without losing any of their most intimate features' (p. 49).
45 Soane, 1830, and 1832, p. 25.

9 *Anthony Alan Shelton: Cabinets of Transgression: Renaissance Collections and the Incorporation of the New World*

1 M. Hodgen, *Early Anthropology in the Sixteenth and Seventeenth Centuries* (Philadelphia, 1964); B. Keen, *The Aztec Image in Western Thought* (New Brunswick, 1971); L. Laurencich-Minelli, 'Museography and Ethnographical Collections in Bologna during the 16th and 17th Centuries', in O. R. Impey and A. G. MacGregor, eds, *The Origins of Museums* (Oxford, 1985); J. Le Goff, *The Medieval Imagination* (Chicago, 1988), p. 10.
2 J. Huizinga, *The Waning of the Middle Ages*, trans. F. Hopman (Harmondsworth, 1965), pp. 254–5; U. Eco, *Art and Beauty in the Middle Ages* (London, 1986), p. 12.
3 Cited in Eco, p. 13.
4 K. Pomian, *Collectors and Curiosities: Paris and Venice, 1500–1800* (Cambridge, 1990), p. 17.
5 J. Burckhardt, *The Civilisation of the Renaissance in Italy* (New York, 1958), I, pp. 154–5. See also P. Geary, 'Sacred Commodities: The Circulation of Medieval Commodities', in *The Social Life of Things, Commodities in Cultural Perspective*, ed. A. Appadurai (Cambridge, 1986), p. 169.
6 Pomian, op. cit., p. 17.
7 Burckhardt, op. cit., I, p. 155.
8 Eco, op. cit., p. 16.
9 Ibid., p. 98.
10 According to Robert Grosseteste, Bishop of Lincoln in the first half of the thirteenth century: 'beauty is a concordance and fittingness of a thing to itself and of all its individual parts to themselves and to each other and to the whole, and of that whole to all things' (cited in Eco, op. cit.).
11 Eco, op. cit., p. 53.
12 Ibid., p. 95.
13 Le Goff, op. cit., p. 27.
14 Ibid., pp. 27–8.
15 Pomian, op. cit., p. 271.
16 Ibid., p. 48.
17 Ibid., p. 35.
18 Ibid., p. 47, and p. 78.

19 Ibid., p. 48.
20 Ibid., pp. 58–9.
21 A. Lugli, 'Inquiry As Collection: The Athanasius Museum in Rome', *RES*, XII (1986), p. 114.
22 Pomian, op. cit., p. 35.
23 Ibid.
24 Ibid., p. 69.
25 Ibid., p. 70.
26 Hodgen, op. cit., p. 119.
27 Pomian, op. cit., p. 76.
28 Laurencich-Minelli, op. cit., p. 22.
29 G. Olmi, 'Science – Honour – Metaphor: Italian Cabinets of the 16th and 17th Centuries', in Impey and MacGregor, op. cit., p. 5.
30 Hodgen, op. cit., p. 123.
31 Ibid.
32 Ibid.
33 A. Aimi, V. Michele and A. Morandotti, 'Towards a History of Collecting in Milan', in Impey and MacGregor, op. cit., p. 27.
34 D. Heikamp, 'American Objects in Italian Collections of the Renaissance and Baroque: A Survey', in *First Images of America: The Impact of the New World on the Old*, ed. F. Chiappelli (London, 1976), pp. 455–6; and M. Ryan, 'Assimilating New Worlds in the 16th and 17th Centuries', *Comparative Studies in Society and History*, XXIII (1981), pp. 526–9.
35 Olmi, op. cit., p. 13.
36 Hodgen, op. cit., p. 127.
37 Heikamp, op. cit., p. 471.
38 Laurencich-Minelli, op. cit., p. 18.
39 Ibid., p. 19.
40 S. Stewart, *On Longing: Narratives of the Miniature, the Gigantic, the Souvenir, the Collection* (London, 1984), p. 152.
41 Burckhardt, op. cit., p. 161.
42 Cf. Lugli, op. cit., p. 112.
43 Aimi, et al., op. cit., p. 27.
44 Heikamp, op. cit., p. 458.
45 Aimi, et al., op. cit., p. 24.
46 Olmi, op. cit., p. 11.
47 D. Heikamp, *Mexico and the Medici* (Florence, 1972), p. 11.
48 Hodgen, op. cit., p. 119.
49 See *Mythen der Neuen Welt: Zur Entdeckungsgeschichte Lateinamerikas*, exhibition catalogue by K.-H. Kohl; Berliner Festspiele (Berlin, 1982), p. 45.
50 D. Robertson, 'Mexican Indian Art and the Atlantic Filter: Sixteenth to Eighteenth Centuries', in *First Images of America: The Impact of the New World on the Old*, ed. F. Chiappelli (London, 1976), p. 489.
51 S. Greenblatt, *Marvelous Possessions: The Wonder of the New World* (Oxford, 1991), p. 14.
52 See Keen, op. cit., Hodgen, op. cit.; H. Konning, *Columbus: His Enterprise* (New York, 1976); J. H. Elliott, *The Old World and the New, 1492–1650* (Cambridge, 1970); L. Hanke, *Aristotle and the American Indians: A Study in Race Prejudice in the New World* (London, 1959); and A. Padgen, *The Fall of Natural Man: The American Indian and the Origins of Comparative Ethnology* (Cambridge, 1986), and *European Encounters with the New World, from Renaissance to Romanticism* (New Haven, 1993).

53 See T. Todorov, *The Conquest of the New World: The Question of the Other* (New York, 1984); and Greenblatt, op. cit.

54 This last-mentioned sought to situate the phenomena of the world by reconstructing its evolution from the biblical creation story.

55 Le Goff, op. cit., p. 40.

56 Bernal Díaz, *The Discovery and Conquest of Mexico*, ed. G. García, trans. A. P. Maudslay, intro. I. A. Leonard (New York, 1979), see pp. 226, 214 and 192.

57 Keen, op. cit., p. 60.

58 Ibid., pp. 95–6.

59 See P. Cabello Caro, *Coleccionismo americana indigena en la España del siglo XVIII* (Madrid, 1989), p. 25.

60 Pal Kelemen in *Art of the Americas, Ancient and Hispanic* (1969), p. 182, recounts an amusing incident when, in 1935, while working in the British Museum, he was shown a feather mosaic picture of the Christ at the Column. Since the Museum could not itself afford to purchase the picture, the 'curator' asked Kelemen whether he would be interested in acquiring it! Another picture, representing St Antony and the Christ Child, was offered the Museum in 1988, but this too was refused.

61 This is not intended as an exhaustive list of surviving examples of featherwork. For a more detailed description of these works, readers are directed to 'Tesoros de Mexico, Arte plumario y de mosaico', *Artes de Mexico*, no. 137 año 17 (1970), Z. Nutall, *Ancient Mexican Featherwork at the Columbian Historical Exhibition in Madrid*, Washington D. C.(1895), and the works of Heikamp listed in the bibliography.

62 A. P. Maudslay, 'Montezuma's Gifts to Cortez', in Díaz, *The Discovery and Conquest of Mexico*, p. 165.

63 Díaz, op. cit., p. 62.

64 Ibid., p. 70.

65 Ibid., p. 71.

66 Ibid., pp. 74–5.

67 Ibid., p. 76.

68 Ibid., pp. 95–6.

69 Cortéz, cited in Keen, op. cit., p. 59.

70 Ibid., p. 196.

71 Ibid., p. 250.

72 P. Muller, 'The Old World and Gold from the New', in *The Art of Pre-Columbian Gold: The Jan Mitchell Collection*, ed. J. Jones (London, 1985), p. 18.

73 Keen, op. cit., p. 64.

74 Ibid., p. 65.

75 Díaz, op. cit., p. 222.

76 Heikamp, 1972, p. 8.

77 S.K. Lothrop, *Inca Treasures as Depicted by Spanish Historians* (Los Angeles, 1938), p. 48.

78 Ibid., p. 50.

79 An inventory of the articles received by Charles V, summarized by Medina and quoted in Lothrop, op. cit., p. 50, lists the following items: 'Thirty-four jars of gold, of varying standards and weights. . . . Three of them were provided with covers also of gold. Two bags, small, as they weighed between them two pounds and ten ounces. A stalk of maize, of gold, with three leaves and two ears. Two kettle drums (atabales) or drums (tambores), of four pounds, four ounces. A panel of gold and silver, which enclosed the figures of an Indian man and woman, both of medium size. Two platters, which weighed seventeen pounds, and five ounces. A sack, of thirty-three pounds and fifteen ounces. An idol with the figure of a man, of eleven pounds, eleven ounces. A vase like a pitcher of twenty-seven pounds weight. Of silver objects 100 jars were

enumerated, the largest weighing 161 pounds and 12 ounces; and the smallest of 45 pounds and 4 ounces.'

80 Medina, cited in Lothrop, op. cit., p. 61.

81 Ibid., p. 46.

82 Díaz, op. cit., p. 248.

83 Díaz, op. cit., p. 249.

84 Cabello, op. cit., p. 25.

85 Surviving examples include the winged lizard pendant in the Wernher Collection, Luton Hoo, Bedfordshire, an 8th-to-12th-century frog pendant with shell inlay at the Metropolitan Museum of Art, and a sixteenth-century frog pendant at the Baltimore Museum of Art. An eighteenth-century niche figure, now in the Schatzkammer der Residenz, Munich, has a head made from an Aztec mask remodelled from a pre-Columbian sculpture.

86 Cabello, op. cit., p. 27.

87 Cited in Cabello, op. cit., p. 26.

88 Muller, op. cit., p. 16.

89 In I. Bernal, *A History of Mexican Archaeology: The Vanished Civilizations of Middle America* (London, 1980), p. 131.

90 As a consequence of these disasters, most of the existing American collections are no earlier than the 18th and early 19th centuries when the Bourbons commissioned expeditions to Palenque and other archaeological sites.

91 Cabello, op. cit., p. 27.

92 Robertson, op. cit., p. 491; and Heikamp, 1976, p. 456.

93 For Aldrovandi, see Heikamp, 1976, and Laurencich-Minelli, op. cit.; for the Medici, see Heikamp, 1972.

94 Heikamp, 1972.

95 E. Umberger, 'Antiques, Revivals, and References to the Past in Aztec Art', in *RES*, XIII (1987); and C. Gonzalez and B. Olmedo Vera, *Esculpturas Mezcala en el Templo Mayor* (Mexico, 1990).

96 Heikamp, 1972, pp. 34–5.

97 Heikamp, 1976.

98 Laurencich-Minelli, op. cit., p. 18.

99 Important collections in the Musées Royaux d'Art et d'Histoire, Brussels, and the Museum of the American Indian, New York, were recovered from caves in the Mixteca-Puebla area of Mexico, and are late arrivals to Western museums (see Shelton, note 101, below).

100 All but one were destroyed in World War II.

101 Maudslay, in Díaz, op. cit.; E. Carmichael, *Turquoise Mosaics from Mexico* (London, 1970); and A. Shelton, 'In the Realm of the Fire Serpent', *British Museum Society Bulletin*, LV (1988), pp. 20–25.

102 It is regrettable that the results of subsequent research on the history of this collection advertised in Carmichael, op. cit., p. 9, have never been made public.

103 Ryan, op. cit.

104 Ibid., pp. 527–8.

105 Letter from Bram Hertz to Henry Christy dated 5 February 1858 (in Carmichael, op. cit.).

106 In H. J. Braunholtz, *Sir Hans Sloane and Ethnography* (London, 1970), p. 31.

107 Díaz, op. cit., p. 158.

10 *Susan Stewart: Death and Life, in that Order, in the Works of Charles Willson Peale*

I would like to thank the Getty Center for Art History and the Humanities, Los Angeles, the Center for Literary and Cultural Change at the University of Virginia, Charlottesville, and the DIA Center for the Arts, New York, where preliminary versions of this essay were read.

1 See R. S. Buck, ed., *Plato's Meno* (Cambridge, 1961), esp. pp. 408–11, and R. McKeon, ed., *The Basic Works of Aristotle* (New York, 1941) – 'On the Soul', pp. 535–603, and for Daedalus, p. 544. I have considered the theme of animation more generally in *On Longing: Narratives of the Miniature, the Gigantic, the Souvenir, the Collection* (Baltimore and London, 1984; 2nd edn Durham, NC, 1993). A suggestive parallel to the case considered here is Annette Michelson's study of the iconography of Lenin's death, 'The Kinetic Icon in the Work of Mourning: Prolegomena to the Analysis of a Textual System', *October*, LXX (1990), pp. 16–51.

2 The relation between countenance and oblivion is outlined in E. Levinas, *Totality and Infinity, An Essay on Exteriority*, trans. A. Lingis (The Hague, 1961; reprinted Pittsburgh, 1969).

3 The major groups of the Peale Family papers are held at the American Philosophical Society and the Historical Society of Pennsylvania in Philadelphia; additional materials drawn on for this essay are located in the American Philosophical Society Library and the Library Company in Philadelphia. See also L. B. Miller, ed., *The Selected Papers of Charles Willson Peale and his Family*, 3 vols (New Haven, 1983–88); C. Coleman Sellers, *Charles Willson Peale* (New York, 1969); *idem, Mr Peale's Museum: Charles Willson Peale and the First Popular Museum of Natural Science and Art* (New York, 1980); *idem*, 'Charles Willson Peale with Patron and Populace: A Supplement to "Portraits and Miniatures by Charles Willson Peale"*, with a Survey of his Work in Other Genres', *Transactions of the American Philosophical Society*, LIX/3 (1969); *idem*, 'Portraits and Miniatures by Charles Willson Peale', *Transactions of the American Philosophical Society*, XLII/1 (1952); *Catalogue of an Exhibition of Portraits by Charles Willson Peale and James Peale and Rembrandt Peale*, Pennsylvania Academy of the Fine Arts (Philadelphia, 1923); E.P. Richardson, B. Hindle and L. B. Miller, eds., *Charles Willson Peale and his World* (New York, 1983); J. T. Flexner, *America's Old Masters: First Artists of the New World* (New York, 1939), pp. 171–244; L. B. Miller and D. C. Ward, eds., *New Perspectives on Charles Willson Peale: A 250th Anniversary Celebration* (Pittsburgh, 1991).

4 Charles W. Peale, *Discourse Introductory to a Course of Lectures on the Science of Nature with Original Music composed for, and Sung on, the Occasion. Delivered in the Hall of the University of Pennsylvania, November 8, 1800* (Philadelphia: Zachariah Poulson, Jr, 1800), p. 34.

5 Richardson, Hindle and Miller, op. cit., p. 101; and Sellers, *Mr Peale's Museum*, p. 19. Peale's skill at mounting skins on woodwork derived from his apprenticeship as a saddler.

6 Zebulon Pike had given two grizzly cubs, male and female, to President Jefferson, who in turn gave them to Peale for the museum zoo. One severely injured a monkey and later entered the Peale kitchen in the Hall basement. Peale contained the animal and shot it. He later killed the mate, and mounted them both: see Sellers, *Mr Peale's Museum*, pp. 206–7. Peale records the event in his *Autobiography*, typescript by Horace Wells Sellers, 2 vols, 1896, in the American Philosophical Society Library, Philadelphia, II, p. 373.

7 On this subject, see J. A. Leo Lemay, ed., *Deism, Masonry, and the Enlightenment* (Newark, 1987); P. Byrne, *Natural Religion and the Nature of Religion: The Legacy of Deism* (London, 1989); K.S. Walters, *The American Deists: Voices of Reason and Dissent in the Early Republic* (Lawrence, 1992); *idem, Rational Infidels: The American Deists* (Wolfeboro, NH, 1992).

8 See R. Grimsley, ed., *Rousseau: Religious Writings* (Oxford, 1970), for a discussion of

motion and will in 'Profession de foi du Vicaire savoyard' (1762), pp. 107–200 (131). In his *Autobiography* (Wells Sellers typescript, 1, p. 12), Peale mentions Rousseau's *Confessions*.

9 See Anthony Ashley Cooper, 3rd Earl of Shaftesbury, *Characteristics of Men, Manners, Opinions, Times* (1711), ed. J. M. Robertson (Indianapolis, 1964), 1, pp. 268–9, who held the belief that future rewards and punishments were immoral; and Benjamin Franklin, letter to Ezra Stiles, 9 March 1790, in Walters, *Deists*, p. 105: 'the soul of Man is immortal, and will be treated with Justice in another Life respecting its conduct in this'.

10 See J. T. Flexner, *The Light of Distant Skies: The History of American Painting, 1760–1835* (New York, 1969), p. 12.

11 Peale also copied West's copy of Titian's *Venus*; see L. B. Miller, ed., *The Selected Papers of Charles Willson Peale and His Family, I (Charles Willson Peale: Artist in Revolutionary America, 1735–1791)* (London, 1983), p. 87n.

12 Sellers, *Mr Peale's Museum*, p. 101.

13 The best essay on *Rachel Weeping* is P. Lloyd, 'A Death in the Family', *Philadelphia Museum of Art Bulletin*, LXXVIII (1982), pp. 3–13. Lloyd connects the painting to European mourning portraits and the conventions Peale may have drawn from Charles LeBrun's *Traité des Passions* (1649), and adds a detail that links the painting to the artifice of *Elisha Restoring the Shunamite's Son*: 'The telltale indication that Peale did not observe his wife from life is to be found in the whites of the eyes visible below the rolled up iris, after the example of LeBrun. This glance is nearly impossible to hold, especially with the head held straight'. An interesting parallel to the separation of Rachel's figure from the foreground can be found in Peale's complex *Self-portrait with Angelica and a Portrait of Rachel* (1782–5), where the depiction of the *portrait* of Rachel appears slightly larger than the other two figures and is positioned beyond the picture plane. David Steinberg relates the structure of this work to 'images of supernatural aid [given] to the artist in the moment of creation', a pun on *Angelica/angel* as the daughter reaches out to guide her father's hand. But such an interpretation of divine intervention would seem to be contrary to Peale's Deism, unless perhaps it can be read as a playful allusion or parody. See D. Steinberg, 'Charles Willson Peale: The Portraitist as Divine', in Miller and Ward, eds., *New Perspectives on Charles Willson Peale*, p. 132. John Adams was 'prodigiously' affected by the picture of Rachel mourning when he saw it on 20 August 1776. See Miller, ed., *Selected Papers*, 1, p. 382n, and L. Butterfield and others, eds., *The Adams Papers, Series II: Adams Family Correspondence* (Cambridge, Mass., 1963), 11 (June 1776–March 1778) p. 103: 'Yesterday Morning I took a Walk, into Arch Street, to see Mr. Peele's Painters Rooms. Peele is from Maryland, a tender, soft, affectionate Creature. . . . He showed me one moving Picture. His wife, all bathed in Tears, with a Child about six months old, laid out, upon her Lap. This Picture struck me prodigiously.' In the same letter Adams notes that Peale's head 'is not bigger than a large Apple. . . . I have not met with any Thing in natural History much more amusing or entertaining than his personal Appearance.'

14 Richardson, Hindle and Miller, op. cit., p. 66.

15 'On Transience', in P. Rieff, ed., *Freud: Character, and Culture* (New York, 1963), pp. 150–1.

16 'An Essay on Vital Suspension', pp. 7–11.

17 Peale himself records several incidents of ambiguous death and successful revival of corpses in the account of Rachel's death in his *Autobiography*; see the typescript, 1, pp. 135–6.

18 See J. McManners, *Death and the Enlightenment* (Oxford, 1981), for a survey of French 18th-century practices regarding death; M. M. Coffin's *Death in Early America* (New York, 1976), is an anecdotal account of a variety of folkloric customs regarding

death, mourning and burial; see also D. E. Stannard, ed., *Death in America* (Philadelphia, 1975), especially Philippe Ariés's contribution, 'The Reversal of Death' (pp. 135–58), which sees the eighteenth century as the turning-point in the historical movement toward the denial of death and suppression of mourning characteristic of modern society. Yet Peale explicitly rejected the common mourning customs of his day: 'If we are free agents to act as our best reason shall direct, then to [not] follow any custom which we deem absurd or even useless, must be laudible' (*Autobiography*, typescript, I, p. 137). The ambivalent status of the corpse is given much attention in chapters 5–7 of Charles Brockden Brown's novel on the yellow fever epidemic in Philadelphia, *Arthur Mervyn, or Memoirs of the Year 1793* (1799).

19 See Miller's note in her edition of Peale's *Selected Papers*, II, pt 1, pp. 14–15.

20 Ibid., p. 21 n.4. Miller notes that 'only one incident of the exhibition of an embalmed body is known, that of the English philosopher Jeremy Bentham (1748–1832), who, toward the end of his life, suggested that people have themselves exhibited after death so that their remains would become a statue, or "auto-icon". On his death, Bentham's corpse was mummified, dressed, and placed in a chair for display at the University of London.' It is still there.

   Among the miscellaneous papers at the American Philosophical Society Library relating to Peale's Museum is a document (dated 28 July 1825) attesting to the authenticity of two Egyptian mummies sold to the Museum.

21 Ibid., p. 21 n.4.

22 Flexner, *America's Old Masters*, pp. 195–6.

23 Miller, ed., *Selected Papers*, I, p. 380.

24 Ibid., pp. 382–3 (letter to Joseph Brewer, Philadelphia, 15 January 1783). Peale had four children by this time: Raphaelle, Angelica Kauffman, Rembrandt, and Titian Ramsay. His worries about his mother-in-law's will may have stemmed, Miller suggests, from financial difficulties. Phoebe Lloyd, 'A Death in the Family', sees this period as a key to the ways in which Peale concentrates on 'making the most of a loss', including the altered mourning portrait of Rachel and Margaret, throughout his career (p. 5).

25 See Richardson, ed., *Charles Willson Peale and His World*, p. 88. Peale recorded in his *Autobiography* (typescript, II, p. 338) that 'If a painter . . . paints a portrait in such perfection as to produce a perfect illusion of sight, in such perfection that the spectator believes the real person is here, that happy painter will deserve to be caressed by the greatest of mortal beings.'

26 Flexner, *The Light of Distant Skies*, p. 140.

27 See L. E. Hinsie and R. J. Campbell, eds., *Psychiatric Dictionary* (London, 1970), p. 205, for a useful summary of derealization.

28 Peale describes the moving pictures in his *Autobiography* (typescript, I, pp. 79–83). The presentation of 'Pandemonium', after Milton's description, is accompanied by a note that 'Before the scene opened the following words were sung with musick: To raise by art the stately pile / we will essay our skill / . . . Yet great the task to make the glow / that burning sulphur does bestow / Yet great the task to make the glow / That burning, that burning sulphur / Does bestow. . . .' (typescript, I, p. 81). In the American Philosophical Society copy of the typescript, a 1785 notice of the exhibit of moving pictures is inserted in volume I, between pp. 79–81.

29 Peale to West (17 November 1788), in Miller, ed., *Selected Papers*, I, p. 544.

30 Peale, *Discourse Introductory to a Course of Lectures on the Science of Nature with Original Music composed for, and Sung on, the Occasion* (Philadelphia: Zachariah Poulson, Jr, 1800); Library Company copy, p. 48.

31 Ibid., pp. 39–40.

32 Ibid., pp. 6–7, and 46.

33 Ibid., p. 47.

34 Sellers, *Charles Willson Peale and his World*, p. 305.

35 Peale to Elizabeth DePeyster Peale (28 June 1801), in Miller, ed., *Selected Papers*, II, pt 1, p. 335.

36 Peale to Andrew Ellicott (12 July 1801), Philadelphia, in Miller, ed., *Selected Papers*, II, pt 1, pp. 343–4.

37 Peale to West (16 December 1807), in Miller, ed., *Selected Papers*, II, pt 2, pp. 1052–4. This letter is discussed briefly in an article in the *Pennsylvania Magazine of History and Biography*, IX (1885), pp. 130–2. At the left of the tent, standing with arms folded, is Peale's fellow naturalist Alexander Wilson (author of *American Ornithology*). Climbing a ladder in the foreground is John Masten, the farm's owner. Peale himself stands with arms extended, holding a large drawing of the bones. Next to him, from left to right, are Mrs Hannah Peale in a Quaker cap, possibly Mrs Rembrandt Peale, and members of the Peale family: Rembrandt, Sybilla, who is pointing up to heaven to explain God's plan for the universe and the meaning of the discovery to her little sister Elizabeth, Rubens (with glasses) and Raphaelle. James Peale stands between the two poles at mid-picture. In the group to the right of Wilson, Peale's deceased second wife, Elizabeth DePeyster, scolds her youngest son, Titian Ramsay II; her sister and brother-in-law, Major and Mrs John Stagg, stand behind her. Other relatives are behind the green umbrella, while the two younger Peale boys, Linnaeus and Franklin, push a log into the pit with a long pole.

38 Rembrandt Peale, *An Historical Disquisition on the Mammoth, or Great American Incognitum, an Extinct, Immense, Carnivorous Animal, Whose Fossil Remains Have Been Found in America* (London, 1803). Reprinted in Miller, ed., *Selected Papers*, II, 544–81.

39 For Peale's estimation of Catton's *Noah and his Ark*, see the *Autobiography* (typescript, II, pp. 428–9). See also Sellers, *Mr Peale's Museum*, p. 246. It is interesting to note that in Manasseh Cutler's Journal, in which he records meeting Peale when visiting the studio in 1787, he draws an analogy between Peale and Noah; see W. P. Cutler and J. P. Cutler, eds., *Life, Journals and Correspondence of Revd Manasseh Cutler* (Cincinnati, 1888), p. 261.

40 M. Praz, *Conversation Pieces: A Survey of the Informal Group Portrait in Europe and America* (University Park, PA, 1971), pp. 209–23.

41 Peale to Rembrandt Peale (11 and 18 September 1808), in Miller, ed., *Selected Papers*, II, pt 2, p. 1136.

42 By the time the picture was finished, St George had died (in 1778); Peale's mother had died in 1791; his young daughter Eleanor (here on his mother's lap) had died in infancy in 1772; Rachel had died in 1790 and Margaret, in infancy, in 1772; Peale's sister Margaret Jane died in 1788, and the family's nurse Margaret Durgan (on the right), had died in 1791.

43 Several times in his career Peale was called upon to paint memorial portraits of dead or dying children; See Miller, ed., *Selected Papers*, I, p. 415n. It is a theme we see not only in the relation between Titian's death and the museum's establishment, but also in the controversies surrounding the life and death of Raphaelle Peale. In his thorough analysis of *The Artist in his Museum*, Roger B. Stein adds a note that poses a somewhat ironic reading of Peale's citation of Luke 15 ('For thy brother was dead, and is alive again, and was lost and is found') in his 'Essay to Promote Domestic Happiness' of 1812. Stein sees the quotation as an admonition to Peale's own prodigal son, Raphaelle. Raphaelle died in 1825 after years of physical and mental instability, probably brought on by arsenic poisoning as a result of taxidermic work. See Stein, 'Charles Willson Peale's Expressive Design: "The Artist in His Museum" ', in Miller and Ward, eds., *New Perspectives on Charles Peale*, pp. 167–218 (217 n.95). For an

account of Raphaelle's poisoning, see P. Lloyd, 'Philadelphia Story', *Art in America*, LXXVI (November 1988), pp. 154–71, 195–203. Further, there is an uncanny echo between the passage from Luke and the 1783 breakdown, for it is *Raphaelle* who cannot be remembered at the time. And it is obviously Raphaelle's drinking and tumultuous marriage that are the thinly veiled referents of passages on the 'hideous form of drunkenness' that makes 'the proud form of man . . . degraded below the brutes' described in Peale's *An Essay to Promote Domestic Happiness by Charles W. Peale* (Philadelphia Museum, 1812), Library Company copy, p. 4. The meaning of the Luke passage can also be taken to refer to the position of St George in *The Family Group*, where Peale's painting situates himself and James in conversation and in positions of observation in relation to the dead – but here revived – St George. And the theme of the lost brother also recalls, of course, the traumatic aftermath of the Battle of Trenton – James's disfigurement, and Charles's inability to recognize him.

44 See Miller, ed., *Selected Papers*, II, pt 2, p. 1136.
45 Peale to Rembrandt Peale (23 July 1822), in L. B. Miller, ed., Peale Family Papers, microfiche, American Philosophical Society Library.
46 It is suggestive to consider that in his last years Peale, in fact, seemed to undertake a repetition or review of his earlier work. In January 1821 he began a large historical work on a theme directly also taken up by West and in contrast to Deist tenets on miracles and revealed religion, *Christ Healing the Sick at the Pool of Bethesda*. In 1823 Peale made a new version (untraced) of *The Staircase Group*. In this work, which measured 8 × 6 feet, he showed himself descending a short flight of steps with a palette and maulstick in hand, and with his saddler's hammer in the foreground. His movement is the opposite of the earlier staircase group, inverting the generations and inverting the direction of movement. He wrote: 'The steps will certainly be a true illusion, and why not my figure? It is said that Apelles painted grapes so natural that the birds came to pick them, that he then painted a boy to protect them, but the birds still came to take the grapes'. In a letter to Rubens (25 August 1823) Peale said that Thomas Sully was fooled by the new *Staircase* painting, thinking that the bottom step was a real step, as in the first *Staircase* group. See Sellers, *Charles Willson Peale and his World*, pp. 409–11. His plans for the work are also described in the *Autobiography* (typescript, II, pp. 452–3).

11 *John Forrester: 'Mille e tre': Freud and Collecting*

1 Swann's valediction, in Marcel Proust, *Remembrance of Things Past*, trans. C. K. Scott Moncrieff and T. Kilmartin (Harmondsworth, 1983), II, pp. 728–9.
2 Sigmund Freud, 'Notes Upon a Case of Obsessional Neurosis' (1909), in *The Standard Edition of the Complete Psychological Works of Sigmund Freud*, edited by J. Strachey in collaboration with A. Freud, assisted by A. Strachey and A. Tyson, 24 vols (London, 1953–74), X, p. 176. This edition is hereafter cited as *SE*.
3 Freud, *Civilization and its Discontents* (1930), in *SE*, XXI, pp. 70–1.
4 Freud, 'Fraülein Elisabeth von R.', *Studies on Hysteria* (1895), in *SE*, II, p. 139.
5 *The Complete Letters of Sigmund Freud to Wilhelm Fliess, 1887–1904*, ed. J. M. Masson (Cambridge, Mass., 1984), 6 December 1896, pp. 207–8. This edition is hereafter abbreviated to *Freud/Fliess*. For the evolutionary dialect, see F. J. Sulloway, *Freud: Biologist of the Mind* (London, 1979); for the philological dialect, see J. Forrester, *Language and the Origins of Psychoanalysis* (London, 1980).
6 And the fact that the portion of his library that Freud sold was the 'professional' one, mainly psychiatric, neurological and psychoanalytic books – very few books on archaeology or editions of the classics were sold – is an indication of what lay closest to his heart; see E. Timms, 'Freud's Library and his Private Reading', in E. Timms and

N. Segal, eds., *Freud in Exile: Psychoanalysis and Its Vicissitudes* (London, 1988), pp. 65–79.

7 P. Gay, *Freud: A Life for Our Time* (London, 1988), p. 635.

8 Freud to Jeanne Lampl-de Groot (8 October 1938), quoted in E. L. Freud, L. Freud and I. Grubrich-Simitis, eds., *Sigmund Freud: His Life in Words and Pictures*, with a biographical sketch by K. R. Eissler, trans. C. Trollope (London, 1978), p. 313.

9 Bruno Bettelheim, 'Berggasse 19', in *Recollections and Reflections* (London, 1990), p. 22.

10 Freud to Zweig (7 February 1931), *Letters of Sigmund Freud, 1873–1939*, ed. E. L. Freud, trans. T. and J. Stern (London, 1970), p. 402.

11 'Freud ne trompe pas sa femme. C'est scandaleux! C'est anormal.' See M. Choisy, *Sigmund Freud: A New Appraisal* (London, 1963), p. 47.

12 For this topic, see E. Hooper-Greenhill, *Museums and the Shaping of Knowledge* (London, 1992); R. Lumley, ed., *The Museum Time Machine: Putting Cultures on Display* (London, 1988); S. M. Pearce, ed., *Objects of Knowledge* (London, 1988); K. Pomian, *Collectors and Curiosities: Paris and Venice, 1500–1800*, trans. E. Wiles-Portier (Cambridge, 1990); T. Richards, *The Commodity Culture of Victorian England* (London, 1991); D. K. Van Keuren, 'Cabinets and Culture: Victorian Anthropology and the Museum Context', *Journal of the History of the Behavioral Sciences*, XXV (1989), pp. 26–39.

13 J. J. Spector, *The Aesthetics of Freud: A Study of Psychoanalysis and Art* (New York, 1972), p. 17.

14 See S. M. Pearce, *Museum Objects and Collections: A Cultural Study* (Leicester and London, 1992), pp. 34–5.

15 Freud to Abraham (18 December 1916), *A Psychoanalytic Dialogue: The Letters of Sigmund Freud and Karl Abraham, 1907–1926*, ed. H. C. Abraham and E. L. Freud (London, 1965), p. 244.

16 *Freud/Fliess* (6 December 1896), p. 214; translation adapted in accordance with Lynn Gamwell, 'Freud's Antiquities Collection', in L. Gamwell and R. Wells, eds., *Sigmund Freud and Art: His Personal Collection of Antiquities*, exhibition catalogue introd. by P. Gay; Freud Museum, London; State University of New York, Binghamton; 1989, p. 24.

17 Freud, *The Interpretation of Dreams* (1900), in *SE*, IV, p. xxvi.

18 *Freud/Fliess* (24 January 1895), Draft H, p. 110; the juxtaposition of old maids and bachelors is repeated, within the context of a somewhat different argument, in *The Interpretation of Dreams*, in *SE*, IV, p. 177.

19 *Freud/Fliess*, (24 January 1895), Draft H, p. 110.

20 See M. Balmary, *Psychoanalyzing Psychoanalysis: Freud and the Hidden Fault of the Father*, trans. and introd. by N. Lukacher (Baltimore, 1982).

21 See L. Appignanesi and J. Forrester, *Freud's Women* (London, 1992), esp. Ch. 4; 'sexual megalomania' is the phrase Freud used in a letter to Karl Abraham, *Freud-Abraham Letters* (9 January 1908), p. 20.

22 And it should be noted that Krafft-Ebing borrowed these terms from an anonymous Berlin correspondent; see Krafft-Ebing's *Neue Forschungen auf dem Gebiet der Psychopathia Sexualis: Eine medizinische-psychologische Studie* (Stuttgart, 1890), pp. 19–20, quoted in R. I. Hauser, 'Sexuality, Neurasthenia and the Law: Richard von Krafft-Ebing (1840–1902)', unpublished PhD dissertation, University of London, 1992, p. 240.

23 M. Benedikt, *Hypnotismus und Suggestion: Eine klinisch-psychologische Studie* (Leipzig, 1894), p. 76, quoted in R. Hauser, *Sexuality, Neurasthenia and the Law*, p. 45.

24 *Freud-Fliess* (22 June 1897), p. 254.

25 Freud, *The Interpretation of Dreams*, in *SE*, IV, pp. 194–5; the series of 'Rome' dreams of which these anecdotes form a part are dated to January 1897 in Didier Anzieu, *Freud's Self-analysis* (1975), trans. P. Graham (London, 1986), p. 182.

26 See Freud, *The Psychopathology of Everyday Life*, in *SE*, VI, and J. Forrester, 'What the Psychoanalyst Does with Words: Austin, Lacan and the Speech Acts of Psychoanalysis', in Forrester, *The Seductions of Psychoanalysis: Freud, Lacan and Derrida* (Cambridge, 1990), p. 152.

27 Freud, 'Screen-Memories', in *SE*, III, p. 304.

28 *Freud/Fliess* (6 August 1899), p. 366.

29 *Freud/Fliess* (28 May 1899), p. 353.

30 Anna Freud Bernays, 'My brother, Sigmund Freud', in H. Ruitenbeek, ed., *Freud as We Knew Him* (Detroit, 1973), p. 141.

31 Freud, 'Psycho-Analytic Notes on an Autobiographical Account of a Case of Paranoia (Dementia Paranoides)' in *SE*, XII, p. 71.

32 *Minutes of the Vienna Psychoanalytic Society*, ed. H. Nunberg and E. Federn, trans. M. Nunberg, 4 vols (New York, 1962), I, 19 February 1908.

33 Freud, 'On Narcissism: An Introduction', in *SE*, XIV, p. 89.

34 L. Andreas-Salomé, *The Freud Journal*, trans. S. A. Leavy, with an introduction by M.-K. Wilmers (London, 1987), p. 89.

35 Jean Baudrillard, *Le système des objets* (Paris, 1968), p. 126.

36 One might connect this with Freud's often quoted account (Freud to Ferenczi, 6 October 1910; quoted in Gay, *Freud*, p. 275) of how he had employed his homosexual drives to enlarge his ego, whereas his friend Fliess had failed in this task and thus succumbed to a paranoia; the accent is as much on Freud's transformation of his homosexual bond with the close friend as it is on Fliess's paranoia.

37 Freud, 'Notes upon a Case of Obsessional Neurosis', in *SE*, X, p. 176.

38 H.D., *Tribute to Freud: Writing on the Wall, Advent*, foreword by Norman Holmes Pearson (London, 1985), pp. 96–8.

39 H.D., *Tribute to Freud*, p. 14.

40 H.D., *Tribute to Freud*, p. 9.

41 W. H. Auden, 'In Memory of Sigmund Freud', in *Collected Poems*, ed. E. Mendelson (London, 1976), pp. 215–18.

42 See Spector, *The Aesthetics of Freud*, and E. Gombrich, 'Freud's Aesthetics', *Encounter* (January 1966), pp. 30–40.

43 C. Ginzburg, 'Morelli, Freud and Sherlock Holmes: Clues and Scientific Method', in U. Eco and T. A. Sebeok, eds., *The Sign of Three: Dupin, Holmes, Pierce* (Bloomington, 1983), pp. 81–118.

44 Freud, *The Interpretation of Dreams*, in *SE*, IV, p. 217, n.1.

45 Philip Rieff's classic work, *Freud: The Mind of the Moralist* (New York, 1959), is the indispensable guide to this aspect of psychoanalysis.

46 See Wells's Preface in Gamwell and Wells, eds., *Sigmund Freud and Art: His Personal Collection of Antiquities*, p. 11.

47 Freud, 'Thoughts for the Times on War and Death' (1915), in *SE*, XIV, p. 277.

48 Karl Marx, *Grundrisse: Foundations of the Critique of Political Economy* trans. M. Nicolaus (Harmondsworth, 1973), p. 218.

49 Freud, 'Thoughts for the Times on War and Death', p. 279.

50 Baudrillard, *Le système des objets*, p. 139.

51 See D. E. Allen, *The Naturalist in Britain: A Social History* (London, 1976).

52 Susan Stewart, *On Longing: Narratives of the Miniature, the Gigantic, the Souvenir, the Collection* (Baltimore and London, 1984), p. 152.

53 Excellently analysed by Adam Phillips in his 'Freud and the Uses of Forgetting' in a seminar series given on Memory at King's College, Cambridge, on 10 June 1993.

54 Freud, 'Negation' (1926), in *SE*, XIX, pp. 235–9.
55 *The Freud/Jung Letters*, ed. W. McGuire, trans. R. Manheim and R.F.C. Hull (Princeton, NJ, 1974), item 147F (18 June 1909), p. 235.
56 H.D. *Tribute to Freud*, p. 14.
57 Marx, *Grundrisse*, p. 221.
58 Marx, *Grundrisse*, p. 216.
59 See J. Miller, 'Interpretation of Freud's Jewishness, 1924–1974', *Journal of the History of the Behavioral Sciences*, XVII (1981), pp. 357–74; E. Oring, *The Jokes of Sigmund Freud: A Study in Jewish Humor and Jewish Identity* (Philadelphia, 1984).
60 Baudrillard, *Le Système des objets*, p. 124.
61 As described in Gay, *Freud*, p. 543.
62 Freud, *The Interpretation of Dreams*, in *SE*, V, p. 583.

12 Naomi Schor: Collecting Paris

All the postcards reproduced here are from my personal collection. A longer version of this essay first appeared in *Critical Inquiry*, XVIII (Winter 1992), pp. 188–243, under the title '*Cartes Postales*: Representing Paris 1900'. My thanks to Janell Watson, my resourceful research assistant (1989–92), for her help in preparing that text. Abigail Solomon-Godeau provided expert editorial assistance and Richard Klein patient logistical support, for which I thank them both. Special thanks are due here to Anna Gilcher, my new research assistant, and especially my editors, John Elsner and Roger Cardinal, for their help in crafting this (light) version of my earlier text.

1 Benjamin's childhood collection included one of postcards; see *Sens unique: Précédé de enfance berlinoise et suivi de paysages urbains*, trans. J. Lacoste (Paris, 1978), p. 61, also pp. 67, 105. Included in the series called *Topographie de Paris*, which Benjamin worked on at the Bibliothèque Nationale's Cabinet des Estampes, were postcards of Paris, no doubt the same ones still available there today.

   Incidentally, Benjamin raises the question of the conflict between stamp and postcard collecting, that is between the two sides of the postcard: 'Sometimes you come across them on postcards and are unsure whether you should detach them or keep the card as it is, like a page by an old master that has different but equally precious drawings on both sides' (*One-Way Street and Other Writings*, trans. E. Jephcott and K. Shorter, London, 1985, pp. 91–92).

2 In *Illuminations*, trans. H. Zohn, ed. H. Arendt (New York, 1968), p. 60; hereafter abbreviated to 'U'.

3 One anamnesis provokes another. Recently, as I was preparing this text, my sister Mira Schor said to me 'You know you really should take a look at the postcards in Mama's drawers'. There, to my surprise, I found a small group of postcards my parents had brought with them in the rucksacks, as they called them, which was their baggage on arriving in the United States. Mostly the cards were disappointing, poor-quality pre-war reproductions of paintings my artist parents had preciously saved. But among these 'worthless' cards was a small series, no doubt incomplete, of hand-painted cards representing the costumes of Provence, where my parents had spent a year waiting for visas. They have become, retroactively, the matrix of my collection.

4 S. Stewart, *On Longing: Narratives of the Miniature, the Gigantic, the Souvenir, the Collection* (Baltimore and London, 1984), p. 135; hereafter abbreviated to *OL*.

5 D. MacCannell, *The Tourist: A New Theory of the Leisure Class* (1976; New York, 1989), p. 79.

6 Jean Baudrillard, *Le Système des objets* (Paris, 1968), p. 125; hereafter abbreviated *SO*; all translations mine except where otherwise noted.

7 See E. Apter, 'Splitting Hairs: Female Fetishism and Postpartum Sentimentality in the

Fin de Siècle', in her *Feminizing the Fetish: Psychoanalysis and Narrative Obsession in Turn-of-the-Century France* (Ithaca, 1991), pp. 99–123. The literature on female fetishism is growing rapidly; see also my 'Female Fetishism: The Case of George Sand', in *The Female Body in Western Culture: Contemporary Perspectives*, ed. S. Suleiman (Cambridge, Mass., 1986), pp. 363–72; Elizabeth Grosz, 'Lesbian Fetishism?', in *Fetishism as a Cultural Discourse*, ed. E. Apter and W. Pietz (Ithaca, 1993), pp. 101–15; and M. Garber, 'Fetish Envy', *Vested Interests: Cross-Dressing and Cultural Anxiety*, (New York, 1992), pp. 118–27.

 8 See E. Apter, 'Cabinet Secrets: Fetishism, Prostitution, and the Fin de Siècle Interior', *Assemblage*, IX (June 1989), pp. 7–19, esp. pp. 15–16.

 9 W. Dûval with V. Monahan, *Collecting Postcards in Colour, 1894–1914* (Poole, Dorset, 1978), p. 28; hereafter abbreviated *CP*.

10 J. H. Smith, *Postcard Companion: The Collector's Reference* (Radnor, PA., 1989), p. ix; hereafter abbreviated *PC*.

11 G. Neudin, *Les Meilleures Cartes postales de France* (Paris, 1989), p. 324: 'One meets specialized collectors for every street, every quartier (e.g. Montmartre, the Bièvre), or every *arrondissement*'. All translations are my own, except where otherwise noted.

12 B. Martin and C. T. Mohanty, 'Feminist Politics: What's Home Got to Do with It?', in *Feminist Studies/Critical Studies*, ed. T. de Lauretis (Bloomington, 1986), p. 196.

13 Ibid.

14 Such is the claim made in some of the LL promotional literature. Basing himself on information available at the Bibliothèque Nationale, José Huguet of the Sociadad Valencina de Historia de la Fotografia traced the origins of the Maison Lévy back to one Charles Soulier. In 1864 Soulier turned over his business to his students and assistants, Léon and Lévy (LL?). Nothing much more is known of Léon. I want to take this opportunity to thank both Huguet and Yves Beauregard (editor of *Cape-aux-Diamants: Revue d'histoire du Québec*) for generously sharing with me what information they had already gleaned regarding LL and the Maison Lévy before I undertook my research.

15 M. Alloula, *The Colonial Harem*, trans. M. Godzich and W. Godzich (Minneapolis, 1986).

16 The issue of *auteur*-ship is a tricky one. The tendency to transform heretofore anonymous producers of 'documentary' or commercial photographs into authors of an *œuvre*, thereby endowing them with the prerogatives of the romantic artist (genius, individual vision, originality, self-expression, aesthetic value, and so on) has been fiercely resisted by critics who want to stave off the invasion of photography by the commodification endemic to the fine arts. See, for example, R. Krauss, 'Photography's Discursive Spaces: Landscape/View', *Art Journal*, XLII (1982), pp. 311–19; A. Sekula, 'Photography between Labour and Capital', in *Mining Photographs and Other Pictures, 1948–1968: A Selection from the Negative Archives of Shedden Studio, Glace Bay, Cape Breton*, ed. B.H.D. Buchloh and R. Wilkie (Halifax, NS, 1983), pp. 193–268; and Sekula, *Photography against the Grain: Essays and Photo Works, 1973–1983* Halifax, NS, 1984).

At the same time, my attempt to reconstitute the LL series on Paris and to obtain some minimal information about its producers has been constantly impeded by their non-status as artists. Whether in the archives of the library (Bibliothèque Nationale, Bibliothèque Historique de la Ville de Paris) or in the market-place, postcards of Paris are organized topographically, by *arrondissements*, irrespective of editors. Searching out the cards produced by a single editor – when they are not the highly prized 'Petits Métiers' or 'Paris Vécu' series – is tedious work, which goes against the grain of conventional classification.

The question that arises is how can one reconstitute the discursive network within which the LL cards were produced and circulated without claiming for them some sort of privileged status, which may or may not enhance their value? View-cards remain one of the last sanctuaries of photography untouched by the gilding hand of aestheticization. The price of Parisian (and other) view-cards is based strictly on their value as social documents (*studium* here is prized over *punctum*) and, of course, their scarcity, and according to this scale of values, architectural renderings of buildings (especially those still standing), however prolix in details, represent a degree zero of value. As it will become apparent below, for me the discursive and the aesthetic are inseparable, for part of what constitutes the interest of the LL series is its distinctive and ideologically inflected aesthetics.

17 J. Douglas, cited in F. Staff, *The Picture Postcard and Its Origins* (London, 1966), p. 81; hereafter abbreviated *PP*.

18 Griseline, *Le Cartophile*, III (December 1900), p. 7.

19 See Guy Feinstein's introduction to M. Cabaud and R. Hubscher, *1900: La Française au quotidien* (Paris, 1985), p. 6.

20 C. Bourgeois and M. Melot, *Les Cartes postales: Nouveau Guide du collectionneur* (Paris, 1983), p. 28.

21 It would be wrong to proceed as though the postcard were merely a minor mode of photography, because what constitutes the specificity and the fascination of the modern illustrated postcard is, of course, its bilaterality: it has two sides, two faces – the pictorial and the scriptural. It is the perfectly reversible semiotic object, a virtual analogon of the sign. Just as the image face of the postcard provides visual representations of the street scenes of Paris *c.* 1900, the message side records the millions of exchanges between the men and women of that time, which often refer quite explicitly to the choice of image, for the sides are not sealed off from one another any more than are the signified and signifier. As one author puts it, the relationship between the two sides is 'never gratuitous, even if it sometimes remains ambiguous' (F. Vitoux, *Cartes postales*, Paris, 1973, p. 34). It is in reading those communications, which range from laconic formulaic greetings to virtual letters in the crabbed microscopic handwriting the French call 'pattes de fourmi', that one is placed in the position of the voyeur, or better yet the eavesdropper on everyday life. From the backs of these cards emerges a murmur of small voices speaking of minor aches and pains, long awaited engagements, obscure family feuds; reporting on safe arrivals and unexpected delays; ordering goat's cheese; acknowledging receipt of a bouquet of violets, a bonnet; in short, carrying on millions of minute transactions, the grain of everyday life.

22 M. Normand, 'Coup d'oeil sur L'Exposition', in *Les Grands Dossiers de l'Illustration: Les Expositions Universelles; Histoire d'un siècle 1843–1944* (Paris, 1987), p. 134. Cf. J.-J. Bloch and M. Delort, who write: 'Paris is a woman who welcomes her visitors at the main door of the Exposition . . . with a monumental statue. . . . She is neither an allegory nor a goddess, she is la Parisienne, which Paquin the couturier has dressed according to the latest fashion. One can ironize at length about this woman with arms outstretched but she is the very symbol of the Belle Epoque' (Bloch and Delort, *Quand Paris allait 'à l'Expo'*, Paris, 1980, p. 105).

23 P. Greenhalgh, *Ephemeral Vistas: The 'Expositions Universelles', Great Exhibitions and World's Fairs, 1851–1939* (Manchester, 1988), p. 118, 119.

24 A. Albalat, *Le Cartophile*, III (December 1900), p. 5.

25 P. Hamon, *Expositions: Literature and Architecture in Nineteenth-century France*, trans. K. Sainson-Frank and L. Maguire (Berkeley, 1992), p. 71.

26 MacCannell, op. cit., p. 63.

27 D. Oster and J. Goulemot, *La Vie parisienne: Anthologie des moeurs du XIXe siècle* (Paris, 1989), p. 6, 5; 'Classifying, declassifying, outclassing, such are the obsessions of

the era. . . . Flânerie and classification keep post-1848 literature alive' (p. 7); the discourse on Paris is 'a descriptive discourse with totalizing claims' (p. 19).

28 Hamon, op. cit., p. 96.

29 See R. Sennett, *The Fall of Public Man* (New York, 1978), p. 135.

30 Ibid., p. 160.

31 J. Wolff, 'The Invisible "Flâneuse": Women and the Literature of Modernity', in *Feminist Sentences: Essays on Women and Culture* (Berkeley, 1990), p. 34–50.

32 Thanks to the kind cooperation of Alan Bonhoure of the Roget-Viollet photographic agency, which inherited the complete Lévy-Neurdein archives – consisting mainly of thousands of glass plates – when the Compagnie des Arts Méchaniques (who had taken over Lévy-Neurdein in 1932) went out of business (*c.* 1974), I was able to consult the albums containing the complete, or near-complete, sequence of LL cards of Paris. Based on the sartorial evidence provided by some of the most recent views included in these albums, they were assembled sometime in the Twenties. Though the albums, with postcards pasted three by three on their crumbling pages, are not themselves complete and are occasionally unreliable, they provide extraordinarily precious information about the organization of the series. Even though the cards are numbered, and certain numbers correspond to sites whose image was repeatedly re-photographed and updated, others do not: a single number may in fact correspond to two wildly different sites (for example, 256: 'La Rue Saint-Jacques' and 'L'Entrée du Bois de Boulogne'). Though the collection strives toward exhaustiveness, its representation of Paris is anything but systematic, shifting, for example, without any apparent logic from the fancy rue de la Paix (81) to the less elegant Pigalle (82).

33 In terms of urban representations, one might usefully contrast this transitional age with the age of decadence that immediately precedes it, and which is marked by the absence of a reassuring historical sense. In the words of Marie-Claire Bancquart, who has written extensively on literary representations of *fin de siècle* Paris, 'all the writers of the *fin de siècle* experience an unease, feel that intimacy with the Self is impossible; . . . and this malaise is projected onto Paris, a disassociated Paris which has forgotten its history. Intermittencies of the heart of the city: one is struck by the small number of evocations of the past, of monuments, in this capital where money has replaced culture' ('Du Paris Second Empire au Paris des écrivains fin-de-siècle', in *Ecrire Paris*, ed. D. Oster and J. Goulemot, Paris, 1990, p. 48).

Today's postcards can be said to represent a new shift in representations of Paris as nostalgic; even retro-postcards (always black and white, or a grainy, milky grey) of a fast disappearing 'Vieux Paris' (chiefly that of the Twenties and Fifties) are juxtaposed on the racks with bright colour images of the new Paris, the Paris of Mitterand with its I. M. Pei Pyramid and Arche de la Défense. It is through this ubiquitous postcarding of our *fin de siècle* Paris that the naturalizing functions of the postcard are most clearly displayed.

34 G. Guyonnet, *La Carte postale illustrée: Son histoire, sa valeur documentaire* (Nancy, 1947), p. 19.

35 See S. Buck-Morss, *The Dialectics of Seeing: Walter Benjamin and the Arcades Project* (Cambridge, Mass., 1989), pp. 304–7.

Select Bibliography

There are inumerable articles, monographs, guides and catalogues that focus on specific public and private collections, or particular collectors, not to mention the teeming bibliography on such related topics as taste, taxonomy, museology, exhibitions, archives, trading in works of art, antiques and ephemera, and so forth.

Intended strictly as a working guide to what is both significant and reasonably accessible, the following list covers the classic studies and some major recent contributions to a general theory and history of collecting.

J. Alsop, *The Rare Art Traditions: A History of Collecting and its Linked Phenomena* (New York, 1982).

J. Baudrillard, *Le Système des objets* (Paris, 1968). This has never been translated in full, but selected passages can be found in this volume, in Baudrillard's *Selected Writings*, ed. M. Poster (Oxford, 1988), pp. 10–29, and in his *Revenge of the Crystal*, ed. P. Foss and J. Pefunis (London, 1990), pp. 35–61.

W. Benjamin, 'Unpacking My Library: A Talk about Book Collecting', in *Illuminations*, ed. H. Arendt, (London, 1970), first published, in German, in 1931.

P. Bourdieu, *Distinction: A Social Critique of the Judgement of Taste* (London, 1984).

J. Clifford, *The Predicament of Culture: Twentieth-century Ethnography, Literature, and Art* (London, 1988).

B. Danet & T. Katriel, 'No Two Alike: Play and Aesthetics in Collecting', *Play and Culture*, no. 2 (1989), pp. 253–77.

R. Harbison, *Eccentric Spaces* (New York, 1977).

F. Haskell, *Rediscoveries in Art: Some Aspects of Taste, Fashion and Collecting in England and France* (London, 1976).

F. Herrman, *The English as Collectors* (London, 1972).

L. Hoole, *Hoole's Guide to British Collecting Clubs* (Bradford, 1993).

E. Hooper-Greenhill, *Museums and the Shaping of Knowledge* (London, 1992).

O.R. Impey, & A.G. MacGregor (eds), *The Origins of Museums: The Cabinet of Curiosities in Sixteenth- and Seventeenth-century Europe* (Oxford, 1985).

I. Jenkins, *Archaeologists and Aesthetes in the Sculpture Galleries of the British Museum, 1800–1939* (London, 1992).

Journal of the History of Collections (1989–)

J. Lewis, *Printed Ephemera*, 2nd edn. (Woodbridge, 1990).

W. Muensterberger, *Collecting, An Unruly Passion: Psychological Perspectives* (Princeton, NJ, 1994).

E. Paolozzi, *Lost Magic Kingdoms* (London, 1985).

S.M. Pearce, (ed.), *Objects of Knowledge* (London, 1988).

——, *Museums, Objects and Collections: A Cultural Study* (Leicester and London, 1992).

K. Pomian, *Collectors and Curiosities: Paris and Venice, 1500–1800* (Cambridge, 1990).

M. Rheims, *Art on the Market: Thirty-five Centuries of Collecting and Collectors from Midas to Paul Getty* (London, 1961).
——, *The Glorious Obsession* (London, 1980).
S. Rosen, *In Celebration of Ourselves* (San Francisco, 1979).
R.G. Saisselin, *Bricabracomania: The Bourgeois and the Bibelot* (London, 1985).
S. Stewart, *On Longing: Narratives of the Miniature, the Gigantic, the Souvenir, the Collection* (Baltimore and London, 1984).

Index